The English
Administrative
System
1780–1870

THE ENGLISH ADMINISTRATIVE SYSTEM

1780–1870

SIR NORMAN CHESTER

CLARENDON PRESS · OXFORD
1981

Oxford University Press, Walton Street, Oxford OX2 6DP

OXFORD LONDON GLASGOW
NEW YORK TORONTO MELBOURNE WELLINGTON
KUALA LUMPUR SINGAPORE HONG KONG TOKYO
DELHI BOMBAY CALCUTTA MADRAS KARACHI
NAIROBI DAR ES SALAAM CAPE TOWN

Published in the United States
by Oxford University Press, New York

British Library Cataloguing in Publication Data

Chester, Sir *Norman*
The English administrative system 1780–1870.
1. Great Britain — Politics and government — 1760–1820
2. Great Britain — Politics and government — 19th century
I. Title
350'.00941   *JN309*   *80–41310*

ISBN 0–19–822643–8

ℓ

Printed in Great Britain
at the University Press, Oxford
by Eric Buckley
Printer to the University

Preface

Five or six years ago I became aware of the growing literature on the organization and working of government departments during the nineteenth century. As a teacher and practitioner of public administration for some forty years I decided to read the various monographs largely to see what light they threw on the problems of the current system. As a result I became increasingly interested in administrative history.

Though learning a very great deal from the various studies I found some of them not entirely satisfying. First, because the author in many cases was concentrating on a small part of a total picture — for example, the working of one department — he could not put his findings in the context of what was happening not merely in other departments but also in Parliament and the general world of political activity. Second, there was a tendency in a few cases to start from the present day and explain the past in terms of the present, usually to the disparagement rather than the understanding of the late eighteenth and early nineteenth century. So as a result I decided to try my hand at a general administrative history that would, I hoped, avoid both these pitfalls.

To achieve my aim I needed a base year. To my dismay I found that the latest year as a starting-date was 1780. To start much later was to miss many of the political and administrative changes which heralded the modern system. When I came to study the period around 1780 I found myself in a world of very different ideas and institutions, made more difficult to understand and explain because many of the words then in use have by now either changed their meaning or convey a very different content of ideas. Thus the word 'ministerial' was in general use as meaning the administration of non-judicial affairs. The terms central or local government and civil service were not in vogue and to use them in describing the administrative system of 1780 would inevitably conjure up for the reader ideas associated with the present use of the words.

I therefore first wrote the analysis and description of the system of 1780 as though I were living in December of that year. In that way I avoided using terms and ideas that were not in general use at the time. I also avoided the practice of some historians of explaining the past in terms of the present. However, I was told that my attempt to write contemporary history would be unlikely to find favour with professional historians and that readers might find it confusing. So I converted what I had written into the past tense. Nevertheless the discipline of writing in contemporary terms was very valuable and I trust that no anachronisms have crept into the revision.

My aim has been to explain the way the system changed and developed primarily from the viewpoint of the practitioner rather than of the political historian. Occasionally I mention Pitt, Palmerston, Gladstone, and other leading statesmen but their important contribution to British history lay in the formation of national policy rather than in the perfection of administrative machinery. Indeed the implication of the study is that the system developed the way it did more as a result of general forces, e.g. increase in size of and pressures on departments, and not because this or that Minister was a managerial innovator. Nor, for that reason do I accord Bentham the amount of space and importance granted to him by some historians. I was impressed by the article by Henry Parris in the *Historical Journal* for 1960 entitled 'The Nineteenth Century Revolution in Government: A Reappraisal Reappraised'. I do not deny that Bentham influenced the content of legislation. But there is little or no evidence that he was significant in the development of the administrative system.

The completion of this work was greatly eased by the award of an Emeritus Fellowship by the Leverhulme Trust. I am most grateful for their help.

My debt to those who have already shown their expert knowledge of this field is obviously very great: to my friend and former pupil Henry Parris, to Gillian Sutherland and the group which contributed to her volume of Essays, and to John

Sainty and Michael Collinge whose painstaking volumes covering 1660–1870 have opened the way for much further work.

I have been very fortunate in the help I have been given by other scholars. I must most warmly thank the following for having read all or part of the typescript: Gerald Aylmer, Michael Collinge, Nevil Johnson, George Jones, Bryan Keith-Lucas, Betty Kemp, Henry Roseveare, John Sainty, Maurice Wright, and David Yale. A. P. Donajgrodzki, Sammy Finer, Geoffrey Finlayson, Freddie Madden, and Barry Supple have very kindly helped me on particular points.

John Davis gave great assistance both generally and in checking most of the quotations and footnotes. For the translation of my handwriting into clear typescript I am indebted to Margaret Hunt and Mrs K. Rogers. Finally I must pay tribute to the library staff and resources of the Bodleian and Nuffield College.

CONTENTS

Part I The Administrative System in 1780

Part I
The Administrative
System in 1780

I

The Constitutional and Legal Basis

Anyone writing in 1780 would have regarded it as a disservice to those who wished to understand the working of the English system of government, not to start with the authoritative Commentaries of Sir William Blackstone. These were first delivered as lectures in Oxford when Sir William Blackstone was Vinerian Professor of English Law, the first volume being published in 1765. So influential were they that eight editions had appeared by the time of his death in 1780.

THE BALANCE OF FORCES

The Constitution of 1780 had emerged out of the troubles of the previous century, still vivid in many people's thoughts. The English people had experienced the tyranny and the threat to liberty which occurred when the king tried to assert the supremacy of the prerogative over all the other institutions of government and, equally so, when a similar claim was made for Parliament to the exclusion of the royal authority. The events of 1688 had led to the royal power being curtailed, but by no means extinguished. The power of Parliament was greatly enhanced but certain limitations came to be recognized. As Blackstone explained, the

true excellence of the English government [is] that all the parts of it form a mutual check upon each other. In the legislature, the people are a check upon the nobility, and the nobility a check upon the people; by the mutual privilege of rejecting what the other has resolved: while the king is a check upon both, which preserves the executive power from encroachments. And this very executive power is again checked and kept within due bounds by the two houses, through the privilege they have of inquiring into, impeaching, and punishing the conduct, (not indeed of the king, which would destroy his constitutional independence; but, which is more beneficial to the public,) of his evil and pernicious counsellors. Thus every branch of our civil polity supports and is supported, regulates and is regulated, by the rest.[1]

Elsewhere he explained that the independent position of the courts was the most essential safeguard of constitutional liberty:

In this distinct and separate existence of the judicial power in a peculiar body of men, nominated indeed, but not removable at pleasure, by the crown, consists one main preservative of the public liberty; which cannot subsist long in any state, unless the administration of common justice be in some degree separated both from the legislative and also from the executive power. Were it joined with the legislative, the life, liberty, and property of the subject would be in the hands of arbitrary judges, whose decisions would be then regulated only by their own opinions, and not by any fundamental principles of law; which, though legislators may depart from, yet judges are bound to observe. Were it joined with the executive, this union might soon be an over-balance for the legislative. . . . Nothing therefore is more to be avoided, in a free constitution, than uniting the provinces of a judge and a minister of state.[2]

THE ROYAL PREROGATIVE

'The supreme executive power . . . is vested by our laws in a single person, the king or queen: for it matters not to which sex the crown descends; but the person entitled to it, whether male or female, is immediately invested with all the ensigns, rights and prerogatives of sovereign power . . .'[3] The powers inherent in the king were known as 'the prerogative' and like much of the common law had been so recognized from time immemorial. He did not owe them to Acts of Parliament. A most important constitutional function of the courts had been to interpret the limits of the prerogative. Parliament had also played a significant role in this matter. Several important Acts had restricted its scope. At the same time Parliament had on occasion vested fresh powers in the hands of the king, i.e. beyond those he possessed by ancient usage.

The law ascribed to the king 'the attribute of *sovereignty* or pre-eminence' and, in his political capacity, 'absolute *perfection*, The king can do no wrong' and an 'absolute immortality, The king never dies.' The law invested him with 'a number of authorities and powers; in the exertion whereof consists the executive part of government.' He was 'not only the chief, but properly the sole, magistrate of the nation; all others acting by commission from, and in due subordination to him.' With regard to foreign concerns, the king was delegate or representative of his people. He had 'the sole power of sending ambassadors to foreign states, and receiving ambassadors at home.' It was also his prerogative to make treaties, leagues, and alliances with foreign states and princes. He had 'the sole prerogative of making war and peace.' In domestic affairs he was 'a constituent part of the supreme legislative power; and, as such, [had] the prerogative of rejecting such provisions in parliament as he judged improper to be passed.' He was not bound by any Act of Parliament, 'unless he be named therein by special and particular words.' Yet an Act expressly made for the preservation of public rights and the suppression of public wrongs, and which did not interfere with the established rights of the Crown, was said to be binding as well upon the king as upon the subject. The king was 'the generalissimo, or the first in military command, within the kingdom.' In this capacity he had 'the sole power of raising and regulating fleets and armies.' He had the prerogative of appointing ports and havens, also the erection of beacons, lighthouses, and sea marks. He was also 'the fountain of justice and general conservator of the peace of the kingdom.' 'Justice is not, however, derived from the king, as from his free gift, but he is the steward of the public, to dispense it to whom it is due.' The king was likewise 'the fountain of honour, of office and, of privilege.' He had the inherent right of 'erecting and disposing of offices.' Finally, he was the arbiter of domestic commerce. Public marts, or places of buying and selling, such as markets and fairs, with their tolls, could only be set up by virtue of the king's grant. He was the regulator of weights and measures and it was he who gave authority to the coining of money and its currency.[4]

The king did not have absolute discretion in the use of these powers:
(i) The revolution which put William on the throne led to the Declaration and Bill of Rights of 1689 (1 Wm. and M., St.2, c.2) which implied that the monarch had entered into a kind of contract with the nation. An Act (1 Wm. and M., St.1, c.6) passed at that time modified the coronation oath and George III, at his coronation in 1760, solemnly promised and swore

'to govern the People of this Kingdom of England, and the Dominions thereto belonging, according to the Statutes in Parliament agreed on, and the Laws and Customs of the same.' In other words, his prerogative did not entitle him to act contrary to the statute and common law. Thus Parliament could at any time pass legislation with, of course, the king's consent, restricting the royal prerogative. It was, for example, the Mutiny Act, passed annually, not the prerogative, which provided legal authority for the maintenance of a standing army in time of peace and for the infliction of the death penalty or other punishment by a court martial for certain offences. Again an Act of 1701 (1 Anne, St. I, c.7) deprived the king of the power to grant any crown land or property in perpetuity, but only for a limited terminable period. Another example was the limitation contained in an Act of 1708 (6 Anne, c.7 re-enacting 4 Anne, c.8) whereby no greater number of commissioners could be made or constituted for the execution of any office (e.g. the boards of the revenue departments) than had been employed in its execution before 14 June 1705, i.e. the first day of that Parliament.

(ii) The prerogative did not include the right to impose taxation. The king still possessed certain hereditary revenues, but George the Third had handed over the bulk of these in return for a fixed annuity. It had long been accepted that the raising of additional revenue by way of taxation or borrowing required the approval of Parliament. There still remained some doubts, however, whether the king, by virtue of his prerogative to regulate trade and define the privileges of alien merchants, could levy an additional duty on foreign trade. In 1689 the Bill of Rights enacted 'That levying Money for or to the use of the Crown, by Pretence of Prerogative, without Grant of Parliament, for longer Time, or in other Manner than the same is or shall be granted, is illegal.' This was clearly a very great limitation when applied to an authority responsible for the administration of the laws of the land and the conduct of wars. It also made the House of Commons an important partner in the executive power.

(iii) The prerogative did not entitle the king to legislate without the consent of Parliament. The Bill of Rights declared that the 'Pretended Power of suspending of Laws or the

Execution of Laws, by regal Authority, without Consent of Parliament is illegal'. Acts of Parliament to be valid, i.e. recognizable by the Courts, required the assent not only of the king but also of the two Houses of Parliament — Lords and Commons. The prerogative gave the king the right to refuse to give his assent to any Bill, just as either House had the right to refuse to pass a Bill approved by the other or asked for by the king.

(iv) The prerogative did not extend to the making of judicial decisions. True, judges and their officials were his 'servants' and in so far as not met out of fee income, their stipends in part were paid by the king as was the cost of their buildings and supplies. In Blackstone's words 'though the constitution of the kingdom hath entrusted him with the whole executive power of the laws, it is impossible, as well as improper, that he should personally carry into execution this great and extensive trust.'[5]

It was also generally accepted in 1780 that the royal prerogative did not extend to the creation of new courts or changing the jurisdiction of any existing court or altering the number of judges in any such court or the mode of their appointment. These things could be done only by Act of Parliament. Judges were still appointed by and received their commissions from him. But they no longer held their appointments at the royal pleasure (*durante bene placito*), the form of tenure for most of his chief servants. The Act of Settlement, 1701, laid down three important rules:

(a) in future judges were to hold office during good behaviour (*quamdiu se bene gesserint*);

(b) they were not to be removable save upon an address of both Houses of Parliament i.e. they could be removed only by Parliament; and

(c) their salaries were to be ascertained and established. Thus the king would not be able to alter them and so bring financial pressure, either way, on a particular judge.

THE CROWN

Though Blackstone usually spoke of the king possessing this or that attribute or power, he sometimes used the term 'the crown', for example, in the phrase, the judiciary are 'nomi-

nated indeed, but not removable at pleasure, by the crown.'
The term was also used in Acts of Parliament. There was no
difference at law between the king and the crown, but the
former was not uncommonly used to distinguish those acts
which the king performed as a natural person — such as
eating, hunting, and marrying — from those he performed by
virtue of being the king.

Lawyers had, for a very long time, recognized that the king
had two capacities — natural and politic — and that in his
politic capacity he never died. So his natural death was
usually referred to in law as the demise of the king, an
expression which signified merely a transfer of property.
Basing himself on Plowden, Blackstone stated 'when we say
the demise of the crown, we mean only that, in consequence of
the disunion of the king's natural body from his body politic,
the kingdom is transferred or demised to his successor.'[6]

Nevertheless neither the Courts nor legal theory had been
prepared to treat the king, for the purposes of the constitution,
as what Coke called a corporation sole, distinguishing thereby
between his acts as an ordinary person and his acts in his
official capacity. The logic of the maxim — the king never dies
— was not followed by the courts, for if he did not legally die
then nothing would follow from his natural death. All those
who held office of the deceased king would automatically hold
office from his successor, for they would hold office from the
king as a permanent legal entity, not from any particular king
as a person. Instead, the stress was on the king as a living
person. As such he was capable of dying but when he did so
his office did not become vacant, for his successor was already
known and came immediately into it. As, however, all the
dead king's acts were personal to him, even though undertaken in his capacity as king, they died with him. The power to
make these decisions was immediately handed over or
demised to his successor, but not the actual decisions. At one
time this doctrine had applied even to cases pending in the
Courts, many of which, being started in the name of the king as
the fountain of justice, had to be started afresh upon his death.
Legislation in 1547 and 1692 had removed this consequence.

Parliament was summoned by the king and, until an Act of
1696 (7 and 8 Wm. III, c.15), ceased to exist when he died,

but that Act enabled it to sit for six months after his demise unless sooner prorogued or dissolved by his successor. Should no Parliament be in existence when the king died the last Parliament would have to be immediately convened. An interim arrangement for six months minimized the inconvenience without throwing doubt on the capacity of the successor to exercise his personal choice and rule.

At one time the death of the king also dissolved the Privy Council and put an end to the tenure of all the officers of state and all commissions in the army. In effect it left the country without an executive government and without an effective army. The inconvenience could be very serious if the successor were likely to be out of the country at the time, or there were to be a rival claimant. This situation was envisaged as a possibility when Queen Anne died. In 1708, therefore, Parliament enacted (6 Anne, c.7) that the Privy Council should remain in office for six months unless sooner determined by the successor. The same provision was applied to the Lord Chancellor, Lord High Treasurer, Lord President of the Council, Lord Privy Seal, Lord High Admiral, and to any other 'of the Great Officers of the Queen or King's Household for the time being.' Nor was 'any Office, Place or Employment Civil or Military . . . to become void by Reason of the Demise or Death of [the Queen] . . . [but all] shall continue in their respective Offices, Places, and Employments, for the Space of six Months next after such Death or Demise, unless sooner removed and discharged by the next in Succession . . .'. The same Act provided that the Great Seal, Privy Seal and Signet, and all other public seals were to continue to be used as the Seals of the successor until he gave orders to the contrary. This law was extended in 1760 (1 Geo. III, c.23), the six months' limit being removed so far as the Judges of the Common Law Courts were concerned. The basis of this legislation was that these servants owed their office and allegiance not to the Crown or to the State, but to the king in person. The prerogative powers were not vested in something called the crown, they were vested in the king as a person. It was the king as a person who jointly with the Lords and Commons passed legislation. It was the king as a person to whom money was voted by Parliament for both the civil government and the armed forces: it was not voted to the Boards of Treasury or of Admiralty, nor even to the Administration. All this had two important consequences.

It meant in the first instance that no clear distinction was drawn at law between what the king did as a person and as the Executive power. In most matters the domestic affairs of the king and what was sometimes referred to as the civil government were inextricably mixed. The Civil List included the costs of the royal households as well as salaries for the judges and the clerks in the Treasury. Payments in respect of these very diverse items were handled by the Treasury and the Exchequer in the same manner. The Secretaries of State used the Signet for the king's personal affairs as well as for matters of great public significance. True the king had a number of officers responsible for the effective running of his household arrangements. But there was no legal difference between the Treasurer of the Household and the Lord Chamberlain on the one hand and the Treasurer of the Navy or the First Lord of the Treasury on the other. All were officers of the king, appointed and removable by him. The king was one and indivisible, whether making a declaration of war or refurbishing one of his palaces

THE SEALS

Secondly, it followed that the exercise of the prerogative powers and the spending of the money possessed by or voted to the king required his personal action. In most cases this meant his personal signature or Sign Manual. Should the king be ill or for some reason unable to sign the necessary documents, or should he refuse to sign, no other signature would suffice at law. Though the Sign Manual was an essential element in the use of the king's powers, it was not in itself sufficient legal authority. The law required at least one officer to be involved in any of the formal acts of the king. Thus an essential element in any formal expression of the king's will was the use of one of the Seals. And because the Seals were so essential those Officers of State who had custody of them had a special character and importance.

The sealing of a document to provide formal proof that it carried the authority of the person or body originating it goes back to very early times. Use was not confined to the king. The Commissioners for the Treasury and for the Admiralty, for example, had their own official seals for the authentication of certain kinds of business. Peers of the realm, municipal corporations, and most corporate bodies had their own seals which they used to solemnize their more important acts, particularly where these involved documents whose legal validity might otherwise be questioned in the courts.

In the case of the king, three Seals were recognized by the law. The Great Seal was the oldest and most important and had been styled the *clavis regni* or key of the realm. The Privy Seal developed next and was mainly used for two purposes: as a major part of the process whereby the use of the Great Seal was authorized and for the issue of money from the Exchequer. Finally in time came the Signet, used, mostly in association with the Sign Manual, for a wide range of public business.

In most cases custom had established which Seal was sufficient to ensure legal recognition of the great variety of instruments and expressions of the royal will. Formal correspondence was normally satisfied by the Signet, but grants of Charters or of important Offices usually required the Great Seal in accordance with the Act of 1535. The Commissions establishing the Admiralty and the Treasury boards, and the appointments of the Secretaries of State, the Clerk and the Under Clerk of Parliament, and the Treasurer of the Navy were examples of royal decisions conveyed by Letters Patent* under the Great Seal.

The full process whereby the Great Seal was affixed to a Treaty, grant of Office, or Charter, was as follows. A warrant was first made out at the office of the Secretary of State, or at the Treasury, according to the nature of the Instrument, which was signed by the king and countersigned by the Secretary of State or the Lords Commissioners of the Treasury. The Warrant then went to the Attorney- or Solicitor-

---

* Letters Patent are open letters, *literae patentes*, so called because they are not sealed up but exposed to open view, with the Great Seal pendant at the bottom. They were usually directed or addressed by the king to all his subjects at large, and the patent-rolls on which they were recorded were open for public inspection.

General, who prepared a bill to the same effect which was sent to the Secretary of State who obtained his Majesty's signature thereto. This bill was then transmitted to the Clerk of the Signet in waiting, who prepared a transcript and addressed it to the Lord Privy Seal, the Signet being affixed thereto. In consequence of this Signet bill a like transcript was made at the Privy Seal Office, with the Privy Seal affixed and directed to the Lord Chancellor. He ordered Letters Patents to be prepared accordingly, to which the Great Seal being affixed, the Instrument was then complete.[7]

Certain very senior officers of the king had, however, been given the right for certain matters to proceed direct without going through the Offices of the Signet or the Privy Seal. Thus Commissions of the Peace were normally prepared by the Clerk of the Crown in Chancery upon authority of a fiat signed by the Lord Chancellor and then submitted to the king. Again the Lord High Treasurer could apply directly to the Chancery for the issue of a Letters Patent for many of the Treasury appointments, e.g. in the Customs. The rights of the Lord Chancellor and the Lord High Treasurer were specifically protected by the 1535 Act even though its basic purpose was to safeguard the interests of the Clerks of the Signet and the Privy Seal.

Money could, however, only be legally released from the Exchequer upon the authority of an instrument under the Great or Privy Seals. At the commencement of each reign General Letters of Privy Seal gave the Treasury Board a general authority to make issues out of the Exchequer in accordance with the tenor of Sign Manual warrants. When money was needed for any particular service a warrant was prepared in the Treasury, presented by the First Lord to the king for signature, and afterwards countersigned by at least three of the Lords Commissioners of the Treasury. In pursuance of the Sign Manual a Treasury warrant was prepared, addressed to the Auditor of the Receipt of the Exchequer, requiring him to draw an order for paying the sum mentioned. The Order, prepared in the Auditor's office and signed by himself, was returned to the Treasury with the warrant upon which it was founded. Both this warrant and the associated Order were then signed by the Lords Commissioners, and were subsequently lodged at the Auditor's office. These were not, however, by themselves sufficient authority for the payment of the money. Discretion as to the balance of cash to be retained in hand and as to priority of payments, rested with the Treasury Board. Before taking further action the Auditor of the Receipt required a formal Letter (of Direction or of Issue) from one of the joint Secretaries of the Board. More than one such Letter was likely to be needed to authorize payment of the whole amount of the sum covered by one warrant. In the case of money granted by Parliament for the Navy and the Ordnance, a Privy Seal was needed to authorize its issue. Money for military purposes required a slightly different process: the primary instrument needed for each issue being the Sign Manual, but the final payment out of the grant had to be made under the Privy Seal.[8]

A great deal of time and effort went into these formalities. Documents had to go through successive stages, each of which might involve some redrafting, and always records needed to be kept, usually involving a summary. These documents and records had to be prepared and copied, sometimes in a special script and quite often involving lengthy and somewhat archaic legal language.* Most of the time of the small number of clerks in the offices of the Secretaries of State, the Lord Privy Seal, and even of the Treasury were spent on this formal paper work.

---

* An Act of 1731 (4 Geo. II, c.26) required that after 25 March 1733 'all writs . . . patents, charters, pardons, commissions, statutes . . . shall be in the English tongue and language only, and not in Latin or French . . . and shall be written in such a common legible hand and character as the Acts of Parliament are usually ingrossed in . . . and not . . . Court hand, . . . and in words at length and not abbreviated;'. But an Act of 1733 (6 Geo. II, c.6) excluded the Court of Receipt of the Exchequer from the requirement.

II

Offices, Officers and Employees

Though the Executive power was vested in the king it was obviously physically impossible for him single-handed to conduct even a small part of the public affairs. Indeed, with the country almost continuously at war and with the expansion of the overseas possessions government had become increasingly complex and time-consuming, requiring a big increase in the number of the king's servants. Even, however, for that part of the Executive which lay within the physical capacity of the king he always had to act through others. The king might grant offices, he could not execute them himself.

Blackstone stated 'That the king can do no wrong, is a necessary and fundamental principle of the English constitution: meaning only . . . that in the first place, whatever may be amiss in the conduct of public affairs is not chargeable personally on the king; nor is he, but his ministers accountable for it to the people . . .' It must also be borne in mind that the king could not be sued in his own courts. True the common law provided the methods of petition and plea of right whereby the subject might attempt to obtain possession or restitution from the crown of real or personal property. But even here the law was concerned with 'detecting the errors or misconduct of those agents, by whom the king has been deceived, and induced to do a temporary injustice'.[9]

There had always to be some person who could be held responsible at law for the public acts of the king. These servants of the king had at law a different status from that of a delegate, deputy, or assistant, entitled to plead that he was acting in accordance with the wishes or instructions of his principal. As was shown in the case of Lord Somers it was no defence against impeachment to plead that one was acting on the king's instructions. Thus a fundamental feature of the administrative system was that the functions which in law the king were deemed to perform were distributed among many offices. As England developed and the responsibilities undertaken by the king widened, successive kings proceeded to create particular offices to fulfil particular duties. Each holder was endowed with powers, obligations and rights, the grant usually being embodied in an imposing legal document. Since the fifteenth century the main instrument used had been Letters Patent issued under the Great Seal.

The functions of these offices were usually distinguished by their titles, for as Coke said the 'names of men in great places should put them in mind . . . of their duty: as the treasurer of England to have special care of the king's treasure.' Many were of great antiquity and importance, such as the Lord High Treasurer, the Lord High Chancellor, the Secretaries of State, the Lord Chamberlain, the Lord Chief Justice. Outside the immediate entourage of the Court there were the Sheriffs, Lords Lieutenant, and Justices of the Peace. But one could draw up a very long list including the Groom of the Stole, the Clerk of the Pells, the Clerks of the Signet, the King's Assay-Master, and so on. Some of these offices, being primarily concerned with the king as a person, had remained inside the Court — such as the Master of the Jewel Office and the Lords of the King's Bedchamber. Others, because the duties related to the king as Executive and head of the country, had moved more and more into the public sphere and were engaged in the administration of the government of the country.

Where more than one person needed to be named to exercise the same powers, the Letters Patent set out the names of the various people so commissioned — for example, the Commissioners of the Treasury and of the Customs, and the Commissions of the Peace for each county.

Though a grant by Letters Patent under the Great Seal was the highest authority for the holding of particular offices, there were other forms and instruments in use. Commissions in the Army, for example, were granted by the king's signature and the Signet. In some cases letters under the Privy Seal were regarded as sufficient. Again, the Lords Commissioners of the Treasury, acting presumably under authority delegated by the king, appointed many officers in the financial and revenue spheres. Thus the Auditor of the Receipt and the Clerk of the Pells, both important officers of the Exchequer, were appointed for life by a Constitution under the Hands and

Seals of the Commissioners of the Treasury. In the Customs some officers were appointed by Treasury Constitution, others by Treasury Warrant. The difference was that a warrant only nominated a person, leaving it to the Commissioners of Customs to make the actual appointment, whereas a Constitution both nominated and appointed.

A substantial number of officers, particularly those concerned with the conduct of local affairs, derived their authority not directly from the king, but from the Common Law or from Acts of Parliament. High and Petty Constables, Parish Clerks, and Coroners, owed their existence, rights, and duties to ancient custom, for constant usage had not only sanctioned their first establishment but also had prescribed and settled the manner in which they were to be exercised. Even offices created by Letters Patent owed some of their rights and responsibilities to customary usage and by no means depended wholly on the wording of the instrument. The most numerous offices created by Act of Parliament were the Overseers of the Poor and the Surveyors of Highways.

The holder of an office was entitled to certain rights and incurred certain duties and obligations.

LEGAL RIGHTS

(i) *Remuneration and other Financial arrangements*
Though some important officers were remunerated solely by way of a fixed salary, e.g. the Treasurer of the Navy and the Lords Commissioners of the Treasury, the fullest and most ancient concept of office was usually associated with the right to collect fees. Whilst a salary was often attached to an office, this might be quite small in relation to its total pecuniary value. Thus the salary of the Clerk of the House of Commons according to his Patent was £10 a year 'together with all and other rewards, dues, rights, profits, commodities, advantages and endowments whatsoever to the said office, after what manner soever, or however now or heretofore, anciently appertaining, incident, accustomed, incumbent, or belonging.' The post was reckoned to be worth some £5,000 a year. In the Customs, a Patent officer might receive less than £100 a year as a salary, but have an income from fees of £500–£700 a year.

The Chief Clerks in the Offices of the Secretaries of State and in the Treasury, the Clerks in the Privy Seal Office, and the joint Secretaries of the Treasury Board were not paid a salary but drew their ample remuneration from the fees charged.

To be remunerated from the fees charged for the work performed had important implications for the status and role of an officer. Being paid by those who benefited from his services implied that he was in their service, not in that of an employer. His position was not very different from that of a merchant or a shopkeeper in relation to his customers: it was as though the particular function had been farmed out to him. In contrast, if he were to receive only a salary, his obligation must be towards those who paid his salary — his primary aim would be to please his employer rather than his clients.

The right of an officer to collect income from fees emphasized in another important way the independence and self-contained character of his office. For the implication was that the fee income was for the execution of the duties of the office. Should the public demand on these duties grow beyond the personal capacity of him or his deputy, the consequential increase in the fee income was available for the employment of clerks and other assistance. In other words, the fee income was not just for the remuneration of the officer, it was for the adequate conduct of his office. The growth in the number of clerks engaged on the processes arising from the use of the royal seals, the care of the king's treasure, and legal proceedings in the Courts, had been financed out of the growth in fee income.

Even where the grant of office entitled the holder only to a fixed salary he might nevertheless be expected to meet out of it the cost of some assistance and subordinate staff. The financial arrangements attaching to the offices of the Secretaries of State were interesting in this respect. The salary stated in their Patent was only £100 but each received a salary at pleasure of some £5,000 or so a year also from the Civil List. To these payments were added to each a share of the fees of the Office and of the profits of the London Gazette, bringing their gross income up to some £8,000. Out of this, however, in addition to paying certain taxes, each had to meet bills for coals, candles, and turnery ware and part of the salaries of the clerks and others in the department, leaving him with a net income of about £5,000. In the counties the fees payable to the Sheriff were numerous and substantial enough to enable him to meet the cost of the Under-Sheriffs and the staff of bailiffs. A somewhat different but nevertheless relevant example was to be found in the administration of the army. Officers received funds from the government and supplied themselves and their men with what was needed, making a profit if they could. Some items of equipment were supplied by the government from its own stores, but officers had to see to and pay for the repair, storage, and transport of what they received and the replacement of certain items when worn out.

Where an office involved the receipt of public money, whether in course of being passed on to the Exchequer or being used to meet the cost of a service, the holder normally had responsibility for its safe custody. He might use any balance in hand as though it were his own money. He might, for example, keep any interest the money earned from a bank or for a short-term loan. Such interest, or the free use of the money, thus constituted part of the pecuniary benefits of the office. The amount involved might range from the millions which passed through the hands of the Paymaster of the Forces to the small sums handled by the Receivers-General of the Land Tax in each county. An officer engaged in the collection of taxes would generally be able to draw upon the receipts for the costs of his office, or even for expenses laid on the tax by Act of Parliament. Thus, the Militia Act required the Receivers-General of the Land Tax to meet certain costs incurred in respect of the mustering of militia in their area, paying into the Exchequer only the net proceeds of the tax after this and other charges had been met. These and similar financial arrangements gave many offices the character of a sub-treasury. Not only did the officer perform certain functions which only he could perform, not only did his remuneration derive directly from those for whom he performed the functions, but also he might handle and have under his control for a time the whole of the moneys arising out of his activities. These features further emphasized his independent status.

(ii) *Exercise by Deputy*[10]

It was quite common for the Patent to empower the holder to exercise his office by means of a 'sufficient deputy'. It was obviously necessary to allow an officer to secure the performance of his office while he was sick, or for some other good reason unable to carry out the duties personally. But the right to appoint a sufficient deputy had come to be used to enable the officer to farm out, as it were, the work even though he was perfectly fit to perform the duties himself. The power greatly increased the attractions of the office, for it enabled the officer to derive an income from the office whilst performing none of the duties: he merely appointed a deputy on financial terms which left a surplus to himself.

The practice was most prevalent in the more ancient offices, for example, the Exchequer, the Privy Seal Office, and the Courts. Thus, in the former, the Clerk of the Pells, the two Chamberlains, the Usher of the Exchequer, the two Auditors of the Imprest, and the four Tellers of the Receipt of the Exchequer, all exercised their offices by deputy. Most of the patent officers in the Customs service were also so empowered. Indeed most officers appointed by Letters Patent were given that right except where the office was clearly granted because of the particular qualities of a person, e.g. a judge or where the holder had to have close personal contacts with the king. In the counties the ancient office of Clerk of the Peace was usually exercised by deputy, probably a leading lawyer of the town, but that of the Justice of Peace could not be deputed.

The financial arrangements were a matter to be settled between the officer and the deputy in very much the same way as rent is agreed between the owner and the lessee of a farm or a house. In this transaction, however, the right to the income of the office, however profitable, remained with the holder, not with the deputy, who received either a fixed salary or a stated proportion of the fees received. Should a person be appointed as a deputy without an allowance he had no remedy except against his principal.

The use of a deputy was not confined to profitable offices. At the other extreme there were offices which were both distasteful and unpaid, e.g. local constables and surveyors of highways. A person chosen to perform such an office might even pay a deputy to perform the duties for him.

The choice of the deputy usually rested with the officer. This underlined both the property character of the arrangement and the continuing general responsibility of the officer. The Letters Patent normally used the phrase 'sufficient deputy' which implied an obligation on the officer to appoint somebody suitable and adequate for the exercise of the duties. In some cases, however, the instrument required the officer to obtain the approval of some other officer or board. Some of the patent officers in the Customs required the approbation of the Treasury Board to the persons they might wish to appoint as their deputies. An Act of 1697 (8 and 9 Wm. III, c.28) required the chief clerks of the patent officers in the Exchequer, i.e. their deputies, to be put on oath for the 'due, just and faithful performance' of their tasks and their appointment to receive Treasury approval.

(iii) *Office as a Property*

It was well accepted that an office constituted a form of property, particularly the longer and more certain its tenure and the more pronounced the rights and pecuniary benefits attached to it. By 1780, though some offices were still granted for life, most were granted at pleasure, i.e. at the discretion of the grantor. But in practice the difference was not very great. Apart from the holders of 'political' offices close to the king, who had no expectation of remaining long in them, for most office-holders, appointment at pleasure meant in practice appointment for life. The holder still needed an income in his old age and if he had given the main years of his life in faithful public service it was considered just that he should continue to be provided with the wherewithal on which to live and, where necessary, make provision for his family.

Because the Letters Patent or other instrument gave the office-holder a legal right to certain pecuniary benefits it is little wonder that Blackstone could speak of 'Offices, which are a right to exercise a public or private employment, and to take the fees and emoluments thereunto belonging' as being incorporeal hereditaments.[11]

In as far as an office might ensure its holder a future income it was not dissimilar from a corporeal hereditament in that any purchaser was buying, for a capital sum, a series of future annual incomes. The holder might wish to sell the remaining years of his tenure or the reversion to the office, i.e. the purchaser to come into possession upon the death of the holder.

Some offices had not been saleable, for a long time, for example those of the judges or of the king's senior advisers. Generally speaking the practice was not so prevalent in 1780 as a century earlier. It was in any case more associated with tenure for life than 'at pleasure'. There was, however, one form which was known as 'Quartering'. In the Post Office, for example, it was a common practice for officers, though forbidden to sell their place, to make private bargains with their successors. By this process they continued to receive a proportion of the earnings of their office even after they had retired from it, thus providing for their old age.

The principal statute concerning the sale of offices was that of 5 and 6 Edw. VI, c.16 'For avoiding of corruption which may hereafter happen to be in the officers and ministers in those courts, places, or rooms, wherein there is requisite to be had the true administration of justice or services of trust, . . .' The Act declared that any bargain, or sale of any office or deputation, or the receipt of any money or reward for such a purpose shall be void and the person disabled from holding the office. The Act was not, however, as clear or as comprehensive as it would appear or else there were many transgressors. Nevertheless the Earl of Macclesfield, then Lord Chancellor, was impeached in 1725 and charged with selling the offices of Masters in Chancery. In his defence he argued that an office could be considered in respect to the duty and to the profit and advantage. Only the former was the concern of the public and provided the officer discharged his duty well, without extortion or other misbehaviour, the public were little concerned whether his profit be more or less. In the matter of appointing a deputy, provided the deputy behaved himself well, the public had never concerned itself about the salary or allowance he might receive from his principal. 'The public', he claimed, 'is concerned only in the goodness of the officer, not how advantageous to him the grant of office is, nor in the inducement which he that appointed him had to put him in; whether friendship, acquaintance, relation, importunity, great recommendation or a present.' The Noble Earl was expressing a widely held view but nevertheless he was fined £30,000.[12]

To regard an office as a form of property rather than a public trust could have two undesirable consequences, for the administrative system. First, it could lead many to regard the appointment of an officer or deputy not as the selection of the one most capable of performing certain duties, but as conferring a benefit upon that person, a kind of favour or reward.

Second, it could lead to the continuance of offices long after they had ceased to be necessary. Thus, under the Secretaries of State, the offices of Keeper of State Papers and Secretary for the Latin tongue no longer had work attached to them but were still remunerated. The continuation of these sinecures was sometimes justified as providing a pension for a public official who had had to retire, or as enabling another officer's income to be supplemented. But a major reason was the great difficulty of abolishing them, even where there was a will to do so. It could hardly be done during the lifetime of the holder, at least not without the payment to him of adequate compensation. It might not even be possible to do it upon his death without infringing property rights, for the reversion of the office might already have been promised to another, or by tradition the current holder might be felt to have the right to appoint his successor. Edmund Burke, hardly a friend of sinecures, pointed out in his speech on Economical Reform, certain offices 'have been given as provision for children; they have been the subject of family settlements; they have been the security of creditors.' 'What the law respects,' he went on, 'shall be sacred to me. . . . If the discretion of power is once let loose upon property, we can be at no loss to determine whose power, and what discretion it is, that will prevail at last.[13]

LEGAL DUTIES AND RESPONSIBILITIES[14]

Each office had imposed on it by the instrument of appointment, by Act of Parliament or by usage, specific duties and obligations. It was, therefore, a matter of some concern to the public that the holder performed these in a satisfactory manner. The law attempted to achieve this in several ways.

First, by indicating the qualities that ought to be possessed by an officer. Thus Coke had laid it down that

> if an office either in the grant of the king or a subject, which concerns the administration, proceeding, or execution of justice, or the king's revenue, or the commonwealth, or the interest, benefit, or safety of the subject, or the like; if they or any of them be granted to a man that is inexpert, and has no skill and science to execute the same, the grant is merely void, and partly disabled by law and incapable to take the same, . . . for only men of skill, knowledge, and ability . . . are capable

of serving the king and his people. Coke had also said that the policy of prudent antiquity was that officers did ever give grace to the place, not the place only to grace the officer.

An Act of 1388 (12 Ric. c.2) laid it down that none shall obtain offices by suit or for reward but upon desert. It specifically required certain Officers, e.g. the Lord Chancellor, Lord High Treasurer, and Lord Privy Seal 'that they make all such officers and ministers of the best and most lawful men, and sufficient, to their estimation and knowledge.

The courts tried to regulate the granting of offices and the conduct of their holders. Thus they had held to be void the erection of a new office which did not define the jurisdiction or authority of the holder. The courts had also held that it did not lie within the prerogative to create any new office inconsistent with the constitution or prejudicial to the subject. No officer constituted by Act of Parliament had more authority than the Act which created him or some subsequent Act might have bestowed on him: he could not prescribe as could an officer at common law. The courts had, as might be expected, been particularly strict about offices relating to the administration of justice, which must be exercised by persons of sufficient capacity and by the persons themselves to whom they were granted, unless the right to appoint a deputy was specifically granted by Letters Patent.

Second, the solemnity of the duties and obligations undertaken by the officer were usually emphasized by requiring him to swear an oath on first taking up the office. This was, of course, additional to the usual oaths of allegiance and supremacy required by the Test Act (25 Car. II, c.2). It was quite usual for an officer on appointment to be sworn and take an oath for the due, just, and faithful performance of his duties. Even the Commissioners first appointed in 1780 by Parliament for the purpose of examining the Public Accounts were required to swear before the Chancellor of the Exchequer 'That, according to the best of my Skill and Knowledge, I will faithfully, impartially and truly execute the several Powers and Trusts vested in me . . .' (20 Geo. III, c.54).

Third, there were a variety of legal remedies available. It was laid down in general that if an officer acted contrary to the nature and duty of his office, or if he refused to act at all, the office was forfeited. The grant of any office implied that it would be executed by the grantee faithfully and diligently. On the breach of this condition the office was forfeited or became liable to be seized. This principle was well accepted, the difficulty lay in its application. As Coke stated: 'in general, all wilful breaches of the duty of an officer are forfeitures of it, and also punishable by fine, etc., for since every office is instituted not for the sake of the officer, but for the good of some other, nothing can be more just than that he, who either neglects or refuses to answer the end for which his office was ordained, should give way to others who are both able and willing to take care of it, and that he should be punished for his neglect or oppressive execution.' He mentioned three causes of forfeiture or seizure of offices:

(a) by abuser, e.g. by a gaoler permitting escapes;
(b) by non-user, i.e. where it was the duty of the holder to attend without request but did not do so; and
(c) by refusal, i.e. where requested to exercise his office but did not do so.

A principal might forfeit his office if he put in a deputy who was ignorant and unskilful. Where an office was granted upon 'good behaviour' it could be forfeited by a breach of that condition. Misbehaviour included a conviction for any infamous offence which, although not connected with the duties of the office, rendered the offender unfit to exercise it. The question whether there had been misbehaviour rested with the grantor of the office. An office might also be lost if the holder accepted an incompatible office: e.g. if a coroner were made sheriff he ceased to be a coroner.

To secure compliance or forfeiture usually involved formal legal proceedings, and various processes, including the prerogative writs of mandamus and quo warranto, were available. If an officer holding office by Letters Patent committed an act incurring a forfeiture, he could not be turned out without a scire facias, nor could he be said to be completely ousted or discharged without a writ of discharge; for his right being of record had to be defeated by a matter of as high a nature.

The method of ensuring that public accountants presented their accounts in due time and returned any money due to the Exchequer involved a whole paraphernalia of writs starting with a writ of Distringas ad computandum, issued by the King's Remembrancer Office, and culminating in a Long Writ, which included every compulsive process known to the law.[15]

The use of judicial and legal processes to secure proper performance was perhaps even more marked in the case of the officers and bodies in the counties, parishes, and boroughs. Thus, when the County of Derby failed to comply with the Militia Acts, a writ of mandamus was issued against the Justices to compel them either to raise their statutory quota of 560 men, or pay £5 per man. On the issue of this writ the Justices ordered the sum of £2,800 to be raised, but nothing was done until another mandamus was threatened in 1773.[16] The basis of such actions was that an official or a community had failed to fulfil his or its legal duty. The courts were, however, rightly reluctant to interfere with the exercise of discretion vested in the Justices or other local officer or body. In this sphere as in the case of officers more closely associated with the king, the judges' task was to see in particular that the law was obeyed and, in general, that the liberty of the subject was not endangered.

In local administration many of the duties placed on officers, communities and even individuals were enforced by the ancient machinery of presentment and indictment. Thus, if a constable were thought to be neglecting his duties in a certain matter, or a parish failed to repair its highways, the constable or the parish could be presented at Quarter Sessions and could be punished. The process was used by the Justices to ensure that bridges, gaols, and other county buildings were maintained and became so normal that an Act of 1739 (12 Geo II, c.29) provided that no money was to be spent on the repair of bridges, gaols, prisons, or houses of correction without a presentment of the grand jury at the assizes, or at Quarter Sessions. The procedure gave the local inhabitants who served on the grand jury a chance to express their opinion about whether the repairs, etc., were so needed that money should be spent on them.[17]

It would be quite wrong to assume that the public were constantly taking legal action to ensure that particular officers fulfilled their obligations. That would imply that the holders of the large number of offices were either ill-chosen or unwilling or unskilled, which would not be true. The use of a sufficient deputy met the need where the principal suffered from one or all of these defects. It was, moreover, not easy to find grounds for taking successful legal action in the case of the more important of the king's officers. If an officer refused to carry out his duties there was clear cause for legal action but the more likely situation was for the officer and the public to differ on what was a sufficient performance, or for example, as to the speed at which he performed them. In matters of that kind the courts were unlikely to interfere.

In any case two important developments had begun to cast doubts on the effectiveness of this essentially legal method of conducting the country's affairs. The first was the increasing number of persons employed in the public offices who could not be regarded as officers in the normal legal sense of the term. Second, there was the growing belief in political quarters that political rather than legal accountability was the better safeguard of the public interest. The two developments reinforced each other.

EMPLOYEES

The bulk of those engaged in the non-military services of the Crown in 1780 were engaged on the levy and collection of taxes. Their number and the character of their work had during the eighteenth century changed the public service out of all recognition. The Customs duties had been levied for a long time but had become much more complex. Excise duties were more recent and even more so were the Stamp and Salt duties and the Land tax. Very few of the ten thousand or so engaged in these departments were officers. Because of its ancient origins there were several hundred patent officers in the Customs, a great many of whom exercised their office by deputy. But in the other revenue departments only a very small number were appointed by Patent: usually the Commissioners and one or two departmental heads, for example, the Secretary of the Stamp Office, the Solicitor of the Excise, and the Comptrollers of the Stamp and Salt Offices. Other senior appointments were usually made by Treasury Constitution or Warrant or even by the Board.

The difference between the Customs and the other revenue departments was largely due to the new boards being created and staffed at the end of the last century when the concept of office had perhaps lost its main force. There were, however, two more fundamental reasons. For one thing, it was clear from the beginning that none of the taxes could be administered by a single Officer; considerable numbers would have to be engaged mainly on work of a similar character. There was no chance, therefore, for the slow growth and change that had taken place in, for example, the Treasury. For another, the concept of office at its fullest depended on a system of fees accruing to the holder for the duties he performed. The administration of the new taxes could, however, be financed out of the receipts and, in any case, the compulsory payment of a tax was hardly a service for which the public would be willing to pay a fee.

A similar development though on a very much smaller scale had taken place in the offices of the Treasury, of the Principal Secretaries of State, and of the Admiralty. At the beginning of the century, apart from the five Commissioners and a Secretary, the Treasury consisted of a dozen or so clerks and a few messengers. By 1780 there were some thirty clerks and a dozen or so messengers, housekeepers, and similar employees. The rate of growth in the office of the Principal Secretaries of State had been somewhat similar so that, in addition to the three Principal Secretaries, there were some fifty clerks, office keepers, and others. Apart from the political heads only a handful of these officials were formally appointed by the king and these held such ancient offices as the Secretary for the Latin Tongue and the Keeper of the State Papers. The great bulk of those engaged in the public offices were appointed by the political heads.

The fact that some of these officials possessed attributes generally enjoyed by officers did not thereby put them in that category. The clerks in the Treasury and in the Office of the Secretaries of State were, for example, remunerated out of fee income. No doubt many of them regarded their post as a form of property. The necessary woman in the office of the Secretaries of State even executed her duties by way of a deputy. Their functions, however, were to assist an officer — the Lords of the Treasury or Principal Secretary — to fulfil his duties and responsibilities. They did not in themselves possess powers which only they could exercise. At one time most clerks were in the personal employ of the officer, paid by him out of the fees or income he derived from the office. Thus the Secretary of the Treasury originated as the personal servant of the Treasurer of England and so did the Under-Secretaries to the Secretaries of State and the Secretary to the Lord High Admiral. In other words they were neither servants of the king nor paid by him, any more than one of the gamekeepers on the estate of say, the Duke of Newcastle, was anything more than a private employee. As the volume of work increased, more assistants had to be engaged and came to be differentiated as Chief, Senior, and Under clerks, and even Extra clerks.

Most of the secretaries, clerks, and other subordinates had by 1780 ceased to be dependent on their original patron. Whereas in earlier days a secretary or clerk would follow his patron in and out of office, they were now normally appointed for what was in effect life, or until they were driven by old age or ill health to retire. The need for permanence arose from the increasing complexity and volume of the work of the great officers. It would not be easy for a new Secretary of State to find friends and protégés skilled and experienced enough to replace the existing clerks, even if he were in mind to do so. In the case of the Treasury only the two Secretaries were likely to change, with changes in the person of the First Lord of the Treasury. When a man had worked in a department for twenty or thirty years, even longer in some cases, he had acquired a value and an importance which overrode the fact that he was a servant of the officer at the head of the department and did not derive his authority from an instrument under the king's hand and seal.

The clerks, excise men, and others in the public offices were not deputies, for the officer they assisted was also active. But the parallel with the deputy was relevant for when an officer exercised his office by means of a deputy, legal responsibility remained with him and did not pass to the deputy. A deputy was one who exercised an office in another man's right, whose forfeiture and demeanour could cause the officer whose deputy he was, to lose his office. Should the deputy not be sufficient the officer could be required to answer in civil actions. If this were true of deputies how much more true must it have been of the clerks and others who assisted the political heads of the important public offices.

The increasing number of clerks and other assistants had another important implication for the system of administration. For inevitably it led to a hierarchy of authority. When an officer needed only the help of one or two others to exercise his office, the relationships were highly personal and there was little or no need to delineate the powers of each assistant. But as the number of clerks increased, they could not all work direct to the officer and some had to be given greater responsibilities than others. Thus the increase in the size of the Treasury resulted in a hierarchy of clerks, their degrees of importance and power being reflected in their remuneration. In this respect the civil administration was beginning to take on one of the features of the organization of the Navy and the Army, that of a series of levels of authority and command, each answerable to those at a higher level and able to give orders to those at a level below them.

The concept of office did not fit easily into such a hierarchical system. For the legal basis of an office was that the holder was answerable at law for the performance of his duties. He could hardly be held answerable if that performance were dictated by somebody of superior authority. It was incompatible with the concept of office that the holder should be wholly subordinated to another officer. This would certainly be true if the other could exercise the office of the holder without his authority, or if the holder could only exercise his duties on the instruction of the other. If these circumstances existed, and particularly if the person who apparently held the office had no authority to exercise any powers except those deputed to him by the other, then he must be deemed to be an employee and as such not legally liable for the service he performed.

There were, however, cases where the instrument of authority required an officer to obey the instructions of another officer. Thus officers in the Navy and Army must obey the instructions of their superior officers. For discipline is an essential element in the conduct of war and is provided in a hierarchy of authority. But that did not take away the authority which a subordinate officer derived from his commission from the king. Civil government is not, however, based on such hierarchy of legal authority. Officers in civil government were not normally made subordinate to officers with higher levels of authority. This was the characteristic arrangement of the Secretaries, Chief Clerks, Clerks, and so on, and that is why they constituted quite a different administrative system than one based on the concept of office.

The character and form of an appointment was a legal indication of its status and its relationship with other appointments. In the management of the various taxes, for example, all the Commissioners, with the exception of the unimportant Office for Hawkers and Pedlars Licences, were appointed by royal Letters Patent. Most of the clerks and subordinate staff were appointed by their respective boards, or by a senior officer of the Board. There were, however, always several who were given a special status by being appointed not by a board but by either Letters Patent or by Treasury Constitution or Warrant. Thus the Comptrollers of the Stamp, Salt, and Excise departments were appointed by Patent, as were the Receiver-General of the Customs and the Receiver of the Stamp Office, whereas in the case of the Excise, Tax and Hackney Coach Offices they are appointed by Treasury Warrant.

The existence of a few special posts with the status implied by Letters Patent, need not interfere with a department being organized according to a hierarchy of degrees of authority and subordination. For such offices as Receiver-General, Comptroller, and Solicitor were sufficiently individual and important to be entitled to a special position in any hierarchy. But the effect would be different if the post was one of several undertaking the same kind of duties. If, for example, one of the four chief clerks in the Treasury had been appointed by royal Patent, he could hardly have fitted easily into the organization of the department.

In the Customs most of the Collectors were patent officers and though the Letters Patent appointing the Customs Commissioners enjoined such officers to be obedient to the Board, the Commissioners had no power over them, nor over their deputies, except the power of suspending them in order to prevent any prejudice to the revenue and to give time for representing their conduct to their principals.[18] Even less prestigious methods of appointment could affect the degree of control exercisable by a revenue Board: a person appointed by Treasury Constitution was also in a more independent position than one who was appointed by the Board direct. There was indeed an important distinction in the case of the revenue departments and possibly in other departments between staff appointed internally and those appointed by an external authority. In the former category there was a further distinction between those appointed by the Board and those appointed by an officer of the Board. It was by no means unusual for an officer in the service of a Board to appoint his own immediate clerks and assistants.

The significance of the type of appointment to those charged with the management of a service can be illustrated by an exchange of views between the Commissioners of Customs and the Treasury Board in 1778. It concerned the office of the Receiver of Fines and Forfeitures. When created in 1728 it had been filled by Treasury Warrant, but since 1765 by Constitution. The Commissioners pointed out that their Patent gave them full powers over officers appointed by them, but made no mention of their powers over those appointed by Treasury Constitution. If the Constitution did not contain a clause of obedience to the Board's orders, the person would not come under the Board's management but would be solely under Treasury direction. Even where the Constitution contained the usual clause of obedience it was doubtful whether the Commissioners could enforce it by suspension, let alone by dismissal, i.e. by cancelling the Treasury commission. They asked that either the Patent be altered to give them the same control over Constitution as they had over Warrant appointments, or to change this particular appointment to that by Warrant. The Treasury continued to grant the office by Constitution which, however, now contained a clause requiring obedience to the Commissioners of Customs.[19]

III

Ministers and Parliament

There was no sharp distinction in legal theory between the First Lord of the Treasury, the Master of the Horse, or the Secretary of the Stamp Office. All were servants of the king, owing their legal authority to royal Letters Patent. In reality, however, there was an extremely big difference between the First Lord of the Treasury and the others. For though appointed by the king his real authority was derived from his position in Parliament and, in particular, from the support accorded to him by the House of Commons and from his position in relation to his colleagues. There were a number of officers with a political status: the Principal Secretaries of State, the First Lord of the Admiralty, Lord President of the Council, Lord Privy Seal and half a dozen or so others. The relation of these officers with the king had changed over the past fifty or so years and the trend continued. One sign of the change was the emergence of a smaller 'effective' cabinet confined to these officers and not presided over by his Majesty.

The Privy Council was a large body composed of some one hundred members of whom some two-thirds were Peers of the Realm. Its business was, however, conducted by a small number of members summoned by the king to advise him on a particular matter. It was 'By the Advice and Consent' of the Privy Council that the king issued Proclamations and Declarations of War and summoned or dissolved Parliament. It had been customary for a good many years for the king to rely on a small group of Counsellors for regular advice and this group was known as the Cabinet Council, or simply, as the Cabinet. At one time the group included not only the principal officers of State already mentioned but also such important dignitaries as the Archbishop of Canterbury, the Lord Chief Justice of the King's Bench, the Lord Chamberlain, and the Master of the Horse. A smaller body had, however, emerged, an 'efficient' in distinction to a 'nominal' Cabinet, composed solely of a handful of 'political' officers. It was this smaller body, at which the king was not present, which discussed major issues of national policy and advised the king on such matters. In so far as the word 'Administration' had any collective meaning it was to be found in the group of politicians who held certain great Offices of State and who met together in this Cabinet.

In 1780 the House of Lords was composed of three Peers of the Royal Blood, twenty-two Dukes, one Marquis, seventy-eight Earls, fourteen Viscounts and seventy-two Barons, all of whom had the hereditary right to be summoned. To these were added the two Archbishops and twenty-four Bishops and sixteen members elected from the Scottish Peerage. The House of Commons contained 558 Members elected from time to time, 513 representing England and Wales and 45 representing Scotland. Each House was responsible for its own affairs, but their joint approval was needed for legislation. Each House debated such matters as it thought to be of interest and importance and passed such resolutions as the majority found agreeable . Their constitutional position in respect of legislation was set out in the preamble of each general Act of Parliament: 'be it enacted by the King's most Excellent Majesty, by and with the Advice and Consent of the Lords Spiritual and Temporal, and Commons, in this present Parliament assembled, and by the Authority of the same . . .'

The king had two prerogative rights *vis-à-vis* Parliament. First, he could refuse to sign a Bill agreed by the two Houses. William III used this power in 1693 and 1694 in respect of the Triennial and the Place Bills. Queen Anne used it only once, against a Bill for Scottish Militia in 1708. Though still part of the prerogative, it was a power unlikely to be used lightly. But as Lord Ilay said in 1743 in the House of Lords: 'when those who have the honour to serve the crown find a Bill brought into this House, which they think the king ought not to give his assent to, it is certainly their duty to oppose the bill in its progress, and to endeavour to have it rejected by the House, in order to prevent their sovereign's being subjected to the invidious task of refusing it the royal assent.'[20]

Second he might dissolve Parliament, a course of action he had taken as recently as September 1780. In constitutional theory the king had complete freedom to dissolve and call Parliament, for it was but one of several advisory councils available to him, and, therefore, in theory he was free to dispense with its advice — and by the same theory he was not under any obligation to arrange for regular elections. But since 1695 (6. Wm and M., c.2) Parliament had to be called at least once in three years and, since 1715 (1 Geo., Stat. 2, c.38), a general election had to take place at intervals of not more than seven years.

In their turn the two Houses had powers which they could use against the king. Either House could refuse to pass a particular Bill even though the measure was known to have His Majesty's support. As the High Court of Parliament it could impeach any one of the king's advisers. Parliament could remonstrate and complain to the king 'even of those acts of royalty which are most properly and personally his own; such as messages signed by himself or speeches delivered from the throne'.[21]

Finally, the Commons could refuse to grant supply to the king, a power which put that House in a position superior to that of the Lords, and a power of increasing significance. At one time the hereditary revenues, perhaps with a small supplementation, were sufficient to satisfy the old maxim that the king should live of his own. Even had the Stuart kings been less prodigal, these revenues would still have been wholly inadequate to finance the Executive in times of war. The king had, therefore, to come year after year to Parliament for the money needed for the conduct of the various wars, and even sometimes for the civil government.

By a Resolution of 1678 the Commons had stated that the grant of supply to the king was their sole gift and that neither taxes nor grants should be changed or altered by the Lords. The preamble to any Act imposing taxation or granting supply made it clear that this was done by the Commons even though the Act, like other Acts, required the consent of the king and the Lords.

The king's powers to refuse his assent to Bills approved by the two Houses or to dissolve Parliament before the normal end of its life, just as the Commons' powers to refuse supply or to impeach one of the king's advisers, were not for everyday use. On the whole, the relations between the king and his advisers and the House of Commons were usually co-opera-tive. The Commons recognized that the Constitution vested the Executive function in the king and had therefore been reluctant to take actions which could be said to encroach upon the prerogative. Equally, the king had reacted sharply to any such attempts by the Commons.

Some part of the willingness of the Commons to accept the king's policy was due to 'the influence of the crown'. Even Blackstone displayed some concern over the power of this 'influence most amazingly extensive.'[22] This influence was made up of several elements. First, a number of Members of the House of Commons were office-holders or placemen. In the House elected in September 1780 there were some 40–50 Members holding effective government posts, some 30 who held sinecures, some 25 or so who held appointments at Court, and nearly 60 who held commissions in the armed forces. Second, the Crown had various means of obtaining the support of particular Members. The First Lord of the Treasury, in particular, had a large number of posts, mainly in the Customs, which needed to be filled each year and even if a Member might not want one for himself he might have relations and friends who did. There was also money in the hands of Ministers, particularly the Secret Service money, which was used to support the government's friends at elections. Finally, the needs of war had greatly increased the public purchase of stores and borrowing of money and here again the government could favour their friends and suppor-ters.[23]

It is not suggested that this influence purchased the unwil-ling support of Members. Probably David Hume saw the matter in proper perspective in his Essay of 1741 on The Independence of Parliament:

The crown has so many offices at its disposal that, when assisted by the honest and disinterested part of the house, it will always command the resolutions of the whole so far, at least, as to preserve the ancient constitution from danger. We may, therefore, give to this influence what name we please; we may call it by the invidious appelations of *corruption* and *dependence*, but some degree and some kind of it are inseparable from the very 'nature of the constitution and necessary to the preservation of our mixed government.[24]

The day-to-day link between the king and Parliament was furnished by those of his advisers who were active in one or other chamber. But because of its special position in respect of the grant of Supply membership of the Commons was becoming more significant. Unless the policies and actions of the king had at least the tacit support of the Commons he could face considerable friction and even outright opposition. In practical terms this meant that unless the king's chief political advisers, principally the First Lord of the Treasury, had the confidence of the Commons they were not of great value to him and he would have to change to others who had.

The possibility of a close working relationship between Ministers and the House of Commons would not have emerged had the Act of Settlement of 1701 remained on the statute book. For that Act contained a section which baldly declared that 'no Person who has an Office or a Place of Profit under the King, or receives a Pension from the Crown, shall be capable of serving as a Member of the House of Commons'. Before, however, that prohibition could come into operation it was repealed.

There were a good many Members who believed in this total exclusion but others preferred a more affirmative and ambitious solution to the problem of influence. This was to enable a limited number of specified household officials and working Ministers to sit in the Commons but to exclude the great bulk of minor placemen, sinecurists, pensioners, and officers in the armed forces. The House of Lords, which was heavily weighted with the king's supporters were against exclusion and argued that exclusion was

inconsistent with the nature and constitution of the English government. For to enact, that all persons employed and trusted by the Crown shall, for that reason alone, become incapable of being trusted by the People, is in effect to declare that the interests of the Crown and of the People must always be contrary to each other: which is a notion no good Englishman ought to entertain.

The Lords would have liked to have limited the disability to any person holding an office or place of profit under the

Crown created thereafter. That clause was agreed by the Commons, the date being 25 October 1705, along with three other provisions: (1) a member of the House of Commons who accepted an office automatically forfeited his seat but was eligible for re-election, and, if re-elected, could retain the office; (2) Certain named offices the duties of which were thought to be incompatible with a seat in the House were excluded e.g. Pensioners during Pleasure, Comptroller of Accounts of the Army, Governor or Deputy Governor of any of the Plantations; and (3) members of the House who were officers in the Navy or Army were not to be disqualified. The new policy was incorporated in an Act of 1705 (4 Anne, c.8) and re-enacted in the Succession to the Crown (or Regency) Act of 1707 (6 Anne, c.7).

The Board of Commissioners and officers of Excise had been excluded by an Act of 1699 (11 and 12 Wm. III, c.2) and of the Customs by an Act of 1701 (12 & 13 Wm. III, c.10). In 1742 a Place Act (15 Geo. II, c.22) increased the number of officials who were ineligible for membership of the Commons. The Act particularly concentrated on the deputies and clerks in such main public offices as the Treasury, Exchequer, Admiralty, and Secretaries of State. It specifically excluded from its coverage such posts as the Secretaries to the Treasury and the Admiralty and one Under-Secretary to any of the Principal Secretaries of State.

Had the policy embodied in the Act of Settlement not been modified, presumably the great officers of State would have been treated by the Commons in the same manner as it treated all who are not Members. Thus, when an officer of the Exchequer or the Customs came to present a return at the command of the House, he was called to the bar and was treated, for what he was, as an outsider. It would hardly have made for close relations if, for example, the First Lord of the Treasury or one of the Principal Secretaries of State, had been so treated. It might have had the effect of increasing the importance of the House of Lords for that chamber had never excluded placemen, and, indeed, in 1780 the majority of the holders of the great Offices of State were still members of that House.

It had become recognized that two or three must be in the

Commons, quite apart from such junior office-holders as the two Secretaries to the Lords Commissioners of the Treasury. At the end of 1780 the First Lord of the Treasury, the Secretary-at-War, the Paymaster of the Forces, and the Treasurer of the Navy, were Officers with seats in the Commons.

In the House of Commons it had become customary to reserve places for the king's Ministers on the front bench on the right of Mr Speaker, commonly known as the Treasury bench. It was they who explained and defended the government's policy and who steered through the measures necessary for its fulfilment, in particular the measures imposing taxation, and authorizing loans and expenditure. The leader was usually referred to as His Majesty's Minister in the House of Commons. From time to time Parliament became unhappy or disenchanted with the course of events, for example, the failure of British military efforts in North America, and this was reflected in criticism of and lack of support for Ministers. While the Commons could not presume to dictate to the king whom he should chose to serve him it could and did show an unwillingness to grant the king's wishes when put forward by Ministers who had lost its confidence. Such unpopularity might also be reflected in the lessened success of the government's supporters at a general election.

In those spheres of public affairs in which the king was advised by and his policy carried out by this small number of political officers, the doctrine that the king can do no wrong could only mean that these Ministers were legally accountable. In their case the established process was by impeachment. The High Court of Parliament was the supreme court in the kingdom. The Commons were entitled to impeach any one of the king's officers and it was for the Lords to consider the charges and the defence and pass judgment. The process had, however, not been used since 1746.

Without implying in any way that more Ministers should have been impeached it has to be recognized that it was a cumbersome and unsatisfactory device. It was by no means easy to determine which Minister was legally responsible at law for any particular policy or decision. Such great Officers of State as the Principal Secretaries derived little or none of their authority from the Statutes. For this reason Blackstone did not deal with them: the powers and duties, he says , of 'the lord treasurer, lord chamberlain the principal secretaries, or the like' are not 'in that capacity in any considerable degree the subjects of our laws, or have any very important share of magistracy conferred upon them'.[25] Many matters were discussed in the Privy Council or in the Cabinet and the Commons could hardly proceed by impeaching all present at a particular meeting, even if it could be proved that the decision in question had been taken there. The simplest legal test had been the affixing of the appropriate seal and the countersigning of the king's authority, the test applied in the impeachment of Lord Somers in 1701.

It had long been recognized that custody of a Seal was an office of considerable trust and constitutional significance. The Keeper of the Great Seal had developed into the office of Lord High Chancellor; of the Privy Seal into the Lord Privy Seal and the Keepers of the Signet, of which there were now three, were the Principal Secretaries of State. Custody of a Seal carried with it responsibility for its use. When they affixed it to a document the Lord Chancellor, the Lord Privy Seal, or one of the Secretaries were not just subordinates acting in accordance with the king's commands. True, such commands were not lightly to be disregarded, but should the act so formalized be in fact illegal, or be likely to arouse strong Parliamentary criticism, then the officer authorizing the use of the seal might find himself held personally liable. The countersignature of one of the Principal Secretaries to a warrant, for example, signified in effect his approval of the document, and so Parliament could rightly hold him responsible for its contents. Nor was it a valid defence to plead that he had acted under the king's orders. Personal responsibility arose at each stage in the process of authorizing the use of the Great Seal. The Lord Chancellor could not plead, for example, that he was merely following the decisions already made by a Secretary of State and the Lord Privy Seal, though no doubt it was a comfort to him to know he was in such good company. Sometimes the process started by the Signet was stopped at the next or even at the final stage because the officer responsible for that superior Seal had doubts about the merit or validity of the act.

Because the use of the Seals extended over the whole range of the king's actions, so did the responsibility of their custodians. This was particularly significant in the case of the Signet, which was needed for a very wide range of business. The Secretaries of State authorized its use to seal warrants issued under the Sign Manual for such matters as commissions in the Army, instructions to colonial governors and formal directions to, say, the Master-General of the Ordnance to issue arms. As a result they were aware of and involved in a whole range of matters. Their influence was correspondingly great, and most of the opportunity to exercise it was derived not from powers vested in them personally, but almost wholly from their responsibility for the use of the Signet.

Impeachment was a legal, not a political, process and the accusers had to prove that the accused had acted or advised the king contrary to the law. Yet in many cases what concerned those who supported a particular impeachment was not that the Minister has committed some crime or breach of the law but that his advice to the king had been unsound or contrary to the advice which the majority would have preferred him to have seen offered. In the case of Walpole, for example, the effective remedy was found to be not impeachment but the withdrawal by the Commons of their support. The limits to any major policy being pursued by the king and his Ministers could be set by the willingness of Parliament, and in particular of the Commons, to vote the money and approve the measures essential for the implementation of that policy. To be effective, however, the departmental arrangements would have to be such that Parliament could know clearly which Minister could be held accountable for any particular action or policy. Use of the Seals was too general an act to suffice. Each Minister would need to have publicly assigned to him a particular sphere of public affairs, for which he would have to answer in public.

By 1780 the constitutional and administrative arrangements had proceeded much less far in the direction of individual than of collective responsibility. The Prime Minister and few of his most senior colleagues such as the Secretaries of State and the First Lord of the Admiralty, met quite regularly as a Cabinet without the attendance of the king. This inevitably added substance to the claim that these ministers had a collective responsibility. Lord North apparently accepted this doctrine when defending the Secretary of State for the American Colonies (Lord G. Germain) in the House of Commons on 14 December 1778. He said that the attack on the noble lord about the war in America concerned 'measures of state, originating in the King's counsels, and were of course no more the noble lord's measures than they were of any other member of the cabinet: the crimes or faults, or errors committed there, were imputable to the whole body, and not to a single individual who composed it.'[26]

The success or failure of the war in America was a matter of great national significance. It was obvious to all that blame for any lack of success could hardly be laid solely at the doors of the most junior of the Secretaries — it reflected discredit on the king, Lord North, and all his senior political colleagues. The same argument could hardly be used for lesser faults or errors.

The development of a Prime Minister had not so far meant that all other ministers acted under his direction. Lord North felt that there should be one directing Minister who should plan the whole of the operations of government and control all the other departments of administration so that they co-operated zealously and actively. But neither the king nor the other senior Ministers were prepared to accord this degree of authority to one Minister. The king dealt with many Ministers directly to seek their personal advice. Grenville insisted that none of his colleagues should consult with the king unless he knew of it, but he did not last in office very long. Lord North was much more amenable· to the king and did not attempt to dictate to his colleagues.

It was natural, however, that anybody invited to become the king's chief Minister, should want some say in the choice of the people who were going to hold some of the main political offices. He might make his acceptance dependent on two or three of his political allies being given office and the exclusion of one or two others whom he disliked. In these matters as in all human relationships, there were no constitutional rules. The king had to have a few senior ministers who were able and reasonably popular. To get them he might have to accept a particular line of foreign or domestic policy, though, left to his own devices he would have preferred a rather different line. He might have to appoint one or two politicians as the price for obtaining and keeping his Prime Minister. But he was equally entitled not to give way on any matters and appointments about which he felt strongly and in those cases Ministers usually accepted his views. But the time was not far off when the stresses and strains resulting from maintaining a collective front against strong public criticism would require Ministers in the Cabinet to be chosen from amongst those with similar political principles and aims.

IV

Public Offices and Boards

It is not possible even to list let alone explain every public office or authority existing in 1780. There were, for example, scattered throughout the land a great number and a great variety of manorial courts, most in decay but some like the Manchester Court Leet still active. Even at the national level there were too many public officers and offices to mention individually. We will, therefore, concentrate attention on the main institutions and particularly on those which illuminate the ways in which the administrative system worked in practice. For this reason we will not deal with the officers of Parliament, as being more relevant to the Legislature than to the Executive, nor with the Church of England, as not being part of the civil administration.

We will also say but a few words about those who ministered to the royal dignity and comfort, in other words officers in the Royal Household and in the separate households of the Queen and the Prince of Wales. Chief among these were the Lord Chamberlain, the Master of the Horse, and the Lord Steward, who were often invited by the king to attend his Cabinet Council. As might be expected, the Royal Household contained a large number of offices with such ancient sounding titles as Lords of the Bed Chamber, Groom of the Stole, Master of the Jewel Office, and Clerks of Board of Green Cloth. Their salaries and the cost of upkeep of the Households were a charge against the Civil List.

Chief among those who occupied the offices concerned with the conduct of the public affairs of the country was the First Lord of the Treasury who was Prime Minister and in 1780 also Chancellor of the Exchequer. The three Principal Secretaries of State, the Lord President of the Council, the First Lord of the Admiralty, the Lord Chancellor, and the Lord Privy Seal were usually members of the effective Cabinet presided over by the Prime Minister. Other officers on the fringe of this group were the Master-General of the Ordnance,

Secretary at War, Chancellor of the Duchy of Lancaster, Master of the Mint, and Attorney-General.

Membership of the Cabinet was a good indication of the political but not of the executive significance of an officer, The Lord President of the Council, Lord Privy Seal, Chancellor of the Duchy of Lancaster, and Master of the Mint occupied offices making few claims on their time. The Lord Privy Seal, for example, was assisted by four patent clerks who exercised their duties by deputy. In contrast the First Lords of the Treasury and of the Admiralty had responsibility and authority for a number of important activities.

The simplest way of describing the main structure of the executive is in terms of finance, defence, overseas affairs, and domestic affairs.

In the financial sphere the Treasury Board had superseded the Exchequer in significance because of the overwhelming importance of taxation and borrowing as a means of financing the nation's wars. Since 1714 the ancient office of Lord HighTreasurer had been in commission. The five Commissioners were appointed by Letters Patent, the first named being known as the First Lord. The Chancellor of the Exchequer or Under Treasurer was always a member but the office was held by the First Lord when he was in the Commons. The business of the Board was to superintend every branch of the public revenue and to this end could give directions to all boards and persons entrusted with its receipt or expenditure. Closely linked with the Board were the revenue departments, the Royal Mint, and the Lottery Office.

There were seven Boards of Commissioners responsible for the levy and collection of the ever increasing volume of taxes: Customs, Excise, Stamps, Salt, Taxes (for the Land Tax), Hackney Coach, and Hawkers and Pedlars. Their instruments of appointment and the legislation which authorized the creation of the Boards made them generally subordinate to the Lord Commissioners of the Treasury. Members of the revenue boards were prohibited from sitting in the House of Commons. The other major revenue department was the General Post Office under a Postmaster-General, an office shared by two holders in 1780. There were also Receivers for the Sixpenny Civil List and the Shilling Pension Duties.

The Mint manufactured the coinage: it did not decide the value, form, or number of different coins to be minted. Like the Exchequer it was a collection of officers rather than a department, with a head, clerks, and other assistants. The officers had such picturesque names as Warden, Master and Worker, Chief Engraver, Clerk of the Irons, and King's Assay Master. Many of the offices were executed by deputy. The coins were minted by the Moneyers over whom the Warden and Master had little control and who were in a contractual relationship with the Treasury.

State Lotteries had been used since 1693 in association with the raising of loans. Subscribers to the loan had the right to participate in a lottery, the prizes usually taking the form of an additional allotment of stock. After 1769, however, the prizes were usually paid in cash. An Act authorizing the raising of money in this way was passed in most years, e.g. in 1780 (20 Geo. III, c.16). Each lottery was under the general control of the Treasury who appointed Managers and Directors otherwise known as Commissioners to handle the arrangements for making the draw and settle disputes. The tickets were sold in offices which after 1779 (19 Geo. III, c.21) required a licence costing £50 from the Managers.

The Exchequer, though closely linked with the Treasury, is more appropriately dealt with as part of the section on Finance.

The sphere of defence was dominated by the Board of Admiralty. The ancient office of Lord High Admiral had been in commission continuously since 1718. Usually seven Commissioners were appointed by Letters Patent, the first named being the First Lord. The business of the Board of Admiralty was to consider and determine upon all matters relative to His Majesty's Navy and the departments belonging thereto. It was empowered to give directions to any of the departments or branches for the performance of all the services that might be required. Next in significance was the Navy Office under ten or so Commissioners who were responsible to the Admiralty for the well-being and regulation of the civil establishments of the navy; they made contracts for stores of all kinds, prepared all the estimates for the expenses of the navy, directed all money for naval services into the hands of the Treasurer of the

Navy, and examined and certified his accounts of expenditure. There was the Sick and Hurt Office usually under three Commissioners and a Victualling Office usually under seven Commissioners.

Responsibility for the Land Forces was nothing like so concentrated. The king was in effect his own Commander-in-Chief and had the assistance of the Secretary at War. This officer was, however, of a status far inferior to that of the Principal Secretaries of State and it was through these that the main conduct of the army was regulated. There was a Paymaster-General for the Land Forces who handled the money voted by Parliament for this purpose. The arms, ammunition, and military stores for both the army and the navy were provided by the Board of Ordnance.

In the spheres of both overseas and domestic policy the Principal Secretaries of State were the dominant Ministers though their responsibility was rather different in kind from that of the First Lord of the Treasury and of the Admiralty. Because of their closeness to the king they were likely to get involved in all aspects of his activities. In legal theory there was only one office of Secretary of State, each holder being able to undertake any part of its duties according to the wishes of the king. In 1768 a Principal Secretaryship had been created specifically to deal with colonial business. The other two Secretaries had a joint responsibility for domestic affairs but divided foreign affairs between them on a North–South basis, hence they were usually referred to as the Northern and Southern Departments.

Finally, reference must be made to the Council of Trade and Plantations consisting of eight Commissioners, the first named being the First Lord. Originally the Board's duties had been to promote the trade of the kingdom and to inspect the king's planations in America and elsewhere. At various times the king, by Order in Council, had revised the powers of the Board. The establishment of a separate Secretary of State for Colonial affairs in 1768 took away almost its only executive functions and left it largely as an advisory body. As such the paid Commissioners, who were usually Members of Parliament, had little or nothing to do and the economical reformers wished to abolish the Board.

Having dwelt so long on the independence and status of the officer it may appear paradoxical to be referring constantly to boards and commissions. But in effect the boards were collective offices. The general idea was that the members should act collectively and therefore no distinction was drawn between them. Thus the members of the Treasury Board, of the Board of Admiralty and of the Board of Trade were treated in their Letters Patent as having equal authority. In each case, however, the person named first in the Commission, i.e. the First Lord, was regarded as by far the most senior and most important member.

There were, however, several boards constituted on quite a different principle. The Board of Ordnance[27] was an interesting mixture of individual and collective responsibility. The Master-General and the Lieutenant-General acted in two capacities. In their military capacity they were Commander-in-Chief and second in command respectively over the Artillery and Engineers. In his civil capacity the Master-General had the entire management and control of the whole Ordnance department. He, the Lieutenant-General, and four other principal Officers were appointed by separate Letters Patent and constituted the Board of Ordnance. All warrants from the king, Privy Council, or, in sea affairs, from the Board of Admiralty, and all letters from the Secretaries of State conveying orders relative to the Ordnance, were directed to the Master-General. The Board carried them into execution under his authority and in consequence of his direction. He could do alone any act which was within the power of the Board, but an order to issue money had to be signed by three Board members. During his absence or during a vacancy, the whole executive power devolved on the Board. Next in importance was the Lieutenant-General. His duty was to superintend all the officers and others in the various departments of the Ordnance. There were four other principal officers: the Surveyor-General (or Master Surveyor), Clerk of the Ordnance, the Principal Storekeeper, and the Clerk of the Deliveries. Independently of being a Board member each had a separate and distinct branch of business committed to his management.

The Navy Board was another example. Known both singly

and collectively as Principal Officers and Commissioners of the Navy, the Navy Board was composed of officers of theoretically equal standing some of whom supervised the conduct of special areas of business and some, known as Commissioners at Large, performed general duties. The six who had particular duties allotted to them besides their general duty as Commissioners were the Comptroller, Surveyor, Clerk of the Acts, and the three Controllers of the Treasurer's Accounts, of the Victualling Accounts, and of the Storekeeper's Accounts. Four Commissioners were specially appointed to reside at the dockyards of Chatham, Portsmouth, Plymouth, and Halifax in North America. The Comptroller presided over the meetings of the Board. The Ordnance and the Navy had had the longest experience of the management of a large enterprise, in contrast to the giving of general advice or the supervision of finance.

There were several reasons for the popularity of the use of boards and commissions. An early motive was a desire on the part of the king to spread the risk and reduce the power in the hands of one man. This was certainly an important factor in placing the offices of Lord High Treasurer and Lord High Admiral in commission, for these had responsibility for two of the most important and complex branches of the king's business.

Most of the boards were working boards, each Commissioner usually performing regular administrative work and not just attending occasionally to discuss big issues of policy. Both the Treasury Board and the Board of Admiralty required a good deal of effort from their members, the former meeting several times a week. The work of the revenue boards varied. The Customs and the Excise Commissioners usually met on five days a week, whereas those dealing with Hackney Coaches and Hawkers and Pedlars met only once or twice weekly.

Again the availability of a number of paid offices with little work attached to them was useful for securing political support and helping friends and relations. The Board of Trade was a good example. Since members of the revenue boards had been disqualified from holding a seat in the House of Commons it was sometimes the practice for the Government, wishing to find a seat for one of its supporters, to offer a vacant Commission to a serving Member who, on acceptance, had to vacate his seat. But by 1780 in most cases the Commissioners were active administrators and not sinecurists and the Crown had to pay regard to the need for efficient management.

Finally, it must be remembered that boards were a form of administration popular both in Parliament and in the country at large. For example, the Private Madhouse Act 1774 (14 Geo. III, c.49), established a body of five Commissioners for the purpose of regulating madhouses in the London area. The five were elected by the President and Fellows of the Royal College of Physicians from among their number. A more exotic example is to be found in a 1753 Act (26 Geo. II, c.22) which originated the British Museum. The list of ex-officio trustees reads like the nominal Cabinet: First Lords of the Treasury and Admiralty, the Principal Secretaries of State, Lord Chancellor, Archbishop of Canterbury, Lord Privy Seal, Lord Chief Justice of the King's Bench, Speaker of the House of Commons, and so on — plus the Presidents of the Royal Society and of the Royal College of Physicians and several named persons closely associated with the negotiations leading to the purchase of the museum and collections. Their task was to appoint fifteen associate-trustees for life who, along with the Lord Chancellor, Speaker of the House of Commons, and the Archbishop of Canterbury, managed the trust.

Throughout the country a large number of corporate bodies were continuously being created, mainly by Local Acts of Parliament, e.g. bodies for the paving, lighting, and cleaning of particular areas, turnpike trusts, etc. Each Act usually established a board or commission by naming the first members and perhaps including some ex-officio members. Thus an Act of 1762 (2 Geo. III, c.21) for the paving, cleaning, and lighting of Westminster, set up a board which included, ex officio the Chancellor of the Exchequer, the Speaker of the House of Commons, the Members for Westminster and Middlesex, and the Surveyor of the Board of Works. The numerous municipal corporations were also corporate bodies, and so in a sense were the Justices of the Peace when meeting in Quarter Sessions.

Finally, one general point about the administrative arrangements. There was usually a difference in the freedom which the king had in administering his prerogative powers and administering those conferred by Act of Parliament. In the former case he had considerable freedom of choice, whereas, in the latter, Parliament often prescribed the administrative arrangements in detail. Thus the annual Act imposing the Land Tax not only named the Assistant Commissioners who were to levy the tax in the various counties, boroughs, and other places, but went into great detail about how they should go about their business. Most of the Acts providing for taxes contained provisions about management. For example, an Act of 1694 (5 and 6 Wm. and M., c.21) required the Commissioners for Stamp duties to keep their head office within the Cities of London or Westminster; to keep distinct books of receipts and pay the duties collected into the Receipt of the Exchequer on Wednesday of every week, and so on.

Nevertheless, when, during the strongly opposed passage of the Militia Bill of 1756, the Commons wished to use the Assistant Commissioners for the Land Tax to perform the same functions in respect of each county's quota of men, the House of Lords refused to agree. They said 'such Acts of Magistracy should not be vested by Act of Parliament in any Set of Men; this being the Executive Part of Government, and undoubtedly, by the Constitution, a peculiar and natural Right of the Crown, which this Practice has doubtless entrenched upon, and the Lords cannot agree on this Occasion, to countenance another Precedent of that sort.'[28] The militia being part of the country's defence was within the king's prerogative, whereas taxation was a matter for the House of Commons.

THE COURTS OF JUSTICE

There were three principal common law courts. Broadly speaking the Court of King's Bench dealt with cases in which the king's interest or prerogative was concerned, including criminal cases; the Court of Common Pleas dealt with suits between subjects; and the Court of Exchequer dealt with cases arising out of the collection of the revenue. But there was no rigid demarcation of functions and suitors tended to try in the court in which they thought they had the best chance. The King's Bench also had superintendence over the due observation of the law by officers and others mainly be means of the prerogative writs. The first two courts were each presided over by a Lord Chief Justice and the last by the Lord Chief Baron. Each had three other judges. All received a salary from the Civil List augmented from the proceeds of a stamp tax specially imposed for the purpose. In addition each received some income from fees, particularly the two Lord Chief Justices. The Lord Chief Justice of the King's Bench was also an important Officer of State and a regular member of the nominal Cabinet.

The three courts developed out of the Curia Regis, yet leaving some residual judicial power to the king. Those who were dissatisfied with the decision of one of the courts could petition the king in Parliament, alleging error. Hence came the appellate jurisdiction of the House of Lords. But sometimes the petitioner did not allege error but complained that he could not afford the needed redress. The king came to refer these petitions to the Lord High Chancellor and so developed the important Court of Chancery and with it the development of equity jurisdiction.

The Lord Chancellor as well as being head of the judiciary was Keeper of the Great Seal and sat on the woolsack in the House of Lords. His responsibility for the Great Seal brought him into close touch with many of the significant acts of government. He had the main say in the appointment of Justices of the Peace, usually being advised by the Lord Lieutenant. He thus combined judicial and political activities and responsibilities.

Each court had jurisdiction over its own officers and staff, thirty to forty, for example, in the Court of King's Bench. The administration of the courts was a supreme example of the combination of officers and fees. It had long been the practice that those who had recourse to the courts should pay not only for their own lawyers but also for the services provided by the court. The availability of an ample fee income meant that the House of Commons had not to be asked for financial aid other than to supplement the salaries of the judges. The fee income and the number of officers increased not only because of a general increase in business but also by reason of the growing elaboration of procedure and pleading. The staff of the courts, particularly in Chancery, showed many examples of richly rewarded sinecures and the worst effects of too great an emphasis on the earning of fees.

There were several other courts, for example, the Admiralty Court which had limited jurisdiction relating to certain offences committed at sea. There are also a number of courts with local jurisdiction other than the Justices of the Peace.

V

The Administration of Local Affairs

Historians usually concentrate on the king, his leading Ministers, and Parliament. But to do this for the administrative system of 1780 would give a most one-sided impression. For the activities of the king and all his highly paid officers touched very little on the everyday life of the great mass of the people, except as collectors of a widening range of taxes and of men for the militia or in respect of friends and relatives in the Navy or Army. The prerogative powers were all important in foreign affairs, in dealing with the colonies and overseas possessions and in providing a basis for the working of Parliament and the constitution generally. They made very little contribution to the law concerned with domestic affairs. The people's everyday lives were much more likely to be affected by their local Justices of the Peace and parish officers.

The common law provided the basis for a whole range of public action, principally in respect of the prevention of nuisances and the maintenance of the peace. Also Parliament had enacted, for example, that the poor should be looked after, that roads and bridges should be maintained, and that various practices designed to harm the consumer should be prohibited. The administration and enforcement of these laws were not imposed either by the common law or by Parliament on the king or his immediate advisers. They were made the responsibility of the parish officers and the Justices of the Peace throughout the length and breadth of the land. It was these officers and these officers alone who possessed the great variety of general statutory powers. The results could be readily seen in the frequent editions of Mr Burns's invaluable 'The *Justices of the Peace and Parish Officers*'. Their duties, powers, and responsibilities were there described under nearly two hundred headings, from Alehouses and Apprentices to Weights and Measures, Witchcraft, and Woollen Manufacture. To these ancient offices Parliament had added a number of bodies of commissioners, e.g. Turnpike Trusts, Paving and Lighting Commissioners. Created by and provided with constitutions by

Local Acts, these bodies were invested with important powers, rights and duties each in a defined locality.

The Lords Lieutenant and Justices of the Peace in the Counties held their offices from the king 'at pleasure'. In that sense, therefore, they were in no different position *vis-à-vis* the king than were the Secretaries of State, the First Lord of the Treasury, or the Lord Privy Seal, who also were appointed and removable by the king. In 1780, for example, two Lords Lieutenant were dismissed from office by the king for voting against the government. They were all part of the king's government, which was not confined to external affairs or London, but spread throughout the realm. Nevertheless there was this very big difference: the Justices of the Peace were exercising powers conferred on them by Act of Parliament, or derived from the common law. They may have been appointed by virtue of the prerogative, but their powers did not come from that source.

It is interesting to consider the relative contribution of national and local officers in quantitative terms. Of the very large sums voted by Parliament in 1780 the great bulk of the £22·6 million was spent on the armed forces (nearly £15 million) and in the payment of interest on the ever-increasing national debt (nearly £6 million). Of the Civil List annuity, fixed at £900,000, more than half was spent on maintaining the various royal households and over £100,000 went in the payment of various pensions. Probably less than £200,000 was spent on officers and others who executed and enforced the law domestically.

Statistics of expenditure incurred by the counties, municipalities, parishes, and other local bodies, are less easy to come by. The receipts from the poor rates, the county, and other rates, were about £2 million a year, most of which was spent on the relief of the poor. But money was not wholly adequate as a measure of comparison for, whereas most of those engaged directly in the service of the king other than the armed forces, received substantial remuneration, most of those who administered local services did so with little or no payment: the Overseers of the Poor, the Surveyors of Highways, and the Petty Constables were mostly unpaid, and so were the Lords Lieutenant. The Justices of the Peace received a very small fee for attending each Quarterly Session. Probably only the Clerks of the Peace were remunerated on a scale anything like comparable to officers near to the king.

It is an odd reflection on the state of affairs at the time that the nearer a person's office took him to the king, the more he expected to be remunerated for it. The government of the country away from the Court was based on an entirely different principle, that of compulsory unpaid service. With a few exceptions all residents in a parish had an obligation to serve that parish, and to take their turn in holding one or other of the parish offices: Surveyor of Highways, required by an Act of 1555, Overseer of the Poor, required by an Act of 1601, or Constable referred to in many Acts of Parliament. As there were probably more than 10,000 parishes or townships, in England and Wales this meant some 30,000–40,000 persons carrying out local public responsibilities. To these must be added the Justices of the Peace, those who take part in the municipal corporations, and the several hundred Improvement Commissions, Turnpike Trusts, etc., probably another 5,000 or so.

There were, of course, some 12,000 civil officers and clerks engaged directly in the king's service, the great majority of these, however, being engaged in the Customs, Excise, and Post Office. Some 500 were employed in the various offices for the Navy, Army, and Ordnance. Of the remainder a substantial part were engaged in processing the public revenue and expenditure or, spent their days preparing, copying, and summarizing the great amount of paperwork. Very few were concerned with either law enforcement or the provision of services for the general public.

The Land Tax was an interesting departure from the rule that national taxes were managed and collected by Boards of Commissioners appointed by the king. Being a levy on the income from property and public office it raised administrative problems quite different from those presented by the Customs and Excise duties. For those were levied on tangible objects — gallons of beer, wine, or brandy, pounds of tobacco, tea or coffee. The object of the taxation was readily verifiable and it remained only to apply the statutory scale to its volume or other basis of measurement. Moreover, Customs duties were levied on foreign trade and even the Excise dealt only with a limited number of brewers and manufacturers. In striking contrast the value of property or even the income derivable from it were not easy to measure; there was plenty of room for the assessment to be disputed by the potential taxpayer. Moreover, the tax was mainly payable by the landed interests, the gentry, and the holders of the better-paid public offices. As they resented the imposition of the tax, they were not easily handled by comparatively unimportant officials. Experience in the seventeenth century had shown the impossibility of levying a tax on personal property and the great difficulties of assessing the value of real property. In 1693, therefore, Parliament fixed the amount of the tax which had to be paid each year by each county. The quota of each county had then to be apportioned between all the prospective payers — in other words, individual assessments had to be made which in the end produced the amount of money prescribed for the county in the Act. The supervision of the assessments was placed by the Act in the hands of local commissioners, actually named in the Act, for each county and borough. The commissioners were drawn predominantly from the Justices of the area. In the boroughs usually the mayor, aldermen, and common council were nominated. The Treasury appointed a Surveyor in each area to watch their interests. The administrative assumption was that the only way incomes from property could be taxed was by securing the active co-operation of the propertied class, first by gaining their consent in Parliament, and then by drawing men of substance into local administration. The clerk to the local commissioners was usually a local solicitor and the duty of assessment and collection often went by rota among the farmers. The clerk and the collectors were allowed a poundage on the sums paid over.

The money for the county was paid to a Receiver General appointed by the Treasury. These were quite often merchants or country gentlemen, and were remunerated by a small poundage fee. There was a Board of Taxes, commissioned by the king, but it had no control over either assessment or collection. A taxpayer could appeal against his assessment and this was heard by the local Commissioners whose decision was final. Here once again we find the Justices of the Peace and the substantial men of the counties and boroughs being charged with administrative responsibility for a particularly difficult piece of legislation.[29]

Just as each county had to provide its quota of money for the Land Tax, so it had to provide its quota of men for the militia. In this case primary responsibility for seeing that the requirements of the Militia Acts were met fell on the Lord Lieutenant of the county, who appointed a number of deputy lieutenants. As with the Land Tax the county quota was divided among the various divisions and parishes. For assessing and exacting the burden of service, the lieutenants used the ordinary local machinery. The general and sub-division meetings which directed the work were simply military equivalents of Quarter, Petty, or Local sessions. Justices of the Peace attended and did most of the business, provided at least one deputy lieutenant was present. Their orders were carried out by the civil officers of parish.[30]

LAW ENFORCEMENT AND THE COMMON INFORMER

The method of law enforcement in 1780 provides a final example of the very small part played by Ministers and those based in London in the administration of local affairs. It was the duty of every citizen both to know the law and to see that it was obeyed. This was the origin of the Grand Jury, twelve or so citizens who brought to the notice of the judges cases of wrongdoing. The ordinary citizen could fulfil his duties in various ways, by bringing a matter to the attention of a Grand Jury or of a local Justice. For felonies and criminal acts reliance had to be placed on the local constable of each parish. This machinery was reasonably adequate for the mass of small rural parishes and for the more obvious crimes. But it had many shortcomings, particularly in the developing towns where there was much talk, and some action, of strengthening the police.

Unless the breaking of the law affected a person directly, few were inclined to go to the trouble or incur the odium of bringing charges against their neighbours. The practice grew up, therefore, of encouraging private individuals to undertake the discovery and conviction of offenders by the granting of rewards or other benefits. All kinds of offences were handled in this way: robbery, murder, the regulation of hawkers and pedlars, pawnbrokers, licensed premises, immorality, selling bread or other commodities deficient in weight, and so on. A common informer was a person who instituted proceedings, not because he personally was aggrieved, or wished to see justice done, but because under the law he was entitled to a part of any fine that might be imposed. In Blackstone's words 'these forfeitures [usually] created by statute are given at large to any common informer; or in other words, to any such person and persons as will sue for the same. And hence such actions are called *popular* actions . . .' Once an informer instituted proceedings he acquired what Blackstone called an 'inchoate imperfect degree of property'. Nobody else could pursue the matter, but his right to the property (forfeiture) did not become absolute until he had secured the verdict.[31]

It became usual for Acts creating offences to contain a provision whereby anybody securing a conviction under it received either a fixed payment or a share (generally a moiety) of the fine imposed. For example, an Act of 1777 (17 George III, c.56) prescribed that persons having in their possession, or removing during the night, materials which had been stolen or embezzled, were liable to a fine of £20, £30, or £40, on a first, second, or third offence, and in each case half was to go to the informer who secured the conviction, the other half to the poor of the parish.

An Act of 1699 (10 and 11 Wm. III, c.23) provided an unusual form of reward or benefit. Anyone apprehending and successfully prosecuting an offender guilty of burglary, housebreaking, horse stealing, or thieving in shops, warehouses, or coach-houses, of goods to the value of five shillings or more, was entitled to claim a certificate exempting him from all offices in the parish in which the offence was committed. Since these offences carried the death penalty, a conviction for any one of them was likely to send the guilty person to Tyburn — hence the certificate came to be known as the Tyburn ticket. The certificate was signed by the judge or justices and enrolled in the office of the Clerk for a fee of one shilling. It could be assigned to another person who would then acquire the exemption, but not after it had once been used to avoid office.

VI

Finance

The arrangements for the spending of the public moneys were very much like the administrative system generally, indeed they had emerged from the same origins and reflected a similar set of ideas. Both the administrative and the financial arrangements were dispersed.

The ancient maxim compatible with the prerogative was that the king should 'live of his own'. He had large estates and certain feudal rights and the general belief was that these should be sufficient to maintain him and his household and the servants he needed to carry out his kingly duties. It was only when 'his own' proved insufficient for any reason — extravagance or war — that the king had to resort to taxation. The history of the constitution and, in particular, the growing strength of the House of Commons, turn very largely on the controversies and struggles in respect of the right to impose taxation. For taxation was seldom popular with those whose money was to be taken.

Even so the issue would have meant much less to the position of the king in the Constitution had the country remained at peace. For the hereditary revenues, well managed, supplemented from time to time by comparatively small Aids, would have been more than sufficient to meet the needs of the king's government. Instead, the country had been at war for half of the previous eighty years. The cost of the armed forces and of the National Debt had reached alarming heights. The need for Parliament to impose new and heavy taxation to meet such expenditure had led to important constitutional innovations.

There was little or no point in Parliament authorizing the king to incur expenditure on the army or navy or indeed on any major new purpose without making a corresponding sum available either from fresh taxation or from new borrowings. There was no large uncommitted fund at the disposal of the House of Commons out of which new expenditure could be met. It was therefore natural for Parliament to be concerned that the proceeds of the additional taxation they were voting should be spent only for the purposes which justified the new levy. What was once an occasional decision justified by the peculiar circumstances of the expenditure had by 1780 become a regular feature of the financial system: the appropriation by the House of Commons of their aids and supplies to purposes specified by statute.

The Appropriation Act of 1780 (20 Geo. III, c.62) empowered the king to spend not more than £5½ million on Naval Services; £1½ million on paying off the Navy Debt (i.e. overspending in earlier years); over £6½ million on the Land Forces; £438,136 and £591,466 (for 1779) on the Ordnance. Of these very large sums only that voted for the Land Forces was appropriated for more specific purposes, e.g. £946,176 for defraying the charges of 35,000 effective men and officers and 4,213 invalids for Guards, Garrisons, etc., in Great Britain; £367,893 for 13,471 troops of Hesse Cassel; £94,174 for 4,300 Brunswickers, and so on. The Act also listed a number of non-military items, for example, £25,000 for carrying on the building of Somerset House, £6,997 for new roads in the Highlands of Scotland, and £14,348 for maintaining Convicts. It declared that 'the said Aids and Supplies . . . shall not be issued or applied to any Use, Intent, or Purpose . . . other than the Uses and Purposes before mentioned.' It stated the sources out of which the expenditure so authorized could legitimately be met. They included the proceeds of certain specified taxes, £650,457 surplus on the Sinking Fund, savings and balances from the previous year, and the sale of French Prizes.

Though, because of the large sums needed by the Armed Forces, the Appropriation Act of 1780 provided for a major part of the public expenditure, it by no means covered all of it. The principal exclusions were the sums involved in funding the ever-growing National Debt and the Civil List annuity. Willingness to lend money voluntarily depends on a lender's confidence in the borrower's capacity to pay the interest due on the loan and its ultimate repayment. The Bankers Case (1689–1700) had cast doubt on this certainty so far as the king was concerned and so Parliament had itself to take responsibility for providing security. Thus, whenever a new loan was raised or an unfunded loan was funded, it was necessary for Parliament to specify the precise source from which the new obligation would be met.

The expenses of the royal households and of those officers and charges traditionally met by the king out 'of his own', were largely paid out of a lump sum settled by Parliament at the beginning of each reign. In 1760 George III surrendered the bulk of his hereditary revenues in return for a Civil List annuity of £800,000. This proved insufficient and in 1777 a further £100,000 a year was made available. The sum of £900,000 refers solely to England and Wales. There remained for the king's use and outside the Civil List annuity (i) the Crown revenues in Scotland and Ireland and of the Duchy of Lancaster; (ii) the Four-and-a-half per cent duty, payable mainly on sugar produced in Barbados and the Leeward Islands (so called the Kings Sugars); and (iii) certain prerogative revenues principally the droits of the Crown and of the Admiralty.[32]

For some years there had been a growing tendency for the House of Commons to provide, out of annual Supply, for civil expenditure which might at one time have been regarded as falling on the Civil List or the remaining hereditary revenues. In some cases this was done by submitting an Address to His Majesty asking that a specified item of expenditure should be met out of the Civil List revenues on the understanding that the House would vote the necessary money in next year's Appropriation Act. In 1779, for example, the House provided by this arrangement some £20,000 towards paying off the debts of the Earl of Chatham and some £4,000 for his funeral. These were additional to the several items of civil expenditure included in the annual Appropriation Act.

A good example of the earmarking of the proceeds of a particular tax for the satisfaction of stated items of expenditure occurred in 1758, when Parliament decided to augment the salaries of the judges. An Act (32 Geo. II, c.35) provided for the cost of imposing an additional stamp duty on vellum, parchment, and paper used for legal matters. When that imposition failed to provide sufficient revenue for the purpose, Parliament increased it in 1762 (2 Geo. III, c.36) and again in

1765 (5 Geo. III, c.47). In some cases Parliament avoided imposing a new tax for a specific purpose by making the cost a direct charge on an existing source. Thus a number of pensions to former public figures were charged against the revenue of the Post Office.

Earmarking was the main cause of two features of the system of national finance. The Appropriation Act did not cover the whole of the public expenditure. There was indeed no account or Parliamentary Return from which it was possible to obtain the total public income and expenditure of the country. Second, it meant that a large number of detailed separate accounts had to be kept. More than a hundred revenue accounts were required to deal with the debt funding system.

This very short and therefore elementary survey needs supplementing in two respects. First, the expenses of carrying out and enforcing the law in the various localities were not met out of national taxes, nor are they covered in any way by the foregoing exposition. Various local bodies, had, by particular Acts, some of them confined to a particular locality, been authorized to raise money compulsorily from the inhabitants of their area. The Poor Relief Act of 1601 (43 Eliz., c.2) under the powers of which most of the money was raised, required the Overseers of the Poor to raise it 'by taxation of every inhabitant, parson, vicar, and other, and of every occupier of lands, houses, tithes impropriate or propriations of tithes, coal-mines, or saleable underwoods.' Other Acts used different wording and indeed there was a considerable variety of practice.

FEES

Second, something needs to be said about the use of fees which as we saw earlier met all or most of the expense of a number of quite important branches of government. The system of fees was an ancient and integral feature of the whole system of government and was based on an acceptance of two principles:

(1) The expenses of civil government should mainly be met by those who benefited by the services provided;

(2) Officers who provided the services should be remunerated

by those who used their services and to the extent that they did so.

The two are not ways of saying the same thing for it would be quite consistent with the first for the users of the public services to pay fees, e.g. into the Exchequer, yet for the officers to be paid fixed salaries, i.e. for the second principle not to operate. Indeed such a policy found increasing support in the 1770s. There were, however, aspects of the second precept which went beyond anything needed to satisfy the first, particularly the arrangement whereby fees were paid by one public officer to another out of public moneys.

In origin the first principle arose from the legal character of much of the early business of the king's government. It had long been customary to remunerate by fees those who practised and administered the law. Even when the functions of some of the royal courts and councils became more administrative than judicial the custom continued. It seemed fair that those who had recourse to the law should meet the expense of providing the courts, for presumably they hoped to advantage themselves by such recourse. The same argument was applied to those who benefited by a royal grant under Letters Patent or from the passing of a Local Act. They should meet the cost of the preparation of documents, the sealing of instruments, and the processing of Bills through Parliament.

The application of this financial principle to the administrative process generally was made easier by the large number of formal documents which had to be prepared and copied. Indeed the fee system had no doubt encouraged that feature. Fees were often based on the character of the document and the number of pages that had to be prepared and copied.

In the course of time the fee system was shown to have one great financial advantage. As the demands on a Court or an Office grew so did the income derived from fees, so providing some or all of the money out of which to pay for more clerks and assistance.

Unfortunately, for those who wished to avoid taxation, a great part of the expansion of the public services could not be financed in this way. It was hardly practical to charge fees to those who lent money to the king, or those who paid taxes, or those against whom the navy and army fought. The large sums involved in these three elements had to be met out of taxation. Fortunately, whereas Parliament was reluctant to vote more money for the Civil List it was always willing to vote substantial sums for the Navy.

From time to time, however, there were public protests about the system, indeed there was a major enquiry into the practice in the 1730s. One major objection arose from doubts about the legal authority for the scales of charges and uncertainty as to what was the proper scale, many fees being based on usage rather than prescribed by Parliament: those charged in the office of the Principal Secretaries of State went back to the middle of the seventeenth century.

More reprehensible was the need to pay gratuities in some offices. Fees were paid for the attendance of the officer at his place of employment at the legal times, whereas gratuities were paid for work done at a time or place not legally required of the officer. It was, however, a form of reward very liable to abuse. It could be for civility, favour, or extra service, but it could also purchase undue preference. There was always the possibility that what had once been a spontaneous gesture became by custom another burden on the user of the public services.

Probably the most frequent criticism in 1780 was directed at the big increase in the income of those remunerated by fees as a result of the abnormally high level of government activity due to the American War. This was particularly noticeable in the Exchequer of Receipt where fees were calculated as a poundage of the money which passed through the officer's hands. This basis dated back to the time when the Exchequer had to handle coins of various denominations possibly clept or of doubtful weight. In these circumstances it was twice as much trouble to handle £10,000 as it was to handle £5,000 and therefore to charge a poundage was fair and proper. By 1780, however, most money transactions were conducted by Notes, Drafts, or Bills to any amount with little trouble or labour to the Exchequer. In 1780 some £62,000 was paid in poundage, a serious misuse of the fee system as well as a waste of public money.[33]

What was hallowed by long usage had a firm basis in law. But there was strong opposition to the creation of new opportunities to claim fees: in many people's minds, fees had come to be regarded as a form of taxation. Thus Blackstone cites Coke to the effect that the king may create new offices 'but not with new fees annexed to them, nor annex new fees to old offices; for this would be a tax upon the subject, which cannot be imposed but by act of parliament'.[34]

It was also a sign of the times that legislation establishing a new public activity which might have created new opportunities to impose fees, specifically prohibited them. Thus the Acts empowering the raising of revenue by the issue of Exchequer Bills usually provided that 'no Fee, Reward and Gratuity, directly or indirectly, shall be demanded or taken of any of His Majesty's subjects . . . by any of His Majesty's Officer or Officers, their Clerks or Deputies, on Pain of Payment of Treble Damages to the Party grieved by the Party offending with full Costs of Suit' (20 Geo. III, c.62).

THE REGULATION OF THE REVENUE AND EXPENDITURE

There were two main elements in the system of regulation — the Exchequer and the public accountants.

The Exchequer was both a Court and an essential part of the process for ensuring the safe keeping of the king's revenues and preventing their use for unauthorized purposes. For these administrative purposes it was divided into the Upper Exchequer or Exchequer of Account and the Lower Exchequer or Exchequer of Receipt. The former was concerned with making certain that public accountants fulfilled their financial responsibilities: the latter was concerned with the receipt and issue of money.

A public accountant was an officer legally responsible either for paying into the Exchequer money collected on behalf of the king by way of taxes or other revenues or for paying the cost of salaries, supplies, and other expenses incurred on behalf of the king's government and household.

The receipts came mainly from the Customs, Excise, and other revenue departments. Usually the Receiver General to the board was the public accountant but the Commissioners of Excise were collectively responsible. In the case of the Land Tax the Receiver General for each county was the public accountant. The money was paid to the office of one of the four Tellers, but for some years the practice had been for it to be received by a Bank of England clerk stationed permanently in the Exchequer who gave the payer a ticket of acknowledgement. The receipt was recorded both in the Waste Book and on a tally stick (involving the Tally Cutter) and was checked by the Clerk of the Pells and by the Auditor of Receipt.

The arrangements for the issue of money started with the Treasury and has been outlined earlier. In the Exchequer the key officer was the Auditor of Receipt. It was he to whom the Treasury addressed their warrants and letters of direction. He assisgned the Order for payment to the appropriate Teller and it was delivered to the Pells office. Having been checked against the superior authorizing instrument the money was then issued to the appropriate public accountant.

The procedure both for the receipt and issue of money, and particularly for the latter, involved a complex system of checking and counter-checking and of making entries at each step. It was based on an Act of 1697 (8 and 9 Wm.III, c.28) and on usage. Such care was clearly desirable where the public finances were concerned but inevitably it meant delay. The processes of the Lower Exchequer were further complicated by the unusual language and notation used in the records. Thus the Imprest Roll containing a record of the sums to be issued on account to satisfy either the King's Warrant or Act of Parliament used figures that were a corruption of the old text and used only in the Exchequer. They were impossible to cast up and had to be reduced to common figures before the Roll could be made up.[35]

When an ordinary individual is confronted by a bill from his grocer, garage, or tailor, he pays it direct by cash or by a cheque on his bank account. In the case of the king an intermediate stage was usually introduced. The Exchequer did not in general pay the creditors of the king direct, the money necessary for this purpose being issued to an Officer, not a member of the Exchequer, who took responsibility for paying the salaries and other expenses. The arrangement had the advantage of enabling the Receipt of the Exchequer to concentrate on their function of being the king's bankers. The other advantage was that responsibility for the proper spending of the money was clearly fixed on an individual and the systems of accounting and audit were arranged accordingly. The Exchequer issued money usually by imprest and on account to a paymaster, e.g. of the Land Forces, who used it to meet the costs of his branch of the government. He was a public accountant. The records of the Exchequer were designed to show how much had been issued to each public accountant. At the end of each year he had to show the Upper Exchequer how he had spent the money issued to him. His expenditure in most cases would be audited by one of the Auditors of the Imprests. When he had proved to the satisfaction of the Upper Exchequer that his accounts were in order he was given his Quietus, which discharged him of any further liability, the discharge being full and sufficient at law, the Upper Exchequer being for this purpose a court of law.

The proper performance of the duties of each public accountant was vital to the proper and safe conduct of the king's finances. For this reason he was sometimes appointed by a royal warrant or Treasury Constitution or even by Letters Patent. It was obviously desirable that a person of standing, sometimes even of substance, should be appointed, for he had a personal responsibility as the holder of that office.

VII

Conclusion

The essence of the system lay in the diffusion of authority. The concentration by historians on North, Pitt, and other major figures is inclined to give the impression that the administrative system was completely in the hands of a small group of powerful politicians. The situation was completely different in reality. Instead it was in the hands of a large number of more or less independent legal entities or officers. To state this is not to say that the First Lord of the Treasury and the Principal Secretaries of State were not very powerful men particularly when they had the king's full support. But in themselves they possessed very few legal powers so far as domestic affairs were concerned and had little direct control over most of those who administered the laws.

This system of diffused authority was ideal for a country whose people were concerned about the threat to their liberties which could come from a concentration of authority in the hands of the king or of his senior advisers. It was now threatened by great pressures and changes: the large increase in public expenditure with the consequent big increase in the number of government employees, and the development of new commercial methods. Indeed, some would claim that the system we have described was no longer dominant, and indeed had broken down. The unfortunate turn of events in America had stimulated criticism not only of Lord North and his government, but even of the king himself. Some critics were demanding changes in the methods whereby the House of Commons was elected, but others concentrated on the waste and extravagance which was said to account for some part of the ruinous level of taxation. In particular attention was directed at the many pensioners paid out of public funds, the existence of many sinecures, and the excessive remuneration received by some officers. Some of the critics concentrated their attentions on the influence wielded by the king because of the patronage he possessed and the number of officers dependent on his goodwill.

Lord North accepted the need for some form of inquiry and secured the appointment of a Commission to Examine the Public Accounts by Act of Parliament (20 Geo. III, c.54). None of the seven commissioners named in the Act was a member of either House, and the Act excluded place-holders.

The Act empowered the Commissioners to examine on oath the officers of the Exchequer, Treasury, Admiralty, and other departments. They were required to report on the state of the public accounts; to report what balances were in the hands of accountants which might be applied to the public service; what defects there were in the mode of receiving, collecting, issuing, and accounting for public money, and in what more expeditious and effective and less expensive manner the financial arrangements could in future be regulated and carried on for the benefit of the public. These generally worded purposes offered the Commission a good deal of scope. The Act was only for one year, but was renewed annually until the Commissioners finished their task at the end of 1786[36]

Some commentators thought it possible to remove the worst blemishes in the system without destroying it. But an Executive system based on the king and legal processes was not compatible, in the opinion of many, with the achievement of their goal — to bring the Executive entirely under the control of the House of Commons. Such control pointed towards a concentration, not a diffusion, of authority. It also implied control exercised politically rather than through the law and the courts.

Part II
1780–1870

I

Population, Wealth and Public Finance
1780–1870

The trend of a country's population and wealth is particularly important in understanding the course of its government.

Population. The population of England and Wales for 1780 has been estimated at between 7½ and 8 million. At the first census (1801) it was 8.9 million and thence rose rapidly to 15.9 million in 1841 then declined, and by 1871 had fallen to 5.4 trebled in the period covered by this book. The population of Scotland followed a somewhat similar course from 1.6 million in 1801 to 3.36 million in 1871. In contrast the population of the whole of Ireland after rising from 4 million in 1781 to 8.2 million in 1841 then declined, and by 1871 had fallen to 5.4 million.

Wealth and Prices. The national income of Great Britain rose quite markedly. In 1780 it has been estimated at £97.7 million, in 1800 at £232 million, in 1831 at £340 million and in 1871 at £917 million. Thus it increased more than ninefold during our period.

The increase partly reflected the rise in population and partly the level of prices. For 1780 the national income per capita has been estimated at £9.3, which had become £11.5 in 1801, £18.5 by 1831, and £30.5 by 1871. These estimates are at constant prices, i.e. allowance has been made for price changes.

The level of prices was greatly affected by the Napoleonic War. It has been estimated that by 1800 the cost of living was about 75% above the average for the 1780s. It fluctuated around this level until the end of the war, reaching some 100% around 1810. After 1815 it fell fairly rapidly. By the beginning of the 1830s it was only some 15% higher than in the 1780s and despite various fluctuations, was still around this level by 1871. Not only must the course of public finance be judged in the light of this trend but so also must the level of salaries in the public service.

National Public Expenditure. War was also the most important factor in determining the level of government expenditure. This is shown in Table 1.

TABLE 1

Principal Items of Government
Expenditure 1780–1870

£ millions

	Debt Charges	Naval and Military	Civil
		Net. Great Britain	
1780	6.0	14.9	1.2
1800/1	16.7	31.7	2.1
		Gross. United Kingdom	
1815	30.0	72.4	5.8
1821	32.0	16.7	5.4
1831	29.2	13.9	4.9
1841	29.5	13.9	5.3
1851	28.3	14.7	6.8
1861	26.3	28.3	10.7
1871	26.8	21.1	12.0

Source: Abstract of British Historical Statistics by B. R. Mitchell and P. Deane (1962). Their source was the memorandum by H.S. Chisholm, PP 1868–9 Vol. XXXV.
(The reason for the different basis of the 1780–1800 figures from the later figures is partly the addition of Ireland and partly reflects the later practice of showing gross receipts. Unfortunately Mr Chisholm did not provide the data whereby the two periods could be put on the same basis.)

The most noticeable features are:
(1) Debt charges rose from £6 million to £30 million between 1780 and 1815. The debt was very slow to be paid off and so the charges remained the major element in national expenditure. This can be seen from the following figures of the National Debt.

National Debt — Funded
and Unfunded, United Kingdom
1780–1871

		£ million
1780		167.2
1801		456.1
1815		744.9
1819	(Peak)	844.3
1831		786.2
1841		790.2
1851		789.7
1861		805.7
1871		738.1

Source: Mitchell and Deane.

(2) Expenditure on the armed forces was more adjustable.
Though it rose from £14.8 million to £72.4 million between
1780 and 1825, it then fell away rapidly to a level below 1780.
The increase after 1850 no doubt reflects the growing involve-
ment of Great Britain in an expanding empire and the peace
keeping responsibilities of the major power in the world.
(3) Civil expenditure did not begin to rise until after 1841.
The apparent rise between 1800–1 and 1815 largely reflects a
difference in the compilation of the figures.

The money to finance this expenditure, other than by
borrowing, came from a variety of taxes.

Table 2 shows the great reliance placed by Chancellors of
the Exchequer on the Customs and Excise Duties. The
Property and Income Tax made an important contribution
during the years 1799–1815 when it was repealed and again
after it was reimposed in 1842.

Though the level of expenditure and taxation looks so much
higher in 1871 it was, in terms of population and national
income, lower than in 1780. Between 1780 and 1800 the revenue
raised by taxes in the United Kingdom, at constant prices, rose
per capita from £1.2 to £1.56 and as a percentage of national
income from 12.9 per cent to 13.4 per cent. By 1821 for Great
Britain it was £3.5 per head after which it fell away until it was
only £2.3 per head in 1871, still about twice the level of 1780. In
terms, however, of the share of the national income taken by
taxation there was a marked reduction. At the height of the
Napoleonic War it was 25 per cent or more but by 1831 it had
fallen to 16 per cent, by 1851 to 10.9 per cent and by 1871 to 7.4

TABLE 2

Receipts from the main Taxes
£ million

Net. Great Britain

	Customs	Excise	Stamps	Land and Assessed Taxes	Property and Income	Death Duties
1780	2.8	6.1	0.5	2.5	–	–
1800–1	6.8	10.6	2.6	5.1	4.5	–

Gross. United Kingdom

	Customs	Excise	Stamps	Land and Assessed Taxes	Property and Income	Death Duties
1801–2	8.8	11.6	3.2	4.6	5.8	–
1815	14.8	29.5	6.5	8.0	14.5	–
1821	11.9	29.6	6.9	8.2	–	–
1831	19.4	20.0	7.3	5.4	–	–
1841	23.4	14.9	7.4	4.2	5.5	–
1851	22.0	15.3	6.7	4.6	10.9	–
1861	23.3	19.4	8.3	3.1	6.4	–
1871	20.2	22.8	3.6	2.7		4.8

Source: Mitchell and Deane.

per cent. By this measurement the burden of taxation was less in 1871 than it was in 1780 and indeed even earlier in the eighteenth century.

Similar information is not available for the numerous local authorities. The earliest reliable figure of local expenditure in England and Wales is £5,348,000 in 1803. Of that figure £4,077,000 was on Poor Relief, which rose to £6,910,000 by 1817 bringing total expenditure in that year to some £10 million. Expenditure on Poor Relief rose to nearly £7.9 million in 1818, then fell to £5.7 million in 1824, after which it rose to between £6 million and £7 million until the drastic measures introduced by the Poor Law Amendment Act 1834 brought the cost down to around £4½–5 million in the period 1836–46.

By 1870 total expenditure had reached £27.3 million and was £29.9 million in 1871. By then expenditure on Poor Relief, though it had risen to some £7 million a year, no longer dominated local budgets. The County rate was running at over £1½ million, of which some £550,000 was in respect of Police. Borough Councils were spending some £2¾ million a year. In London the Metropolitan Board of Works was spending over £2 million, the Metropolitan Police over £800,000.

Not all the increased expenditure was being met out of rates. Local authorities were meeting most of the capital expenditure on sewers, street improvements, and other public works out of loans. Out of a total expenditure of some £30 million about £5½ million was met by borrowing. By the end of the period grants from the Treasury were becoming a significant feature at £1¼ million of which some £0.4 million went to Boards of Guardians and £0.3 million to the Metropolitan Police.

Sources

The main source of information for this section is the Abstract of British Historical Statistics (1962) by B. R. Mitchell and P. Deane. There is also a useful chapter on 'Taxation and Industrialization in Britain, 1700–1870' in *The Transformation of England* (1979) by Peter Mathias.

The fullest information about local taxation and expenditure is contained in the Return of Local Taxation made in August 1870 by G. J. Goschen, President of the Poor Law Board, assisted by R. Giffen (PP (1870), LV). The annual Local Taxation Returns did not start until 1871.

II

From King to Crown

Blackstone[1] claimed that 'The supreme executive power of these kingdoms is vested by our laws in a single person, the king or queen'. And again, 'The king of England is therefore not only the chief, but properly the sole, magistrate of the nation; all others acting by commission from, and in due subordination to him.' This did not mean, however, that the king had an absolute power as supreme executive for 'the true excellence of the English government [is] that all parts of it form a mutual check on each other.' The 'executive power is . . . checked and kept within due bounds by the two houses [of Parliament], through the privilege they have of inquiring into, impeaching, and punishing the conduct of his . . . counsellors.'

Critics have said that, by concentrating on the law and ignoring the political realities, Blackstone misled his audience by placing the king on more or less an equal footing with the House of Commons. But the lectures were first published in 1765–9 whereas some of the critics had a later period in mind. The period 1760–1870 saw a very substantial shift of constitutional power from the king to the House of Commons. Miss Kemp[2] labels the years 1716–83 as the period of Balance between King and Commons and the years 1784–1832 as the period of decline in the influence of the King.

It would be simple and dramatic if one could state that in 1780 the king was in practice as well as in constitutional theory the Executive whereas by 1870 this role had passed entirely into the hands of the Cabinet: that in 1780 the Monarch both reigned and ruled, but in 1870 only reigned. Such a stark contrast would be inaccurate. In 1780 Ministers were not without influence and therefore power and in 1870 the Queen was not without influence over the Ministry. Nevertheless there was a very substantial shift in authority from the Sovereign to the Cabinet during this period. Much of the shift was not obvious to the onlooker, for the institutions and the terms in which they were referred to remained outwardly unchanged.

DECLINE IN STATUS AND AUTHORITY

Whilst no king or queen, however gifted or admired, could have held his or her ground against the rising power of the House of Commons, particularly after the Reform Act of 1832, certain features of the monarchy after 1780 hastened the decline in the status and authority of the Sovereign.

The first factor was the waning of the influence of the Crown over Parliament.

Critics of the 'influence' advocated two alternative methods of reducing it. The first was to curb the political power of those who held office or employment under the king or enjoyed government contracts. The Place Act of 1742, for example, had already excluded a wide range of officers and clerks from eligibility to a seat in the House of Commons. In 1782 Parliament went even further and disenfranchised the Commissioners of the Excise, Customs, Stamp Duties, and the Salt Tax and their subordinates, and the Postmaster-General and his subordinates (22 Geo. III, c.41). In the same year another Act, (22 Geo. III, c.45) excluded from the House of Commons all persons who held contracts from the Treasury, Navy or Victualling Office or Board of Ordnance, or from 'any other person or persons whatsoever, for or on account of the public service.'

The second method was to cut down or control the money at the disposal of the king for these purposes. This approach obviously found favour with those who were primarily alarmed at the high and increasing level of taxation and expenditure. The movement for economical reform was particularly strong and most likely to succeed with those proposals which reduced both public expenditure and the influence of the Crown. Thus attention was focussed on sinecures, useless offices, and pensions, all of which cost money without any apparent service to the public. And so the critics were mostly interested in the Civil List, even though it was a comparatively small and relatively stable element in total national expenditure. For it was out of the Civil List revenues that the Secret Service money, the bulk of the pensions, and many of the office-holders were paid. Moreover, even in 1780 the House of Commons had no say in the spending of this money, indeed they did not even have current information as to how the money was spent.

The elimination or reduction of the various forms of influence reduced the power of Ministers to control the House of Commons and were a factor in the rise of the power of that House and the greater dependence of the Executive upon it. The change, however, had a particular significance for the position of the king in the constitution. First, it had been easier for him to control or dominate Ministers who were not wholly dependent on the support of the House of Commons than those who were, for the latter could justifiably claim that they were not free agents and that however much they might agree with the king they could not carry out his wishes. Even in the eighteenth century Ministers, on occasion, could use this plea and the king had to accept the inevitable. As the nineteenth century progressed this became increasingly the case.

Second, some of the forms of influence involved the king personally. Most of the attractive offices were held by formal instruments bearing the king's signature. The Civil List was in effect the personal purse of the king and within limits he could use it to reward those he favoured. In 1780 the king was the centre of a network of officers, mainly owing their appointments to him, whereas by 1870 the great mass of the public service, although still Crown servants, were appointed by their departments to whom they thereby owed their first loyalty.

The public status of the king was also reduced by the increasing distinction being made between the royal household and the civil government. In earlier times all the great officers of state were housed in the Court or adjacent parts of the king's properties. But, though most of them had moved out of court, their salaries and expenses remained inextricably mixed with those of the Household. The Civil List provided, *inter alia*, all or part of the salaries, wages, and expenses for the royal households, for officers in the Treasury and for the Judges. In the details of the expenditure supplied occasionally to the House of Commons, the Masters of His Majesty's

Tennis Courts, Hawks, and Revills rubbed shoulders with the First Lord of the Treasury and the Lord Chief Justice. Parliament assumed that the lump sum granted to the king would enable him to conduct the government of the country. The fact that large sums had also to be voted for the armed forces and for the servicing of the national debt did not seriously weaken that assumption. The removal of expenditure on civil government from the List in 1831 carried the implication that those hitherto dependent on the king's money and favour were now dependent on that of the House of Commons.

The force of these institutional factors was strengthened by the declining health of George III and particularly by the form of his illness. In the summer of 1788 he became mentally deranged and quite incapable of dealing with any business. However before a Bill to establish a regency could be agreed and passed, the king made a sudden recovery. He was stricken with the same illness in 1801 and 1804 but each time recovered. However, in 1810 it was clear that he was now permanently insane.

As such he became incapable of signing and, therefore, of authorizing certain acts without which the government of the country could not be carried on. There were some who thought that the situation should be handled in accordance with the precedent of 1688, in other words that the two Houses should, by resolution, simply offer the Regency to the Prince of Wales. For various reasons it was decided to follow the procedure agreed in 1788, that is by an Act of Parliament. Both Houses resolved that a commission should be issued under the Great Seal for opening Parliament. When the Bill had been agreed both Houses then authorized the issue of Letters Patent under the Great Seal and for the giving of the royal consent by commission.

Under the Regency Act of 1811 (51 Geo. III, c.1) the Prince of Wales became Regent 'to exercise and administer the Royal Power and Authority of the Crown of the United Kingdom . . . and to use, execute and perform all Authorities, Prerogatives, Acts of Government and Administration of the same, which lawfully belong to the king . . . to use, execute and perform' subject, however, to certain prescribed limitations.

The significant clause in the Act, without which there would have been no transfer of authority, declared that the Sign Manual of the Prince Regent 'shall be as valid and effectual, and have the same force and effect as His Majesty's Royal Sign Manual, and shall be deemed and taken to be, to all Intents and Purposes, His Majestys ... and be obeyed as such'. There was, however, a period during which the king was incapable of signing and the Regent was without authority.

Supply voted to the king could only be issued from the Exchequer with his formal authority. The Lord Privy Seal was willing to incur the responsibility for affixing the Privy Seal to the warrant although by the terms of his oath he was restrained from using it 'without the king's special command'. But the deputy Clerks of the Privy Seal who had to prepare the essential documents held themselves precluded by their oath of office from preparing letters to pass the Privy Seal in the absence of a warrant signed by the king. In January 1811, therefore, two warrants signed by the First Lord and four other Lords of the Treasury were addressed to the Auditor of the Receipt directing him to draw one order on the Bank of England for £500,000 on account of the army, and another of the same amount for the navy. The Auditor, Lord Grenville, doubting the validity of the warrant asked that the opinion of the Law Officers be obtained. They confirmed his doubts and, though the Treasury Commissioners expressly assumed the entire responsibility for the issue, Lord Grenville refused. He could not obey the Treasury without 'a high and criminal violation both of a positive statute, and also of the essential principles of our Monarchical and Parliamentary constitution ...' Thereupon the Chancellor of the Exchequer moved a resolution in the House of Commons by which the Auditor and officers of the Exchequer were 'authorized and commanded' to pay obedience to Treasury warrants for the issue of such sums as had been appropriated for the services of the army and navy, as well as money issuable under a vote of credit for £3 million. The resolution was agreed to by both Houses but only because of the immediate necessity of the occasion. It was argued that the resolution involved a further assumption of the executive powers of the Crown and in the

Lords' *Journals* a protest to that effect was entered having been signed by twenty-one peers, including five royal Dukes.[3]

Precedents of this kind were hardly helpful to the maintenance of the claim of the king to be an equal partner with the two Houses. True, insanity is not an everyday disease and when it occurs it may justify exceptional measures. But it was apparent, particularly to those in informed circles, that for some years George III had been nothing like as commanding a figure as he had been in his early years on the throne.

The Prince was Regent for nine years and, as George IV, king for ten years. He was 'a clever, versatile, lazy man ... always a liar, always selfish, bad in his private and public conduct, and without the least understanding of his age ... the English monarchy could hardly have survived a successor of his kind'.[4] He was succeeded by his brother — William IV who was aged 65 and reigned only seven years to be succeeded by Victoria who was barely 18. These were hardly a series of individuals to sustain the idea that the Executive power of the country was exercised by the king.

Writing in 1858 Earl Grey could state without fear of contradiction that Blackstone's assertion that Executive power belonged exclusively to the King, while the power of legislation was vested jointly in the Sovereign and the two Houses of Parliament had ceased to be correct, unless it were understood as applying only to the legal and technical distribution of power. The distinguishing characteristic of Parliamentary government, Grey said, required 'the powers belonging to the Crown to be exercised through Ministers, who are held responsible for the manner in which they are used ... and who are entitled to hold their offices only while they possess the confidence of Parliament, and more especially of the House of Commons.'[5] The Executive power and the power of Legislation were virtually united in the same hands. According to Bagehot, writing a few years later, popular constitutional theory involved two errors as to the Sovereign — that she was a separate co-ordinate authority with the Houses of Lords and Commons and that she was the Executive. The Queen, he stated, 'must sign her own death warrant if the two Houses unanimously send it up to her.'[6]

Nevertheless the major shift of power did not alter the legal basis of the constitution nor did it require the promulgation of new laws concerning the organs of government and their relationships. The administrative system continued to be based on the assumption that nothing legally had affected the Sovereign's powers and status: they remained with the king *de jure* even though they had passed to the Cabinet *de facto*. This brought advantages and disadvantages to Ministers, who inherited the royal powers and privileges.

ADVANTAGES DERIVED FROM THE TRANSFER

The main advantage was that without the need for legislation Ministers found themselves able to use the substantial prerogative powers. Had they been obliged to obtain them by legislation the measures would almost certainly have been delicate to draft and controversial in passage, for example, the right to declare war.

The simplest way of assessing the significance of these powers is to note what Ministers had power to do without the need for legislation. There was, for example, no legislation which empowered the Cabinet or any Minister to declare war or to make peace, to have a navy or an army, to hold possessions overseas, to make binding treaties with other countries, to control the movements of aliens, and to create new honours. The prerogative provided for most of the simpler elements in the administrative system, for example, the appointment, dismissal, and conditions of the mass of public servants. The government's powers as regards justice and the courts were largely derived from the prerogative.

In terms of the limited scope of governmental action in the early nineteenth century the prerogative powers provided the Executive with most of the authority it needed, assuming Parliament was willing to vote sufficient financial support. But they were not of much help when the country and Parliament demanded governmental action in respect of such matters as the regulation of trade unions and friendly societies, child labour, poor relief, and public health. These were matters which could be dealt with only by legislation. Yet even in 1870 an important part of ministerial authority particularly in foreign and colonial affairs, defence and public safety was still dependent on the royal prerogative.

Less tangible but in some ways more significant was the continued role of the king in the working of the country's political institutions. Thus, as Blackstone said, 'no parliament can be convened by it's own authority, or by the authority of any, except the king alone'.[7] Indeed in order to give life and existence to Parliament and enable it to proceed to perform its functions the personal presence or the delegated authority of the sovereign is required at the opening of the Session. Similarly the prorogation and the dissolution were legally matters for the king. Another royal responsibility was the choice of Prime Minister. Legislation on these matters would have been particularly delicate to draft and most contentious to pass. Had the monarchy been abolished decisions about these and similar matters would have had to be taken presumably by Parliament who would probably not have agreed to place them in the unfettered hands of the Cabinet. Either some person, say a President, would have had to be given the powers with some discretion as to their exercise or else as with the written Constitution of the United States little or no room would have been left for judgement and discretion.

A third advantage to Ministers was that they inherited the special position the king held in the judicial system. It had long been recognized that the king could not be sued in his own courts. But it was admitted that, as the fountain of justice, he could not refuse to redress wrongs when petitioned to do so by his subjects. Thus it became established that though the subject could not sue the king he could bring a Petition of Right which, acceded to by the king would enable the courts to give redress. Among the incidental prerogatives were several that gave the king certain procedural privileges in the courts. He could, for example, not only make use of nearly all the actions open to one his subjects but he also had much easier and more effectual remedies.

The extension of the functions of government led to the growing use of the remedy by Petition of Right and in 1860 (23 and 24 Vict., c.34) the procedure was simplified and the remedy made more generally available. Under that Act a Petition of Right could be submitted to the Home Secretary who, if he thought fit, submitted it to the king for his fiat. In practice the fiat was never refused when the petitioner had the shadow of a claim but there was no legal means of compelling the Home Secretary to act. The remedy was available for the recovery of property and for breach of contract but not for torts.[8]

The special position in the courts applied not only to the king but was extended by the lawyers to cover the king's servants. There was never any attempt to define precisely who were covered by the terms — 'king's servants' or 'servants of the Crown'. In the 1860s two decisions by the House of Lords[9] arrested the tendency to bring an even wider range of public bodies within the umbrella of the legal privileges enjoyed by the Crown. The Act of 1601 under which poor rates were levied did not name the king and therefore it followed that property occupied by him was not rateable. By the middle of the nineteenth century it was established that not only buildings occupied by the great departments of state but also buildings occupied by the police or for the administration of justice were exempt from rates because they were occupied by the Crown. Lord Chief Justice Ellenborough in 1803 even appeared to extend it to include 'any public body or [body] . . . for the exercise of any public duty'. However in 1865 the House of Lords held that the Mersey Docks and Harbour Board though a statutory body and performing duties of public importance were not Crown servants. Only the king and 'the direct and immediate servants of the Crown whose occupation is the occupation of the Crown itself' came within the exemption. The exemption, therefore, did not extend to property occupied by local government bodies or by similar autonomous public bodies. The same distinction was drawn in the following year as regards liability for torts. It was held that though it was correct that a person acting as a public officer on behalf of the government and having the management of some branch of the government business, was not responsible for the neglect or misconduct of public servants, though appointed by himself, this only applied where the officer was directly appointed by the Crown, and was acting as a servant of the Crown: it had no application to the case of Trustees incorporated for the purpose of public works. Thus the Manchester City Council was liable but not the Home Secretary[10]

Judges and legal commentators were ready to provide the public offices with protection against the use of legal remedies normally available. Their attitude reflected a deference for the king; the vagueness of such ancient concepts as the king can do no wrong; and a practical view of the day-to-day problems of the public services. Ellenborough, when Lord Chancellor was in effect part of the Executive. As the century wore on and new departments and offices were established by statute and the statutory powers of the Executive were extended, the courts began to take a more limited view both of the legal privileges of the king and of the extent of the public services which should enjoy them. But tied as judges were to decisions made in previous cases and in any event, slow to change, the law continued to favour Ministers and Crown servants. It was not therefore until the Crown Proceedings Act of 1947 (10 and 11 Geo. VI, c.44) that the Crown was made subject to the law applying to private person, and even then only with serious reservations. It seems rather unlikely that all these legal privileges and exemptions would have been available had they had to be provided initially by Act of Parliament.

In passing it should be noted that the independence of the judges from the Executive owes a great deal to the continuance of the constitutional role of the king. For that independence dated from the time when the king exercised the Executive power and the judges, by their limited interpretation of the extent of that power were seen as allies of Parliament.* It was Parliament, therefore, which insisted on the measures insulating the judges from royal pressures. Even the provision that a judge could not be removed by the king save on a resolution of both Houses was seen as a restriction on the king rather than as a device for Parliamentary control By the time Ministers became *de facto* the Executive the independence of the judiciary was so well accepted as a basic feature of the constitution that the fact that the Executive had now become responsible to the House of Commons did not

* The immunity of the King from actions against him in the Courts did not apply to cases involving the interpretation of the scope of the prerogative. In the Case of Proclamations (1611) it was clearly laid down that 'the king has no prerogative, but that which the law of the land allows him'.

change the attitude. Had the monarchy been abolished the precise relations between the Government, particularly one popularly elected, and the judiciary would have been reopened and might have led to some degree of subordination to the 'people'.

Fourth, there were three procedural devices, or arrangements, which governments found particularly useful for the administrative system. They were the Order in Council, the committees of the Privy Council, and the Secretaryship of State.

An Order in Council is, practically, a resolution passed by the king in the Privy Council by and with the advice of the Privy Councillors present who assume responsibility for the decision taken. The instrument has the advantages of providing a formal link with the Cabinet and of avoiding the need for legislation. It can, however, only be used for matters lying within the royal prerogative unless specifically authorized by Act of Parliament — for example, in respect of municipal charters.

The Orders were used for a wide range of governmental acts. They were, for example, the instruments of government for the colonies and were used to confirm or disallow the acts of colonial legislatures. They gave effect to treaties and granted charters to companies and municipal bodies. They were the formal means for the call, prorogation, or dissolution of Parliament. Internally they were used to regulate the business of the public offices, e.g. the establishments of the major departments and the terms of the public service.

Orders in Council could occasionally be used as an alternative to asking Parliament to pass possibly highly controversial legislation. In 1839, for example, the government wished to take some action to further elementary education but knew that the strong feeling on the religious question made it unlikely that a Bill would pass the House of Lords. They, therefore, secured the authority of the Appropriation Act, which did not need the approval of the Lords, for the spending of money, and of an Order in Council to establish a Committee of the Privy Council for Education. It was not until 1856 that legislation was needed (to appoint a paid Vice-President), and not until 1870 that any statutory powers were granted to the Department of Education. i.e. to the Lords of the Committee of the Privy Council on Education. The Minutes of the Committee were used to promulgate such matters as the regulations for the use of the money voted.

The other striking example concerns the civil service. In their report, Northcote and Trevelyan were convinced that changes of the importance they were recommending could only be carried into effect successfully by a short Act of Parliament. Sir James Stephen was, however, emphatically opposed to such a procedure. 'From time immemorial', he stated, 'the constitution of the Civil Service of the Crown has been regulated by Royal Orders in Council.'[11] It was also argued that an Act might prove too inflexible. So the establishment of the Civil Service Commission and the system of examinations was made by an Order in Council in 1855. Incidentally, as Cornewall Lewis pointed out, some expenditure would have to be incurred and the annual vote would 'give the House of Commons a practical veto upon the system once in every session.'[12] Subsequent major changes, e.g. the introduction of open competition, were handled by Order in Council. Indeed the only legislation regulating the civil service *per se* in 1870 was the Superannuation Act of 1859.

An Order could not however be used to extend the law. Early in 1866, for example, immediate legislation being needed to deal with a cattle plague but its drafting requiring careful consideration, Lord Derby suggested that three or four resolutions be adopted in both Houses embodying those points on which there were no differences of opinion and authorizing the Government to deal with the subject by Orders in Council accordingly, such Orders to cease to be valid by 25 March. The Prime Minister (Russell) and Earl Grey objected strongly, saying that it would be a dangerous principle, and it was not pressed.[13]

The earlier model of the use of a committee of the Privy Council for the management of a public office was the Board of Trade constituted by Order in Council in 1786. As with the later Board of Education the payment of the Ministerial heads had to be provided by Act of Parliament. Another example was the transfer in 1858 of certain public health powers vested in the General Board of Health to the Privy Council. The powers could be exercised by three or more members of the Council, one of whom had to be the Vice-President of the Council's Committee for Education.

The office of Secretary of State is an excellent example of a legal position derived from usage rather than from Act of Parliament. As the work of being secretary to the king became too much for one man a second was added. Their work was not, however, divided in any formal legal manner. They possessed no powers of their own, it being purely a matter for the king to decide how the work they performed for him should be divided between them. Thus either could do the other's work should he be absent or ill. For that reason it was usual for George III to see them together (at least before 1783) whereas he would see other Ministers individually.[14] When Parliament started to confer statutory powers and duties on particular Ministers the character of the Secretary-ship of State was continued as if its holders exercised only prerogative powers. Thus, with rare exceptions statutory powers were conferred on one of His Majesty's Principal Secretaries of State not on a particular Secretary. If the power concerned police it was inferred that the Home Secretary was the Minister, if the army, then the War Secretary. By 1858 there were five Secretaries of State, each capable of performing the functions of any of the others, save for the rare cases when Parliament had conferred a statutory power on a particular one of them.

The fifth and more general benefit which Ministers derived from taking over intact the royal prerogatives was the concept of the Executive. Montesquieu, Blackstone, and others had explained and stressed the existence of three functions which the constitution had to perform: the legislative, judicial, and executive. The first was performed by Parliament and the second by the courts. It might be thought that by the middle of the nineteenth century that the Cabinet might have been recognized as performing the executive function. But the Cabinet did not exist legally either as the Cabinet or as the government: there were no references to it in the statutes and it had not existed long enough to be hallowed by usage. Nor did the Cabinet or even the government as such possess any powers, at least powers that could be substantiated in the Courts. At law its members were servants of the king appointed by him: they were a collection of individual officers not a corporate body. The Cabinet did not replace the king. He remained the Executive and they were his advisers, his position at law not being affected by any decline in his power to make his own decisions. At law the king was just as much the Executive in 1870 as in 1780 or 1720.

The attitudes which over the years had developed in respect of the king as the Executive were inherited and used by the Cabinet. They were very useful whenever the House of Commons showed too great an interest in the detailed working of the administration. The danger, as Ministers saw it, was that Members would attempt to govern, i.e. would take on some of the executive work. No doubt there were sufficient men of sense in and out of Parliament to appreciate that an assembly of over 600 members was not likely to be at its best in making decisions on everyday administrative matters. In the words of Cobden 'the House can interfere with great advantage in prescribing the principles on which the Executive Government shall be carried on; but beyond that it is impossible for the legislature to interfere with advantage in the details of the administration of the country.'[15]

To govern, the House would have had to be able to give orders or directions to the permanent officials. They might have tried to do this, as did the Long Parliament, by the establishing committees with executive functions, in other words by operating in a way similar to that developed by Municipal Councils. Instead the emphasis was placed on the fullest rights of Members to criticize and enquire into the actions of Ministers and to declare their sense and opinions. In the words of Erskine May 'Parliament has no direct control over any single department . . . It may order the production of papers . . .; it may investigate the conduct of public officers; and it may pronounce its opinion upon the manner in which every function of the government has been, or ought to be, discharged. But it cannot convey its orders or directions to the meanest executive officer in relation to the performance of his duty.'[16]

Whenever Members appeared to be going beyond criticism

and discussion Ministers were ready to quote the prerogative and role of the king. Lord John Russell in his book on the English Constitution stated the point quite bluntly: 'the two Houses of Parliament constitute the great council of the King; and upon whatever subject it is his prerogative to act, it is their privilege and even their duty to advise. Acts of executive Government, however, belong to the King, and should Parliament not interfere, his orders are sufficient.' He wrote those words originally in 1823 but he did not alter them in the edition published in 1865[17] Writing in 1858 Earl Grey stated: 'any direct interference on the part of either House of Parliament with the management of the army, would undoubtedly be a violation of the principles of our Constitution; but the same observation applies to every branch of the executive authority.'[18]

In 1842 it was proposed that the advantage of having the Board of Admiralty completely composed of naval officers should be considered. Peel, then Prime Minister, protested against the House 'laying any restrictions on the exercise of the royal prerogatives. If you begin thus on the navy you may next go on with the army . . .' and so 'to any branch of the public service.'[19]

POSSIBLE DISADVANTAGES

Public acts of the king involved the use of one or more Seals and a variety of formal instruments, a use encouraged by the grandeur associated with the royal court, e.g. the grant of office by Letters Patent under the Great Seal, and by the fee income which accrued to the officers and clerks who prepared the various instruments.

The suppression of a large number of sinecures and patent offices reduced the number of royal appointments. The severing of the link between fees paid and remuneration reduced support for the continuation of many of these formal procedures. In any case the ritual had less appeal to the nineteenth century. And the fact that in most cases the appointment was in effect made by a Minister not by the Sovereign no doubt reduced the dignity of even Letters Patent.

In 1849 the Treasury appointed a Committee on the Signet and Privy Seal Offices. It made a number of recommendations for reducing the use of these two Seals, for example, that appointments to offices held during pleasure should be made not by Letters Patent: a Sign Manual Warrant would be 'amply sufficient.' Statutory authority was given for a number of important changes in 1851 (14 and 15 Vict., c.82). These enabled the offices of Clerks of the Signet and of the Privy Seal to be abolished, the residual duties of the former being transferred to the Home Secretary.

Until 1862 it was the practice that all commissions in the Army* should pass under the royal Sign Manual. At that date 15,000 commissions had accumulated and were awaiting the Queen's signature. It was said that there were precedents, whereby the Queen could, by virtue of her prerogative, depute others to sign for her. It was however pointed out that when George IV, in the last weeks of his life, found it difficult and painful for him to affix his signature to documents it was considered that neither the king of his own authority, nor the king in Council, could make valid the expression of the royal will in any other way than by the actual royal signature. An Act of 1862 (25 and 26 Vict., c.4) empowered the Queen by Order in Council to declare that her signature would not be necessary in the case of appointments and promotions and that of the Commander-in-Chief or a Principal Secretary of State would be sufficient.

Other examples of the same trend were: in 1869 (32 and 33 Vict., c.97) the appointment of all members of the India Council was transferred from the Queen to the Secretary of State. Whereas before 1830 it was usual for Ministers to be appointed by Letters Patent in later years a Royal Warrant or an Order in Council was thought to be sufficient. In 1868 the practice whereby Secretaries of State received their appointments by Letters Patent was discontinued.[20] In the case of the issue of money the formal act continued to be needed. The Appropriation Acts continued to vote supply to the king, his heirs and successors. The Exchequer Act, 1834 (4 and 5 Wm. IV, c.15) reaffirmed the arrangement whereby the Sovereign by Royal Order under the Sign Manual, countersigned by any three Commissioners of the Treasury, authorized and

* Commissions in the Navy were granted by the Board of Admiralty.

required the Comptroller of the Exchequer to issue part of all of the sums granted by Act of Parliament or voted by the House of Commons. The Royal Order was not needed for Consolidated Fund Charges. In a memorandum to the Select Committee on Public Moneys in 1857 the Chancellor the Exchequer said

However necessary the Royal Order may be as a legal authority to the Treasury to apply the grants of Parliament, it must be admitted that it is only a form, prepared by the Treasury itself, and that in reality it is no check upon the Government; it is not desirable therefore to multiply unnecessarily these formal authorities, for the purpose of giving them the appearance of a check which does not belong to them.

He suggested therefore that there should be but one Royal Order for the Supplies of each Session: 'The purport of it should be to give to the Treasury the sanction of the Crown to their applying all sums already granted or to be granted by Parliament during the session, in conformity with the specific appropriations directed or to be directed by Parliament.'[71]

The suggestion was strongly attacked by the Comptroller of the Exchequer. 'It would be in fact,' he said, 'the putting of the Royal authority in commission for the entire Session, to be acted on by letters of the Secretary, the Assistant Secretary, and occasionally, a Senior Clerk of the Treasury.' He went on:

As well might there be one Patent at the opening of every Session, authorising the Lord Chancellor to give the Royal Assent to all Bills which may, during the Session receive the assent of both Houses; or to affix the Great Seal to any Patent laid before him, with the signature of the Private Secretary of the First Lord. The Sovereign of England is not a pageant and a legal fiction. Our Sovereign is an essential reality in the constitution . . .[22]

Lord Monteagle also thought the suggestion impracticable. Like some others of the Chancellor's suggestions it did not find favour with the Committee. What neither the Chancellor nor the Comptroller appear to have considered was for the money to be voted by Parliament not to the king but to the Exchequer or even to the government. The need for a Royal Order was continued by the Exchequer and Audit Departments Act, 1866.

The other disadvantage was the inconvenience caused to those in the employ of the Crown by the death of the king or queen. Parliament had already taken various steps to reduce the consequences for the political and administrative system.

In 1817 (57 Geo. III, c.45) the obligation to renew patents of offices held during pleasure was removed. In 1830, the grace of six months granted in 1708 was extended to eighteen in the case of those holding office or employment in the colonies (1 Wm. IV, c.4) and in 1837 it was enacted that commissions in the Army and the Marines were to continue in force unless cancelled by the successor (7 Wm. IV and 1 Vict., c.31). In 1867 it was enacted (30 and 31 Vict., c.102) that the duration of Parliament should not be affected by the demise of the king.

THE CROWN

By the 1860s there was an increasing tendency on the part of politicians and even of lawyers to use the term 'the Crown'. In some cases it was used as an impersonal description of the monarch and had the advantage of not referring to any particular occupant of the throne. Thus Earl Grey could write

Ministers of the Crown should obtain its direct sanction for all their more important measures. The Crown . . . seldom refuses to act upon the advice deliberately pressed upon it by its servants . . . But the Sovereigns . . . generally [have] exercised much influence over the conduct of the Government . . . and in extreme cases the power of the Crown to refuse its consent . . . may be used with the greatest benefit to the nation.[23]

It is not clear what was gained by talking in terms of giving advice to the Crown and the Crown refusing its consent, except that it avoided him speaking directly of the queen. The term, however, could be useful as meaning the king in his capacity as king and not as an individual. It could also be used to avoid referring to the government or Ministers. Thus the Royal Commission on the State of Large Towns and Populous Districts in 1845 recommended 'that the Crown [should] possess a general power of supervision'[24] over the local administrative bodies. It went on to recommend that 'the Crown be empowered to define and to enlarge . . . the area for drainage.' Though the Chairman was the Duke of Buccleuch it is doubtful whether he envisaged Queen Victoria taking on these duties.

It might be thought that when the need arose to supplement

the prerogative powers Parliament would have conferred the new statutory powers on the king. Instead from the 1830's onwards Parliament gave powers to individual Ministers rather than to the king. The reasons would appear fairly obvious. By that time it was generally accepted that the king acted on the advice of his Ministers and that a particular Minister was answerable for advice in a particular field. One did not criticize the First Lord of the Admiralty for the conditions in Newgate prison, nor the Home Secretary for the inadequacy of the Navy. It was more open and direct, therefore, and more in keeping with the increasing emphasis on individual ministerial responsibility for new powers and duties to be conferred on the Minister who would have to administer them and to take public responsibility for their performance. It also had the practical merit of avoiding the need for a formal instrument involving at least the Sign Manual. An alternative might have been to confer powers on the Crown or some legal embodiment of the State. But 'the Crown' was not a legal entity. In his celebrated essay: The Crown as Corporation F. W. Maitland said,

Whether the State should be personified, or whether the State, being really and naturally a person, can be personified, these may be very interesting questions. What we see in England, at least what we see if we look only at the surface, is not that the State is personified or that the State's personality is openly acknowledged but . . . that the King is 'parsonified.' Since that feat was performed, we have been more or less explicitly, trying to persuade ourselves that our law does not recognize the personality or corporate character of the State or Nation or Commonwealth, and has no need to do anything of the sort if only it will admit that the King, or, yet worse, the Crown, is not unlike a parson.[25]

The linking of the king with the parson is a reference to Coke's statement that they were both artificial persons, corporations sole, created not by God but by the policy of man'. But there were, as Maitland points out, difficulties in the way of any real and consistent severance of the king as a man and as a corporation. It would lead to the 'execrable and detestable consequences' that allegiance is due to the corporation sole and not to the mortal man. After the King's lands had been made inalienable George III had to go to Parliament in 1800 (39 and 40 Geo. III, c.88) to hold some land not as a King but as a man, a consequence that would not have followed had the original Act of 1701 made the distinction. Other legislation was needed in order to secure 'private estates' for the king.

In Holdsworth's opinion[26] the failure of the attempt to apply the conception of a corporation sole to the Crown was due not so much, as Maitland suggested, to the conception itself as to the course of British constitutional history. If the Stuart kings and the prerogative lawyers had had their way king and State would have been identified. The result of Parliament's victory was that the Crown, though it remained a corporation sole with many extraordinary qualities, did not become coextensive with the State.

The decisions quoted earlier limiting the scope of the terms 'servants of the Crown' had a similar effect. It was therefore possible to have public bodies with different degrees of legal independence from the State unlike, for example, the position in France. This was to prove particularly important in view of the increasing concentration of power in the hands of the Cabinet when assured of an effective majority in the House of Commons.

In practice if not in law, both king and Crown came to represent the power of the State or the nation. One talked of the king's Peace or the king's Highway, the armed forces swore allegiance to king and country. Civil servants were servants of the Crown not of the State nor even of the government: in any case, members of the government were also servants of the king or Crown. In the courts, actions taken by the government were in the form of *Rex or Regina* v. John Doe.

The increasing volume of statutory powers received little recognition. In his Constitutional History Maitland was probably the first lawyer to call attention to the change.

The new wants of a new age have been met in a new manner — by giving statutory powers of all kinds, sometimes to the Queen in Council, sometimes to the Treasury, sometimes to a Secretary of State, sometimes to this Board, sometimes to the other. But of this vast change our institutional writers have hardly yet taken any account. They go on writing as though England were governed by the royal prerogatives, as if ministers had nothing else to do than to advise the king as to how his prerogatives should be exercised.

In my view, which I put forward with some diffidence and with a full warning that it is not orthodox, we can no longer say that the executive power is vested in the king; the king has powers, this minister has powers and that minister has powers. The requisite harmony is secured by the extra-legal organization of cabinet and ministry.[27]

Maitland gave his lectures in 1887–8. There had thus been nearly twenty years further legislation beyond the end of our period. Nevertheless the truth of his statement was already becoming apparent in 1870.

CONCLUSION

In 1870 Queen Victoria was unpopular. The monarchy, as a political institution, was at its lowest ebb. In that year Gladstone in a letter to Earl Granville[28] even expressed doubts whether the monarchy could survive. It still had, he thought, a large fund of goodwill created in the earlier part of Queen Victoria's reign but this was diminishing. Nor did he see from whence it was to be replenished: the Queen was invisible, the Prince of Wales was not respected. It was increasingly difficult to get the Queen to perform formal ceremonial duties to the public and her reluctance would, he thought, grow with age. The outlook for ten, twenty, thirty, or forty years hence was a very melancholy one.

The chief cause was the withdrawal of the Queen from public affairs upon the death of her husband in December 1861. There was a widespread feeling that she was neglecting her national duty and was not earning the large grants made by way of the Civil List. In France the king had just been replaced by a republic but there was not a large public demand for such a change in Britain. In any case the recovery of the Prince of Wales at the end of 1871 after a serious illness evoked a burst of enthusiasm which increased the popularity of the royal family. Thenceforward the Queen's reputation grew rapidly until towards the end of the century it became almost a religion.

In his English Constitution[29] Bagehot started his account of the Monarchy by stating 'The use of the Queen in a dignified capacity, is incalculable'. Under a constitutional monarchy, he went on, the sovereign had three rights: to be consulted, to encourage, and to warn. In the course of a long reign a sagacious king would acquire an experience with which few Ministers could contend. He would have the advantage which the Permanent Under-Secretary has over his superior the Parliamentary Under-Secretary — that of having shared in the proceedings of the previous Parliamentary Secretaries. The analogy is revealing.

The withdrawal from public life no doubt confirmed the general belief that the Queen had ceased to be a significant part of the Executive. In practice, however, she continued to be an important factor all Ministers had to take into account. She was, for example, extremely reluctant to sign the Order in Council of June 1870 subordinating the Commander-in-Chief to the Secretary of State for War, regarding this as an encroachment on her prerogative. But the position was a very long way removed from that of George III in his heyday. There was no suggestion in Bagehot that the Ministers of the Crown were responsible for the Queen.

Pride of place in both Bagehot and Lord Grey's expositions published about the same time is given to the responsibility of Ministers to Parliament and in particular to the House of Commons. In Bagehot's eyes it was this feature which gave the British constitution superiority over that of the United States. Grey, as a working politician, saw some of the difficulties, but he is equally clear that the British political system was based on ministerial responsibility.

III

The Changing Character of the House of Commons

From the 1780s onward the work of the House was characterized by two new features: a very strong desire on the part of the ordinary Member to inquire into every aspect of the activities of the Executive and a growing dominance of Ministers in the procedure of the House.

INQUIRIES AND INFORMATION

Initially, the great increase in the interest of Members in the detailed work of the Executive arose out of a concern at the high level of public expenditure. Though a large part of wartime expenditure was financed by borrowing, not by increased taxation, this resulted in higher debt charges which left total expenditure higher even after the wars were over.

Whether called 'economical reform', 'economy' or 'retrenchment' the search for means of reducing public expenditure was a popular activity throughout our period. Though occasionally linked to party politics it was generally a cry which united all Members. No item of expenditure was too small to be investigated. In 1815, for example, the Clerk of the Stables provided the House with details of the number of horses kept by the king for each of the six years 1792–7 and for 1815 and a very detailed account of the expenses incurred in the department of the Master of the Horse for each of the three years, 1813–15.[1] The pursuit of economy took Members into every nook and cranny of the nation's adminstration. It led the House to use the Treasury as its agent and handmaiden. It coloured thinking on most administrative matters.

Members were, of course, in their strongest position when concerned with public expenditure. For it had long been accepted that the House had the sole right to vote taxation and to approve how the money should be spent. Yet, even in this vast sphere of activity the rights of Members were essentially those of enquiring into and criticizing, not of initiating. By a resolution of 1706, made a Standing Order in 1713, the House had denied itself the right to consider new or increased expenditure 'but what is recommended from the Crown'. Though initially introduced to prevent individual Members from irresponsibly raiding the public purse the arrangement had by the nineteenth century come to coincide with the general view about the relative roles of Ministers and Members. It was the prerogative of the former to take or initiate all Executive action, the function of Members being to investigate, criticize, and if they saw fit, condemn any such action. In the 1820s and particularly after 1832, Members became more actively interested in social and economic problems.

The House could exercise its right to information in several ways. The simplest procedure was for a Member to move that a return should be made to the House providing statistical or other information about a specific subject, for example, about the collection and management of the revenue, public expenditure, including salaries and pensions, and general statistics about trade and industry. But information about the exercise of the prerogative, e.g. treaties with foreign powers, dispatches to and from the Governors of colonies, and returns connected with the administration of justice or the activities of one of the Secretaries of State, could be obtained only by an address to the Crown: the House could not simply order the return to be made, it had to ask the Sovereign politely to provide it. Ministers were not in a strong position to oppose either motion, because of the belief in the right of Members to be provided with information. It was on particularly weak ground in attempting to refuse information about revenue and expenditure.

The government also made information, reports, etc., available to the House without any action on the part of Members, e.g. papers circulated by command of his or her Majesty. This was the usual arrangement for the reports and evidence of Royal Commissions.

A requirement to provide returns and annual reports became a regular feature of Acts of Parliament. As early as 1787 an Act (27 Geo. III, c.13) placed an obligation on the Treasury to lay before Parliament annually an account of the produce of the duties of Customs, Excise, Stamps, and the Expenses. Also an account of all additions to the annual charge of the public debt. The purpose of the return was to enable Parliament to judge whether the Fund was able to meet the first priority charged against its resources. The requirement was repealed in 1802 (42 Geo. III, c.70). Instead, after 5 January 1803, the Treasury was to submit each year an account of the total revenues of Great Britain (i.e. not just those mentioned in the 1787 Act), together with an account of the Consolidated Fund, of the public funded debt, of the arrears and balances due from all public accountants; of the exports and imports of Great Britain; and of how the moneys given for the service of the country had been disposed of. The information had to be provided for a year to end on 5 January and be submitted to both Houses on or before 25 March or, if Parliament were not sitting, then within 14 days after the next sitting.

It also became usual for the House to require the provision of regular information about the activities of the Executive in some area of current concern. There was indeed a strong belief that bad government and ill-founded policies could not last for long under the strong light of publicity. When for example, the House became greatly concerned about the number, pay, and pensions of public servants an Act of 1810 (50 Geo. III, c.117) laid it down that there should be laid before both Houses an annual account of every increase and diminution that had taken place within the preceding year in the number employed in all public offices and departments, and in the salaries, emoluments, allowances, and expenses in respect of all officers and persons so employed.

The number of these requests and their haphazard character increased the work of the departments. The Secretary of the Post Office complained to the Treasury that Robert Wallace's latest inquiry (1837) had required 'looking through eighteen folio volumes and eight large chests of papers in London alone' involving the employment of several extra clerks.[2] In 1848 Trevelyan told a Select Committee[3] that 'the extent to which the time of the public establishments is consumed in preparing the returns is very great'. It was, however, one of the questions of which the Treasury had not considered themselves 'authorized to interfere in the usual official way'. The Treasury had already recognized the growing importance of these demands by the appointment in 1812 of a Superintendent of Parliamentary Returns. Through allowing the post to lapse in 1821, they created in 1824 a post of clerk of Parliamentary Accounts, in view of the increasing complexity of the returns.[4] It was hoped thereby that a Member, thinking of 'calling for papers', would consult this official as to the form and scope of the request so that trouble and expense could be saved. Doubts were, however, expressed at the time about whether any officer not belonging to the House and easy of access to Members at all times could answer the purpose. The Commons' Librarian came, therefore, to be cast in this role. In 1830 the Library Committee of the House suggested that Members intending to move for Returns should in the first place find out from the Librarian whether the same or similar return had not already been moved and printed. Members might thus reword their request to cover only new material. The Select Committee of 1841[5] made this a recommendation and also proposed that the Speaker should be consulted.

It came to be appreciated that a good deal of the demand might be met by the regular publication of statistics. In 1832 the Treasury had agreed that a statistical branch should be opened in the Board of Trade under G. R. Porter with three clerks to assist him. Beginning the next year Porter began to publish each year consolidated returns covering a wide range of topics. He was given an established position as Superintendent of the Statistical Department in 1834[6]

A requirement to provide regular reports to Parliament came to be laid on newly created agencies and boards and even on local councils. Though occasionally a body might be required to submit an annual report direct to Parliament it was more usual for the report to have to be submitted to a specified Minister who was then required to submit it within a limited time to both Houses of Parliament. Thus the Inspectors of Prisons appointed under the Act of 1835 (5 and 6 Wm. IV, c.38) were required on or before 1 February of each year to make a report to the Secretary of State on the state of every gaol they had visited and he was required to lay every such report before Parliament within 14 days after 1 February. The Registrar of Joint Stock Companies, established in 1846 (7 and 8 Vict., c.110) had to report on his activities annually, the Act prescribing in some detail the points his report had to cover. The Board of Trade had to lay the report before both Houses within six weeks.

In many cases the requirements appeared to be using the Secretary of State or other Minister largely as a post office, as a means whereby the report reached the House of Commons. But the implication was that the body in question was in effect reporting both to a particular Minister and to Parliament. Even if the Minister had little or no powers in respect of the matters dealt with in the report he could not deny that he was not properly informed if so asked by a Member. In some cases it was made clear that the report was but part of the right of the Ministry to demand information. Thus the Act of 1836 (6 and 7 Wm. IV, c. 71) required the Tithe Commissioners to give the Secretary of State such information about their proceedings as he might require and also to submit to him an annual general report.

Under Bentham's influence, so strong was the belief in the value of regular reports to Parliament and therefore to the public, that the government might submit them even when not compelled to do so. Thus the reports of the Factory Inspectors to the Home Secretary were printed and submitted to Parliament even though there was no statutory obligation in the 1834 Act. This was also the case of the reports of the Inspectors of Schools required to be submitted to the Minister by Minute of the Privy Council. The Post Office published its first annual report in 1855 followed two years later by the Customs and the Inland Revenue departments.

A demand for returns was, however, not suitable for the treatment of subjects requiring the questioning of witnesses and the formulation of recommendations. A task of this kind had to be deputed to a small committee of Members. For these purposes the Select Committee became a very popular device and was greatly used by Members wishing to investigate in depth the cost and organization of the public offices. Composed wholly of Members, including Ministers occasionally, they demanded and obtained written and oral evidence, from

officials, sometimes from Ministers, and from knowledge-
able members of the public and outside experts. Their reports
were published and provided a mass of information not
only for Parliament but also for the Press and the general
public.

Between 1797 and 1803, for example, a Select Committee
on Finance issued 36 reports. This was followed in 1807–12 by
13 reports from a Select Committee on Public Expenditure,
and in 1817–19 by 11 reports from another Select Committee
on Finance. The device was used by the House to investigate
sinecures, the Civil List, and even official salaries. Later the
scope of the inquiries widened to cover areas of general public
concern such as the employment of children, emigration,
usury, friendly societies, and foreign trade.

These Committees were, however, appointed for one Session at a time and as they could not rely on being renewed,
might hurry their work or submit an inadequate report. If a
Select Committee did not have time to complete its work the
evidence it had taken was usually published and so sometimes
was the draft report prepared by the chairman. Thus the
Select Committee on the Income and Property Tax whose
members included Cobden, Disraeli, and Baring, published
two volumes of evidence in 1851 and 1852 but only a draft
report prepared by its Chairman, Joseph Hume. The Committee were of the opinion that there was 'not sufficient time
for discussing and preparing a Report that can do justice to
this complicated subject'.[7] Had the Committee had the time,
or the inclination to agree a report, it would probably have
been very different from Hume's draft. The report of the
Select Committee on Public Moneys was substantially different from the draft prepared by its Chairman — Sir Francis
Baring.[8]

Such Committees[9] were, therefore, not the most certain or
convenient device for exploring such subjects. Nor was the
composition of the Committee always the most suitable for the
task in hand. Choice could be haphazard and ill balanced.
Again Select Committees were confined in their inquiries to
the precincts of Parliament or, by special leave, to other parts
of London. They could not investigate matters on the spot in
other parts of the country, they could only summon witnesses

to London. Finally the fact that many such Committees sprang from private Members' motions meant there was no government commitment to do anything about their recommendations.

For certain kinds of inquiry, the Royal Commission proved a more suitable device. It usually remained in being until it had fulfilled its terms of reference, it could be composed wholly of non-Parliamentarians, and it could be invested with wider powers. In the thirty years from 1832 some 190 new Royal Commissions were appointed to deal with such subjects as Poor Relief, Municipal Corporations, Education, Military Promotions, and County Courts. It was moreover a government not a House of Commons device. Any Member could put forward a motion for the establishment of a Select Committee with his terms of reference, naming, with their permission, its members. Ministers might oppose the motion but if there were a general wish in the House for an inquiry of some kind it was not easy for them to resist the House performing one of its primary functions. They might even be driven to resign when the proposal was carried, for example, in 1830 when the House agreed to appoint a Select Committee to report on the Civil List.

In contrast the members and terms of reference of a Royal Commission were decided by the government and formally appointed by the King, either by Letters Patent under the Great Seal or by the royal Sign Manual. It was an exercise of the royal prerogative. It was natural, therefore, for Ministers to prefer Royal Commissions to Select Committees.

Quite often the appointment of a Select Committee or a Royal Commission coincided with an attempt by a small but active group of Members to secure legislation. In 1831, for example, Michael Sadler, meeting strong opposition to his Ten Hours' Bill, secured the appointment of a Select Committee of which he became Chairman, to inquire into the facts underlying the Bill. This sat for 43 days and examined 89 witnesses. No report was issued but the published minutes of evidence created a profound sensation. After the general election the House, by a majority of one, secured the appointment of a Royal Commission of which Chadwick was one of the three members. Its report led to the passing of the Factory

Act, 1833 (3 and 4 Wm. IV., c.103), the Bill being prepared by Chadwick.[10]

The Royal Commissions on the Poor Law and the Municipal Corporations established about the same time employed well-paid, itinerant Assistant Commissioners to investigate and to take evidence about conditions in various parts of the country. The Factory Commissioners did their own local investigations. In each case, the three 'central' commissioners were strongly opinionated, indeed they could be said to be biased in favour of a particular solution. They were part of the government's plans to secure early legislation and led to major measures in 1833, 1834, and 1835. They were not the model adopted for later Commissions which were usually larger with a representative membership.

There also began to come into occasional use committees appointed by the Treasury or a Secretary of State to inquire into and report upon a matter of importance to their departments but not deemed sufficiently significant to warrant the appointment of a Royal Commission with its special status and powers. They were usually composed of two or three officials and there was no obligation to publish their reports. In 1837, for example, the Treasury appointed a Committee to inquire into the Fees and Emoluments of Public Offices. The Northcote–Trevelyan Report was another example. Departmental Committees were not, however, a popular device before 1870.

CHANGING COMPOSITION

Two other changes were taking place during the nineteenth century. First, particularly after 1832, the composition of the membership changed, so that the House was increasingly influenced by outside opinion. Second, there emerged a more disciplined two-party system. The former encouraged Members to be more active, the latter, however, provided a framework to the procedure of the House which increasingly concentrated time and attention on subjects agreed by the leaders of the two parties. The full effects of these two changes did not come about until after 1870.

The unreformed House was composed of 658 Members of

whom 513 were returned by constituencies in England and Wales, 45 in Scotland, and 100 in Ireland. The franchise in England and Wales varied between the counties and the boroughs. The former was uniform, an Act of 1430 having given the vote to owners of freehold land or property worth 40s. a year. There was, however, no uniform franchise for the boroughs. In some cases voting was confined to the freemen of the town, in others any man who paid poor rates could vote, and in some the Member was returned by the corporate officers of the town. In the great majority of the boroughs the corporation played an important role. The number of counties and boroughs had remained almost the same for a long time. Small towns with shrinking populations retained their Members whilst large towns emerging out of the industrial revolution continued to be excluded. In 1830, of 202 English Boroughs, 77 had 100 or less voters and only 43 had over 1,000 voters. In these circumstances it was not difficult for the person who owned most of the land and property in the town to 'control' the results. Hence a substantial number of Members were in effect nominated to the seat by some large landowner.[11]

The Reform Act did not change the number of Members but spread them more evenly over the population. It also granted the power to vote, broadly speaking, to all men with freehold or copyhold land or property assessed at £10 or more, thus increasing the electorate by almost 50 per cent.[12] The changes greatly reduced the power of the large landowners and others who had control of the small boroughs which lost some 140 Members. The newly developed industrial areas of the North and the Midlands received representation. It was a shift of political power from the large landowners to the middle classes. The Act affected the working of the political system in three ways.

First it was no longer possible for a small number of large landowners to control the composition of the House of Commons, so further reducing the power of the king over the Commons for usually they favoured the king and were prepared to use their influence to sustain him and his Ministers in the House of Commons. Coming on top of the measures reducing patronage and other inducements meant that within a few years after 1832 it was no longer possible for the government to control the House.

Second, the effective choice of the Prime Minister and his leading Cabinet colleagues passed out of the hands of the king and became a major role of the House of Commons. For a long time, of course, the House had been an influential factor in the king's choice of his Ministers. But whilst substantial patronage and other forms of influence were at his disposal and, provided he had sufficient support from the Peers who controlled so many constituencies, a Cabinet which had his confidence had to become very unpopular before he needed to change it. Even in the late 1820s George IV was able to avoid a Whig government and to prevent legislation which he disliked for he had the means and support to win any consequential election.[13]

Third, there was a change in relations between the king and Cabinet on the one hand and the House of Commons on the other. Members could more rightly claim that they were returned to represent the views of their constituents and that, as long as they enjoyed the confidence of their electors they need not be beholden to any Minister.

The changes in attitudes and relationships did not, however, take place immediately. Their impact took some time to work out. It was not until after the Second Reform Act, 1867 that the effective voice in the choice of government passed from the Commons to the electorate. That Act disfranchised some of the small borough constituencies or reduced their representation from two Members to one, using their seats to increase the representation of London and the growing urban areas. It also increased the electorate by almost 90 per cent so that nearly 2½ million adult males in England, Wales, and Scotland became entitled to vote.[14]

PARLIAMENT AND THE PEOPLE

The conduct of Ministers and Members became increasingly influenced by the greater publicity given to the proceedings of the House. Though Members disliked the publication of reports of their debates, fearing misrepresentation but also disliking the publicity,* they tacitly abandoned in 1771 their right to prevent such publication. In 1803 the House recognized the right of the Press by reserving special seats in the public Gallery for the use of reporters, and the first series of Hansard's *Debates* start in that year. The interested public continued to learn of what was being said in the House of Commons from the very full reports published inthe newspapers. The proceedings in the House ceased to be the preserve of the few. Moreover as Ministers and Members knew they were speaking to a very much wider audience than the few present in the Chamber, they became more sensitive to public opinion. Members were encouraged to seek publicity by making a speech or at least asking a Question.

The newspapers were more than records of news, they usually supported one side or the other either in general or on particular issues. Ministers came to accept the criticisms and comments of particular newspapers as part of the public opinion which they had to take account of, ignore, or influence in their speeches. Some were better at it than others. Lord Derby, as Prime Minister, was said 'never to have been able to realize the sudden growth and power of the political Press for which he has no partiality . . . a fatal error in men who wish to obtain public power and distinction'.[15] As newspapers and periodicals became almost as much part of the political arena as the chamber of the House of Commons so most permanent officials learnt to keep away from them.

The House of Commons also disliked publicity being given to the names of Members who had voted for or against particular motions. The results of divisions were of course recorded in the Journals but not the names. Until 1853, the House even insisted that the Strangers' Gallery should be cleared for a division. The division lists that appeared in the Press were compiled from information gathered by reporters from Members. In 1836, however, the House started to publish official division lists and so it became clear to all how particular Members had voted. This made Members more consciously answerable to their constituents or to outside groups interested in the outcome of their vote.

* The Commons *Journals* record only the formal proceedings and decisions.

Finally, in the 1830s the Papers submitted to Parliament and the proceedings and reports of its Committee were made more readily available. Until then the prints of Bills and Reports were officially circulated only to those directly concerned but were also placed in public libraries if their subjects were likely to be of general interest. In 1835 a Select Committee recommended that Parliamentary Papers and Reports printed for the use of the House should be made accessible to the public by being put on sale 'at the lowest price they can be furnished'.[16] This was done, making a mass of information available to the interested public.

CONTROL OF THE TIME OF THE HOUSE

In 1780 there was ample time available for the business which Members wished to transact in the Chamber. The volume of general legislation was quite small and most of the measures were short and uncomplicated. Civil government was almost wholly financed out of the Civil List and only a handful of votes of Supply was required to meet the large expenditure on the Navy, Land Forces, and Ordnance. Beyond that there were occasional major debates mainly about the war or overseas affairs. All this was changed by the increased activity of Members and the addition of a hundred Irish Members in 1800 followed by a reduction in the length of the Session. The essential business of the country and the measures and motions which the majority of Members wished to discuss and hear discussed were thereby put at risk. Procedure had to be changed to give some priority to such items.

In 1811 the House agreed that on Mondays and Fridays, days usually devoted to Supply, Orders of the Day should have precedence over Notices of Motion. The distinction was largely between business which the House had agreed to discuss, i.e. ordered to be taken on a particular day, and any other public business. Much of the business so ordered was government business but by no means all, for Bills not promoted by Ministers could also be covered. On days when ample time was available to deal with Orders of the Day business not ordered would come up late, usually at a less attractive time, and the Government were not obliged to keep a House for it. But as the business of Supply and of general legislation increased quite often notices were not reached or Members were discouraged from moving them at the late hour.[17]

In 1835 Orders of the Day were also given precedence on Wednesdays. About this time 'by courtesy of the House' it came to be accepted that on Mondays and Fridays the government should have precedence for their business. Thus for the first time a distinction came to be drawn in the proceedings of the House in favour of those Members who held Ministerial Office. Previously all Members whether the First Lord of the Treasury or the newest recruit, could claim equal access to the time of the House.[18]

The status of Ministers was furthered by their increasing role in the formulation and passage of general legislation. At the beginning of the century Ministers confined themselves to preparing and handling Bills essential to the carrying on of the country, e.g. the Appropriation Act, measures imposing taxation or essential to the conduct of the war and defence, e.g. the Militia Act. Beyond that, legislation, whether general or private, was very much the province of the ordinary Member: the Acts were sometimes known by the names of their promoter, e.g. Gilbert's Act of 1782. Even quite significant measures might be drafted and steered through the House by such Members. The Middlesex Justices Act of 1792 (32 Geo. III, c.53) was brought in by an ordinary Member with the support of the Home Secretary.[19] The Passenger Act of 1803 (43 Geo. III, c.56) was based on the ideas of a good cause group — the Highland Society of Scotland.[20]

The wording of public Acts came increasingly under criticism. In 1796 a Select Committee reported that the style in which the statutes were composed was for the most part 'verbose, tautologous and obscure'.[21] The Treasury had established a post of Parliamentary Counsel as early as 1769 who was responsible for drafting its Bills and, in the course of time, those of other departments. On the death of the then holder in 1841 the office was discontinued. A year later it was agreed that the work should be undertaken by Parliamentary Counsel to the Home Office who had been appointed by Peel in 1835 for the improvement and consolidation of the criminal law. The Home Office Counsel remained the principal government draftsman until 1869 when the post and its occupant (H. Thring) were transferred back to the Treasury.[22]

Recognition of the advantages of expert drafting coincided with a changing attitude towards legislation. The successful conduct of wars, foreign and colonial affairs depended on finding the correct policy; little or no legislation was needed. When, in the 1830s, the emphasis shifted to the amelioration of social or economic problems fresh legislation became essential. The increasing number of measures mainly promoted by the government took up more and more of the prime time of the House. There was therefore less and less chance of a private Member's measure passing through all its stages in the Session, indeed not even all government Bills succeeded in doing that though given priority. He was therefore driven to try and obtain government support for his measure. In 1850 Peel was 'disposed to think the principle an excellent one, so far as independent members were concerned, that the duty of preparing measures of legislation should in all cases of general interest be undertaken by ministers.'[23] By 1861 a Select Committee concerned with procedure could state:

Although it is expedient to preserve for individual Members ample opportunity for the introduction and passing of Legislative measures, yet it is the primary duty of the Advisers of the Crown to lay before Parliament such changes in the law as in their judgment are necessary; and while they possess the confidence of the House of Commons, and remain responsible for good government and for the safety of the State, it would seem reasonable that a preference should be yielded to them, not only in the introduction of their Bills, but in the opportunities for pressing them on the consideration of the House.[24]

The last fifty years of our period are characterized by a struggle for the control of the use of the time of the House. Its elaborate procedure had been developed to encourage Members to participate and to enable any minority or opposition to criticize and delay. In 1848, in order to pass a Bill through the Commons eighteen different questions had to be put the last two being 'That this be the title of the Bill' and 'That Messrs A and B do carry this Bill to the Lords'. Each motion provided an opportunity for a debate so delaying the passage of the measure and taking up the time of the House. The Speaker stated 'the progress of Public Business has been impeded of late years partly by the unusual number of Members who speak in debate . . . and partly by the virtual abuse and evasion of the Rules of the House'.[25] The remedy adopted was to reduce the opportunities, for example, by requiring that many of the formal motions should be put to a vote without debate. Even so by 1861 government Orders of the Day were still only given precedence on two days (now Mondays and Thursdays) but a third Order Day was usually conceded towards the middle of the Session. In the meantime the changes made in 1854–5 whereby various charges were removed from the Consolidated Fund and along with the expenses of the Revenue departments had now to be voted each year had 'made a large deduction from the time available for Government Bills'. The numerous opportunities presented to every Member worked reasonably well when few wished to take advantage of them. But when a procedural device became so popular as to take a large share of the time the House very soon agreed to its suppression or limitation. The rise and decline in the use of public petitions is a major example.

It had long been the right of any aggrieved person to present a petition to Parliament. From the late eighteenth century petitions were mainly used to express views on a current issue or to gain redress for some grievance. In 1779–80 no less than twenty-four counties and many other constituencies presented petitions against the corrupt influence of the Crown. The number submitted grew with the increased popular political awareness and dissatisfaction with the unrepresentative composition of the House of Commons. From some 200 a year in 1800–5 the number presented grew to 900 a year during 1810–15, to almost 5,000 a year in 1826–31, and reached over 14,000 a year during 1836–41. They came to be used as forms of mass action, attracting tens of thousands of signatures, dealing with Parliamentary reform, factory conditions, slavery, and a great variety of issues which aroused popular indignation.

Each petition gave the Member presenting it to the House four chances to speak. With the help of a few friends he could thus exact a full debate on the subject-matter. Ministers were expected to attend for the presentation, which took place at the beginning of the sitting. Between 1833 and 1842 the House agreed to drastic curtailments of this opportunity and after 1839 debate upon presentation was forbidden save in rare instances.[26]

Even before the middle of the century the Minister 'who conducted the business of the Government' was being called 'leader of the House'. The leader was increasingly expected to determine the sense and feeling of the Chamber and give a positive lead, e.g. whether a motion for a Select Committee should be accepted.

Though the procedural changes had the appearance of placing the agenda of the House under the control of the government this was only superficially so. The problem which confronts any large debating assembly is how to concentrate on issues which the majority wish to discuss without suppressing completely the rights of an individual Member to raise matters of interest only to himself and perhaps to a few others. Thus it was not just a case that a dozen or so Ministers wished to use the time to secure the grant of Supply or the passage of a measure, it was also the wish of their supporters who constituted the majority of the House. In many cases it was also the wish of most of those opposed to the government; indeed the motion may have initiated by the leaders of the opposition. The organization of the agenda to accord with the demands of the majority was incompatible with allowing every Member access to it at any time and on any matter. The wishes of the majority could be achieved only by giving priority to Ministerial use or to a use agreed between representatives of the government and of the opposition. By the 1830s each Party had Whippers in or Whips with a view to securing the support of Members.

The procedural changes did not necessarily point to the subordination of the Commons to the Cabinet. The increased independence of Members and other factors resulted in six changes of government in the 1850s. It was not until after 1870 that the development of party organization and discipline gave the two front benches growing control over their supporters. In one very important respect the Cabinet lost the freedom the king and his advisers had enjoyed at the beginning of the century: the uncontrolled moneys, the loopholes, and the flexible arrangements which earlier characterized the national financial arrangements had all disappeared by 1870.

Since the eighteenth century[27] the bench on the right-hand side of the Speaker's chair had been left for the Lords of the Treasury, the Secretaries of State, and other important Officers. The privilege had been conceded by the House so that Ministers could be certain of a seat without having to attend the House early in the day in order to claim it. The bench was retained for them, even in their absence. For a similar reason the leading opponents of the government came to sit on the front bench on the Speaker's left hand directly confronting the Treasury bench.* The seating arrangements were convenient for the House for the small number of leading statesmen who occupied them spoke regularly, caught the Speaker's eye readily and were well placed to be heard by Members. Otherwise no places were particularly allotted to Members.

The seating arrangements and the changes in the conduct of the affairs of the House showed the increasing acceptance of a two-party system with its loyalties and practices. It was recognized well before the middle of the century that the political leaders who could command a majority in the House were entitled to form a government, take the executive decisions, and try to put their policies into practice by legislative and other means. The attention both of the House and of the country was thus focussed on the actions and statements of these leaders or Ministers. This governing group had a collective responsibility in that no member of it could for long pursue a policy at variance with the views of his colleagues. But, in day-to-day terms, his responsibility was more limited and personal. If Members were concerned about taxation then their attention focussed on the Chancellor of the Exchequer, if factory conditions were their concern then on

---

* H.J. Hanham says the term "His Majesty's Opposition" was first used in the House in April 1826' (*The Nineteenth Century Constitution* (1969), p.114).

the Home Secretary, if the navy then on the First Lord of the Admiralty, and so on.

The practice and procedure of the House came to conform to this emphasis on the responsibility of particular Ministers for particular spheres of policy and action. By the 1860s the Estimates for example, came to be formulated and presented in accordance with Ministerial responsibilities. Two devices developed for the use of the ordinary Member also had the effect of emphasizing the accountability of individual Ministers. These were motions arising out of the Committee of Supply and Questions to Ministers.

The presentation of the Estimates in great detail did not lead Members to spend much more time discussing small items in Committee of Supply. The increased clarity and information appeared to satisfy most Members, or, if it did not then they had to be that much more the master of the facts than in the days when all kinds of maladministration and waste could be concealed by the large, vaguely designated demands of the government.[28] Instead they preferred to set up a Select Committee of Members from time to time to examine particular areas of expenditure, e.g. that of 1847–8 on Miscellaneous Expenditure.

However as procedural changes steadily reduced the opportunities open to the ordinary Member to raise an issue of his own choice, the Committee of Supply emerged as a new and important opportunity. By using the old doctrine of 'grievances before supply' Members could raise matters which they or their constituents wished to see aired either on the formal motion* which converted the House into a Committee of Supply or afterwards when particular Estimates were moved.

QUESTIONS[29]

In order to provide for orderly debate the basic rule of the House was that Members could speak in the Chamber only when a motion had been moved. It had, however, proved

---

* Mr W. E. Forster's complaint abut the alleged censorship of the reports of Inspectors of Schools (p.319) was raised on the Motion that Mr Speaker do now leave the Chair.

convenient to allow a Member to ask another Member a question providing this did not lead to a debate. At first these were usually inquiries about the business of the house, e.g. about the introduction of some Bill, and were addressed to any Member so concerned, not solely to Ministers. Even the First Edition of Erskine May, published in 1844 goes no further than stating that 'questions are frequently put to ministers of the Crown concerning any measure pending in Parliament, or other public event; and to particular members who have charge of a Bill, or who have given notices of motion; . . .'[30]

Increasingly the attention of Members was focussed on the activities of individual Ministers, not just in respect of measures they proposed to introduce but in respect of the actions they had taken or had the power to take in their departments. The change was partly the result of increasing statutory powers but it was encouraged because a Question took less time than the alternative of a motion. The aim of Ministers and leading members of the House from 1830 onwards was to avoid time being frittered away or the progress of important business being jeopardized by masses of casual motions, particularly those for the adjournment of the House.

In 1835 the practice began of Members giving notice of Questions to Ministers, which appeared on the Order Paper under the head 'Notices of Motions'. In April 1869 for the first time the Order Paper listed them under the separate heading 'Questions'. By 1865 Dod's *Parliamentary Companion* could state 'At half-past four public business begins when the leading Members of the Government are expected to be in their places to answer the questions of which notice has been given'. At that date the Speaker took the chair at 4 p.m. so the arrangement left thirty minutes for Petitions and Private Business. The presence of Ministers in their places at a set time was a formal acceptance of the importance of this new device. The scope of Questions was still being worked out. Questions to Members other than Ministers became confined 'to any Bill, Motion or any public matter connected with the business of the House in which [they] may be concerned'. The Tenth Edition of Erskine May (1883) stated for the first time: 'Questions addressed to ministers should relate to the public affairs with which they are officially connected, to proceedings pending in Parliament, or to any matter of administration for which the minister is responsible.'

LOCAL LEGISLATION[32]

Until well into the nineteenth century the promotion and passing of private Bills continued to be a significant role of the non-Ministerial Member. A private Bill, also called a local or personal Bill, was for the particular interest or benefit of an individual, company, corporation, or a locality and therefore contrasted with General or Public Bills. Procedurally the distinction turned on the manner in which a measure was brought before the House. Private Bills had to be brought in by way of a petition. Private Acts generally exceeded the number of general Acts. In the 15 Sessions of 1801–13/14 Parliament passed 1,967 general and 2,393 local or personal Acts. In the 1860s when the number of Public Acts averaged around 120–30 a year the number of Local and Personal Acts was running at over 200 a year, being 372 in 1865. In addition there were quite a number of unsuccessful private Bills.

The handling of these measures was very much a function of the House of Commons not of the Government; of ordinary Members not of Ministers. Members of the government were exempt from serving on Private Bill Committees. Indeed as late as 1840 the Chancellor of the Exchequer (Baring) could say that it would be contrary to all established practice for Ministers to give an opinion on a private bill.[33]

Each Bill was initiated by a petition. The petitioners i.e. the person or group outside the House, had to find a Member (usually from the locality covered by the Bill) who would present the petition and take charge of the Bill through its numerous stages in the House. In most cases the interests of others, not merely those of the promoters, were involved. The most important stage was the examination of the Bill in each House by a Select Committee. In the Commons it was the practice to include the representatives from the counties and towns in the area affected by the Bill, but generally speaking, the only regular attenders were Members whose constituents were affected. The Committees were quite large, consisting in the 1820s and 30s of some 120 Members, but the size could be larger for railway Bills where the proposed line passed through several counties.

The procedure was supposed to be judicial in character, in that Members were expected to weigh impartially the merits of the case put forward by the promoters in the light of the criticisms and objections of the opponents. It was almost impossible to achieve this with Committees mainly composed of Members interested in one way or another in the outcome. Nevertheless for a long time the House refused to exclude local Members from membership, who, it was argued, were the most competent judges of benefits to arise from measures affecting their own communities. However in 1839 a Committee of Selection was appointed thus making it easier for the House to appoint the Chairman and members of Private Bill Committees without reference to their local interests.

In 1844 when the House was faced with no fewer than 248 railway Bills a system of small Committees of five Members was adopted, each of whom had to declare that his constituents had no local interest, with three as the quorum. The custom of choosing the Member who had moved to introduce the Bill as Chairman of the Committee and who naturally was active in the Bill's favour was dropped in 1840. In 1855 local representation disappeared from all Private Bill Committees. The handling of this kind of legislation became increasingly professionalized and judicial in temper with much less scope for the ordinary Member.

It is indicative of the increasing use of officials that about the middle of the century departments should become involved in the consideration of such Bills. It had always been open for the Treasury, for example, to raise a question about a clause in a private Bill. Their *locus standi* was, however, little different from that of other opponents of the Bill. In the 1840s and 1850s the Departments came to have a more general status. They began to propose amendments and make criticisms from their own general viewpoint.

In his Third Edition (1851) Erskine May greatly amplified his section on private Bills. He said: 'They [i.e. the promoters of the Bill] are frequently in communication with public boards or government departments, by whom amendments are also proposed; and who, again, are in communication with the chairman of ways and means, or the chairman of the Lords' committees.' He went on to refer to the Commissioners of Railways* re railway bills, the Home Office re turnpikes, the Commissioners of Woods and Forests re Crown property, the Board of Trade re bills affecting trade, patents, and shipping, and the General Board of Health for the improvement and sewerage of towns.[34]

While the Committees paid due regard to the views of departments there was no suggestion that the Bills thereby became government measures. Their contents still remained essentially matters to be settled by the House of Commons. What governments could do, however, was to promote general legislation making it easier for local authorities and others to obtain the use of the powers granted in local Acts.

In the 1840s 'model Bills' were prepared for several classes of private legislation, e.g. railways and town improvement, to secure greater uniformity and cohesion in such measures. In 1845 three Clauses Acts embodied model forms for Land (compulsory purchase), Railways, and Companies, and two years later covered several other areas of private Bill legislation, e.g. Markets and Fairs, Gasworks, Waterworks, Cemeteries, and Police. These Acts not only improved the drafting, they also made the powers more readily available. The town, for example, still had to promote its own Bill but this need only adopt all or any of the clauses set forth in the revelant Clauses Act. The Town Improvement Clauses Act, 1847 (10 and 11 Vict., c.34) made more readily available in 216 sections the provisions contained in earlier private Acts for paving, draining, cleansing, lighting, and improving towns.

Many of the powers made available by the Public Health Act of 1848 were founded upon provisions in local Acts. The Act also used a new Provisional Order procedure. Where a Town, Borough, or other place petitioned the General Board of Health to apply all or part of the Act to the area within its boundaries and there was no Local Act in force for paving, lighting, cleansing, etc., for that area, and the Board reported

* A primary purpose of the Railway Board set up in August 1844 was to exercise some supervision of the large number of Bills for the extension of railways.

favourably on the petition the powers could be conferred by Order in Council. Where these conditions did not apply, e.g. where a Local Act was in force, the Board could proceed by making a Provisional Order 'under their Hands and Seal of Office'. Copies of the Order had to be deposited with various officials in the area, e.g. the Town Clerk, but no such Provisional Order had any force or effect without the previous authority of Parliament. If any Order were opposed it was treated in the same way as an opposed private Bill. But the fact that it was put forward by an impartial body after a thorough examination resulted, in practice, in most Orders being passed unopposed, so saving a large amount of time and expense. Between 1845 and 1869, for example, the Inclosure Commission made 958 Provisional Orders of which 842 were confirmed by Parliament without opposition.[35] Had this procedure not been introduced there would probably have been 958 private Bills, many of which would have been opposed.

MINISTERIAL ACCOUNTABILITY

It is now convenient to bring together a number of the points already mentioned and show their impact on the administration of the public services. The lessening of Members' inhibitions about investigating or discussing in detail the operation of the Executive combined with their greater freedom from the influence of the Crown meant that every aspect of the work of the departments, however trivial, was open to scrutiny and criticism. In order to avoid the Commons attempting to perform the functions of the Executive, Ministers had to accept, indeed stress, that the functions of Members were to investigate, criticize, and approve or disapprove. This interpretation also suited those responsible for arranging the most effective use of the time of the House, providing devices could be made available which, while enabling back-benchers to exercise their rights did not put at risk the passage of the main elements of public business. The main general device which emerged was the right of Members to question Ministers on the floor of the House. Other opportunities, e.g. to move the adjournment of the House at any time, remained but were not liked by the two front benches.

Increasingly after the middle of the century the working life of the Commons was based on the principle that Members could hold a particular Minister answerable for every act or failure to act in that section of the total powers of government for which he had a recognized authority. This remained true even though it was becoming increasingly difficult for any Minister personally to make all the decisions and be fully conversant with the whole of the work of his office. The House grew increasingly intolerant of administrative arrangements which obscured who was answerable for what, for example, in the management of the armed forces. Members wished to know who was responsible, meaning which single Minister. If, as in the case of the Poor Law Amendment Act, 1834, no Minister was responsible for a controverisial area of public activity this could lead to annoyance and frustration. The principle thus had important consequences both for the structure of the administrative system and for the internal working of the public offices.

In as far as answerability was a matter of providing information the point might have been met by giving Members direct access to officials. At the end of the eighteenth century statistical and other returns were sometimes presented to the House by a Treasury clerk or by a member of one of the revenue boards. Not being members of the House these officers could not enter the Chamber but stood at the bar to deliver their documents. This was hardly a convenient procedure for everyday use. Moreover the clerks in the public offices had no responsibility vested in them, they were there to help the political head of their Office. To have given Members access to them might have faced them with the problem of divided loyalties. Apart from the occasions when they were called to give evidence before a Select Committee permanent officials did not deal directly with Members. Members had access to them only through the Ministers they served.

The increasing emphasis by Members on individual accountability meant that all Ministers whose work was of continuous political interest had to be in the Commons. Thus, whereas in the Cabinets of Pitt and Addington at the beginning of the century only two or three of the ten or so members were in the Commons Gladstone's first Cabinet of 1868–70 contained nine Commoners out of fifteen members. The ancient offices of Lord Chancellor, Lord President of the Council, and Lord Privy Seal remained firmly based on the Lords. Of the Secretaries of State only the Foreign Secretary was regularly in the Lords, the assumption being that major issues of foreign policy would be handled by the Prime Minister and the Commons was not very interested in the day-to-day work of the Office. When new Ministerial offices were created it was usual to empower the holder to sit in the Commons. The disqualification of the Postmaster-General was removed in 1866. From the 1850s it was not unusual for a group to demand the creation of a Minister in the Commons with responsibility for a particular subject, for example, Scotland, education, agriculture, and justice.

The answerability or accountability of each Minister was a political not a legal device. If a Minister broke the law he could be brought before the ordinary Courts. The device of impeachment had proved to be cumbersome and unsatisfactory. The impeachment of Warren Hastings (not a Minister) in the 1780s had lasted for seven years and had pleased neither the lawyers nor the politicians. Henry Dundas, (Lord Melville), who was impeached in 1805, was acquitted, but had already resigned. In any case, the Commons were hardly likely to cherish a device which put the final control of Ministers in the hands of the Lords. It was simpler and more in keeping with the new relations between the Commons and the king's advisers that Members who disliked the policy or actions of a particular Minister or regarded him as incompetent could make their displeasure felt by voting against him.

Even if their criticism did not lead to his defeat, because his Cabinet colleagues came to his support, his reputation and political career might suffer and at some covnenient time he might be moved or dropped by the Prime Minister. A Minister who showed that he had mastery of the affairs of his office, who could hold his own in debate, yet was sensitive to the feelings of the House, particularly of his own supporters was likely to achieve the highest Ministerial posts. Political accountability had replaced legal accountability.

IV

From Officer to Employee

In the ninety years after 1780 there was a further marked increase in the number engaged in the public services. As in the eighteenth century this increase took the form of the appointment of clerks and other subordinate officials and only rarely in the creation of new offices In the earlier part of the period two administrative changes at the national level were reducing the number of officers with personal legal responsibility for the execution of their duties. They were:

(i) A considerable number of ancient offices were suppressed and some disappeared as the result of administrative reorganization, e.g. the merging of the revenue departments.

(ii) The legal character of most of those which remained was so changed that the status of their holders became little different from that of employees.

At the level of local administration a similar move from a system based on a concept of office to one based on a concept of employment took place. But this came about not by the suppression of offices but by the replacement of officers with statutory or common law duties by paid employees answerable to an elected body.

Suppression

The term 'sinecure offices' was used to cover three broad categories of office: (i) offices without duties or responsibility attached to them i.e. its original sense; (ii) offices with insignificant duties compared with the very high level of remuneration enjoyed by the holders; and (iii) offices with useful business but executed by a deputy.

To the number of offices without duties, the Commissioners for Examining the Public Accounts and the economical reformers were ready to add many others which still had duties attached to them, but of a character no longer regarded as useful, necessary, or sufficient and certainly not worth the rewards they obtained. The third category existed because of the practice common since the fifteenth century of empowering an officer to exercise the functions of his office by a sufficient deputy.

The attraction of sinecure offices to their holders depended partly on their status in the service of the king and in the public regard and partly on their pecuniary value. Where only a salary was provided, varying from £1,000 or £2,000 down to £30 or £50, because these were usually paid out of the Civil List, pressures on the king's resources had inhibited increases in their level during the latter half of the eighteenth century. Increasingly, therefore, the most attractive offices became those with fees attached to them for, with the high level of war expenditure and activity, fee income rose markedly. The relative attractiveness of offices executed by a deputy depended on the difference between the earnings of the office and what needed to be paid to the deputy and his assistants to execute the office — in other words, its net profitability. In the Exchequer, for example, the value of the offices of the Clerk of the Pipe was £100 to the deputy and £720 to the principal; of the Comptroller of the Pipe £160 to each; and of the King's Remembrancer £1,500 to the deputy and £991 to the principal.[1] Where the offices were remunerated by fees, the fee income remained the right of the office-holder and did not devolve to the deputy; the amount the deputy received being a matter of agreement between him and the office-holder. In general, deputies were remunerated by a fixed stipend, the office therefore showing an increasing profitability to its holder as the fee income rose.

In 1780 sinecures were concentrated in the oldest parts of the administration, particularly those closest to the king, and in the courts. They were less often found in the new departments or in those which had expanded rapidly during the century, for the expansion of the staff in those cases had taken the form of additional clerks rather than the creation of new offices. Thus they were prevalent in the Exchequer and the Customs, but not in the Treasury and the Excise. They were more likely to be found where there was a large and growing income from fees than where remuneration was mainly by salary and allowances — in other words, in the Law Courts and in the ancient Offices of the Privy Council and Privy Seal rather than in the Admiralty. While political attention tended to focus on some of the most glaring cases, for example, a nobleman received substantial emoluments for holding an office which involved him in no work — the system operated throughout the whole range of the king's service. In the Treasury one of the solicitors drew a net salary of £130 a year in spite of 'no duty or attendance having ever been required either of him or his predecessor'; two messengers received net salaries of £262 a year but executed their offices by deputies; and a clerk drew his Civil List salary of £100 but had been superannuated from the office.[2] Several of the clerks held other appointments, which added to their remuneration. And all this under the authority of the Treasury Board. In the Home department of the Secretaries of State the 'necessary woman' (housekeeper) with a fixed salary of £48 executed her office by deputy to whom she paid £28 and the benefit of the perquisites.[3] Most of those affected by Burke's Civil Establishment Act of 1782 were in receipt of quite small salaries or pensions.

For fifty or so years a good deal of Parliamentary energy went into securing the suppression of sinecures. The reformers, however, were faced with a major difficulty — the existence of proprietary rights in these offices. Even the enthusiastic Commissioners for Examining the Public Accounts had to pay regard to this fact. After arguing that sinecures should be abolished, they had this to say in their Eleventh Report of June 1784:

We do not mean to violate in the slightest Degree, any Right vested in an officer by virtue of his Office. The Principles which secure the Rights of private property are sacred, and to be preserved inviolate; they are Land Marks to be considered as immovable. But the Public have their Rights also; Rights equally sacred and as freely to be exercised . . . If a useless and expensive Office cannot be suppressed, nor the Redundancies of an Office curtailed, be the Necessities of the State ever so urgent, without intrenching upon the right of the Possessor, and violating the Public Faith, the Evil must be endured, until the Power of the Legislature can, without the Imputation of Injustice, be exerted for the Relief of the State.

Nevertheless, being determined that sinecure offices should be abolished, they sought arguments to justify such a course of action. They went on to claim that 'not the emolument of the Officer, but the Advantage of the Public, [was] the Object of the Institution'. To suppose the officer to have right to object to the regulation, diminution, or annihilation of his profits, would be 'to suppose the Office created for his Benefit'.[4] In their Fourteenth Report of December 1785, they argued:

A Freehold held under the Grant of the Crown, is a solemn Right, to be treated with Respect, Delicacy and Caution; but if the Subject of that Grant be a Public Office, and a Stipend be annexed to it, payable out of the Revenue of the Public; if rendering a service useful to the State, as the Consideration for the Stipend, be of the Essence of such an Office . . . where the Utility of the Service is either wanting at the Time of the Grant, or in the Process of Time ceases to exist, the Grant either had not at first, or has lost, the Quality essential to its Support; and no Power of the Grantor, . . . or Duration of the Interest, can supply the Defect: It cannot be supported in the Shape of an Office; for it has not the Character that distinguishes an Office from an Annuity or a Pension.

They went on to say that the holders may deserve to be rewarded, but, if so, not by an office but by an appropriate payment or allowance, for an office tended to be a perpetual encumbrance on the Revenue and was calculated to mislead the public.[5]

Suppression, however, was said to be an interference with the prerogative and in some cases, where members of the Royal Household or favourites of the king were involved, as being a personal insult to His Majesty. There were also the practical politicians who doubted whether the Executive could function properly without having a number of sinecures at its disposal. Their suppression would mean that reward for political support and public service would have to be given in future by some other means, e.g. by elevation to the peerage or the award of some other honour.

Abolition or modification could be achieved only by paying due regard to the rights of the existing holders. Many of the grants had been made under the Great Seal which was not lightly to be put aside. True an Act of Parliament could override even the Great Seal, but so in effect could it override every public and private decision. The people who held these grants held them in the faith that they would continue to be honoured. In 1797 defending the slow progress of abolition, Pitt reminded the House of Commons that 'sinecure offices are given in the nature of a freehold tenure' and that Parliament had 'expressly said they will respect them as freehold property'.[6] Abolition was achieved in two main ways.

(i) *Abolition when the office became vacant.* An early example was the Act of 1783 (23 Geo. III, c.82) which provided for a number of important changes in the organization of the Receipt of the Exchequer. The offices of the two Chamberlains, the Tally Cutter, and the Usher, were to be abolished 'after the Death, Surrender, Forfeiture or Removal of the possessors' and after the Death, etc. 'of the persons respectively entitled thereto' after the departure of the present possessors.

It was sometimes possible to secure abolition not by statute but by the use of administrative action, i.e. by not filling vacancies as they occurred. This was Pitt's policy in respect of patent officers in the Customs, which were in the gift of the First Lord of the Treasury and numbered 196, some of great value. After the defeat of his Public Offices Regulation and Customs House Bills in 1783, Pitt decided to proceed by the means within his power. He allowed any such offices to remain vacant as they fell in. By the time an Act was passed in 1798 (38 Geo. III, c.86), suppressing this class of office, fifty had fallen in.[7]

(ii) *Abolition during the period of the office, but with compensation.* As in all cases of expropriation, the problem was to decide on the amount of compensation. The two Auditors of the Imprests abolished in 1785 were each paid £7,000 a year for the rest of their lives. Their recent fee income had been much higher, but presumably £7,000 was an acceptable figure. In any case, their offices were hardly redundant, except in the sense that they were exercised by deputies and clerks. The government wished to introduce a different structure. Burke's Civil Establishment Act of 1782 which abolished over a hundred offices and employments and enabled rather more to be suppressed, left the terms of any compensation to be settled by the Treasury. Those who held their office by Patent for life, or who had purchased their place for a valuable consideration, were to receive an annuity equal to the legal emoluments of the office. Other persons who had 'diligently and faithfully' executed their subordinate offices, and who by suppression of their office would be reduced to 'distressful or indigent circumstances' were to receive such annuities as the Treasury 'shall think equitable and just'. It will be noticed that a distinction was drawn between patent offices where the property interest was recognized, and subordinate posts.*

Proceeding by these two methods had two consequences. First, the monetary savings were offset for many years by the annuities paid as compensation. Burke had pressed for the Act of 1782 on the assumption that the savings from the suppression of offices would go a long way towards meeting the annual deficit on the Civil List. He estimated the savings as £72,000 but an estimate for Shelburne, then First Lord of the Treasury, showed only £40,000. Out of this had to be paid pensions and allowances. The main savings accrued when the pensions and allowances ceased.[8]

Second, suppression was a slow process even when Parliament was ready to pass legislation. For, as many of the offices were held for life, many years could pass before the change could take place. Of the four Tellers of the Receipt of the Exchequer in 1783 whose successors were to be paid a fixed salary, one did not die until 1813 and another, Lord Camden, remained in office until 1834 but relinquished a large part of his emoluments in 1812. In 1851 one of the four Clerks of the Signet remained in office, having been appointed in 1802 and, therefore, not affected by the Acts of either 1817 or 1832. He had never attended the office or performed any duties. In part this accounts for the long drawn-out character of some of the changes and for the alternation of periods of reforming zeal with periods of inactivity. The position was reviewed for the House of Commons by its Committee on Public Expenditure

* The suppression of occupied posts in the Customs was usually accompanied by 'just and reasonable' compensation. See for example, the Act of 1811 (51 Geo. III, c.71).

in 1808, by a Select Committee on Sinecure Offices in 1810 and by a Select Committee on Finance in 1817. After a thorough survey of the situation, the Select Committee of 1810 found that throughout the government both at home and abroad there still existed some 250 sinecure offices.[9] A Committee of 1834 listed 108 sinecure offices, but most of these were in the process of being abolished or regulated.[10]

(iii) *Other Changes*. Three other parallel developments either made it easier to secure suppression (by the provision of superannuation) or were in effect a form of suppression (bringing remuneration into line with responsibility and the standardization of titles).

First, it came increasingly to be appreciated that sinecures were often an alternative to a pension. The Commissioners on the Public Accounts had pointed out in 1785 that the holders might deserve to be rewarded, but if so by an appropriate payment or allowance. They regarded the introduction of a superannuation scheme as a necessary part of their attack on the system of offices.[11] The Fee Commissioners recommended in 1786 that every officer who retired on account of age or infirmity should have 'a decent provision made for his future subsistence'.[12] The Customs and the Excise already had a limited form of pension and in 1803 the Treasury authorized a more comprehensive scheme. The awards were two-thirds of the retiring salary after twenty years' service, or after fifteen years, providing the employee was over the age of sixty. Under sixty and with ten to twenty years' service he would get half his salary. The Committee on Public Expenditure of 1808, after commenting adversely on the irregularities and abuses in certain departments, commended the Customs scheme 'as uniting a due consideration towards long and meritorious service, with great attention to economy'.[13] The Treasury applied the scheme to the Excise in 1809 and an Act of 1810 (50 Geo. III, c.117) established the system for other civil staff.

The 1810 Act applied to any person who had held any public office or employment. The qualifying conditions it laid down for a pension were, however, unlikely to be satisfied by those who had held political offices. Their special circumstances were catered for by an Act of 1817 (57 Geo. III, c.65). This empowered the King to recompense the meritorious services of persons quitting or being removed from high, effective civil offices, 'the Abolition and Regulation of Various Offices [depriving] the Crown of Part of the Means by which His Majesty has been heretofore enabled to [do this.].' A life pension of not more than £3,000 could be paid to any former First Lord of the Treasury, Secretary of State, Chancellor of the Exchequer, or First Lord of the Admiralty who had served the king for not less than two years. Lower sums and longer service were fixed for lesser political officers.

Second, it became clear that some offices were not in effect sinecures, but that the holders were merely overpaid for the duties involved. Thus the Committee of 1808 distinguished between offices which should be abolished and those for which the emoluments should be considerably reduced. In most cases this was part of the general problem of remuneration by way of fees.

Third, the opportunity was taken when other changes were being made to replace the distinguishing titles of posts by a general description. The ancient offices usually carried titles which described the function of the holders: Chamberlain, Remembrancer, Warden in Eyre, Protonotary, Surveyor-General of the Green Wax, Surveyor of Subsidies, Tellers, and so on. Even where the word 'clerk' was used it was amplified, e.g. Clerk of the Tally, Clerk of the Signet, Clerk of the Rules on the Plea Side, Clerk of the Pipe. Such titles emphasized the uniqueness of the holder's position.

The practice did not disappear quickly. In the Treasury for example, the post of Auditor of the Civil List was created in 1816 and several new Principal Clerkships had their function included in their title, e.g. the Principal Clerk for Colonial Business. Much of the development of the Board of Trade in the 1830s and 1840s took the form of the creation of posts with specific titles, e.g. Superintendent of the Statistical Department in 1834. But the trend was strongly towards the use of titles such as principal, chief, or first, second or third class clerks which indicated both the generality of their responsibilities and the hierarchical character of the appointments.

Changes in the legal character of the Public Service

Reducing the number employed in the public services could be justified on the grounds both of economy and of reducing the influence of the king. The argument for such action could apply equally well to the junior clerk or messenger as to the holder of an ancient, useless office. As such it was not necessarily an attack on the concept of office, though some of the features of that concept undoubtedly strengthened the hands of the reformers. Even so, in as far as the office was useful, reform could have been directed against those features rather than in favour of suppression. The changes in the legal content of an office and the legal rights of office holders were thus more far reaching than those satisfying the perennial call for economy. They reduced the status of most office-holders to something very little different from that of an employee.

The changes were of six main kinds:
  (i) Abolition of the right to exercise an office by means of a deputy
 (ii) Prohibition of buying and selling of offices
(iii) Prohibition of the use of offices as a political bribe
 (iv) Abolition of the right to grant an office in reversion
  (v) Removal of the banking function
 (vi) Replacement of fee income by salaries

(i) *Abolition of the right to exercise an office by means of a deputy.* There was a good deal of legislation dealing with particular offices. We will quote only three examples. An Act of 1782 (22 Geo. III, c.75) prevented the granting in future of any Patent Office in any Colony or Plantation belonging to the Crown for any longer term than during such time as the grantee thereof or person appointed to the Office shall perform the duty in person and 'behave well therein'. Existing grants were not prejudiced by the Act and any person aggrieved could appeal to His Majesty in Council.* This Act of Shelburne's was

* The Act was extended and strengthened in 1814 (54 Geo. III, c.61) to cover other than patent offices. No office in a colony could in future be granted for any longer time than during the residence of the grantee.

evaded in various ways, e.g. by appointments being made by Sign Manual, instead of by Letters Patent, and by Secretaries of State allowing influential patentees to have prolonged leave of absence.[14] Again in 1817 (57 Geo. III, c.63) it was laid down that after the termination of the present interests the offices of the Clerks of the Signet and the Clerks of the Privy Seal were to be performed in person. In the same year similar provision was made for certain offices in the Court of Exchequer (57 Geo. III, c.60). Two Acts of 1825 prohibited the sale of certain offices in the King's Bench and the Court of Common Pleas and their exercise by deputy (unless for some reasonable cause) for new holders (6 Geo. IV, c.82 and c.83).

(ii) *Prohibition of buying and selling.* Allegations in the House of Commons[15] of corrupt patronage based to a large extent on the work of the Committee inquiring into the conduct of the Duke of York, led to an Act of 1809 (49 Geo. III, c.126). It started by recalling an Act of Edward VI against the buying and selling of offices, which evidently needed restating, or reinforcing. The 1809 Act declared that persons buying or selling or receiving or paying money or rewards for 'any office, commission, place or employment' were guilty of a misdemeanour. This was also true of soliciting, negotiating, or advertising for a sale. The Act excluded (i) commissions in the Army paid for at not more than the sum allowed by the Regulations; (ii) deputies, where lawful to appoint a deputy and paid for out of the fees or profits of the office; and (iii) annual payments out of fees to any person who formerly held the office.

(iii) *Use of office as a political bribe.* In the same year another Act (49 Geo. III, c.118) imposed penalties on any person giving or promising to give any office or an express contract to procure a seat in Parliament. The Member who obtained a seat by these measures forfeited it and so did the receiver of the office. They were also subject to fines of £500 and £1,000.

(iv) *Abolition of the right to grant an office in reversion.* The Committee on Public Expenditure of 1808 criticized the power of the Crown to grant offices in reversion, a practice which 'can never have obtained with regard to efficient Offices, without considerable risk of ultimately producing the effect of converting them, so far as respects the Principals, into Sinecures, or into Offices to be exercised wholly by Deputy'.[16] The proposal did not prove very popular even in the Commons, but when in 1807 a Bill to abolish the granting of offices with a right to the reversion was passed by the Commons it was rejected by the Lords. Whereupon, just before the prorogation, the House of Commons asked the king not to grant any office in reversion until six weeks after the commencement of the next Session. He gave a favourable answer. In the following Session, a temporary Act was passed suspending the granting of offices in reversion, or for joint lives with the benefit of survivorship (48 Geo. III, c.50). It was renewed in 1810 (50 Geo. III, c.88) and again in 1812 (52 Geo. III, c.40). The Lords encouraged by Lord Eldon, the Lord Chancellor, refused to renew it in 1814. The measure did not apply to the Courts of Law.

(v) *Removal of the banking function.* Objection to this right or practice was less strong than against some of the others already mentioned. When it was difficult to move money about the country quickly and easily it was convenient to allow an officer to retain a balance out of which he could meet continuing expenditure. In some cases, for example the Receivers-General of the Land Tax, money earned by way of interest was regarded as part of the emoluments of office. As much as anything, therefore, the change came about with improvements in the banking system and the use of the Bank of England as the government bank. It was hastened by the realization that the fewer the number of separate bank accounts involved in the management of the public income and expenditure the smaller the total balance needed and therefore the lower the cost in borrowing on Exchequer Bills. We show later how the large number of accounts in the names of officers or individuals became a single account at the Bank of England. Other measures included payment in 1822 to the Receivers-General of the Land Tax of a salary in lieu of other emoluments.[17]

(vi) *Replacement of fee income by Salaries.* As we saw earlier, the charging of fees for the performance of public functions had two quite different aspects: as a means of remunerating a particular officer and as a means of financing a service. With the possible exception of the fees paid to the Customs, it was the first aspect which aroused most criticism in the forty years or so after 1780. Fees went on being collected long after they ceased to be the basis of the emoluments of an officer.

The criticisms of fees as a form of remuneration were partly general and partly directed at particular points. In the early part of the eighteenth century the difference in remuneration between fee income and salary was not necessarily very great. But as the century wore on, salaries remained at substantially the same level, whereas fee income rose markedly. For example, the chief clerks of the Treasury shared between them one-third of the fees received in the department. In the 1750s each received about £700 a year from this source, as against about £330 in 1711. By 1770 they were averaging £850 and at the height of the American War of Independence they achieved £1,278 each.[18] There was not always a clear and direct connection between the amount of work involved and fees paid. Indeed it was possible for the fee income to increase whilst the physical load of work decreased, as was the case of those officers in the Exchequer whose income was calculated as a poundage on the cash passing through their hands.

A particular criticism was that dependence on an income from fees and perquisites was derogatory to the dignity of the holders of the highest offices. Thus, in 1780 the remuneration of those very important officers, the Principal Secretaries of State, varied materially according to the fees paid into their departments each year: 'a source of emolument which, besides being precarious, is little consistent with the dignity of [their] situation', was the opinion of the Commissioners on Fees. Dependence on the profits of the London Gazette was 'equally precarious and equally derogatory.'[19] The Act of 1790 (30 Geo. III, c.10) which provided £6,000 a year for the Speaker of the House of Commons, was 'for the better Support of the Dignity of the Speaker . . .' The Committee of 1830–1 thought that remuneration by means of fees was 'derogatory from the high dignity of the office [of Lord Chancellor] and necessarily exposed [him] to the suspicion of occasioning impediments to the exercise of its functions.[20]

Administrative arguments were also used against the system. It was said to encourage public officers to discriminate in favour of the more lucrative parts of their business, a charge which was hard to deny by those who claimed that fees encouraged officers to be more zealous. Most of the fees charged had remained unchanged for at least half a century, much longer in some cases. No doubt many were out of date, and and as a result even within the fee system they may have distorted the zeal and efforts of their receipients. Their influence was very pervasive, as is instanced by the Receiver of the Six Penny Duty who explained that he allowed funds to accumulate before paying his receipts into the Exchequer because the fees charged for the Tally and for Bill Money were the same irrespective of the sum involved.[21] In the case of the courts the existence of officers appointed for life and entitled to fees obstructed the establishment of small debtor courts for many years, indeed until their emoluments were commuted by an Act of 1830 (11 Geo. IV and 1 Wm. IV, c.58). The financial purists disliked the use of fees as a method of remuneration because, being paid to officers and clerks direct, they bypassed the public accounts.

One course of possible action would have been to revise the scales of fees and so bring them into line with a suitable level of remuneration for each recipient. This solution was not tried. Revision would have been a tedious and lengthy process involving a detailed examination of a large number of miscellaneous charges and raising difficult issues, e.g. of property rights. The Treasury were ill-equipped for such a task even had they had the mind to undertake it. Finally it was war expenditure which helped to distort the system and this seemed for some time to be a transitory factor. In the words of the Commission of 1837[22]

We are willing to admit that where a fee is taken for work actually done, and is commensurate with the labour performed, it may constitute an efficient and just mode of payment, but experience in almost every branch of the Administration has proved how difficult it is to exercise such constant revision as may keep the scale of Fees actually received consistent with right principle and free from abuse;

while even if this object should have been attained . . . the system has a tendency to keep up unnecessary forms and labour . . .

Moreover 'fees' were only part of the problem. The word was loosely used to cover a variety of remuneration not directly related to actual services performed. The Exchequer Act of 1783 used the phrase 'fees, allowances, perquisites, gratuities and emoluments'. In the offices of the Secretaries of State the phrase covered *inter alia* a share in the profits of the London Gazette, profits arising from the franking of newspapers, and a guinea a quarter for paying the stationers' bills. In the Navy Department it covered coals and candles and gratuities paid on the appointment of each clerk. The Secretary to the Postmaster-General received a gross salary of £200 a year; an allowance of £75 a year from the bye letter office; a gratuity of £100 a year from the Master of Lloyd's coffee house; £100 a year for coach hire; certain fees on commissions and deputations (£138 12s. in 1783); and a commission of 2½ per cent on the expenditure for packet boats employed at Dover, Harwich and Falmouth (£1,169 11s. 4d. in 1784). He also had an unfurnished house in the Post Office for his residence, 20 chaldrons of coals, 46 dozen pounds of tallow candles and 12 dozen pounds of wax candles, as well as 2 dozen of arrack and 8 pounds of tea from the East Indian Company.[23]

The annual income of most officers and indeed of most clerks and others in the departments was an amalgam of a variety of payments, of which that from fees was only one. The Clerk of the Pells received thirteen distinct allowances amounting to £1,603, of which only £61 13s 4d. was stated in the Constitution by which he was appointed; five others were also paid out of the Civil List and the remaining seven were paid mainly out of the funds for the debt annuities. He also obtained an income from fees.[24]

The multiplicity of sources from which many officers were paid was similar to the system of earmarking practised generally in the national financial arrangements and largely arose from the same circumstances. If for some reason, good or bad, it was decided to increase the remuneration of an office, it was quite often done by leaving the basic stipend unchanged and adding an allowance for this or that specific purpose, possibly paid from a different source, particularly if the main stipend was a charge on the Civil List. In some cases the department charged the allowance to office incidents (i.e. expenses) where, as in the Tax Office, the revenue was available to meet the extra cost.

Even, therefore, had the fee system remained reasonably favoured, there would probably have had to be a rationalization of allowances, etc. The complicated system 'contrary to the Simplicity and Regularity that ought to be observed in every office . . .'[25] could not have withstood for long the process of simplification of the general financial system. In so far as the establishment of the Consolidated Fund implied an intention to cease distinguishing between the sources out of which expenditure was met, the need for doing so in the case of salaries and allowances was greatly lessened — indeed to continue to do so could hardly have been regarded as consistent with the general principle of consolidation.

In contrast a system of remuneration by fixed salaries offered, according to the Commission on the Public Accounts, 'Simplicity and Aptitude to be accommodated to all Offices, however distinguished'. They were of the opinion that

in the Place of all these Salaries, Fees and Gratuities, there should be substituted and annexed to each of these Offices, of whatever Rank or Denomination, One certain Salary, paid to the Officer . . . this Salary should be an ample Compensation for the Service required . . . the Officer will [thus] know his Income, the Public will know their Expense; and Uniformity and Equality will be introduced into the Provisions for Officers of equal Rank and Station in similar Offices . . .[26]

The transfer from a system of fees and allowances to one of salaries did not present so difficult a problem as the suppression of sinecures, nor was there the same degree of opposition to it from office holders. Nevertheless, property or vested rights could be involved. There were two types of case. On the one hand, there were those whose right to take fees for the performance of their office was clearly granted by the Letters Patent or by some other solemn and binding instrument. On the other, there were the clerks and other employees whose income was wholly or mainly derived from fees, but whose rights depended mainly on custom.

The first category had usually to be treated as a root and branch operation, by legislation which affected the office in other ways, e.g. abolition of the right to exercise by deputy. Thus the Act of 1783 (23 Geo. III, c.82) which dealt with a number of sinecures in the Exchequer, provided that after the death, surrender, forfeiture, or removal of the present holders, the payment of 'all salaries, fees, allowances, perquisites, gratuities and emoluments' to, *inter alia*, the Clerk of the Pells, and the four Tellers, should cease and in lieu they should be paid £3,000 and £2,700 each respectively. The Clerks of the Signet and of the Privy Seal were similarly handled.

The second category were easier to handle for they had no personal property rights in the fees, only the right to be appropriately remunerated for the work they did. In these cases the conversion to fixed salaries could be achieved by administrative action within each department. A Minute of the Treasury Board of 30 November 1782 abolished the receipt of fees, gifts, gratuities, and perquisites by individuals in that department. The scale of fees was revised and continued to be paid by the users of the Treasury's services, but the receipts were to be placed in a fee fund out of which the fixed salaries would be paid. However, the salaries named in the Minute were only to be paid if there was sufficient money in the fund: should it be insufficient then the salaries were to be scaled down proportionately.

The dependency of the new salaries on the resources of the fee fund was a reality, for fee income in a year of peace might be insufficient to cover them fully. There was a shortfall in 1783 made good in the following year. The arrangement was inspired partly by Shelburne's anxiety to balance the Civil List accounts and partly by the 'overrighteous desire to punish the beneficiaries of "undue influence".' It was never intended to be anything but a temporary expendient while an impartial examination was made of the offices and until the Civil List could bear the additional salaries made necessary by the suppression of fees.[27] The Fees Commissioners in their report of June 1786 disapproved of this dependency. Officers should not be liable to a reduction upon a deficiency if they were not to benefit from any surplus. The arrangement might prove a temptation to raise the fees. Finally, if the dependency were abolished it would no longer be necessary to maintain the distinction between that part of a salary paid from the Civil List and that part from the fee fund. Instead the cost of the consolidated salary could be charged against the fee fund and any deficit against the Civil List. Any surplus in the fee fund after meeting the full cost of the salaries should accrue to the Civil List revenues.[28] This change was made by Order in Council in June 1793.[29]

The conversion from fee income to salaries, except for the provision making payment dependent on the adequacy of the fee fund, was praised by the Fee Commissioners as being 'wise, judicious and effectual'. The new regulations, they said, had 'diminished the abuses', and 'very much added to the accuracy and dispatch in conducting the business'. They went on: 'how unequivocally it proves that the suppression of such contingent receipts by individuals, far from being inconsistent with the regular and speedy execution of business, may be even instrumental in forwarding it, by preventing any unfair selection of those parts which are most profitable, and holding forth one undistinguished reward for general industry and exertion . . .'[30]

The Treasury's example was slowly followed by other departments. The offices of the Secretaries of State were dealt with in 1795, the Navy Board in 1796, the War Office in 1797, and the Admiralty in 1800. But like sinecures, the system of fees and allowances lingered, particularly in the administration of the Courts and of Parliament. The general financial arrangements were usually similar to those made by the Treasury in 1782. Fees continued to be paid to the department but went into a fund, an officer in each department being designated as receiver of fees. An Act of 1810 (50 Geo. III, c.117) provided *inter alia* that an estimate of the deficiency should be laid before Parliament in all cases where a fee fund was in deficit. Where no fee fund existed an estimate of the money needed to pay the establishment of the office or department was to be laid before the House of Commons and provided for separately, but this requirement was not to apply to the revenue departments, nor in cases where the cost of the establishment was wholly charged on the Civil List.

As salaries rose and fees remained at their old level, or were abolished, it became usual for fee funds to be in deficit. Thus in 1820 the Treasury fee fund showed a deficit of £25,000 and the fee funds of the Home Office, Foreign Office, and Privy Council Office showed deficits of £13,380, £18,500, and £14,420 respectively.[31] The removal of the items of civil government from the Civil List in 1831, e.g. the salaries of the First Lord of the Treasury, and the abolition of many fees, put the funds in even greater deficit. The Estimates for 1847 showed the salary bill of the Treasury as £51,200 and a fee fund income of only £3,300.[32] In 1849–50 following a recommendation of the Committee on Miscellaneous Expenditure of 1847–8 the system came to an end: any income from fees went direct into the Exchequer and departmental Estimates were correspondingly increased.[33]

In passing it should be noted that in some cases, particularly, it would seem, where a surplus of fee income was expected from the suppression of offices, Parliament made different provision. Thus the Exchequer Regulation Act, 1783, provided that two-thirds of the surplus should go to the Sinking Fund and one-third in aid of the costs of civil government. Any deficiency was to be shared in the same proportions. The savings on the regulation of the offices of the Clerks of the Signet and Privy Seal were to go to the Consolidated Fund. Those due to changes in the Customs made by the Act of 1798 were added to the superannuation fund of the Department.

The abolition of the direct link between fees received for services performed and the level of an officer's remuneration was not just a change in the financial system of the country. It completely altered the character and status of the public servants who had benefited from this basis of remuneration. It removed the appearance that the recipient was in effect a provider of services for his clients; instead it emphasized that he was responsible to the department which paid his salary. It made it very difficult, if not impossible, to claim that an appointment was a form of property. Finally, it eliminated the temptation to treat the officer's income as a kind of subtreasury, out of which he paid his assistants and other expenses.

Local Administration

The situation in the administration of local affairs was very different but the same trend from officer to employee was clearly discernible. There were very few lucrative offices, most were unpaid and carried onerous duties. The Clerk of the Peace in the Counties and the Town Clerk in some of the Boroughs were exceptions. The change could not therefore be brought about by the suppression of sinecures or by any of the methods already described.* It was brought about by the replacement or supplementation of unpaid officers by paid staffs responsible to their employers, either the Vestry, the Justices of the Peace, a Board of Guardians, a municipal council, or a body of improvement commissioners. By 1870, of the local officers who flourished in 1780, only the Justices of the Peace and the constables remained with any significant powers. The issue of Tyburn Tickets was abolished in 1827 (7 and 8 Geo. IV, c.27).

Decline in Legal Processes

For some years after 1780 Parliament continued to impose fines on officers who failed to fulfil their duties. For example, the Passenger Act of 1803 (43 Geo. III, c.56) made it lawful for customs officers together with a Justice of the Peace to take action against ship's masters who failed to meet the requirements of the Act, e.g. by not carrying sufficient stores for the voyage. Any customs officer not following the Act was liable to dismissal and a fine of £50. Again the Act of 1814 (54 Geo. III, c.61), which tightened the rules against the employment of deputies by officers in any colony contained a provision whereby the Governor of the Colony who did not report that he had granted the officer leave of absence was to forfeit a sum not exceeding £100. In 1793 (33 Geo. III, c.55) Justices of the Peace were empowered to impose a fine of not more than 40s. on constables, overseers, and other peace or parish officers for neglect of duty or for disobedience of the orders of such Justices.

* Echoes can be heard of some of the practices found at the national level: for example, the agreed emoluments of the County Treasurer of Surrey included interest earned on the balances in his possession (House of Lords Select Committee on County Rates, 1835, p. 18).

The transfer of responsibility from an officer carrying out his legal duties to an employee carrying out the instructions of some elected representative removed the basis for legal enforcement directed at public servants. The relations between employers and employees normally included provision for disciplinary proceedings, e.g. by dismissal. Legal remedies in local government therefore had to be directed against the Council or local board as the employers. There was in any case a growing dislike of the complicated legal devices dear to the eighteenth century. The abolition of the Upper Exchequer in 1833 eliminated the ancient legal processes aimed at securing the probity of public accountants. In local affairs the use of indictment and presentment had become quite rare by the 1850s.

B. THE NEW ARRANGEMENTS

The legislation and administrative action described in the previous chapter were largely negative. They suppressed and prohibited: only by implication did they indicate the character of the public service. Clerks were not to be remunerated in accordance with the fees their services earned but by salaries: but how were their salaries to be calculated and regulated? If appointment by Letters Patent or other formal instrument caused inflexibility in the deployment of public servants and possibly had other undesirable consequences, how should clerks and others be appointed in future and with what tenure? It is the purpose of this chapter to show how these questions were tackled and explain the new arrangements which emerged.

Salaries

The system of remuneration by way of fees earned and allowances for extra tasks was highly individualistic and to a large extent self-regulating. It was not easy to make comparisons between offices and even more difficult to interpret any differences. For the basic element — the approved list of fees that could be charged — was peculiar to the circumstances of each service and in any case its results depended on the volume of business transacted. What possible basis was there fore comparing the Clerk of the Pells with a Clerk of the Signet or with a patent officer in a Customs outpost? This was also a consequence of remuneration being derived from a variety of unrelated sources. Information came available about salaries, particularly those charged on the Civil List, but it is clear that the various Commissions and Committees which investigated remuneration found it a laborious job ascertaining the exact size and character of the total payments received by many officers.

The situation became, however, quite different when all public servants began to be paid a salary. For now the sum attached to each post was fixed and certain and information about it readily available. More important, the change was associated with a simplification of titles. And, though the general title of clerk might conceal differences in the value and load of work undertaken, there was an assumption, at least as a starting-point, that a Chief Clerk in one department was not a fundamentally different occupation from a Chief Clerk in another department. Their salaries should, therefore, be roughly comparable. Thus it was not merely a matter of deciding the right salary for each post in isolation, but of putting the salaries of different posts in proper relation to each other both within a department and between departments.

Before, however, dealing with the structure of salaries, something needs to be said about the Sixpenny and Shilling Duties. The former arose out of the Civil List debt in the reign of George I. The debt was funded and serviced by a duty of 6d. in the £ upon all pensions and annuities charged upon the Civil List, upon all salaries and fees of offices of profit granted by or derived from the Crown and upon all other payments from the King whatsoever. Commissioned and non-commissioned officers and men serving in the Army and Navy were exempt and the Act gave discretion to make other exemptions (7 Geo. I, Stat. 1, c.27). The Shilling Pension duty was imposed in 1758 (31 Geo. II, c.22), also for the service of specific borrowing. It was raised upon the latest Land Tax assessment, at 1s. in the £ and bore upon all salaries and pensions of above £100 a year payable out of any revenues belonging to the King.[1]

As there was no general income tax these two duties were clearly discriminatory levies on certain kinds of remuneration of certain public officers. The question, therefore, was whether attention should be concentrated on the gross or the net salary? The taxes were disliked by those who had to pay them. The Fees Commissioners reported:

The taxes and duties payable out of the salaries of public officers seem very little calculated to answer the purpose of revenue, for which they were intended. For in those cases where the salaries are too high, the obvious and simple mode of deriving an aid from them to the revenue must be by their reduction; . . . In other cases, where salaries are avowedly no more than sufficient, such reductions only recoil upon the public, by creating new claims for consideration, which must in justice be satisfied.

They were, therefore, of the opinion that 'the salaries of offices . . ., when duly regulated, should be exempted by law from all taxes and duties whatsoever; and until such a mode is adopted, such taxes should be paid out of the general fund.' They adopted this principle in the salary scales they proposed[2] The duties had been criticized from a similar point of view by the Commissioners for Examining the Public Accounts, and their opinion was shared by the Select Committee on Finance in 1797.[3] Generally speaking, when salaries were introduced after 1780 they were made free of deductions, the Crown having the power to grant exemptions. For this and other reasons their yield diminished and by the middle of the century they produced less than £300 as against £74,000 in 1796[4]

The regulation of salaries after 1780 followed broadly the same course as the regulation of the public revenues and expenditure. The very diverse mixture of salaries, fees, and allowances was replaced by an increasingly tidy and controlled structure of salaries. In this process the House of Commons took a great deal of interest and the Treasury were the administrative means.

The starting-point, it must be stressed, was the decision to translate the system of fees and allowances into a system of salaries. It was not a matter of deciding *de novo* what salary to attach to an entirely new office, but what account should be taken of the current remuneration of an office in converting those earnings into a salary. From one point of view the 1780s were not a particularly good time to undertake this exercise, for owing to the American War fee incomes were higher than they had ever been. Indeed this was a reason for the campaign to eliminate them as a form of remuneration. The question which, therefore, faced, for example, the Treasury, was how far current earnings could be ignored and, if so, what earlier basis could be used? The answer had to have regard to the acceptability of any changes — those concerned were legitimately receiving higher remuneration for, so they would claim, working harder, even though it could be argued that as soon as the country returned to peace, activity would decline and so would much of the fee income.

The processs and thinking can be seen in the salary scale introduced into the Treasury in November 1782. The joint secretaries, hitherto wholly remunerated from fees, had had an average income of £3,414 during 1769–71 which had risen to £5,114 during the war years 1779–81. Their salaries were fixed at £3,000 a year. The salaries of the four chief clerks, for whom the comparable earlier figures were £853 and £1,278 a year, were fixed at £800. The under-clerks continued to receive £100 a year from the Civil List plus a scale of salaries based on seniority ranging from £50 to £500 a year. All these payments from the fee fund were free of deductions. The remuneration of the Lords Commissioners not being related to the fee income of the Treasury remained unchanged even though their salaries had been fixed very many years earlier. The First Lord continued to receive the net income of £5,000 fixed in 1754 and the 'junior' Lords the £1,600 a year dating from when the post of the Lord High Treasurer was put into commission, his salary of £8,000 a year being divided equally among the five Commissioners. The junior Lords still continued to have £380 a year deducted for taxes and to receive some £30 a year from New Year's gifts.[5]

In 1784 the net income of the Secretary of State for the Home Department was under £5,000, that of the Principal Secretary for the Foreign department being some £500 higher. In 1783 the Treasury Board had in mind a fixed net salary of £4,500 a year 'in lieu of every other receipt of office'. The Fee Commissioners approved of that figure and proposed that the

Chief Clerk should receive £800 a year, i.e. the same as the Chief Clerks in the Treasury, with other clerks being paid sums not very different from those in the Treasury.[6] No action was taken, however, and when the decision was taken in 1795, by Order in Council, it was based on a much higher level of current earnings. The salaries of the Principal Secretaries of State were fixed at £6,000. This compared with a net income of £8,733 from all sources. The salaries of the Under-Secretaries were fixed at £1,500 (as against a total income of almost £2,000 in 1793); and of the Chief Clerk at £1,000 (as against £1,520).[7]

Salaries were generally fixed at a lower level than the total remuneration from all sources at the time of the conversion, the decisions being dominated by the non-salaried content of that total. Offices already wholly or mainly remunerated by a fixed salary usually continued with that salary unchanged and so often ended up at a lower level than those with newly fixed salaries. There does not appear to have been at the time any attempt to have a scale that would apply to all departments. Thus, the First Lord of the Treasury's salary of £5,000 was £1,000 a year below that fixed for the Principal Secretaries of State, even that of the new Secretary of State for War only established in 1794. Again the salaries of the chief clerks in the Treasury, fixed at £800 in 1782, remained at that level even when those in the Offices of the Secretaries of State were fixed at £1,000. The view of the Treasury Board in 1797 was that 'Under the Regulation of 1782 reducing the Incomes of the Secretaries and Clerks, in Peace and War, below the Average of the Profits in Time of Peace, the Emoluments of the Clerks are not proportionate with their Labour and Responsibility, especially compared with those in other Offices'. They, therefore, decided to grant the Clerks an equal annual sum for the loss of the New Year's gifts.[8]

Comparison is made more difficult by the fact that some of the officers concerned also held other paid public posts. In 1796 William Pitt received £5,000 a year as First Lord of the Treasury, some £1,800 as Chancellor of the Exchequer, and over £3,000 a year as Warden of the Cinque Ports. George Rose, one of the Joint Secretaries, in addition to the £3,000 for that office received £3,124 as Clerk of Parliament, and £680 for two offices in the Exchequer. Each of the four chief clerks also held other public offices.[9] There was less opportunity for this in the offices of the Secretaries of State, but it was by no means unknown. In 1796 the Secretaries of State for Foreign Affairs and War voluntarily renounced a substantial part of their salaries. Grenville at the Foreign Office drew £4,000 a year as Auditor of the Receipt, and Dundas at the War Office drew £4,000 a year as Treasurer of the Navy and £2,000 a year as First Commissioner for Affairs of India. Even after this, however, their total salaries were much higher than the £6,000 to which they were entitled as Secretaries of State.[10]

A salary scale once fixed could only be changed by Order in Council, Treasury Warrant, or other formal decision. Remuneration ceased to fluctuate with the business of an office as measured by its fee income. The salaries of the Joint Secretaries of the Treasury were raised to £4,000 a year in 1800. Those of the Under-Secretaries of State were raised to £2,000 in 1799, with a further £500 a year after three years in office, the qualifying period being extended to seven years in 1817. An Order in Council of May 1809 had introduced in the offices of the Secretaries of State a system of 'compensation' for length of service ranging from £80 a year for five to ten years' service, to £400 a year for twenty or more years' service. The salary of the First Secretary to the Board of Admiralty was fixed in 1800 at £3,000 a year in time of peace and at £4,000 a year during time of war, the corresponding figures for the Second Secretary being £1,500–£2,000.[11]

Not only salaries but the numbers employed also increased. This was to be expected in time of increased governmental activity. Even so, it is difficult not to infer that the change in the financial arrangements removed some of the former limits to expansion. When remuneration came from fees earned, new clerks could be appointed only at some loss of income to existing clerks. True, under the new system the resulting increased deficiency on the departmental fee fund had to be made good out of the Civil List. But by the early years of the nineteenth century the House of Commons had accepted that the inadequacy of the Civil List revenues meant that many new items of civil government would have to be financed out of votes of Supply. The old barriers to increased salaries and increased numbers were thus very much lowered.

Conversely, when the war with France ceased in 1815 and public expenditure began to fall rapidly, there were none of the former built in regulators leading to a reduction in salaries and numbers. The pressure now had to come from the House of Commons, aided by the Treasury. Since 1810 the House had been receiving an annual return of the changes in the salaries of all those employed in the various departments. In 1821 the House received a very full account, department by department, of all the changes in salaries since 1793.[12] A return for 1828 showed that between 1797 and 1815 the numbers employed in the Treasury (including the Commissariat), the offices of the three Secretaries of State, and of the Board of Trade had risen from 223 to 259. The number was still 254 in 1827, the big fall in the Treasury due to the ending of the War being offset by substantial increase in the Foreign and Colonial Offices. Including the revenue departments, the largest employers, and the other offices the total numbers employed had increased by a third during 1797–1827 but the total salary bill had doubled.[13] The retreat from the high salary levels started in 1821. Future Secretaries to the Treasury were to get £3,500 instead of £4,000, Chief Clerks were to receive £1,200, fixed and not on a rising scale. The salaries of Under-Secretaries were reduced in 1822 to £2,000 without any increase for years of service. But the scale of the reductions did not satisfy the House of Commons and there was a further agitation at the beginning of 1830 which led to further cuts. For example, in 1831 the Joint Secretaries of the Treasury fell to £2,500, and in 1834 Chief Clerks to £1,000.[14]

In judging the character of these changes it must be borne in mind that prices rose steeply in the thirty years or so after 1780 and then fell to within 15% or so of that level by the 1820s. The purchasing power of £1,000 in 1811 was only about £550 of its value in 1790.

It is not our purpose to trace all these changes in detail. Something must, however, be said about the views that emerged about the general level of public salaries and the relationship that should exist between different posts and different departments. With their love of the high-sounding, even pompous phrase, the Commissioners on the Public

Accounts had said that a salary 'should be an ample Compensation for the Service required; and the Quantum estimated by the various Qualifications and Circumstances necessary for the Execution, and which together form Title to the Reward.' And again, 'it ought to be a full and competent Recompense for the Execution [of the Office], and no more.'[15]

The Committee on Public Expenditure of 1808[16] took the view that the public 'ought unquestionably to be served as cheaply as is consistent with being served with integrity and ability.' The Select Committee on Public Income and Expenditure of 1828[17] interpreted this statement to mean looking at the level of salaries available in the commercial world. To determine the proper rates of salaries in the public offices it was necessary 'first to find out what they are in Commercial and Other Establishments and then to examine whether more talent and trust are required . . . and [if so] then to make the salaries in the Public Offices proportionately higher'. The Committee inquired into the salaries of clerks in the banking and insurance world and came to the conclusion that 'the salaries in the Ordnance Department admit of diminution'.*

The Select Committee of 1830–1 admitted: 'There are probably few subjects open to more varieties of opinion than the precise amount of Salary suited to any given office of Government.' They disclaimed 'all pretensions to any infallible rule on a question necessarily so vague', but went on 'It is impossible not to recognize to its fullest extent the principle, that the People have a right to have their service done at the smallest possible expense consistent with its efficient performance. Whether Public Servants sit in Parliament or not, the principle is the same.'[18]

---

* The Playfair Commission of 1875 tried to ascertain the market value of clerical work by looking at the clerical salaries in four insurance companies, three banks (including the Bank of England), the London and North Western Railway, and several other private concerns. They found it difficult to make a complete comparison, as conditions varied widely, but 'taken as a whole, the pay of the Civil Service, including fixity of tenure and superannuation, compares favourably with that given in private establishments, whilst for the lower class of clerical work it is certainly higher'. (PP 1875, Vol. XXII, p.9).

Notwithstanding the principle being the same, it was the House of Commons which dealt with the salaries of 'political' offices, leaving those of permanent officials to be handled internally by the Treasury and the departments. The Select Committees of 1830–1 and of 1850 were concerned with posts which could be held by members of either House. Their findings and recommendations, however, affected the level of salaries of the top-tier civil servants. For at a time when Ministers conducted the main work of their departments, their assistants could hardly be paid above that level.

What emerged from the examination was the pre-eminence of six political appointments: First Lord of the Treasury, Chancellor of the Exchequer, three Principal Secretaries of State, and the First Lord of the Admiralty. The first remained at the £5,000 fixed before 1780, or £7,500 if also held with the office of Chancellor of the Exchequer. The salary of that office had been made up from several sources but in 1831 was fixed at £5,000, a slight reduction. In that year the salaries of the Secretaries of State were reduced from £6,000 to £5,000.* The salary of the First Lord of the Admiralty had been increased in 1806 from £3,000 to £5,000 only to be reduced to £4,500 in 1831 — £500 being deducted because he was provided with an official residence. Approving of a uniform level of £5,000 a year the Select Committee of 1850 said these six offices had 'always been considered of the great importance in a government', and it was therefore 'requisite to secure the services of men who combine the highest talents with the greatest experience of public affairs.'[19]

Below this level the figure of £2,000 a year emerged as appropriate for the ministerial heads of less important departments, e.g. Lord President of the Council,* Lord Privy Seal,** President of the Board of Trade, and the Paymaster-General. There were a few exceptions — the Secretary at War

* The salary of the Speaker of the House of Commons, fixed at £6,000 a year in 1790, was reduced to £5,000 in 1834 for new holders of the office (4 and 5 Wm IV c. 70).

** The Select Committee of 1830–1 said these two offices were 'of high dignity and of considerable and indispensable duties, but not such as to bear comparison with some other offices . . .' (p.450).

remained at £2,480, a figure which went as far back as 1784, possibly even to 1714, and the Postmaster-General remained at the £2,500 originally fixed in 1789. The Lord Chancellor, who had had a substantial fee income both as head of Chancery and Speaker of the House of Lords had these commuted. In 1802 a salary of £10,000 was fixed for the Lord Chancellor and 1831 a salary of £4,000 as Speaker, both in lieu of all fees. He was thus the highest paid Minister, excluding the Lord Lieutenant of Ireland.

Settling the salaries of subordinate 'political' posts was more difficult, if only because it was being done at a time when the relationship between political and permanent appointments was still being worked out. The Fee Commissioners of 1786 had suggested that one of two Under-Secretaries of State in the Home and Foreign departments should be made 'stationary', the other changing with the Principal Secretary, and that the joint Secretaries in the Treasury should be similarly distinguished. In the former case, however, they did not suggest any differentiation of salaries whereas in the case of the Treasury they proposed that 'considering the advantages of permanency', the stationary Secretary should receive £2,000 a year less, leaving the other on £3,000. The Secretaries of State and the Treasury were not prepared to accept these proposals.[20]

However, the idea of a salary differential was assisted by the introduction in 1799 of an addition of £500 a year after three years' service, extended to seven years in 1817, but ended in 1822. The Select Committee of 1830–1 recommended that the £2,000 a year should be reduced to £1,500 with an addition of £500 after three years' service. The reason they gave for recommending the addition was that 'Under Secretaries, who habitually remain in office during different changes of administration, and who thus make a profession of official life. may be distinguished from those who merely appear there for short periods.'[21] This was the opposite argument to that used by the Fees Commission. The Treasury differed from the Select Committee in this one main respect and set out their objections at great length in a Minute of 15 April 1831. They argued: 'The appointments of the Parliamentary Under Secretaries of State frequently lead to advancement in the higher offices of the Government, whilst to the permanent Under Secretaries those appointments are, generally speaking, the commencement of a laborious course of profession of great trust and of close application'. They also considered that the saving in salary for three years was less important 'than the increased probability of obtaining the services of men of high character, experience and acquirements . . .'[22] The Government did not bother about the three year rule and from 1831 the salaries of 'permanent' Under-Secretaries were fixed at £2,000 and of their 'political' counterparts at £1,500.

The same distinction came about in the Treasury by different means. In 1805 the post of Assistant Secretary was established. He became the permanent head of the Treasury, being given the title of Permanent Secretary in 1867. His original salary of £2,000 quickly became £2,500 in 1807, £3,000 in 1809, and £3,500 in 1815. It was reduced to £2,500 in 1826 for his successor and in 1834 to £2,000 rising to £2,500 after five years. This remained the salary even after the salaries of the Joint Secretaries were reduced to £2,000 in 1851. The general pattern which emerged, therefore, was that the Permanent received £500 a year more than the Parliamentary Under-Secretaries.[23]

It is less easy to follow the rationalization of the salary scales for the clerks and subordinate posts. The process took much longer. In 1848 the Select Committee on Miscellaneous Expenditure suggested a general review of salaries in the course of which 'it would be found advisable also to establish a more uniform rate of payment for similar services in different departments'.[24] A few years later, however, Northcote and Trevelyan in their report could say that the advance of salaries in the public service was regulated upon a two-fold principle. On appointment, each man was paid for one to three years the minimum salary of that class. His salary then increased automatically by a stated annual increment until he reached the maximum salary of the class. He remained at that point unless promoted to fill a vacancy in a higher class, whereupon he started at the minimum salary for that class and again advanced by annual increments. These incremental scales were a reward for long service without regard for relative merit, and reduced the pressure on departmental heads to promote a man merely in order to provide him with a higher salary.[25]

Though this may have been the general principle it still left the problem of how to apply it to different departments. As Wright[26] shows in his illuminating study of the period 1854–74, the Treasury tried to avoid setting salary scales in terms of the relative importance of the various departments. They found comparisons of this kind were mostly used by those who wished to secure a salary increase. For example in 1848 a letter form Clerks in the Poor Law Commission produced a table of the salaries of the Chief Clerks and several classes of clerks in ten departments to show how low were the salaries they were being paid. The table showed a wide range — from £600 to £1,200 for Chief Clerks and from £350–£400 to £850–£1,000 for first-class Clerks. So the permanent head of the Treasury in 1866 could state 'We find uniformity is the usual plea for increased salaries, we disclaim comparisons and the plea of uniformity in such cases and I think rightly so.' Gladstone told a junior Treasury Minister: 'The doctrine that we cannot have two sets of men doing the same work on different conditions . . . is fatal to all retrenchment in the salaries of large bodies of officers.'

There was, however, another difficulty. The nature and quality of the duties and the opportunities for promotion were held to be peculiar to each department. G. A. Hamilton expressed the general Treasury view that 'scarcely any two departments [were] quite alike or capable of being made alike'. This view was fostered by the degree of independence which each department claimed as its right. There did, however, emerge by the 1860s a broad classification of departments. In 1857 the Treasury clearly thought the Colonial, Foreign and Home Offices and themselves as being in the first class. This did not mean that salaries were the same in each of the four departments. The Chief Clerk in the Home Office received £900, in the Treasury he received £1,000 x £50 to £1,200, and in the Colonial and Foreign Offices £1,000 x £50 to £1,250. The range in the salaries of senior clerks was £600 x £20 to £800 in the Home Office, to £700 x £25 to £1,000 in the Foreign Office. The Admiralty was more conveniently linked with the War Office and with the Paymaster-General's Office and, after 1861, with the Audit Office made up the 'second class'. In a third category came the revenue departments. Even though by the 1860s salaries and incomes in the service were some way off a completely uniform pattern they were even further away from the rich diversity prevailing in the 1780s. No public officer, with the exception of the Lord Chancellor, received the very large income that many had then done, the ceiling being set at £5,000 for a few Ministerial posts and £2,000 a year for most of the rest. Below that level, diversity could be measured in terms of £50–£100 a year rather than several thousand. No changes could now take place without Treasury approval and any changes were closely watched by all public servants. To raise the salary of a particular post or class in one department was to stimulate demands for increases in other departments.

Though the fixing of salaries involved having a view about the level of work and responsibility that was normally expected of say a Chief Clerk, it had not by 1870 led to the standardization either of nomenclature or practice between departments. In 1870, for example, the Treasury had immediately under the Permanent Secretary, the Auditor of the Civil List and Assistant to the Secretaries (one post) followed by four Principal, seven First-Class, twelve Second-Class, and seven Third-Class Clerks. It also had several specifically designated clerkships, e.g. Clerk of Parliamentary Accounts and Principal Clerk of Registry. In the same year the Admiralty had one Chief Clerk immediately under the Permanent Secretary followed by six First-Class, twelve Second-Class, twelve Third-Class (First Section) and eight Third-Class (Second Section) Clerks. A single Chief Clerk next to the Permanent Under-Secretary was also the pattern for the Home Office (1866) the rest being divided into Senior, Assistant, and Junior Clerks with Clerks specifically designated for Criminal Business, Signet Business, and for Roads Business. In contrast the Permanent Secretary of the Board of Trade had four Assistant Secretaries immediately under him followed by Senior and Junior Clerks.[27]

The general state of affairs prevailing at the end of our period can be judged by the fact that in 1875 the Playfair Commission was asked to examine 'the possibility of grading the Civil Service as a whole, so as to obviate the inconveniences which result from the difference of pay in different Departments'.

Appointment

One question came increasingly to be posed: should the Minister or other person with the customary authority to make the appointment be free to choose whom he wished or should the appointee have to satisfy certain minimum criteria? This led later to the wider question of whether certain kinds of employment should not be filled by candidates chosen by a body outside the department.

The system of personal appointment, generally described as patronage, has been strongly disliked by many commentators and historians. They assume that when choice is vested in an individual he is bound to use it badly; that, because of the need to gain or reward political support or to please relations and friends, those so appointed must inevitably be of a low level of ability. This, of course, is not the inevitable result: Trevelyan, Stephen, Kay-Shuttleworth, and many other significant and able officials were all appointed by individual Ministers. Nevertheless the more limited the field of choice the greater the likelihood that the person selected will not be as able as if he had been subjected to open competition.

There has indeed been a tendency to exaggerate both the amount and the use of patronage for ministerial heads. Sir Robert Peel, for example, appointed only six clerks during his seven years as Home Secretary. No clerk appointed after 1822 was related to a Home Secretary although there were still men in the office who were relatives of former Home Secretaries. The most useful and financially valuable offices in the gift of the Home Secretary, apart from the Under-Secretaryship, were the stipendary magistracies, factory inspectorships, and places in the office of the Registrar of Births, Deaths, and Marriages, none of which was affected by the Northcote–Trevelyan proposals. Clerkships became less attractive as their work load increased and the salaries decreased. Peel told a Select Committee that he regarded patronage as a great responsibility. By then appointments to clerkships, infrequent though they were, had probably become a nuisance rather than a privilege to Ministers. Nor did patronage enable the head of the department to adapt it to suit his needs. Vacant clerkships were too infrequent for that and precedent was firmly against their dismissing those appointed by their predecessors.[28]

According to the Playfair Commission of 1875 the system of patronage had two advantages. First, it enabled the Head of each department to adapt the qualifications and pay of the clerks in his office to the peculiar wants of that office. Second, the clerks, receiving their appointments as a matter of favour and being appointed to a particular office and not to the service generally, looked for their career to the pay and prospects offered by that office and were therefore less disposed to claim equality with higher-paid offices and to combine for the purpose of urging their claims on the government. The Commission saw the objections to patronage as the danger of jobbery, particularly serious in the case of junior appointments; the tendency to create places in order to satisfy applicants; and the tendency to maintain the system whereby the higher and lower work of an office were mixed up so that the nominee of a Minister entering by a low level examination might be promoted without further test to a superior position.[29]

Patronage was likely to work worst at the most junior level. For by the time a man had reached his thirties or forties he was likely to have shown whether he was suitable for public responsibility. Moreover, if the Permanent Secretary or the head of a new service were inadequate it would quickly be reflected in the work of a department and make the life of its Minister that much more difficult. At the bottom of the ladder neither of these considerations applied. In any case, as a junior clerk, the new entrant would be spending his time on copying and other routine work. In the words of the Northcote–Trevelyan Report

as the character and abilities of the new junior clerk will produce but little immediate effect upon the office, the chief of the department is naturally led to regard the selection as a matter of small moment, and will probably bestow the office upon the son or dependent of someone having personal or political claims upon him, or perhaps upon the son of some meritorious public servant, without instituting any very minute enquiry into the merits of the young man himself.[30]

In the face of general criticism of patronage as a weapon in the hands of the Executive and of particular criticisms about the bad results it could produce, various restraints came to be put on its unfettered exercise. The more important was the introduction of some form of qualifying test or examination by the main departments.* The rigour of these varied. The examinations for entrance to Treasury clerkships started by Melbourne at the suggestion of Sir Francis Baring had tended to become so stringent that they were abandoned by Peel.[31] On the other hand, the Chairman of the Board of Inland Revenue claimed that in the Excise the examination was little more than 'a mere form' to test a candidate's handwriting and arithmetic. In any case the examinations were not open to anyone who wished to compete; they were confined to the nominees of the Minister or whoever had the right to make the appointment; they were designed to secure that such nominees satisfied a minimum standard, not to secure the best qualified for the job. Nevertheless they provided some safe-guard against the serious misuse of patronage.

The other restraint was the imposition of a period of probation. In the Customs a system of probation was already in operation in 1780. After 1825 clerks had been appointed to the Ordnance on a three-year probation and those found unfit for the work were dismissed. A Select Committee of 1828 praised the arrangements of the Ordnance Board: 'The examination before the admission of a Clerk, the period of probation, the rule requiring that each Clerk must be recom-mended by his Chief Clerk before he is promoted to a superior class, and the setting aside of the consideration of Patronage . . . is not only useful with respect to the Department . . . but may also serve as a model for other Departments.'[32] In 1831 the Treasury introduced a system of probation and in 1833 urged other departments to introduce similar arrangements.[33]

* The Northcote–Trevelyan Report mentioned specifically eleven departments which conducted examinations for the admission of clerks, including the Treasury, the Colonial Office, and the Board of Trade but not the Home and Foreign Offices.

The various changes reduced the scope of the appointments available to the Patronage Secretary of the Treasury. The revenue departments and other offices subordinate to the Treasury were the natural places for the exercise of the general patronage of the government. In 1820 Liverpool had handed over Treasury patronage in the Customs to the Board but by the 1840s much had reverted to the Patronage Secretary. Generally speaking he tried to hold on to as much patronage for as long as possible, even when Open Competition was introduced in 1870. There was general agreement in 1855 that such patronage as the Patronage Secretary of the Treasury exercised had been well managed.[34]

The report of 1854 proposed two major changes in the existing system of recruitment. First, that examinations should be compulsory and should be conducted not by each department but by a central board composed of men holding an independent position and capable of commanding general confidence. Second, this examination should be open to all persons of a given age subject only to their producing satisfactory references and medical certificates. Had these proposals been accepted they would have taken appointments to clerkships substantially out of the hands of the individual department.

In addition to the dislike of having their power of appointment so curtailed there was a feeling that the proposals were too sweeping and that notwithstanding Jowett's support, the emphasis on a written examination was not certain to produce the right recruits, for it would not test all the personal qualities required in a good civil servant. Sir George Cornewall Lewis wrote: 'One of the first qualities required in the clerks of a public office is trustworthiness . . . The honourable secrecy which has distinguished the clerks of our superior offices . . . cannot be too highly commended. But this discreet reserve depends on qualities which cannot be made the subject of examination by a central board, or be expressed by marks upon a paper of written answers'. 'Besides', he went on, 'if this principle [of competition] is the most effectual safeguard against corruption, or error in judgment,' why was it not proposed to extend it to the Lord Chief Justice, as well as to the army and navy, and 'above all, why should not the

Church . . . and the tutors and heads of colleges and public schools be chosen by this method of selection?' Like Arbuthnot, Auditor of the Civil List, Cornewall Lewis argued that the public service must of necessity be largely a matter of departmental tradition: It was not 'like a profession in which there is general similarity of duties and qualifications for all its different members; . . . hence the difficulty of finding a common measure for appointments to the several departments and of reducing them to a uniform rule'.[35]

The upshot of the controversy was that the government decided only to proceed with the appointment of a central examining body. An Order in Council of 21 May 1855 appointed a Civil Service Commission for the purpose of 'testing according to fixed rules the qualifications of the Young Men who might from time to time be proposed to be appointed to junior situations in any of Her Majesty's Civil Establishments'. The Order did not alter the existing rights of departments to nominate candidates, but instead of the examinations being conducted by the appointing department they were in future to be held by this independent outside authority. Moreover the Head of each department was left free to appoint, without the Commissioner's certificate, persons of mature age with special qualifications to any situation for which limits of age were not prescribed. The Order did, however, require candidates appointed after success in the examination to satisfy the Chief of the Department of their fitness following six-months probation in the post.

The Superannuation Act of 1859 further limited the freedom of departments by making it necessary for persons appointed after 19 April 1859 to hold a certificate from the Commissioners in order to establish a *prima facie* case for a pension.

The Civil Service Commission had no power to coerce departments to adopt uniform regulations for their entry requirements. By 1870, however, the Commission had established strict requirements of health, moral fitness, and to a lesser degree, of age, which were applicable throughout the service. To a more limited extent the Commission were also able to introduce a measure of uniformity into the tests of knowledge and ability presented separately by each department, but were much less successful in persuading them to adopt some form of competition. Departments continued to be free to make appointments without opening the vacancy to more than one candidate. By 1860, however, a form of limited competition for clerkships was in use *inter alia* in the Treasury, Foreign, Home, Colonial and War Offices, Admiralty, and Board of Trade. In these cases instead of one candidate being nominated for each vacancy, the job of the Commission being merely to decide whether he satisfied the minimum requirements, the Department would nominate say three or four, in which case the Commission would indicate which it thought the best.

In 1860 the Select Committee on Civil Service Appointments recommended that all departments should adopt a system of limited competition. To avoid abuse, they further proposed that there should be at least five candidates nominated for a single vacancy and a ratio of three to one where more than one vacancy was offered for competition at the same time. They also wished to prevent a department putting forward candidates with no chance and so enabling its favoured candidate to succeed. Little more than lip-service was paid to these recommendations.[36]

In June 1870 another Order in Council introduced the principle of open competition. Robert Lowe had become Chancellor of the Exchequer in December 1868 in Gladstone's first Administration. Both were keen on widening the field of entry, but there still continued to be substantial opposition to the idea. As a result the new principle was applied only to the departments of these Ministers who were ready to accept it. Lowe was ready to introduce it at once into the Treasury and all its subordinate departments. The Home and Foreign Secretaries were, however, strongly opposed, both arguing that the character of the work of their offices made it highly inexpedient to apply the proposed new system to them.

The Order[37] stated that the qualifications of all persons proposed to be appointed, either permanently or temporarily, to any situation or employment in any department of the Civil Service shall be tested by or under the directions of the Civil Serice Commissioners and no person shall be so employed until he had been reported by the Commission to be qualified to be admitted on probation. The rules applicable to each department were left to be settled by the Commission and the 'chief authorities' of the department, with the approval of the Treasury. Appointments after 31 August 1870 were to be made by means of competitive examinations open to all persons of the requisite age, health, character, etc. who might wish to attend. The Commissioners were to hold examinations and make the necessary regulations and arrangements subject to the approval of the Treasury. The rule about six-months' probation continued. Schedule A to the Order contained a list of departments to which the principle of Open Competition was to be applied. The list did not include either the Home or Foreign Offices. Schedule B exempted three categories from the operations of the Order: situations (1) for which the holder was appointed directly by the Crown; or (2) included in any Order or Warrant made by the Treasury under the Superannuation Act, 1859; or (3) filled in the customary course of promotion by persons previously serving in the same department.

The Commission started to develop two levels of examination for clerks: a severe one for those recruited under Regulation I; and a simple kind for those recruited under Regulation II. The distinction did not correspond, however, to that which Northcote and Trevelyan wished to draw between intellectual and mechanical work. It was left to the Playfair Commission to emphasize once again the need for such a division of labour.

Tenure and Pensions

Though most public servants enjoyed *de facto* security of tenure, there were some who were appointed temporarily or were not part of the establishment. Each public office had an establishment which designated the number and character of the posts that could be filled. It could be fixed by Order in Council, as in the Foreign Office, or by Treasury Warrant. The business of a department might fluctuate, requiring it to get permission to employ a few clerks temporarily. These did not, however, form part of the establishment and came to be known as unestablished posts. A similar situation could arise if it were uncertain whether an increase in business was permanent. There was a natural reluctance on the part of the

Treasury to increase the number of permanent posts for fear that it would be difficult to reduce should business decline.

At the Treasury a distinction was drawn for a time between Supernumerary and Extra Clerks. Neither category formed part of the establishment but the former were appointed with the expectation, either express or implied, of being placed on the establishment, usually on the basis of seniority, as vacancies occurred. The grade was abolished in 1805. Extra (or Extraordinary) Clerks were introduced into the Treasury in 1777. They were employed on a temporary basis and had no claim to be placed on the establishment. In 1805 their status was redefined: they were to be employed on a strictly temporary basis and were denied the prospect of ever being placed on the establishment.[37] The word 'temporary' did not necessarily imply a few months or so, it merely meant that the post was not on the permanent establishment of the office. J. H. Capper was first appointed as a Supplementary Clerk in in the Home Office in 1794 and went on to spend forty-seven years as Chief Clerk of the Criminal Department created about 1800, but not treated as part of the establishment. It was quite possible for a person to spend all or most his working life as a temporary. However much such people were told on recruitment that they would never be established it was natural that, as the years passed, they should see little difference in their contribution to the department from that of the established staff.

Temporaries or unestablished clerks, sometimes known as Supplementary Clerks, were often used on less responsible, more routine work of an office. This was particularly so from 1850 onward. But this was by no means always the case, for the time-lag in an increase in the establishment to meet increased work could mean that in effect the unestablished were engaged on work similar to that performed by the established clerks. Nevertheless, at least in the Home Office a rigid distinction was made between the two, the unestablished occupying an inferior position in the structure of the office.[39]

There was no age of compulsory retirement and in the absence of favourable pension arrangements clerks stayed on until infirmity made it impossible. Under the Superannuation Act of 1834 allowances were granted to 9,399 who retired in the period 1835–54: of these 823 were aged 70 and over (one was aged 90) and 1,456 were aged 65 to 69. During the same period 213 men were superannuated and 19 compensated after 50 years or more service.[40]

In order for anyone under the age of 60 to qualify for a pension, the Act of 1810 required a certificate from the Heads of his department stating that infirmity of mind or body made him incapable of discharging his duties. Thus by implication sixty became the age at which public servants could retire in the normal way and not on grounds of ill-health. That age had been introduced into the Customs scheme in 1761 as the minimum age of retirement. It was still, however, not the age when public servants were compelled to retire.[41]

The cost of the arrangements increased rapidly and attracted Parliamentary criticism. In 1822 the superannuation scheme was made contributory: officers earning between £100 and £200 a year were required to pay 2½ per cent of their salaries and those earning over £200 a year were to pay 5 per cent (3 Geo. IV, c.113). Those affected were highly indignant and petitioned Parliament. Eventually the complainants secured such strong support that in 1824 the government was induced to repeal that part of the Act which authorized the deductions and even to refund the money already collected (5 Geo. IV, c.104).

One important change introduced by the 1822 Act remained. The age over which no certificate of incapacity was required remained at 65 not 60 as hitherto. Moreover a person wishing to retire on pension before the age of 65 had to produce a certificate of incapacity not only from the Heads of his department but also from two medical practitioners.

The Select Committee on Public Income and Expenditure of 1828[42] attributed the increase in expenditure on civil pensions partly to the misconception that the public servant had an absolute right to his pension and partly to Heads of departments using the scheme 'in order to hasten the removal of the less useful of their clerks'. As a result contributions were again introduced by Treasury Minute but only for entrants after 4 August 1829. The Minute became the basis of an Act in 1834 (4 and 5 Wm. IV, c.24). The scale of pensions was markedly reduced for new recruits, starting at a quarter instead of a third of the salary after 10–17 years service and finishing with two-thirds instead of a full salary after 45 or more years. Moreover the salary on which the pension was to be calculated was based on the average of the person's last three years not on his final year of service. The discretionary power of the Treasury was strengthened. Sixty-five remained the recognized age of retirement. The departments to which the Act applied were scheduled to the Act. Others could be added by the Treasury but the Commissioners of 1857 found that many new departments, e.g. the Education Department and General Board of Health had still not been added. The Act also reduced the scale of pensions for political officers: the maximum for the First Lord of the Treasury and Secretaries of State was reduced from £3,000 to £2,000 and an applicant for such a pension had to declare to the Treasury that his income from other sources was inadequate to maintain his station in life.

The arrangements were reviewed first by a Select Committee in 1856 and then by a Commission in 1857.[43] They formed part of the review of the public service being undertaken around that time. As a result an Act of 1857 (20 and 21 Vict., c.37) abolished deductions from salaries and an Act of 1859 (22 Vict., c.26) established a revised superannuation scheme.

The main features of the 1859 Act were:

(i) a new scale of pensions beginning with 10/60ths of the salary at the date of retirement after ten years' service rising to 40/60 for forty years. This was higher than the scale in the 1834 Act;

(ii) a redefinition of the scope of the scheme. The ordinary rate of superannuation allowance could be granted 'to Persons who shall have served in an established Capacity in the permanent Civil Service of the State, whether their Remuneration be computed by Day Pay, weekly Wages, or annual Salary.' Section XVII stated that for the purpose of the Act no person hereinafter appointed shall be deemed to have served in the permanent Civil Service of the State 'unless such Person holds his appointment directly from the Crown, or has been admitted into the Civil Service with a Certificate from the Civil Service Commission.' The Treasury 'whose Decision shall be final' were empowered to settle any question that might arise as to the claim of any person or class of persons.

The earlier legislation had not specified that service must be of the established kind. The Treasury's interpretation of the wording excluded temporary clerks, copyists and writers. The Act, however, gave the Treasury power to pay allowances in other cases, including those due to the abolition or reorganization of an Office;

(iii) a reduction in the age of retirement to 60. This proved to be a very controversial point. The Select Committee rather favoured the retention of sixty-five but without a compulsory retirement age. The Royal Commission, however, strongly recommended the lowering of the recognized age of retirement from 65 to 60 and the introduction of a compulsory retiring age at 65 with provision for certain exceptions. They did not, however, anticipate that many would retire 'prematurely' at 60: 'industrious and devoted officers, who have spent the greater part of their lives in the service, are not usually found to be desirous of retiring from it so long as their energies remain unimpaired'. They were disposed to think that, when a civil servant had 'reached an age at which bodily or mental vigour often begins to decline, it may be advantageous to the service to give to the Government the power of facilitating his retirement by granting, if they should so think fit, a super-annuation allowance without a medical certificate'. They went on, however, to recommend compulsory retirement at 65, unless the head of the department made a case for keeping a person longer. For it is 'invidious and painful' for the head to remove a meritorious public servant who did not accept that his powers were beginning to fail.[44]

The Bill of February 1859 would have lowered the recognized age to 60 and fixed compulsory retirement at 65. Strong disagreement was expressed with both provisions. The opposition, mainly led by Gladstone, wished to retain 65 and were not happy at imposing an upper limit when a civil servant would be compelled to retire. Fears were expressed about the expected large increase in cost. Northcote, Financial Secretary to the Treasury, said that the retirement age of 65 had been introduced not at the instance of the government but at that of the Royal Commission. 'It would now be necessary to retire at sixty-five, and as a compensation for this, it was thought right to permit public servants to retire at sixty'. The government

secured a majority for the reduction of the minimum age from
65 to 60 but did not put the maximum age to a vote. Raphael[45]
attributes this to a compromise between the parties. During
the course of the Debate the Chancellor of the Exchequer
(Disraeli) said it was contemplated that in future persons over
the age of 25 would not be admitted to the Civil Service.[46] As
the maximum pension could be achieved by forty years'
service presumably it was thought that few would want to go
on beyond this.

Finally, in 1869, the Political Offices Pension Act (32 and
33 Vict. c.60) provided a simpler pension scheme for former
Ministers. Offices were divided into three classes according to
their salaries. Class 1 covered political offices remunerated
with a yearly salary of not less than £5,000; Class 2, less than
£5,000 but not less than £2,000; and Class 3 less than £2,000
but more than £1,000. A Minister was entitled to a pension
not exceeding £2,000 a year if he had served not less than 4
years in Class 1, to not more than £1,200 a year if not less than
6 years in Class 2, and not more than £800 if not less than 10
years in a Class 3 post.

Numbers Employed in the Public Offices

The statistics of numbers employed in the various departments during 1780–1870 are neither plentiful nor reliable. The
series most usually quoted are from the Returns covering 1797
and certain other years up to and including 1829.[47] They
showed the following annual totals (including Ireland).

1797	16,267	[17,640]†
1805	20,221	[21,850]†
1810	22,931	[24,930]†
1815	24,598	
1819	24,414	
1827	22,912	
1828	22,609	
1829	22,367	

† Adjusted.

The figures for the first three years are too low for they do
not include those employed in the Customs for the Port of
London, the returns for those years being destroyed by fire in
1814. In 1815 the Port of London employed 2,043. Assuming

that this section of the Customs department expanded between 1797 and 1815 at the same rate as all the other sections, this would have added some 1,370 to 1797, some 1,630 to 1805, and about 2,000 to 1810.

Notwithstanding doubts of the complete accuracy of the figures certain features are quite clear. First, the effect of the Napoleonic War is very evident. If 1815 is taken as the dividing line the departments directly concerned with administering the war effort showed a big increase up to 1815 then a marked fall but not to their 1797 level.

	1797	1815	1829
Admiralty	45	65	47
War Office	58	208	99
Ordnance	298	708	513

Second, the revenue departments continued to be by far the largest employers, as can be seen in the next table.

	1797	1815	1829
Customs	6,380†	10,807	11,016
Excise	6,580	7,639	6,355
Stamps	521	572	506
Taxes	291	503	336
Post Office (GB)	957	1,214	1,418
Post Office (Ireland)	153	377	325
	14,882	21,112	19,956

† Adjusted.

Thus whilst the main revenue departments accounted for some 84 per cent of total employment in 1797 they had reached almost 90 per cent in 1829. The Customs and the Excise were giants. In contrast the Home, Foreign, and Colonial Departments employed 30, 47, and 33 respectively in 1829. This bears out the point made earlier — in terms of employment the 'central' government was almost wholly taken up by wars and raising the money to pay for them.

In 1833 Parliament was provided with a Return of Establishments for 1821 and 1832.[48] Unfortunately the figures, at least those for 1821, do not appear to have been compiled on the same basis as those just discussed. They showed a total of 26,880 for 1821, far in excess of the earlier figures for 1819 and 1827. The total for 1832, at 21,305 appears to be in line with the trend shown by the earlier Returns. Owing to a fall in the numbers employed in the Customs department the percentage employed in the revenue departments was slightly less than in 1829.

The next reliable figures are for 31 March 1851 supplied to the Northcote–Trevelyan inquiry and based primarily on the 1851 Census.[49] These showed a total of 39,147, excluding artificers and labourers. Without very detailed examination it is not possible to say whether the figures are exactly on the same basis as for 1829 or 1832 but the assumption is that there are some variations. Assuming, however, a reasonable measure of comparability they show an increase of nearly 18,000 over 1832. Most of this is explained by the great increase in Post Office employees — nearly 14,000 more than in 1832. The numbers employed in the other revenue departments showed an increase of nearly 1,500. The percentage employed on these 'revenue' activities still remained at over 86 per cent. The figures for the central offices showed increases not large in actual numbers but large in terms of rate of growth. The Foreign Office showed 85 as against 39 in 1832, the Home Office 86 as against 30, and the Treasury, without the Commissariat, 105 as against 82.

There are no comparable figures for the remainder of our period. The Registrar to the Civil Service Commission submitted a statement to the Select Committee on Civil Service Appointments of 1860[50] which showed a total of 104,884 for 1859. If the 30,437 artisans and labourers and the 20,000 Irish and Metropolitan police are excluded the figure still shows an unaccountably large increase over 1851. Part can be accounted for by the increase of almost 10,000 in Post Office employees. The figures would appear not to be strictly comparable. The Post Office continued to expand and employed over 28,000 in 1870.

The Census of Population of 1871 for England and Wales showed almost 54,000 occupied in the national government and over 51,000 in local government. Of the latter the bulk were police and poor law officials. It would be unwise, however, to relate these figures too closely to those for earlier years.

V

The National Financial Arrangements

The changes which transformed a diffuse and loose financial system into a concentrated and tightly regulated one had two purposes and consequences: to reduce the number of officers with any personal responsibility for the effectiveness of the system and to strengthen and clarify the control of the House of Commons over it. The changes will be dealt with under six headings:

(i) Balances
(ii) Consolidated Fund
(iii) Appropriation
(iv) Virement
(v) The Rise of Treasury Control
(vi) Audit

BALANCES

The money in the hands of the public accountants had either been collected by them from the public as taxes, or been issued to them from the Exchequer to meet the public expenditure for which they were responsible. The bulk of the former came by way of the Customs and Excise duties and the transference of these receipts into the Exchequer does not appear to have been noticeably delayed, having regard to the facilities available at the time. Only in the case of the Land Tax and the Assessed Taxes was there serious ground for complaint.

The Land Tax and the Assessed Taxes (on windows, houses, servants, etc.) were collected locally and paid over to a Receiver-General in each county. By statute this officer was required to pay his receipts into the Exchequer within twenty days (Land Tax), and forty days (Assessed Taxes). Yet on 14 July 1779 the Receivers-General had £398,748 in their hands. Two reasons were given for the delay: the difficulty of procuring remittances to London, especially from the distant counties, and the insufficiency of the remuneration of the

Officers concerned. The Commissioners estimated that at 4 per cent interest, the public were paying some £13,362 a year 'for want of the Use of their own Money'. They laid it down 'The Revenue should come from the Pocket of the Subject directly into the Exchequer; . . . to permit Receivers to retain it in their Hands, expressly for their own Advantage, is to furnish them with the strongest Motive for witholding it. A private interest is created, in direct Opposition to that of the Public; Government is compelled to have Recourse to expensive Loans; and the Revenue itself is finally endangered.'[1]

The Select Committee on Finance of 1797 found the position improved, but still wished to see the balance lower than the Treasury permitted. 'At a Time', they said, 'when the Public Service has called for Supplies greater than at any former Period of our History, the Government has a Right, and it is their Duty, to avail themselves without Delay, of every Farthing which is taken out of the Purse of the Subject, liable to such Deductions only as are necessarily incurred in bringing forward the Sums so raised . . .'[2]

Balances in the hands of those who received money out of the Exchequer, by way of Imprest and on Account, were far more widespread. Each public accountant would imprest on the Exchequer for a sum he thought should be sufficient for the expenditure he would have to meet, up to the limit of the sum voted by Parliament or otherwise authorized. The system was convenient and consistent with the diffusion of responsibility. It ran into difficulties, however, when applied to the finance of armed activity over a large part of the globe.

When military operations were taking place in distant lands, not only did it take some time for the local accounts to reach the Paymaster-General of the Forces, but it was also difficult to determine definitely whether there were any outstanding claims. The Paymaster-General worked through a large number of sub-public accountants in different parts of the world, e.g. garrison commanders. Even when their accounts were received and paid, they still had to be audited, a process rendered more protracted because the audit staff had not expanded to meet wartime conditions. Delay in clearing the annual account was inevitable and until it was cleared and he had received his Quietus the Paymaster was fully entitled to defer repaying any balance in his hands. Moreover when he ceased to be Paymaster- General he was not required to hand over to his successor any balance he held. He was not even required to hand over the account books and papers. Thus the years went by, the proceedings dragged on, and in the meantime the money earned an income for the holder. In 1780 there was still £378,000 outstanding from the four previous Paymasters-General, of which £256,000 was due from Lord Holland (Paymaster-General 1757–65). In 1781 there was still £12,360 due from George Grenville, who had ceased to be Treasurer of the Navy in 1755. An Act of 1781 directed that the balances then in the hands of former named Paymasters-General and Treasurers of the Navy, should be paid into the Exchequer before 24 October 1781. Upon such payment the person named and/or his heirs were to be acquitted and discharged from any further claims (21 Geo. III, c.48).

The system was changed for the Army and Navy by legislation in the early 1780s. All money issued from the Exchequer for Army and Naval purposes had to be paid into the Bank of England* and to the account of the Paymaster-General or Treasurer. No money was to be issued direct from the Exchequer to these officers: they were to draw on the Bank account by a draft which specified the heads of services for which the sums were to be applied. To prevent any unnecessary accumulation of public money in the hands of the Bank, each officer was required to send to the Treasury at the beginning of each month a statement of the balance of money on his account at the Bank and of all outstanding drafts on it but not paid. Upon the death or removal of the officer, the balance of cash to his credit at the Bank was to be transferred to his successor (22 Geo. III, c.81, Army** and 25 Geo. III,

* Even by the end of the 18th century very few Public Accountants deposited their public moneys with the Bank of England. Even when they did, the accounts were in their names personally, not in the names of their departments or offices. Presumably it was more convenient and more remunerative to place the money with one of the smaller banks. Sir John Clapham, *The Bank of England* (1944), Vol. I, pp. 214–15.

** Amended and replaced by 23 Geo. III, c.58

c.31, Navy). Similar provisions were applied for the first time
to the Treasurer of the Ordnance in 1806 (46 Geo. III, c.45).
In the same year Acts were passed for the better regulation of
the Receiver-General of the Excise duties (46 Geo. III, c.75);
of the Stamp duties (46 Geo. III, c.76); of the Post Office (46
Geo. III, c.83); of the Customs (46 Geo. III, c.150). Each of
these Receivers-General had to keep an account at the Bank of
England.

As regards the system generally, an Act of 1800 (39 and 40
Geo. III, c.54) introduced penalties for delay in paying cash
into the Exchequer. Where a public accountant employed in
the collection or receipt of revenues died or went out of office
indebted to His Majesty for £500 or more, interest of 5 per
cent was to be charged from three months after going out of
office, or from twelve months after his death. A right of appeal
to the Court of Exchequer was allowed. Interest not exceeding
5 per cent could also be charged by the Audit Commission at
their discretion where a public accountant held a balance of
£500 or more, the Treasury having the right to allow or
disallow the charge on appeal. Where, however, the Exchequer owed a public accountant £500 or more, the Treasury
were empowered to allow interest at 5 per cent. To make
certain that vigorous action was undertaken to recover outstanding balances, the Act required the Treasury to lay before
both Houses within fourteen days after the commencement of
every Session, a list of public accountants in respect of whom
the execution of any Processor Proceedings for recovering any
balances — principal or interest — had been controlled,
suspended, or prevented by the king's authority and the
causes for such action.

The critics were concerned not only with the large amount of
public money in the hands of public accountants instead of in
the Exchequer, but also that these officers were encouraged to
hold such balances because they could use them to their own
financial advantage. Nevertheless there were quite genuine
arguments in favour of the arrangement. For one thing, it was
still not easy to transmit money from places remote from
London. The revenue receipts were usually sent to the capital
by bills and drafts on London houses. Even those examples of
administrative virtue, the Excise collectors, remitted their net

receipts by Bills at 21 days from the Counties near London, at 30 days from the Counties rather more remote, and at 50–60 days from the most distant. The receivers for the Land Tax, not having money available regularly, found it more difficult to make such arrangements. But the situation was changing. George Rose writing from the Treasury pointed out to the Tax Office in October 1797 'the increasing Facility with which the commercial Intercourse of the Country has been carried on internally for some Years, has lessened the Difficulty of Remittances to London.'[3]

The right to use balances could be a form of remuneration.* This was not a good defence in the case of the Paymaster General of the Forces, for in 1780 he received a net salary of over £3,000 a year. But even the Treasury were prepared to admit that the Receivers-General of the Land Tax were not particularly well paid. In these and other cases any financial advantage gained by an officer by the use of the balance in his hands was part of his remuneration. But for that advantage he might well have had to be paid from public funds in some other more obvious fashion.

In passing, it is worth noting the close connection between the growth in the sums raised by taxes and the rise of the banking system in the second half of the century. As the money collected was not remitted to London daily, or even weekly, but allowed to accumulate by the collector over a period, it was convenient for him to deposit it in one of the many local banks springing up all over the country. He received interest on the money deposited and in return the bank earned money by lending to merchants and others in need of capital. The banks also came to be involved because some of the taxes came to be paid in bank notes or drafts and also they were a major means of transmitting money to London.[4]

* The attraction of earning interest was not confined to the public moneys. At the turn of the century Landsdowne complained that more than ever agents and tenants now kept their money as long as possible before paying it to the landlord 'on account of the number of country banks, which corrupt the whole country, by soliciting the custody of ever so small a sum . . .' (Quoted J. Norris, *Shelburne and Reform* (1963), p.289.

Finally, on the revenue side the arrangement was an aspect of earmarking. Thus the Receivers-General of the Land Tax were not just tax-collectors, they were also responsible for meeting the cost of certain public services. They were in effect used as the local bankers of the government, for example, for meeting the expenses of the Militia in each County. This was obviously convenient administratively, for if it were awkward to transmit tax receipts from say, Cumberland to London, it was no easier to transmit government money from London to Cumberland. Using funds in the hands of the Receivers-General for this purpose avoided these difficulties. The fact that the balance might offer a pecuniary advantage to the holder did not detract from the advantage to the Treasury.

Turning to the expenditure side, the existence of hundreds of independent accounts increased the total sum of money required as a working balance at any one time. For each officer responsible for meeting this or that item of public expenditure would not wish to be found with insufficient funds for the purpose. Moreover, he could not make good any deficiency on his own fund by drawing on another that was in surplus. Even within a large department such as the Customs, it was usual for each fund or account to be treated as separate and accountable to the Auditors and the Exchequer as such.

The system exacerbated the financial problems of the government in two ways. On the one hand it delayed the payment of tax receipts into the Exchequer, and on the other it resulted in more money being issued from the Exchequer than was strictly necessary to meet current spending. The resulting shortfall between expenditure and current receipts (taxes and funded borrowing) had to be met out of short-term borrowing, i.e. by Exchequer Bills. These were negotiable instruments stating a sum payable to the bearer by a specified date. They were used in 'anticipation of revenue'. By the 1780s their annual cost had risen to around £300,000. It was becoming apparent to Burke and others that if all public moneys were handled by the Bank of England instead of by other banks or being left in private hands, the amount that would need to be raised by Exchequer Bills could be reduced.

There were two possible approaches to reducing the

amount of public money held as balances. One was to reduce the number of public accountants, a method which could have the additional advantage of reducing administrative costs. The other was to reduce the number of individual bank accounts. The first method achieved part of the second in as far as it was deemed necessary for each paymaster to have his own bank account. But with improvements in banking and accounting methods it proved possible to move towards a single Exchequer account at the Bank of England even though money passed through the hands of numerous public accountants.

The Commissioners of Public Accounts who reported in 1831, criticized the Exchequer for also being paymaster for a substantial amount of public money (nearly £900,000 in 1829) for salaries, allowances, and pensions charged against the Civil List and the Consolidated Fund. They proposed that this function should be transferred to a new officer. The transfer would satisfy the principle that the business of examining claims for payment and of making the payment, should be in separate hands.[5] In 1834, therefore, a Paymaster of Civil Services was established (4 and 5 Wm. IV, c.15) who relieved the Exchequer of the function of actually paying money. He made all payments from the votes for the Miscellaneous Services and all civil payments from the Consolidated Fund. He rendered unnecessary the system whereby there was a money accountant in each department, usually the chief clerk, who drew from the Exchequer the amount he needed to meet the salaries and expenses of his department.

In 1836, consolidation of the offices of the Paymaster-General of the Forces, the Treasurer of the Navy, the Treasurer of the Ordnance, and the Treasurer of Chelsea Hospital, was made possible by an Act of 1835 (5 and 6 Wm. IV, c.35). The new resulting office of Paymaster-General was, like those it replaced, tenable with a seat in the House of Commons. In 1848 (11 and 12 Vict., c.55), the offices of the Paymaster of Civil Services and of the Paymasters of Exchequer Bills were abolished and their duties transferred to him. This amalgamation led to a reduction in staff from 108 to 73. So by 1848 responsibility for the payment of all army, navy, and ordnance services, all the civil services voted in the Miscellaneous

Services or charged on the Consolidated Fund, and the principal and interest of Exchequer Bills was vested in a single office. Only a few small establishments, e.g. the office of Woods and Forests, conducted their own payments.[6]

This concentration of authority would have been less effective in reducing the number of accounts but for changes in the treatment of public money in the banking system. The 1834 Act (4 and 5 Wm. IV, c.15), which reformed the Exchequer laid it down that after 11 October 1834 all public moneys hitherto payable into the Exchequer were to be paid into the Bank of England to the credit of the Exchequer. All the moneys passing through this account were to be treated by the Bank as forming one Fund. All Warrants and Orders were to be satisfied out of this 'general Fund', but the newly established Comptroller of the Exchequer and the Treasury were to keep accounts of the receipts, credits, and issues according to the Parliamentary authority under which the expenditure was granted. Credits granted to any person were not to be accompanied by the actual transfer of money 'until the same shall be actually paid by the Bank to or on account of [that] person'. All public accountants to whom money was paid out of the account were required to have their bank accounts at the Bank of England.

Lord Monteagle, the Comptroller-General of the Exchequer, strongly criticized this arrangement in his lengthy evidence to the Select Committee on Public Moneys. He claimed that once issued from the Exchequer account at the Bank, the money could be used for any purpose. The fact that a record of the purposes of the issues was made in the books of the Paymaster-General did not in his opinion meet the requirements of the Appropriation Acts. Had his argument been accepted, a separate bank account would have had to be kept for every head of public expenditure. And in turn this would have meant the Paymaster-General having to keep a balance on every such account, leading, the Treasury estimated, to a tenfold increase in total balances.[7] The Treasury admitted that the practice was not consistent with the Comptroller-General's interpretation of the Exchequer Act but was nevertheless correct because no issue was made without being sanctioned by Parliament and, as far as the Pay Office could do so, within the limits of the vote. But in part the disagreement arose, as we will see shortly, from a widely different view of the significance of control being exercised at the point of issue as against at the point of payment. The criticism would have had more weight in the earlier years of the century, but by 1856 a system of appropriation audit had been developed to cover a large part of public expenditure.

The Select Committee supported the Treasury practice. They were 'satisfied . . . that the consolidation of the Pay Departments has been attended with public benefit; that it has diminished the balances left in the hands of the public accountants to the Crown; that it has increased the security of the public money, and promoted economy; and that the regulation which requires the Paymaster-General to make all his payments from a single cash balance has been attended with beneficial results'. Nevertheless, they recommended that the Paymaster-General should, at the end of each month, make up for the Audit Commission a statement of the balances for and against every head of service.[8]

By 1856 informed opinion had moved a long way from the worries of the 1780s about the malpractices of the Paymaster-General of the Forces and the delays of the Receivers-General of the Land Tax. Improvements in the banking system enabled the money collected from the Customs, Excise, and other taxes to be paid daily into the Bank of England. There was no longer any personal advantage in holding a balance of public money. Yet the avoidance of unnecessary or dead balances remained a goal of Treasury policy. When asked in 1856 for his views on the objects of the system of finance the Principal Clerk of Finance in the Treasury, replied: 'the security of the public money, the utmost simplicity of management, and the greatest economy in the employment of the public balances'. He thought these objects were best obtained 'by placing the finances under one undivided control and responsibility, consolidating all the public moneys into one fund, and issuing them from that fund under one direct authority — the direct authority of the controlling department'.[9] In other words the Treasury believed in consolidation.

THE CONSOLIDATED FUND

The financial system of 1780 was characterized by the ear-marking of taxes for particular purposes. Earmarking was partly a device to satisfy lenders that their principal and interest were secure; partly to avoid annual appropriations; and partly because of the belief that some of the expenditure was temporary. An accumulation of fifty or so years had led to a complicated patchwork of a financial system in which authority to incur expenditure was usually closely linked with the source from which such expenditure should be financed.

It was indeed the tangle in which the Commissioners found the Customs duties and accounts in 1785 that led them to propose the creation of a single fund. They had already recommended that the Customs duties should be consolidated and simplified and they suggested that the idea might be applicable to other branches of the revenue 'perplexed with a Multiplicity of distinct Accounts'. This would then open the way to a great measure of financial regulation, the introduction of the most simple of all modes of account: 'the Formation of One Fund, into which shall flow every Stream of the Public Revenue, and from whence shall issue the Supply for every Public Service'. To assure the lenders of money they added 'One great Fund of Revenue, composed of the Annual Income of the State, will be the ample Security to every Public Creditor.'[10]

In 1787 Parliament approved a lengthy Bill introduced by Pitt. It involved 2,537 separate resolutions, so complicated were the matters with which it had to deal. The primary object of the legislation[11] was to abolish all the then Customs and Excise duties and some of the Stamp duties and replace them by a much simpler and smaller number of duties. The produce of these revised duties, along with certain other revenues, was to be carried to eight consolidated accounts, the total then being carried to one 'consolidated' fund. Security for the loans already funded by the earmarking of specific taxes was provided by the declaration in the Act that the annuities constituting the national debt and the £1 million a year contribution to the recently established Sinking Fund, were to have an absolute priority over all other claims on the

Fund. Next in priority was the £900,000 a year for the Civil List. Finally, there came certain other charges, e.g. augmentation of the judges' salaries.

The idea of a single fund was not new. An Act of 1714 (1 Geo. I, Stat. 2, c.12) had established the General or Aggregate Fund into which were paid the proceeds of certain specific taxes and out of which was paid certain specific expenditure. Walpole's Sinking Fund of 1716, (3 Geo. I, c.7) had a somewhat similar aim. The creation of such general funds reflected the difficulty of linking specific expenditure closely with the proceeds of particular taxes. For the linking involved a capacity to estimate exactly both the receipts and the outgoings so that they balanced. It was much easier and administratively more convenient for the proceeds of several taxes to be paid into a fund against which expenditure could be charged as and when authorized. The creation of a Consolidated Fund in 1787 was not merely a simplification of the Customs and Excise duties and of the national accounts, it was also a shift of emphasis from Parliamentary control by way of earmarking of the proceeds of a tax to control simply by the authorizing of expenditure.

The 1787 Act did not provide fully for a fund into which all revenue was paid and out of which all expenditure was met. It was essentially a means of providing for permanent or long-term expenditure. Any surplus of income over expenditure could be and was voted by Parliament towards meeting the cost of other items. But it was not designed to cope with the large temporary expenditure occasioned by the Napoleonic wars. This was met out of the proceeds of taxes imposed mainly on a year to year basis. In 1813, for example, the House of Commons voted almost £72 million as Supply grants (i.e. for expenditure not charged against the Fund) of which only £500,000 was provided for from the income of the Consolidated Fund. The rest was met out of tax and other revenues which were not paid into the Fund.

The charges imposed on the Fund by the 1787 Act grew with the steady increase in the National Debt. The £9 million of 1787 had grown to £18 million by 1800 and to over £30 million by 1820. There was also a lengthening list of pensions and annuities voted by Parliament to members of the royal family and to retiring public servants, for example the £65,000 a year to the Prince of Wales, voted in 1795 (35 Geo. III, c.129). The proceeds of the taxes originally allocated to the Fund were not sufficient to meet the increasing burdens and from time to time Parliament had to add the proceeds of other taxes. As the charges were regarded as permanent, or long-term moral obligations of Parliament, so the taxes paid into the Fund had to be equally permanent. Thus in 1806, when two duties on wine granted a few years earlier were made perpetual, their proceeds were in future to go to and form part of the Consolidated Fund and 'be applied towards making such permanent addition to the publick revenue, as shall be adequate to the encreased charge occasioned by any loan to be raised . . .' (46 Geo. III, c.44). It was most important to ensure that the Fund was never in deficit in respect of the debt and other charges made on it. A deficiency in one quarter had to be made good out of money voted by Parliament and repaid out of any subsequent surplus. Initially then it was a self-balancing fund designed to meet the country's permanent commitments.

The end of the Napoleonic War enabled large reductions to be made in military expenditure and so most of the taxation imposed for war purposes, including the Property and Income Tax, could be abolished. The remaining 'perpetual' taxes were made payable into the Fund, even though its income was already sufficient to meet the charges upon it. Thus in 1816 (56 Geo. III, c.29) certain temporary or war Customs duties were declared to be perpetual and their proceeds payable into the Fund. Before long the numerous votes for military and civil purposes contained in the annual Appropriation Act could be financed by a sum voted out of the Consolidated Fund.

At this point Parliamentary attention was increasingly focussed on ensuring that all the public revenue should be paid into the Fund. The major exception was that the proceeds of the national taxes were paid into it net, i.e. after the payment of any statutory charges and after meeting the costs of collection. Though Parliament was given information about these expenditures, the sums involved were not appropriated nor were they subject to the methods which the House of Commons had now evolved for controlling spending. By the middle of the nineteenth century attention came to be focussed on this gap in the system. In 1848 the House of Commons resolved: 'This House cannot be the effectual guardian of the revenues of the state, unless the whole amount of the taxes and of various other sources of income received for the public account be either paid in or accounted for to the Exchequer'[12]

The main change was made by an Act of 1854 (17 and 18 Vict., c.94), which removed the bulk of the expenditure met by the revenue departments before paying their receipts into the Exchequer and made it specifically chargeable in future either against the Consolidated Fund or against money to be provided by annual votes of Supply. The Act did not, however, specifically mention that the costs of collection and management should in future be met out of annual votes, but this was achieved by a Treasury Minute of August 1854. In practice the Treasury found it convenient for the revenue departments to continue to meet their operating expenses out of their current receipts. The significant change, therefore, was that Estimates of their expenditure now had to be submitted to the Committee of Supply and they had to act within appropriations in the same way as other departments.[13] The requirement was made statutory by the 1866 Act. The 1854 Act dated the change from 1 April 1854, i.e. to take place during the financial year ending 31 March 1855.

Three other changes must be noticed. (i) In 1849/50 the fees received by those departments with fee funds were required to be paid into the Consolidated Fund instead of only the balance of the fee fund; (ii) In the financial year 1855–6 it became the practise to pay into the Fund the proceeds of Exchequer Bills and of any other securities on which the government had raised money; (iii) From 1 April 1857 the few remaining pensions and certain other expenditure not covered by the 1854 Acts and which had continued to be deducted from the tax proceeds were made a charge against the Consolidated Fund or were to be met by annual votes.

By then, therefore, the Treasury could claim that the whole of the public moneys now passed into the Consolidated Fund and all issues for the supply services were met out of it under the authority of the Ways and Means Act.[14] The actual account for the Consolidated Fund, however, continued to show only expenditure charged against it. As a result it now showed a large surplus out of which was met the cost of the expenditure appropriated annually for the Army, Navy, and Civil Services and the revenue departments. The general account was headed 'Cash Account for the whole of the financial operations of the Lords Commissioners of the Treasury.'

By this time, however, the concept of 'One Fund, into which shall flow every Stream of the Public Revenue, and from whence shall issue the Supply for every Public Service' was less dramatic than when advocated in 1785. For there were already national accounts and centralized banking arrangements. Nevertheless not only did it signify the end of earmarking, it was a further simplification of the financial system. Parliament need now provide money only for the Consolidated Fund: payments out of it could be treated as quite a separate operation. It also placed the whole of the national revenues under the control of the House of Commons, for all had to go into the Fund and nothing could be taken from it without their specific authority.

Consolidated Fund Charges

One feature of the original arrangement, however, persisted: certain expenditure continued to be given exceptional treatment. Originally this had been provided by an order of priority with the servicing of the national debt at the top. About the 1830s, however, the original concept of a strict system of priority declined in significance for the proceeds of the Fund were more than ample to meet the prior charges. Instead there evolved the distinction between expenditure which could be incurred without annual approval and that which had to be authorized each year. Debt charges, the Civil List annuity, and royal pensions had always been in the first category. The removal of the costs of civil government from the Civil List and the creation of new offices raised the question of what other types of expenditure should be treated as permanent charges.

There were already several precedents. In 1785 the salaries and expenses of the newly established Commissioners of Audit were made a permanent charge on the Aggregate Fund and continued to be so when it was merged into the Consolidated Fund. The arrangement for the augmentation of judges' Salaries was also incorporated into the 1787 Act.

The items of expenditure covered by the Civil List were very diverse even when separated from the cost of the royal households. They included the salaries of judges before augmentation, the salaries of such senior Ministers as the Lord President and the Lords of the Treasury, numerous pensions, part or all of the remuneration of many clerks, and a whole series of such miscellaneous items as payments to Oxford Professors. Hitherto none of these items had been subject to an annual vote in Committee of Supply for even the lump sum, once fixed, did not require annual renewal. A decision had therefore to be taken as to whether in future all items should be separately voted each year or granted permanently by Act of Parliament.

The salaries of the First Lord and other Treasury Ministers and of the political heads of departments and their staffs were obvious cases for being voted annually. The salaries of judges were, however, made permanent charges on the Fund. So also was the cost of the Diplomatic Services — Salaries, Allowances, and Pensions. It is not clear why expenditure of this latter kind needed to be treated in this way, except perhaps because of the personal relations of the king to his Ambassadors. In 1869, however, it was decided (32 and 33 Vict., c.43) that in future authority for this expenditure should be voted annually, except for pensions already in existence.

A number of other cases arose during the 1830s. The treatment of the Comptroller-General of the Exchequer by the Act of 1834 (4 and 5 Wm. IV, c.15) was very much on all fours with that accorded to the judges. His salary and allowances were made a charge on the Consolidated Fund and he was removable only by an Address of both Houses. The expenses of his office and the salary and expenses of the Paymaster-General (a political office) also established by the same Act, were, however, to be met out of annual votes. When the offices of Comptroller and of the Audit Commission were brought together under a Comptroller and Auditor-General in 1866, the salary of both him and his Assistant, were placed on the

Consolidated Fund. When the County Courts were established in 1846 (9 & 10 Vict., c.95) the salaries of the judges
were to be met out of the fees, any deficiency being made good
by the Consolidated Fund. In 1856, however, the whole of
their salaries were made chargeable on the Fund but their
travelling expenses had to be met by an annual vote (19 and
20 Vict., c.108).

It was not clear, however, why the cost of a number of new
offices was treated as though they needed this special status.
In 1836, for example, the salaries and expenses of the newly
established General Register Office of Births, Deaths, and
Marriages were made charges on the Consolidated Fund.
Similar treatment was accorded the Commissioners in
Lunacy, the Tithe, Copyhold, and Inclosure Commission, the
National Debt Office, and the Public Works Loans Office.
The Select Committee on Miscellaneous Expenditure in 1848
could not find a 'definite principle upon which certain
expenses are charged upon the Consolidated Fund and similar
ones, [e.g. the Poor Law Commission and the Inspectors of
Factories] upon the Estimates.'[15]

The Act of 1854 (17 and 18 Vict., c.94) sorted out the
situation. First, it greatly reduced the number of Officers
whose salaries and expenses were a permanent charge on the
Consolidated Fund.* Those of the Tithe, Copyhold, and
Inclosure Commission, the National Debt Office, the Public
Works Loan Office, and General Register Office of Births,
Deaths and Marriages, for example, were in future to be paid
for out of the annual votes of Supply. Second, in the remaining
cases, only the salaries of the officers or Commissioners were
left as charges on the Fund, the salaries of subordinates and
office expenses being placed on the Estimates. This principle
was applied even to the Audit Commissioners, only their
salaries remaining Consolidated Fund charges. In the case
of the Lunacy Commissioners and the Metropolitan Police
Courts, the original Bill removed the whole cost from the
Fund, but amendments retained the salaries of the Commissioners and of the Police Magistrates as charges on the Fund.

* Forty-four items were removed from the Consolidated Fund.

In his memorandum to the Select Committee of 1857 the Chancellor of the Exchequer could say:

> The principle of not subjecting to the uncertainty of an annual vote the provision for the security of the public creditor, the dignity of the Crown, the annuities to the Royal Family, and those granted for distinguished public services, the salaries of judges and other officers in whose official character independence is an essential element, compensations for rights surrendered, and like charges, although it may have been carried too far, is one the soundness of which is generally admitted[16]

Parliament became increasingly selective in its use of Consolidated Fund charges. By 1870 they comprised the debt charges and the Civil List, a number of pensions to royal personages and distinguished former public servants, the salaries of Judges, of the Speaker of the House of Commons and his Serjeant-at-arms, of the Comptroller and Auditor-General and his Assistant, and a few sundry items, e.g. the expenses of the Inspectors of Anatomy and a grant to the Scottish Clergy. When the annuity for Queen Victoria's Civil List had been settled a sum of £10,000 a year for the Secret Service had been made a charge on the Fund.

APPROPRIATION

By 1780, with the possible exception of the Civil List revenues, the money made available to the king could at law be used only for purposes specified either by the annual Appropriation Act or by some specific Act. Though the principle of appropriation, i.e. that public money should be spent only on the specific purposes authorized by Parliament, was well recognized, its implications were far from being clearly worked out. Many questions still remained to be answered. In what detail should money be appropriated? Did appropriation leave the government with no discretion, or was some flexibility allowable, and, if so, under what conditions? How was appropriation to be enforced and by whom?

In 1780 whilst a single sum was voted each year for Naval Services and a further sum for the Navy Debt, the money voted for the Land Forces had, as early as 1711, been subdivided and in the 1780s remained a peculiar mixture of lump sums and quite small specific items for particular regiments. The Appropriation Act of 1798 (38 Geo. III, c.90) introduced for the first time votes for particular elements in naval expenditure, e.g. £2,645,500 for wages of 110,000 men, including 20,000 marines; £2,717,000 for their victuals; £4,290,000 for wear and tear of ships; and £350,000 for sea service ordnance. After this it became common form to show the total sum voted for the Navy, Land Forces, and the Ordnance, and then, by the use of the introductory term 'viz.' or 'that is to say', set out the items which made up this sum. The number of these items increased and by the 1830s naval and army expenditure was each voted under some twenty or so heads. In both cases a substantial part of the money was related to the authorized number of men. In the case of the Navy the number was translated into expenditure by figures of cost per head for wages, victuals, ordnance, and even wear and tear of ships.

It became usual to avoid bringing rather different elements of expenditure under one general heading. By the 1830s the salaries and expenses of the Admiralty Office, Navy Pay Office, Navy Office, and Victualling Office, were usually shown separately, and other items picked out were the Royal Naval College and in 1830 even a £1,500 Bounty for Chaplains. The Appropriation Act of 1840 (3 and 4 Vict., c.112) showed Naval Services under 24 heads, Army Services under 18 heads, and Ordnance Services under 12 heads.

Until well into the nineteenth century there was no similar framework for the expenditure on civil government, indeed for a long time the Civil List annuity was expected to meet all those costs. However the House of Commons started to provide extra money in three ways:
(i) Specific items in each year's Appropriation Act. At the end of the eighteenth century these were still quite small both in number and amount for expenditure within the United Kingdom. In 1800 they included £900 to officers of the Exchequer 'for extra trouble,' £6,443 for the expenses of the police at Wapping, and £3,000 for the British Museum. The maintenance of Civil Establishments in the overseas possessions were a regular series of items. Occasionally there could

be some very large items, for example, the £197,803 voted in 1796 for the relief of American loyalists.

(ii) Money made available by an Address to the king asking him to meet the cost of specified items of expenditure out of the current revenues of the Civil List, with an undertaking to repay the money out of the following year's Appropriation Act. In theory these items were unforeseen and therefore could not have been included in the current Act, e.g. for the relief of American loyalists or the repayment of the debts of the Earl of Chatham and the cost of his funeral, but some occurred year after year, e.g. the printing of the House of Commons *Journals* and Sessional Papers. These items were not particularized in the subsequent Appropriation Act but lumped together in one sum.

(iii) Specific provision in a number of Acts. Thus, pensions of £3,000 a year had been granted to former Speaker Onslow and his heirs in 1762 (2 Geo. III, c.33) and £8,000 a year had been granted to the Dukes of York, Cumberland, and Gloucester in 1767 (7 Geo. III, c.19)

In 1780 there was no statement available to Parliament, which brought together the total sum made available in these different ways, nothing which could compare for simplicity and coverage with the votes for the armed forces. Before a system of votes for the civil services could emerge, three developments had to take place:

(i) the costs of civil government had to be taken out of the Civil List, leaving it to bear only the King's personal expenses;

(ii) the 'Address' items had to be replaced either by an annual contingency sum, or by their inclusion in the annual Appropriation Act;

(iii) some items of 'permanent' expenditure had to be transformed into annual votes.

Criticism of the Civil List united the economical reformers, those concerned with the 'influence of the Crown' and those whose primary aim was to strengthen Parliamentary control of expenditure and provide a better regulated financial system. Though there were some critics even in the 1780 who argued that a distinction should be drawn between the costs of the King's household and of civil government, the earliest aim was to confine the king to the total voted by Parliament. When faced with accumulated debt on the List, e.g. £618,340 in 1777, Parliament could grumble but had little option but to pay it off. So the important thing was to prevent overspending, or at least secure the earliest possible notice that it was occurring.

Burke's solution was to prescribe a statutory order of priorities for the different elements which made up the List. Should a deficiency emerge it would be the elements with the lowest priority which would remain unpaid, or on which economies would have to be made. The order established by the Act of 1782 (22 Geo. III, c.82) was as follows:

Class 1 Pensions and Allowances to the Royal Family;
2 Salaries of the Lord Chancellor, the Judges and the Speaker of the House of Commons:
3 Salaries of Foreign Ministers (i.e. ambassadors) resident at foreign courts;
4 Tradesmen's bills of His Majesty's Household;
5 Salaries of the menial servants of the Household;
6 Pensions, beginning with the smallest pensions:
7 Other salaries payable out of the Civil List revenues:
8 Salaries and pensions of the Commissioners of the Treasury and the Chancellor of the Exchequer.

The Act required the Treasury to draw up a plan of establishments and payments according to the order of the classes laid down. After 5 April 1783 all sums payable out of the Civil List revenues were to be paid in that order. The Treasury did not provide the information until 1786, when Parliament would hardly have been willing to pay off further arrears of £210,000 without knowing more about how the money had been spent. The first return showed that Class 1 accounted for some £203,000, Class 4 for some £147,000, and Classes 7 and 8 for some £95,000. The Return added an unnumbered class to cover occasional payments of some £138,000 in 1786.[17]

The classification was not a method of appropriation, certainly not at first, though it became increasingly like it. It constituted an order of priority in which particular items were to be satisfied, should the lump sum prove insufficient. It was for that reason that the salaries of the Treasury Board were put last. If the sum proved insufficient to meet Class 8, the Treasury would have an incentive quickly to report the inadequacy to the House instead of allowing a large debt to pile up.

In as far as the object of the Act of 1782 was to reduce the chance of large debts accumulating without the knowledge of Parliament, it was not successful. Those whose duty it was to carry out the Act interpreted it in a way that allowed arrears to arise upon the different classes, except for the first two. Between 1786 and 1802 a debt of £990,053 accumulated and was paid off by Parliament. This led to the Act of 1804 (44 Geo. III, c.80) which added £60,000 a year to the Civil List revenue and stipulated that should any Class become in arrear for more than two quarters the Treasury had to lay an account of such arrears before Parliament. But though expenditure continued to exceed income, yet by the use of the 'Extraordinary Resources at the Disposal of the Crown' i.e. money outside the Civil List revenues, no arrears arose and no returns were therefore laid. That particular loophole was closed by the 1812 Act (52 Geo. III, c.6) which required a report to Parliament within one month whenever the deficiency on the List should exceed the average annual deficit since the 1804 Act, i.e. £124,000, by £10,000. This led to the state of the Civil List being laid before Parliament in the next Session.[18] Even in 1804 a House of Commons' Committee had been of the opinion, particularly in view of the rise in prices, that the revenue available for the Civil List was inadequate for the various services which the estimate of 1786 was calculated to meet.[19] Parliament had increasingly recognized this by voting Supply for many new items. The strict concept of the Civil List was also not helped by the House of Commons borrowing from it for specific items and repaying the money from the next Appropriation Act. The practice was criticized by the Select Committee on Finance of 1797 which pointed out that its use 'must necessarily occasion large and inconvenient Arrears upon some of the numerous Services for which the Civil List is specially intended.' The Treasury were of the same opinion and in future more of these items were included in the annual Appropriation Act.[20] After 1815 many were dealt with out of the vote for Civil Contingencies.*

It was not until the accession of William IV that any progress was made in separating the personal and the civil government elements in the List.* In 1830, on the death of George IV, there being no debt outstanding on the Civil List, the government assumed that an Act in the standard form would be acceptable. The proposal met unexpectedly strong opposition, the main criticism being that the king's personal expenses should not be mixed up with expenditure on the civil government of the country. It was also argued that many of these latter items should be brought under Parliamentary control by being voted annually. In the end the government was defeated on a Motion to establish a Select Committee to inquire into the Civil List and, being already in a weak position politically, resigned.

The Select Committee recommended that 'the Civil List should be applied only to such expenses as affect the Dignity and State of the Crown, and the proper maintenance of Their Majesties' Household.' The expenses of civil government included in the List 'ought to be always under the cognizance, and subject to the constant control of Parliament.' They also argued that while some provision ought to be made in the List 'for such payments as it might be presumed that the Sovereign would be desirous of making, if He had remained in possession of His Hereditary Revenue' the king only had a life interest in it and therefore no pension was legally due beyond the demise of the Crown. As a result they recommended only £75,000 for Pensions, as against £145,700 currently available.[21] The settlement brought into reckoning branches of revenue which hitherto had been 'secured to the sole and unquestioned disposal of The Crown', e.g. the Droits of the Crown and of Admiralty and the 4½ per cent Duties. Altogether then, no less than £696,000, which had previously been 'vested in the Crown for the life of the reigning Sovereign', was brought within the cognizance and control of

* Some potential economies were achieved in 1816 and 1820 by the transfer of certain pensions to the Consolidated Fund, with a corresponding reduction in the Civil List revenues. As a result, upon the death of the persons in receipt of the pensions, the savings accrued to the public revenues, not to the king.

Parliament. The transfer not only opened the way for greater economy, but ensured that any savings would accrue to the public purse.[22]

The net effect was a Civil List of £510,000 divided into five Classes: Privy Purse; Household Salaries; Household Expenses; Special and Secret Service; and Pensions. The power of the Treasury to apply savings at the end of the year on one Class in aid of other Classes, was continued. Six years later the sum settled on Queen Victoria was £385,000, the Privy Purse being cut from £110,000 to £60,000. The Home Secret Service was fixed at £10,000 and made a charge on the Consolidated Fund (1 and 2 Vict., c.2).

Though some of the items taken off the Civil List revenues were made permanent charges on the Consolidated Fund, the bulk had to be voted annually in future. Also, as the range of governmental activity expanded, other votes were required. As a result the annual Appropriation Act came to include an ever lengthening list of votes covered by the heading 'Miscellaneous Services' a thoroughly justified description. The first attempt to bring some order into them was made in 1824 in the Estimates which formed the basis for the votes. The classification was substantially revised in 1843 when the Estimates for Scotland and Ireland were distributed among the appropriate subject classes. The Select Committee on Miscellaneous Expenditure of 1848 recommended that in future the votes for civil establishments at home and abroad should be arranged in the classes used for the Civil Estimates.[23] The Appropriation Act of 1850 (13 and 14 Vict., c.107) for the first time arranged the Civil Services into seven groups, viz. I. Public Works and Buildings; II. Salaries and Expenses of Public Departments; III. Law and Justice; IV. Education, Science, and Art; V. Colonial and Consular Services; VI. Superannuation, Charities, etc.; and VII. Special and Temporary Objects. The vote for Civil Contingencies was shown separately. In 1854 a new, unnumbered class was introduced for the revenue departments.

VIREMENT

Though classification made the Estimates and Appropriations more coherent and easier to understand it had no legal significance. The 'Uses and Purposes' for which, according to the Appropriation Act, the money was only to be issued or applied were not the classes but the heads which made up each class. Thus in 1850 Class I of the Civil Services was made up of 14 heads and Class II of 23 heads. This meant that more than the sum voted could not be spent on any head even if there was an underspending on other heads within the same class.

The arrangements for Army, Navy, and Ordnance expenditure allowed more latitude. Until 1846 the Admiralty took the view that the sanction of the Treasury was not needed for the use of a surplus under one head to meet a deficiency on any other, provided the aggregate grant for Naval Services was not exceeded. This was the practice of virement, i.e. the transfer of funds allotted for one purpose or service to another. In 1846, (9 and 10 Vict., c.116) however, a new section was introduced into the Appropriation Act. Having confirmed that expenditure on Navy, Army, and Ordnance had to be confined to the separate services for which the money had been granted it added the proviso that if the 'Exigencies of the Public Service shall render it indispensably necessary' the Treasury, on a case being made out by the department concerned, could allow a surplus on one head to be used to make good a deficiency under another head provided this did not result in the aggregate sum voted for the Navy, Army, or Ordnance respectively, being exceeded.

After the merging of the Army and Ordnance departments and the Commissariat in 1854–5, the wording of the Appropriation Act remained wide enough to allow transfers within the whole range of the War Office votes. In view of the large sum involved this soon aroused criticism and the Committee of Public Accounts of 1862 quoted a resolution of the House of Commons of 30 March 1849: 'That when a certain amount of expenditure for a particular service has been determined upon by Parliament it is the bounden duty of the Department which has the service under its charge and control to take care that the expenditure does not exceed the amount placed at its disposal for that purpose.'[24] They thought that a deficiency on any vote should normally be met by coming to the House with a Supplementary Estimate but that provision needed to be made for occasions 'when the position of foreign affairs might render the immediate application' for such an Estimate 'injurious to the public interest.'[25]

The criticism led to a tightening up of the discretionary power. The Appropriation Act of 1862 (25 and 26 Vict., c.71) declared, 'if a Necessity shall arise for incurring Expenditure not provided for in the Sums appropriated to Naval and Military Services ... which it may be detrimental to the Public Services to postpone until Provision can be made for it by Parliament in the usual Course ...', the Treasury could authorize such expenditure to be met temporarily out of 'any Surpluses which may have been or which may be effected by the Saving of Expenditure upon Votes within the same Department.' The Treasury were required to report their action to the House of Commons within one month of the department's accounts being rendered to the Audit Board 'in order that such Proceedings may be submitted for the Sanction of Parliament, and that Provision may be made for the Deficiencies ... in such manner as Parliament shall determine.'

The power of virement was not allowed outside the Army and Navy Services. Most of the civil votes were for quite disparate purposes so that a saving on, say, the British Museum was hardly applicable to the civil establishment of New South Wales or the cost of criminal lunatics. Moreover, should it prove necessary to spend more than the sum voted under any head, the vote for Civil Contingencies could be drawn upon. The Appropriation Act of 1815 (55 Geo. III, c.187) had included £200,000 'For such Expenses of a Civil Nature as do not form part of the Ordinary Charges of the Civil List.' In the following year, £300,000 was provided for this general purpose. By 1835 the vote for Civil Contingencies had fallen to £130,000 and between 1844 and 1856 was at the rate of £100,000 a year. This arrangement avoided the earlier untidy system of borrowing from the Civil List annuity for small or unforeseen items of expenditure. Under the 1863 arrangements a Civil Contingency Fund, maintained at a level of £120,000, replaced the Civil Contingency vote, but remained under the direct control of the Treasury.

Finally, votes for the Civil Services were still not limited to being spent in a particular year: money unspent at the end of one year could be carried over and spent in the next year and so on. At 31 March 1856[26] there was some £643,000 unexpended balances carried forward from previous financial years. The bulk (£509,000) had been voted for 1854/5 but there was still £2,462 carried forward from 1841/2. A sizeable part had already been issued from the Exchequer and was available in the Pay Office. The same rule had applied to the Army and Navy votes until Appropriation Audit was introduced for this required the Audit Board to note 'under each Head whether the Expenditure has been exceeded or fallen short of the Sums voted by Parliament for the [Naval] Service of that year for which the Account is so made up' (2 Wm. IV, c.40). In other words, the Audit Board had to compare the money voted for the use of one year with the expenditure during that same year. The Treasury admitted in 1856 that control was deficient in regard to the whole of the Miscellaneous Services. It said ' . . . we have no appropriation account and have never had one for the civil services; grants have been voted from year to year, and the balances carried on; it has been a running cash account'. The main difficulty in the way of treating the Miscellaneous Civil Services in the same way as the Army and Navy, was the much later date at which the Estimates for these services were discussed and voted in Committee of Supply.[27]

An Appropriation Act was usually one of the last pieces of legislation passed in each Session. It could not start on its way through the procedure of both Houses until all the Estimates had been considered and the numerous resolutions agreed in Committee of Supply. On 19 February 1821 the House of Commons had passed a resolution requiring 'during the continuance of peace, whenever Parliament shall be assembled before Christmas, the Estimates for the Navy, Army and Ordnance departments should be presented before the 15th day of January then next following . . . [or] within ten days after the opening of the Committee of Supply, when Parliament shall not be assembled till after Christmas.[28] The latter was the more usual after 1830. The beginning of the financial year was changed from 1 January to 1 April in 1831 in order that Parliament might have the opportunity of voting the

Supplies for the Army and Navy before Easter.[29] It was usual for the Committee to start its work in late February or March and complete it in July. By the time an Appropriation Act became law, usually in August, the financial year was already over four months old. This did not matter so much when a balance unspent from the previous, or even earlier, years was available to meet expenditure in the early months of the year.

When expenditure on the Navy, Army, and Ordnance was made subject to Appropriation Audit and therefore became confined to the vote of the financial year, it had been necessary to find some means of making money legally available for the period April–August. This was achieved by a Consolidated Fund Act passed just before the beginning of the financial year whereby 'such sums of money as shall be raised by exchequer bills' could be issued and applied 'to such services as shall then have been voted by the commons in this present session of Parliament.'[30] It assumed that the votes in Committee of Supply would be formally legalized in the Appropriation Act. It was usual to vote in March the substantial sums in the Estimates for the pay of officers and seamen of the fleet and of the officers and men of the army as a kind of vote on account. Out of the sum under this heading, the departments could meet the early expenditure under any of the other heads.

This arrangement could not be applied to the Civil Services. There was no equivalent vote that could be used and in any case virement was not allowed between different heads. Moreover, many of the Estimates for the Miscellaneous Services were not completely dealt with or voted upon in Committee of Supply until June or July. Various possible solutions were discussed, but it was not until 1863 that Gladstone as Chancellor of the Exchequer could claim 'for the first time in our financial history, all the services were required to surrender the balances standing to their credit.'[31] On 27 March 1863 the amounts voted under a number of heads were in two parts: 'on account' and 'to complete the sum necessary to defray the [total] charges'. The figures for the Board of Trade, for example, were £15,000 and £47,181. The general principle seems to have been that the vote 'on account' should not be more than a quarter of the total vote.[32]

Inevitably the growing unwillingness of the House of Commons to allow a surplus under one head to be used for the purpose of another vote, drew attention to the principles on which the heads were determined. The more numerous the heads the more detailed the control of the House. The general tendency since the beginning of the century had been to multiply the number of heads and by 1850 there were some 110 for the seven classes of Civil Services. From time to time there were arguments as to whether a particular head should be subdivided. In their evidence to the Select Committee on Public Moneys the Treasury expressed the view that 'the whole of the detailed votes are so numerous now, that they extend far beyond what they ought to do . . . the first step should be to classify the Estimates better and reduce the number of votes'. Each of the 200-odd votes needed a separate Royal Order and a separate Treasury Warrant.[33]

There was, however, another aspect: the relation between the sums voted under each head and the Estimates on which the sums were based. By 1850 the Estimates were presented in great detail, but none of this detail found its way into the annual Appropriation Act. Yet the only legal limitation on the Treasury or on the spending department was that it should not exceed the sum stated in that Act. Theoretically, there-fore, it could spend that sum in quite a different way than had been set out in the Estimates. This did not matter a great deal when the sum voted was small and for a clearly defined purpose. In contrast the sum voted for the salaries and incidental expenses of the Board of Trade covered not only the general work of the department but also *inter alia* the salaries and expenses of the General Register and Record Office of Seamen, and the Office for the Registration of Joint Stock Companies. The Estimates showed the proposed expenditure for each section of the Board's work: the Appropriation Act showed only a single sum.

The problem grew with the expanding work of the various departments. The answer was found not in multiplying the number of votes, but in the introduction of sub-heads. In 1867 the recently established Committee of Public Accounts heard evidence from two officials appointed by the Treasury to inquire into various questions of classification and arrangement arising from the application to the Civil Services of the principle of Appropriation Audit by the Exchequer and Audit Departments Act 1866. Foster and Vine, the two officials concerned, recommended that each Vote should be divided into sub-heads — the Estimates for each Vote being subtitled 'sub-heads under which the Vote will be Accounted for'. The recommendation was accepted by the Public Accounts Committee[34] and the Estimates for the year ending 31 March 1868 were the first so divided.

The significant Class so far as Parliamentary control of the main departments was concerned was II. Salaries and Expenses of Public Departments. Each department had a single vote, divided into sub-heads according to its major activities. In 1870–1 the Foreign Office with a vote of £64,814 had only four sub-heads whereas the Home Office with a vote of £87,032 had thirty-four sub-heads to cover its various Inspectorates and other separate activities. The seven Classes of Civil Services were covered by 145 votes which were subdivided into well over a thousand sub-heads. The Army Estimates contained twenty-five and the Navy Estimates seventeen votes, most of which were divided into sub-heads.

This move still left open the degree of the discretion of departments to vary their expenditure between the various sub-heads. For, as the sub-heads were not included in the Appropriation Act, there was legally no barrier against virement between them. It was, however, a moral or political obligation, accepted by the government that a department would not deviate from these sub-heads without very good cause. Deviation was an action which had to be explained to the Comptroller and Auditor-General and possibly, by way of his report, to the Public Accounts Committee,* and, as in all matters of this kind, the Treasury were expected to see that virement between sub-heads was not used improperly by departments.

THE RISE OF TREASURY CONTROL

One of the most important elements both in the increasing authority of the House of Commons and in the concen-

* The Committee even showed an interest in subdivisions of subheads (cf. First Report, PP 1870, Vol. x, Qq 1485–99).

tration of administrative authority was the rise of Treasury control.

The great growth of public expenditure forced the House to take a deep interest in all aspects of the public finances. But it was not well placed to exercise any continuous interest of an administrative character. It could establish Commissions and Committees to investigate and report, it could call for information and returns, and it could debate and pass resolutions. But for subsequent action it needed some permanent executive body: it found this in the Lords Commissioners of the Treasury. The point can be illustrated by an examination and comparison of three of the Acts passed during the heyday of economical reform.

The Act of 1783 (23 Geo. III, c.82) for the better regulation of the Exchequer provided for the abolition of certain sinecure offices and the replacement of fee remuneration by salaries in the case of certain others. It involved no executive action other than obedience to the law, the requirements of which were clear and precise. The salaries had, however, to be fixed and the Treasury was given authority to do this.

The Civil List Act, 1782 (22 Geo. III, c.82) was in striking contrast. It provided for the suppression of certain offices paid from the Civil List, but could not provide in precise legal terms for the consequential details of the suppression, nor for the compensation to be paid to those being dispossessed. The Act, therefore, specified a number of offices to be suppressed, but definition of the offices 'dependent on or connected' which were consequently to be suppressed, was made a responsibility of the Commissioners of the Treasury. The Treasury Board were also empowered to determine the annuities to be paid to holders of suppressed subordinate offices as they thought 'equitable and just' and according to 'his or their Abilities and Merit'.

The third statute, the Exchequer Audit Act 1785 (25 Geo. III, c.52), replaced the offices of the two Auditors of the Imprests by a Commission for auditing the Public Accounts. In this case the amount of compensation to the Auditors and their Deputies was fixed by the Act and so there was no need to bring in the Treasury. The five new Commissioners were to be appointed by the king. The Act contained a number of provisions stating the Treasury's relations with the Audit Commission.

The contents of these three Acts illustrate two important points bearing on the early relations between the Treasury Board and Parliament. In the first place the Lords Commissioners were in an unusual position for the time in that they were exercising statutory as well as prerogative powers. The Treasury was the first department to cease to exist purely or largely on prerogative powers — excluding, of course, the revenue boards.

Secondly, it was not felt to be contrary to the royal prerogative for a particular part of the king's government to be singled out by Parliament to undertake particular tasks. The House of Commons could hardly have dealt with the suppression of the large number of offices and employments it intended in the 1782 Act without help from the Executive. It could have achieved this by making it lawful for the king to settle the details and the individual compensation. But in a sense it was already lawful for His Majesty to do these things, indeed his understanding of the situation was that he was personally going to deal with his Household, leaving the Commons to deal with the 'civil government' posts. The designation of the Commissioners of the Treasury reflected, therefore, the feeling of the House that in all matters affecting finance, the Treasury was the particular and designated part of the Executive on which the House could rely to carry out those wishes which could not be specifically defined in legislation or which required continuing executive action.

The designation of a particular element in the king's government, rather than relying on the Crown in general, also indicated a strong desire on the part of the House of Commons to deal with a single agency in all matters concerning the nation's finances. This was already the role of the Treasury Board in respect of the revenue, whether taxation or borrowing; they wished it to have the same role in respect of expenditure. One of Edmund Burke's four objectives in March 1782 was 'the destruction of *all* subordinate Treasuries, by subjecting every expense in every department to the Treasury.'[35] According to Roseveare, Burke was 'the first statesman to envisage a partnership in government between a sovereign legislature and an omnipotent Treasury. He wanted effective Treasury control as a condition of effective parliamentary control.'[36]

A recurrent theme in the reports of the numerous Parliamentary Committees of the first fifty years of the nineteenth century was the need for centralized control of the various aspects of the financial system. The Committee on Public Expenditure of 1810 were worried that no general power lodged in the Audit Board 'to embrace and comprehend in any degree the whole examination of that important branch of the public concerns', i.e. that of examining and passing the different public accounts. 'Had the public accounts . . .' they said, 'been under the immediate superintendence of any one department possessing authority . . . and immediately responsible to Parliament, it is neither probable or possible, that the defects of inconveniencies of passing accounts according to the useless forms of the Exchequer could have remained to the present day;'. Their belief in a single controlling body did not, however, point clearly in the direction of the Treasury. 'The Board of Treasury, to whom this duty might be conceived more immediately to belong, has at no time exercised a systematic control over the public accounts; neither would such an employment be compatible with the regular functions, and ordinary occupations of that Board, nor consistent with those urgent executive duties in which it is constantly engaged . . .'[37]

There were, however, more general forces at work. One of the great rallying-points was uniformity and unification, e.g. that all the public accounts should be for the same period, or that there should be a single bank account. Writing in 1831 Sir Henry Parnell[38] placed great emphasis on the need for much greater uniformity in the public accounts. There was, he said,

no uniformity in the constitution and organization of the great departments that conduct the public expenditure, nor any uniformity of classification of business in the several branches of these departments. The Crown, even in exercising its prerogative in regard to the issues of money by the Exchequer does so according to no uniform rule — sometimes an issue is made by privy seal, sometimes by warrants; . . . some for issuing at once the whole sum voted by Parliament, some for a part of it, some for the period of a year, and some for a whole reign.[38]

He seemed to be implying that differences in treatment were always wrong, only uniformity was right. But even without going that far the move towards uniformity was undoubted, and uniformity is easier to achieve in a centralized than in a dispersed system of power. The Treasury was to be the centralizing force.

As part of its attempts both to control and to learn more about the public finances, the House of Commons were seldom for long without an important Select Committee. These Committees began to expect the Treasury to express a Treasury view on any aspect of the country's financial arrangements. There is a difference here between the procedure adopted by the Commissioners who inquired into the Public Accounts and into Fees in the 1780s, and that adopted by House of Commons Committees thirty or so years later. The former relied on departmental evidence for the information and on their own knowledge and experience for their recommendations. The Commission inquiring into fees in the Admiralty and the offices of the Secretaries of State did not, for example, call for Treasury evidence or opinion. By the middle of the nineteenth century it would have been hardly conceivable that a Parliamentary Committee should be inquiring into expenditure or establishments without obtaining the view of the Treasury as well as of the departments directly affected.

The Reports of the Select Committee on Finance of 1797–8 are probably a turning-point. The Committee was set up in response to a renewed compaign for economical reform. The House and the Committee wanted to know what progress had been made in carrying out the recommendations of the two Commissions of 1780–6. Shelburne, now Lord Lansdowne, and a powerful figure in the reform movement of the early 1780s, had launched a vigorous attack on Pitt in May 1796 for ignoring the recommendations of the Commissioners for Examining the Public Accounts. He blamed the failings on the unwillingness of the Treasury to take effective action. ' . . . instead of giving the first lord a staff . . . I would give him a knife to cut off every man's fingers that dared thrust his hand into the public purse.'[39] Pitt, however, was not really 'Treasury minded'. The concept of Treasury imperialism, as propounded by Burke and Shelburne, seems to have left him unmoved. No doubt he also remembered the criticism of his unsuccessful Public Offices Regulation Bill of 1783 by Lord Stormont: 'It gave most extraordinary powers to the Treasury, and diminished the necessary power and the dignity of the other offices . . . several of the great offices of the state had ever been distinct and independent; but this Bill gave the Treasury a painful pre-eminence over all of them, and made every one of the rest subject to its control.'[40]

The Select Committee on Finance reiterated many of the criticisms of the two earlier Commissions. The charge that they had not been sufficiently active led the Lords Commissioners to publish in the years 1798–1803 an account of their efforts to follow up the various recommendations. The documents are of considerable interest as showing the relations between the Treasury and the various departments and agencies at that time. Their immediate significance, however, is that the Treasury felt it necessary to explain what it was doing about the implementation of recommendations not only in respect of matters clearly within its departmental competence, but also in respect of those falling within the competence of the Secretaries of State and the Admiralty.

The Treasury claimed to have acted immediately upon the publication of the Select Committee's reports. Where the issue clearly fell within their authority they had made a decision, for example, to abolish New Year's gifts made to the department. In some cases they had called the attention of other departments concerned to a particular criticism or recommendation. They adopted a noticeable difference in tone in their approach to subordinate departments and, for example, to the Secretaries of State. Thus, in their letter to the Tax Commissioners, having pointed out that arrears of taxes from Receivers-General had again attracted the notice of the Committee of Finance of the House of Commons, they directed the attention of the Tax Board to a passage in the report and asked whether more could be done 'for more immediately recovering the said Arrears'. But when the 'senior' of the joint secretaries wrote to the Under Secretary at the Foreign department, he used the wording: the Lords Commissioners 'desire to represent to Lord Grenville that the Reports of the Select Committee on Finance in the last Session will soon be under Consideration of Parliament, and that their Lordships are desirous of receiving his Lordship's . . . Sentiments on any Matters contained in the Sixteenth Report, with respect to the Office of Secretary of State.' Letters in similar terms went to the Under-Secretary at the Home department and to the Lords Commissioners of the Admiralty. The tart replies to the inquiries received from the powerful Ministers justified the Treasury's cautious approach.

The general opinion in the House of Commons clearly favoured the Treasury playing the major role in matters of public expenditure. The Select Committee on Finance of 1817 referred to the Lords of the Treasury 'as the official and responsible advisers of the Crown upon all matters which relate to the superintendence and control over the public expenditure.'[41] In a later report they said

no department of large expenditure ought ever to be placed beyond the controlling superintendence of the Lords Commissioners of the Treasury. From them every other office should expect, and from them the House will require, not a judgment as to the best mode of constructing, maintaining or improving the works respectively belonging to each separate branch; but a judicious and economical allotment to every one of them, of such limited sums as can be assigned with a due regard to the necessary expenses of every other service, and of the necessities as well as of the resources of the country.[42]

This is a classic statement of the central role of the Treasury in securing the proper allocation of limited public resources.

In 1828 a Select Committee on Income and Expenditure drew attention to the fact that 'the ancient and wise control vested by our financial policy in the hands of the Treasury over all the departments connected with the public expenditure, has been in a great degree set aside'. They wanted restored to the Treasury its 'ancient authority'. Though the Committee exaggerated the degree of antiquity they were clear as to what they had in mind,

. . . this control should be constantly exercized, in determining the amount of expenditure to be incurred by each department; in securing the application of each sum voted in the annual estimates to the service for which it has been voted; in regulating any extraordinary expenditure which, upon an emergency, may be deemed necessary within the year, although not included in the estimates; and in preventing any increase of salary, of extra allowance, or any other emoluments, being granted, without a Minute, expressive of the approbation of the Board of Treasury.

Significantly they added that the control could not be restored and made secure against being set aside again 'except by the House of Commons constantly enforcing its application by holding the Treasury responsible for every act of expenditure in each Department.'[43]

There is evidence that in some part the views of these Parliamentary Committees were stimulated by Sir George Harrison,[44] the first Assistant Secretary of the Treasury. He extolled the doctrine that the Treasury 'are responsible to Parliament and the country as the legitimate and only constitutional advisers of the Crown' in all matters relating to 'the powers and authorities which the Crown, by its ancient constitutional prerogative, might exercise with regard to its revenues'. Within the bounds of the common law and the prerogative, and unless specifically limited by Parliament, this was an absolute discretion. The Treasury was the sole constitutional judge of the propriety and expediency of expenditure, and it followed that the Treasury was '*a superintending*, and *directing*, not an *executive* department'. He stressed that supervision and control should be centralized in the Treasury. He expressed views of this nature to the Committees of 1810 and 1819 and seems to have found a champion in Sir Henry Parnell, an active Member on financial matters, and first holder of the revised office of Paymaster-General, 1835–41. As regards the control of the level of expenditure, Harrison based much of his case on treatment of the Ordnance expenditure which, he claimed, was under 'a constant, efficient and *complete* discretion' of the Treasury Board, 'until the tacit assumption of independence by the Duke of Richmond in 1783'.

Reference to the control of expenditure during this period

could mean either of two quite different purposes and processes: either ensuring that money was spent in accordance with Parliament's decisions, i.e. was issued for the purpose for which it had been appropriated or ensuring that the level of expenditure voted for any service was not more than sufficient to enable that service to be performed efficiently. The Committee of 1810 were somewhat concerned with the former concept, whereas the Committee of 1817 were emphasizing the latter. The two raised different issues for the role of the Treasury. In a sense the former had been a Treasury responsibility for a long time in that no money could be issued from the Exchequer without the formal consent of the Lords Commissioners. The latter was a less clearly accepted role for the Treasury. Yet in the course of the nineteenth century it was the latter which came to be stressed as the Treasury's significant role, whilst the former moved away from it into the hands of a Parliamentary Officer. We will therefore deal first with the second meaning.

Three elements in the constitutional arrangements ultimately gave the Treasury pre-eminence. First, the Standing Order of the House of Commons that it would 'receive no Petition for any Sum of Money relating to Publick Service, but what is recommended from the Crown'. Second, the unification of the public accounts and the closing of various loopholes in the use of the public revenues increasingly underlined the fact that total expenditure had to be matched by equivalent revenue. The Chancellor of the Exchequer was the Minister who had to present the demands for taxes and borrowing. In order to do this he had to have early information about what expenditure was being contemplated by departments during the coming year. That and the Standing Order no doubt accounted for the emergence of the internal rule that all estimates required the sanction of the Treasury before they could be submitted to the House of Commons. Third, much public expenditure was in any case the direct responsibility of the Treasury, e.g. the servicing of the national debt, the cost of revenue collection and a large part of the cost of civil government.

Each year the Treasury wrote to departments asking them to provide an estimate of the expenditure they wished to incur in the coming financial year. By the middle of the century some twenty-five letters of request were sent out. The Clerk of Parliamentary Accounts, a Treasury post created in 1824, put the departmental returns into the classes and form in which they would have to be submitted to the House. They then reached the Chancellor the Exchequer, via the Financial Secretary. Sometimes the Chancellor would take exception to certain items or the sums involved and the Estimate would then be returned to the department. In 1848 the whole of the Estimates were returned to departments with a direction asking that they reconsider them and make every reduction possible. The Miscellaneous Estimates were submitted to the Committee of Supply by a Treasury Minister.[45]

The Army and Navy Estimates were prepared in those departments and submitted to the House by their Ministers. The totals were decided by the general decisions, e.g. about the size of the forces, usually taken in Cabinet in the light of strategic considerations. The First Lord of the Admiralty (the Duke of Somerset) told the Public Accounts Committee in 1862 that the Navy Estimates were formally submitted to the Treasury, but the total and the amounts under the main headings had already been settled in his discussions with the Chancellor of the Exchequer. The Treasury did not scrutinize the Navy Estimates in detail and the First Lord did not think they could do so effectively, not having the information available to the Admiralty. He claimed that 'unless the Treasury are prepared to take the whole responsibility of the conduct of the Navy, they cannot possibly take such management of the details.'[46] Should the Chancellor of the Exchequer disagree with any of the main sums put forward by the First Lord, the latter would probably ask the Cabinet to decide the issue. The Admiralty's special position was due in large measure to most of their expenditure being incurred overseas and to the continually changing nature of the Navy's commitments.

Finally, the Commons saw the importance of Treasury control of establishment, pay, and conditions. When in 1810 the House of Commons agreed to the general application of a superannuation formula already applied in the Customs, it also resolved 'that no such Pension or Allowance should either be granted in any Office, or presented by way of Estimate to this House, until it shall have been submitted to the Commissioners of His Majesty's Treasury, and approved by them, . . .' Shortly afterwards the Treasury's position in these matters was given statutory form (50 Geo. III, c.117).

The Select Committee of 1817 in their report on sinecures, pensions, and salaries said

> Your Committee do not feel themselves competent to recommend any general regulation by which the proper scale of salary . . . may be settled . . . Your Committee are therefore of opinion that it should be left to the judgment and responsibility of the Lords of the Treasury . . . as vacancies occur, to place the several offices proposed to be regulated upon such an establishment with respect to the number and rank of the persons requisite for the discharge of the efficient functions of such offices, and the amount of salary to be assigned to each person, as may appear to them adequate, after a full enquiry into the nature and extent of the duties to be performed, and the degree of official and pecuniary responsibility which necessarily attaches to some of them.

They suggested that a requirement to lay before Parliament a comparative statement of the number, duty, and emoluments under the old and new establishments 'would be sufficient to prevent any abuse of a power which seems properly to belong to the Lords of the Treasury, as the official and responsible advisers of the Crown upon all matters which relate to the superintendence and control over the public expenditure.'[47]

In their third Report the Select Committee recognized the repercussions of any salary change in one department upon other departments. 'The desire of equalising their emoluments to those of other departments, is so natural to all offices, that whenever an advance is made in any of them it will be followed by applications and give rise to pretensions in almost every other, and to dissatisfaction if these representations are not complied with.'[48] Here again it was to be the responsibility of Treasury to watch over any increases in whatever department they were first applied.

By 1850 any department wishing to increase its establishment had to seek Treasury approval giving the details and the reasons for the increase.[49] A study of the Colonial Office[50] shows that by 1830 decisions about the salaries and the numbers receiving them had definitely passed out of the hands of the Secretary of State. When in 1836 the House of Commons appointed a Select Committee to enquire into fees and emoluments, the Committee, having met, thought it more appropriate for the inquiry to be undertaken by the government. As a result a Treasury Minute of November 1836 established a departmental Committee of four. The Treasury wrote to all departments telling them to provide the Committee with information and to send representatives to be examined personally.[51]

Whilst the control of numbers in a department involved issues similar to the control of expenditure, the control of pay and conditions involved different considerations. The Treasury was bound to approve expenditure sufficient to enable a department to carry out Cabinet policy effectively. The numbers to be employed were but part of that calculation. But if a department wished to increase the pay of its chief clerk or solicitor, the Treasury had to take account of the repercussions of that increase on the pay of chief clerks and solicitors in all similar departments. This was recognized and accepted more readily than the Treasury's right to control the level of expenditure.

It is little wonder that even by 1855 Sir Charles Trevelyan could claim that the Treasury was 'the chief office of the Government'. He stated 'Two-thirds of the Civil Establishments are directly subordinate to it, and the expenditure of the remaining third is under its superintendence. No estimate can be laid before Parliament, no new appointment can be created, and no alteration can be made in any Civil or Military allowances, without its sanction. The whole Public Service is, therefore, either directly or indirectly subjected to the influence of this Office.'[52]

AUDIT

The elimination of sundry sources of uncontrolled revenue, the closing of the various loopholes in the system of Parliamentary control, and the creation of a single fund for revenue and expenditure made it easier for the House of Commons to control total public expenditure. Increases in any item, unless offset by savings on other items, led to an increase in taxation. Chancellors of the Exchequer, whose Parliamentary and public reputations turned on their annual Budgets, were unlikely to demand increased taxation unless they were very hard pressed by their Cabinet colleagues. The House therefore started to devote more attention to whether the appropriations it made were respected by the Executive. When the king 'lived of his own', the only safeguard needed was provided by the Course of Exchequer as affirmed in the Act of 1697 (8 and 9 Wm. III, c.28). Money was not to be paid out of the Exchequer, but by the king's authority — in other words, in pursuance of 'some sufficient Grant or Authority' from His Majesty under the Great Seal or under the Privy Seal. While the Lords Commissioners of the Treasury were the officers responsible for the proper use of the king's authority, the Act placed a special obligation on the Auditor of the Receipt, the Clerk of the Pells and the Tellers to ensure compliance.

Appropriation introduced a new responsibility. It was no longer just a matter of securing the king's approval to any expenditure, it was now necessary to pay rgard to the intentions of Parliament. By the middle of the eighteenth century it was standard form for each Appropriation Act to lay down quite clearly that the 'Aids and Supplies . . . shall not be issued or applied to any Use, or Purpose whatsoever, other than the Uses and Purposes before mentioned, or for the several Deficiencies or other payments directed to be satisfied thereout, by any Act . . .' (1 Geo. III, c.19). Until well into the nineteenth century the House of Commons had no certain way of knowing whether the money voted for specified uses or purposes had been spent accordingly. This was not because there was no system of audit, for the two Auditors of the Imprests were among the most ancient of the king's officers. Each was empowered to audit and determine, with the advice, authority, and consent of the Commissioners of the Treasury, the accounts of most officials and persons who had received public money by way of imprest and on account. The Excise accounts were audited by separate statutory auditors and those of the Colonial Customs by the Auditor for America. The arrangements worked reasonably well in preventing fraud and peculation. They were, however, unable to cope with the vast increase in war expenditure, much of it overseas. Nor were they and the accounting system designed to deal with the new problems arising from the increasing interest of the House of Commons in the process of appropriation.

Like so many of the changes introduced in the 1780s the desires to economize and to get rid of sinecures were stronger forces than any theoretical ideas about the requirements of Parliamentary control. The Auditors of the Imprests were typical of the officers and administrative arrangements which aroused the anger and scorn of Burke and his followers. In 1783 each received some £16,000 a year in fees, even though their duties were carried out by their deputies and half a dozen clerks. In 1785 (25 Geo. III, c.52) their offices were abolished: but each remained entitled to £7,000 a year until his death. They were replaced by a board of five Commissioners for Auditing the Public Accounts, two of whom were ex officio (the Comptrollers of Army Accounts). In making the change Pitt's primary aims were to achieve an ultimate economy and to reduce the arrears of work. The Act did not change the character or purpose of the audit.

In 1799 the duties of the three Auditors of the Land Revenues were transferred to the Commission (39 Geo. III, c.83). The War with France greatly increased the volume of audit work and in 1805 an additional Board of Audit of three Commissioners was appointed to deal with the arrears on the Army accounts (45 Geo. III, c.91). A year later the two Boards were consolidated. The king was empowered to increase the number of Commissioners to ten. The two holders of the Office of Comptrollers of Army Accounts ceased to be ex-officio members. The Treasury were empowered to divide the Commissioners into sub-boards and apportion the business between them (46 Geo. II, c.141).

The very big increase in public expenditure caused the House of Commons to look at the role and character of the system of audit. In 1810 a Select Committee on Public Expenditure were of the opinion that the present system had failed, even though it had greatly reduced the arrears of work. The Committee claimed that there was practically no general control or superintendence over the accounts of certain departments and that the Audit Board lacked vigour and efficiency. They recommended, *inter alia*, the simplification of all proceedings relative to all accounts and the enlargement of the discretion and powers of the Commissioners.[53]

When the issue was looked at again in 1819 by the Select Committee on Finance, the Treasury were asked why the Audit Board could not be brought into the process of the issue of money and not confined to an examination of its spending. The Treasury, in the form of Sir George Harrison, explained at some length. The Crown by its Sign Manual warrant, countersigned by the Lord High Treasurer or three Lords of the Treasury, directed an issue of money from the Exchequer to a particular officer for the purpose of it being expended by him on a particular service. He went on:

If a power were vested in any independent board of audit of entering into the consideration of the objects or motives of this expenditure, for the purpose of questioning its *propriety* or *expediency*, it would . . . in effect, be vesting in this independent board a power of questioning of all the acts of the crown, and of trying the whole conduct of the executive government in regard to its expenditure . . . would amount to a delegation by Parliament, to this independent board, of those powers and functions which constitutionally belong, and ought to belong to Parliament and to Parliament alone.[54]

The primary concern of the Select Committee of 1810 was with the loss and waste of money due to wrongful acts and mismanagement, and even the Select Committee of 1819 had these very much in mind. It was rather later that the emphasis changed to the role of the auditor in securing proper conformance with the Appropriation Acts. In part this new emphasis arose out of a growing dissatisfaction with the role and working of the Exchequer,that traditional guardian of the public moneys. Such changes that were made — e.g. the abolition of certain offices, the conversion of others from a fee to a salaried basis, and the ending of the use of deputies — simplified but did not materially change the ancient Course of Exchequer.

In 1831, on the initiative of the Treasury, Commissioners of Public Accounts were appointed, under the Chairmanship of Sir Henry Parnell, to inquire into 'the several Modes in which the Public Money is received and paid'. After paying a tribute to the Exchequer as 'the great conservator of the Revenues of the Nation,' they went on to point out that 'notwithstanding the extensive changes and improvements which experience and civilization have so generally introduced into pecuniary transactions the forms of the Exchequer have undergone little or no amendment or alteration'. A much more efficient, economical system could be safely and advantageously introduced. They proposed that the functions of the Exchequer of Receipt should be placed in the hands of a new Officer — a Comptroller-General of the Exchequer, employing a total staff of nine as against the sixty-eight then employed. They also recommended that a committee independent of the Crown should be chosen annually by the House of Commons to examine and report on the general statement of accounts submitted by a Comptroller-General before the Annual Budget was voted.[55]

In 1834 the Auditor of the Receipt (Lord Grenville) died and so removed any awkward obstacle to the reorganization of the Lower Exchequer.* An Act of that year (4 and 5 Wm. IV, c.15) abolished the offices of Auditor of the Receipt and Clerk of the Pells and transferred their powers to a new officer — a Comptroller-General of the Receipt and Issue of the Exchequer. He was to be appointed by Letters Patent under the Great Seal and be removable only on the Address of the two Houses of Parliament. The Comptroller was required to satisfy himself that any Royal Order for the issue of money was in conformity with and did not exceed the amount granted by Parliament and that any Treasury warrant was in conformity with and did not exceed the amount in the Royal Order. The change greatly simplified the Course of Exchequer but left it with most of its authority in respect of the issue of money.

The significant difference between controlling the issue and auditing the spending came to be recognized with the success of the system of Appropriation Audit introduced in 1832–3. The immediate cause of its introduction was the discovery by Sir James Graham, on becoming First Lord of the Admiralty

---

* The structure of the Upper Exchequer had been abolished in 1833 leaving only the offices of the Chancellor of the Exchequer and of the King's Remembrancer and the judicial Court of Exchequer pleas.

in November 1830, that the appropriations for Naval Services had been disregarded for some years. The Navy had been employing more men than were provided for in the votes: in one year as many as 3,100 men in excess. The money had largely come from the votes for timber and the material for building ships. In the case of timber the sums voted over four years totalled £3,705,000 whereas only £2,675,00 had been spent. This discovery, which Graham had to reveal to the House of Commons, and the confused manner in which the Admiralty kept its accounts, led him not only to reorganize the department but also to improve the system of accounts and audit.

It was generally agreed that the causes were loose estimates which did not truly represent the financial requirements of the service; an incomplete system of accounts which did not and could not show the naval expenditure under the heads of the separate grants; a tardy examination of the accounts; and, above all, the absence of any returns to the House of Commons showing how the intentions of Parliament had been complied with.

Without correct accounts of past expenditure it was impossible to prepare current estimates of future expenditure. In the absence of correct accounts of current expenditure it was impossible to regulate properly the application of the annual grants. Without a complete system of accounts . . . balanced accounts of the naval expenditure compared with the separate grants could not be prepared for the information of Parliament.[56]

In 1831 the Commissioners of Accounts had recommended the mercantile system of bookkeeping by double entry the 'peculiar excellency' of which 'consists in the facility with which it embraces accounts, however complex, various and extensive; giving to all their differences of detail a unity of result . . .' They claimed that a system of public accounts founded on this system was the best security 'for the faithful appropriation of the public money'.[57] The system was applied to the Navy.

The Navy Accounts Act, 1832 (2 Wm. IV, c.40) required the Commissioners for Audit to examine the accounts and vouchers for naval expenditure side by side with the votes and the estimates. An annual account was to be placed before

Parliament, certified as to its accuracy by the Audit Board. These arrangements were extended in 1846 (9 and 10 Vict., c.92) to the accounts of the War Office, Commissariat, and Ordnance; in 1851 to the Offices of Woods and Forests and of Works and Building (14 and 15 Vict., c.42); in 1861 to the revenue departments (24 and 25 Vict., c.93), and to the rest of the departmental accounts by the Exchequer and Audit Departments Act of 1866 (29 and 30 Vict., c.39).

In 1856 a Select Committee on Public Moneys was appointed to inquire into the receipt, issue, and audit of public moneys. The Chancellor of the Exchequer (Sir George Cornewall Lewis), a member of the Committee, recognized the need for a check on the issue of money for, if Ministers 'had an uncontrolled power of applying the public revenue' they might after the annual Mutiny Act had been passed, 'induce the Crown to prorogue or dissolve Parliament, and might carry on the Government by expending the public revenue without legal authority.' A check had, therefore, been provided 'by vesting the power of issue in an independent office, the Exchequer.' The present system of Exchequer control was, however, aimed at something beyond this, i.e. to secure the application of the separate grants in conformity with the directions of Parliament. But, he argued, this check was imaginery. A great deal of the money issued took the form of advances or imprests to be spent abroad which could not be appropriated at the time of issue. This imaginary control should be abandoned and a real control substituted. In other words, the Office of the Receipt of the Exchequer under the Comptroller-General should be abolished and reliance placed on something else.

The Treasury were undoubtedly irked by the continual assertion of authority by the Comptroller-General. As T. Spring Rice he had been Chancellor of the Exchequer between April 1835 and August 1839. He was a strong upholder of Parliamentary control and had wanted to be Speaker in 1839: instead he was made Comptroller-General and in 1841 became Lord Monteagle. The Chancellor of the Exchequer claimed that the office had two defects. First, because control took place at the point of issue it meant the retention of a stage in the financial process which the 1834 Act had aimed to simplify. The Comptroller-General was in effect a part of the executive machinery. He received the authorization from the Treasury, scrutinized it, and checked its validity against 'the Parliamentary grant and when satisfied, gave instructions to the Bank of England which held the balances out of which payments were made.' The Chancellor of the Exchequer said: 'The controlling department should not, on principle, be charged with the duty of conducting the executive details of the business.'

Second, and more important, for Parliament, the check took place too early in the financial process. The fact that money was issued to a department for a particular purpose was no guarantee that it was spent in that way. The only real check was an audit of expenditure. The Chancellor declared: 'it is a deception upon the public to maintain a law which imposes upon that department [i.e. the Exchequer] the duty of controlling the application of the votes of Parliament which it is manifestly impossible it can discharge.' Instead of the imaginary control a real control should be substituted which 'should follow the money from its collection from the taxpayer until the final appropriation of it in payment of the public creditor.'

The Chancellor argued that the responsibility for the regular conduct of the public payments should rest on the Treasury alone, the check being provided by a requirement that two of the Audit Commissioners should need to countersign the Treasury Certificate to the Banks of England and Ireland giving those banks legal authority to the extent of the sums so certified. Better control over the spending of the money would also be secured by extending the Appropriation Audit to the whole of the public accounts. There should also be greater publicity. Each quarter the Treasury should, he suggested, publish an account showing the votes of the preceding Session, the cash payments in respect of each vote and the balances remaining unissued. The account should be signed by the Secretary of the Treasury and certified by the Audit Commissioners. Finally, the House should nominate a small Finance Committee of four Members to assist the Speaker in his responsibility for assuring the House that the moneys it had voted had been correctly applied. After the close of the financial year the Committee would receive accounts signed by the Secretary of the Treasury and authenticated by the Audit Board.[58]

The weakness of the Treasury's proposals lay in the uncertain independence of the Commissioners for Audit. Their Patent empowered them to audit and determine accounts 'by and with the advice, authority and consent of the [Treasury Board] and Chancellor of the Exchequer . . .' If, for example, the Audit Board disallowed a sum, the accountant or department concerned could appeal to the Treasury who were empowered to direct by warrant signed by two Lords Commissioners that the sum should be allowed. Again, where the Treasury gave the Paymaster directions to make a payment, the Auditors could not disallow it even if they thought it contrary to an Act of Parliament. Sir Henry Parnell claimed in 1856 that the attempt to make the Audit Board a control over the Treasury had proved a complete failure. 'It could not be otherwise from the nature of things. One cause . . . is the power possessed by the Treasury over all its proceedings; the want of means to give effect to its decisions is another.'[59]

Certainly when Sir George Harrison was Assistant Secretary the status of the Audit Commission suited the Treasury. He jealously guarded the position of the department as a tribunal of appeal from the auditor's findings and as having the power to relieve public accountants.[60] The Chancellor did not deal specifically with the question in his lengthy memorandum nor did the official Treasury in their evidence. But the Principal Clerk of Finance (W. G. Anderson) in his memorandum stated 'Let your system be based on confidence in the Government, and let the controlling and responsible department of the State [i.e. the Treasury] have full freedom of action.'[61] There was an echo of this in the Chancellor's memorandum: it was, he said,

the object of the measures recommended, to supply these deficiencies by providing additional securities for the due fulfilment of the intentions of the Legislature . . . to strengthen the control of the Treasury and of Parliament over the departments of expenditure, and to fix in a more decisive manner the responsibility of the Government for all its financial acts, without fettering unnecessarily the free action of the Executive; . . .[62]

Thus, the Treasury felt that it could and should be trusted. It was on the same side as the House of Commons as regards the control of expenditure. It was not one of those spending departments which had to be watched very carefully both as to the amount of money they were voted and how they spent it. There was also a strong hint that the Treasury wanted a certain amount of freedom and discretion and not be bound too tightly by the Appropriation procedure.

The proposals of the Chancellor of the Exchequer found favour neither with Edward Romily, Chairman of the Audit Board, nor with Lord Monteagle. The former affirmed that the duty of an auditor of public accounts should be to pass in review the acts of an accountant 'after those acts have been completed'. Any interferences, direct or indirect, on the part of the auditors previous to payment being made and recorded, both lessened the responsibility of the accountant and rendered the auditor incompetent to express an opinion on the acts which he advised and sanctioned. He could not agree, therefore, that the control of the Exchequer should be transferred to the Audit Office. The Comptroller-General of the Exchequer seemed to him to be an officer of a purely executive character acting on behalf of Parliament. Should it be considered desirable that direct executive control should be maintained over the advisers of the Crown, it should not be exercised by 'those who are charged with the duty of auditing the public accounts'. The Chancellor's proposals afforded facilities for the conduct of the Executive, but did not 'supply any real check upon its proceedings'.[63]

The Comptroller-General produced a lengthy, somewhat impassioned memorandum. He denied that the system of control he exercised was 'deceptive', 'delusive', or 'imaginary'. The Chancellor's proposal would for the first time in history place the power of issuing public money entirely at the command of the Treasury. In place of the two checks against abuse — at the points of issue and of expenditure — only a single check would exist. The proposal implied 'the grant of unrestrained power and unlimited confidence to the Executive Government', a new principle. He denied that 'such confidence in the Executive Government is, has, or ought to be recognized in any free State . . . it is constitutional jealousy, and not confidence upon which our institutions are founded, and on which the safety of the liberties of England depend.'[64]

The Select Committee did not accept the Treasury's proposal, indeed the Report made no reference to it.* It did, however, recommend that the Appropriation Audit should be extended to the accounts of the revenue departments and to the votes for civil services. Moreover, to increase the independence of the Audit Board it should transmit the audited accounts direct to Parliament instead of through the Treasury, and, in view of the proposed large extension of its powers and duties, the Select Committee thought the Board's composition and relative position 'as a great department of State' should be reconsidered. The Board was to be responsible to Parliament alone. The Committee recommended that the audited accounts should be annually submitted to revision of a Committee of the House of Commons, nominated by the Speaker. The Exchequer's control over the Treasury's warrants for the issue of money was to continue.

A Treasury Minute of February 1858 accepted the Committee's recommendations, including both the principle of submitting all accounts to the revision of 'an independent authority' which should report to Parliament, and the proposal for a Select Committee to examine the results of such an audit. It was not, however, until Mr Gladstone became Chancellor of the Exchequer in June 1859 that action began to be taken. Ideally the extension of the role and status of the Audit Commission and the establishment of a Select Committee should have gone hand in hand. But Monteagle, though seventy in 1860, was still in office. Nevertheless in April 1861 the House of Commons appointed a Select Committee for the examination of the audited accounts. On 31 March 1862, again on Gladstone's recommendation, the House of Commons resolved, 'that there shall be a standing Committee to be designated 'The Committee of Public Accounts" for the examination of the accounts showing the appropriation of the sums granted by Parliament to meet the public expenditure, to consist of nine* members, who shall be nominated at the

* A draft report prepared by the Chairman (Sir Francis Baring) rejected the proposed abolition of the Exchequer.
* Increased to eleven on 28 March 1870.

commencement of every session, and of whom five shall be a quorum. A few days later the House ordered that the resolution 'be a standing order . . .'[65]

In 1865 Monteagle announced his intention to retire, whereupon the government quickly secured the passage of an Act (28 and 29 Vict., c.93) transferring the duties of the Comptroller to the Chairman of the Audit Board. This was somewhat of a stop gap measure and in 1866 the Exchequer and Audit Departments Act (29 and 30 Vict., c.39) was passed. Two new officers were to be appointed — a Comptroller- and Auditor-General and an Assistant. On their appointment the offices of Comptroller-General of the Exchequer and of the Audit Commissioners were abolished. The two departments were amalgamated under the new officer and his assistant, who were given a dual responsibility for confirming the Treasury's instructions to issue money and for auditing the annual accounts of all departments, particularly in relation to the spending of the moneys voted by Parliament.

The Act laid it down that 'every appropriation account shall be examined by the Comptroller and Auditor-General on behalf of the House of Commons.' If an accounting department did not answer any of his objections satisfactorily, he was to refer the matter to the Treasury who were empowered to determine 'in what manner the items in question shall be entered in the annual appropriation account.' He was to report on the Army and the Navy accounts separately and on the Civil Services votes according to the classes into which they were divided by the Appropriation Act.

Various means were used to emphasize the independence of the two officers. They were appointed by the Queen by Letters Patent under the Great Seal. Their salaries were made charges on the Consolidated Fund. Neither was removable except upon an address by both Houses of Parliament. Neither could be a member of either House and neither could hold his office in combination with any other held at the pleasure of the Crown, or under any office appointed by the Crown. They were given free access at all convenient times to the books of account and other documents relating to the accounts of departments. The Select Committee with whom they were to work closely had the power 'to send for persons, papers and records.'

It is fitting to end this section with the Exchequer and Audit Departments Act 1866. For the Act embodied the experience and aspirations of a century or more of those concerned with the establishment of a modern and adequate system of financial regulation. First, it codified and improved the rules for the issue of money and the form and audit of accounts developed since the 1830s. Second, it reaffirmed the dominant role of the Treasury in all matters of internal financial control. Finally, the Act provided the House of Commons with its own officer and technical staff and so made more effective its control over appropriations. In achieving this the Act made the House less dependent on the Treasury, which did not become the sole judge of the propriety of the issue of public money and, to that extent, the arguments of Lord Monteagle may be said to have succeeded. But the argument advanced by the Treasury in 1819 was met, the authority and discretion of the Crown in such matters would not be being challenged by an independent board, but by a Parliamentary officer.

VI

Offices, Departments, and Boards

From the 1830s, there was a marked expansion of governmental activities and functions outside the traditionally important role of the Army and Navy. The expansion affected the structure of the administrative system differently according to whether it was an expansion of functions already being performed or the creation of new functions. In general, the former was handled by the appointment of additional clerks and office staff. When faced with the administration of a new function the government and Parliament had a choice; they could add it to the work of an existing office or they could create a new office for the purpose. If they chose the second they had a variety of structures available, ranging from an extra Minister to an independent board.

Those having to make these decisions were influenced by several general ideas prevalent during the period. There was the insistence on economy, on administering something in the cheapest manner. The reluctance to create new Secretaries of State was in some measure a reluctance to pay £5,000 a year when Presidents could be secured for £2,000 a year. A few principles or rules of good administration were occasionally quoted as the basis of choice. The Commission for Examining the Public Accounts had suggested for example, that departments whose work was of a similar nature should, where possible, be consolidated.[1] But apart from *obiter dicta* of this kind and Bentham's somewhat bizarre Constitutional Code there was no administrative pattern held up as the ideal for all to follow. This is not surprising for even at the present day when there is much talk of principles of management the most quoted maxim is still the couplet from Alexander Pope's 'Essay on Man': 'For forms of government let fools contest; whate'er is best administered is best' first published appropriately enough in the early eighteenth century. In any case the working of the constitution and the climate of political opinion were changing so markedly that a form of administration feasible and popular at one time could have been unworkable at another.

It was customary to use the terms 'public office', 'office', or 'department' as interchangeable, usage determining which word was chosen in a particular case. Thus it was usual to speak of the Colonial, Foreign, and Home Offices but of the Secretary of State for the Home Department. The Treasury and the Admiralty were usually so described but they were also referred to as the Commissioners of the Treasury or Admiralty or as an office or department. The War Office, however, referred to the Secretary-at-War and the War Department to the Secretary of State for War and Colonies.

Neither 'office' nor 'department' carried the implication of covering the whole of what nowadays would be called a ministry, a term not then used with that meaning. The department or office of the Board of Trade comprised a number of departments, e.g. the Railway Department. In the Parliamentary returns covering the period 1797–1827 (stating the numbers employed in the Public Offices) each of the four Tellers in the Exchequer is listed as a separate department, e.g. the Department of the Rt. Hon. Charles Yorke. As a result the number of departments or offices was always much larger than the number of Ministers under whose umbrella they operated.

The major purpose of this chapter is to show how the structure of the central administration came to be moulded so as to concentrate power and responsibility for these numerous offices and departments in the hands of a small group of political Officers. The clearest way of doing that is to deal in turn with the four main areas of Executive action.

(i) Finance (taxation, borrowing and expenditure).
(ii) External Affairs.
(iii) Defence.
(iv) Internal Affairs.

FINANCE (TAXATION, BORROWING, AND
EXPENDITURE(

Throughout the period 1780–1870 this all pervading aspect of government remained firmly in the hands of the Lords Commissioners of the Treasury. The Treasury were more powerful in 1870 than in 1780 if only because of their closer links with the House of Commons in the regulation of all aspects of revenue and expenditure. We have already seen how the numerous semi-independent public accountants and sub-treasuries which existed in 1780 were gradually eliminated and their roles concentrated into the hands of a Paymaster-General. We have also seen how the ancient framework and functions of the Exchequer were dismantled or changed out of all recognition. These developments clarified and strengthened the position of the Treasury in the structure of government. Only in one respect might the Treasury be said to have lost ground, that was by the creation of the Comptroller and Auditor-General as a Parliamentary, not as a Treasury Officer.

Nevertheless there were still questions which had to be answered before Ministerial responsibility for this area of government could be said to be completely clear — these concerned the status of the various bodies and offices subordinate to or linked with the Treasury and the character of the Treasury Board.

In 1780 the Treasury was the focal point of a variety of dependent offices and boards. The most important were the revenue departments, including the Post Office. There was also the Lottery Office and the Royal Mint. The former continued after the last state lottery, held in 1825–6 had been completed.

In the case of the Royal Mint a few changes were made in 1817 (57 Geo. III, c.67), e.g. the office of Warden was abolished after the termination of the existing interest. It was the subject of Parliamentary inquiries in 1837 and 1849.[2] In 1850–1 two major changes were made. First, in December 1850 on the retirement of Mr R. L. Sheil, the office of Master of the Mint ceased to be treated as political, i.e. the holder changing with a change of government. It had never been a significant office but it had helped to finance more significant Ministers. It was, for example, held by the President of the Board of Trade during the years 1807–14; 1830–4; 1835; 1839–41; and 1843–5. In 1870 the office was assumed by the Chancellor of the Exchequer along with a permanent Deputy Master. Second, the old system of officers and indentured contracts ceased in 1851 and the Mint became a manufactory conducted entirely by salaried officials.[3]

The Revenue Boards

In 1780 the management of the national taxes consisted in Binney's words of 'A great swarm of Collectors and Receivers-General working in conjunction with seven Boards of Commissioners.'[4] The seven were: Customs; Excise; Stamps; Salt; Taxes; Hackney Coach and Chair Licences; and Hawkers and Pedlars. The taxes they managed are conveyed by their titles except in the case of the Taxes Board which handled the Land Tax and the several duties known as the Assessed Taxes, e.g. the Window Tax, and Inhabited House Duty.

The Customs and the Excise departments were very large employers. The other Boards, however, were not very significant and the Commissioners on the Public Accounts recommended in 1781 that Stamps, Salt, Hackney Coach, and Hawkers and Pedlars should be merged with the Tax Office.[5] Pitt contemplated action of this kind but nothing changed until 1798 when the modified Salt duties were placed under the Board of Excise. In 1810 the Hackney Coach Board absorbed the Hawkers Board and in 1831 was itself absorbed by the Board of Stamps which was in turn amalgamated with the Taxes Board two years later. In 1849 the Boards of Excise and of Stamps and Taxes were merged to form a Board of Inland Revenue (12 Vict., c.1). It was this Board which also was responsible for the income tax. By 1870 therefore there were only two bodies concerned with the levy and collection of the national taxes. These amalgamations secured substantial economies. When Stamps and Taxes were consolidated in 1833 there was a saving of 50 officers and staff costing over £18,000. Whereas in 1800 there were some sixty revenue commissioners by 1862 only eleven were needed. Even so both bodies of Commissioners were still entitled to two months holiday.[6]

The amalgamations and changes did not effect the character of the boards and their relations with Parliament. The commissioners who constituted each board continued to be appointed by royal Letters Patent which supplemented the duties and responsibilities they derived from Acts of Parliament. They and their staffs were precluded from sitting in the House of Commons. The existence of commissioners with functions and powers affecting the mass of the population did not create any serious confusion as to ministerial responsibility.

First and foremost, Parliament was principally interested in the level and character of taxation. These were not matters for the revenue boards but for the Chancellor of the Exchequer, indeed on occasion for the Cabinet as a whole. In as far, however, as Parliament had any grievances about the manner in which taxes were levied and collected the responsbility of the Treasury had been recognized for a long time. The Commission on Fees of 1786 stated that the business of the Lords Commissioners of the Treasury was, *inter alia*, 'to give directions for the conduct of all boards, and persons entrusted with the receipt, management or expenditure of the said revenues . . . and generally to superintend every branch of revenue.'[7] The subordination to the Treasury of the various bodies of commissioners was usually indicated in their instrument of appointment. It was also stated in general legislation. For example, when in 1816 (56 Geo. III, c.98) the offices of Lord High Treasurer for Great Britain and for Ireland were united the Act provided that all officers and other persons employed in the collection and management of the revenues should be 'in all respects subject to the Orders and Control of the said Lord High Treasurer or the said Commissioners of His Majesty's Treasury.' It should also be noticed that until 1854/5 there were no Estimates submitted for the cost of collection and management and therefore there was not the normal opportunity for discussion in Committee of Supply.

Second, notwithstanding the clear answerability of the Chancellor of the Exchequer both for the levels and forms of taxation and its general management the arrangements did shield him to some extent from responsibility for individual cases. The assessment of the income tax, for example, was in the hands of local General Commissioners, even though the Surveyors employed by the department were playing a more important role. When taxpayers wrote to the Treasury about their tax assessment they were invariably told 'The Commissioners have full jurisdiction in the matter' or 'The decision of the District Commissioners is final.' In 1874 both the taxpayer and the Crown were given the right to require either the General or the Special Commissioners to 'state a case' for the High Court on the ground that their determination was 'erroneous in point of law'.[8]

In the case of the Customs' duties, however, the decisions of the Commissioners were not final. If a merchant or other person felt aggrieved at some action by a Customs official he could petition the Board but failing satisfaction there he could petition the Treasury. There seems to have been a good deal of this kind of business reaching the Treasury, the Chairman of the Board being a frequent visitor to the Financial Secretary.

When in October 1865 Gladstone, then Chancellor of the Exchequer, was asked by Earl Russell to lead the House of Commons he stipulated that some arrangement should be made to relieve him 'of a considerable and singularly disabling class of business, consisting of cases of real or supposed grievance, at all times arising in connection with the collection of the public revenue . . .' He thought the most effective mode of doing this would be a reorganization of the Treasury Board, which for 'prudential reasons' he did not propose at the present moment.[9] Russell ceased to be Prime Minister in June 1866.

Gladstone became Prime Minister early in December 1868 and before the end of the month a 'Third' Lord had been appointed at a salary of £2,000 a year, i.e. twice that of the junior Lords. The Chancellor of the Excheqer (Lowe) explained to the House that the duties of the Third Lord would tend towards those discharged by himself and would be those of looking after the revenue leaving the Financial Secretary the duty of looking after the expenditure.[10]

Though from this and other evidence it is clear that the existence of the revenue boards did not shield the Treasury from a good deal of public responsibility, the position of the Chancellor would have been quite different without the boards. For inevitably he would have been involved in many of the initial decisions whereas only the comparatively small number of decisions which aroused complaints reached his desk.

Not everybody, however, was happy about the relations between the Treasury and the several boards. Sir Henry Parnell,[11] a major critic of the country's financial arrangements, claimed in 1831 that though nominally under the control of the Treasury the boards were

practically, and necessarily, nearly altogether exempt from it, and [were] possessed of powers, either direct or indirect, of incurring any expense they please. Whatever may be the intentions of the Treasury, the superior knowledge which these boards have of details, and the various means they can employ to influence the opinion and conduct of the Chancellor of the Exchequer, enable them in practice, not only to get rid of the control of the Treasury, but to put it under their control.

His remedy was to abolish the 'numerous independent governments' and in their place put a single board of commissioners of which the First Lord of the Treasury and the Chancellor of the Exchequer would be the Ministerial members along with the Postmaster-General and the chairmen of the present revenue boards. The latter would in effect become departmental heads. Nothing came of this suggeston which was part of a scheme for a thorough change in the structure of the Treasury. It is possible that abolition of the several revenue boards would have had the undesired affect of making the two Ministers answerable for every decision in individual tax cases. In 1848 Trevelyan told a Select Committee[12] that the Treasury had never, to his knowledge, considered putting each board under a junior Lord, no doubt on the lines of the Admiralty reorganization of 1832.

A proposal was made to a Select Committee in 1851 that the Board of Customs should be given some measure of independence by allowing its Chairman or another Commissioner to sit in the House of Commons. Spearman, a former Assistant Secretary, said such an arrangement would entirely change the relations of the Board with the government and Parliament. At present the Chancellor of the Exchequer and the Financial Secretary represented the Customs in Parliament. When asked whether it would not be a good thing to make one of the junior Lords an ex-officio member of the Board he replied that this would necessitate the appointment of another junior Lord. He explained that the Chancellor of the Exchequer was head of all the revenue boards. They were all responsible and amenable to him. He exercised his authority in all ordinary cases through the Financial secretary of the Treasury but in all cases of importance he communicated directly with the Chairman.[13]

There were, however, two offices contributing to the public revenues and therefore under the direct control of the Treasury in which revenue collection and non-tax functions were inter-mixed: the Land Revenues of the Crown and the Postal Services. It was ultimately found impossible to treat these like the revenue departments already mentioned: a more direct form of ministerial responsibility had to be accepted.

The two Surveyors-General, originally created by Henry VIII — one for the Land Revenues and one for the Woods and Forests — were united in 1810 (50 Geo III, c.65), the king being empowered to appoint by Letters Patent not more than three persons for executing the offices and duties of the Surveyor-General, to be known as the Commissioners of His Majesty's Woods, Forests, and Land Revenues. The duties could be performed by any two of the Commissioners or, if the Treasury so ordered, by any one of them. They were required to 'observe, perform, fulfil and keep . . . the Orders, Rules, Instructions and Directions, not being contrary to . . . the Act, make or given to them by the Lord High Treasurer'. The king was further empowered to grant a salary of £2,000 a year to the person first named in the Patent, i.e. the Chairman, and £1,200 to each of the others, clear of all fees and deductions. One of the Commissioners could sit in the House of Commons. This rather indicated that the body was not considered to be simply concerned with the collection of revenue.

In 1832 the duties of the Surveyor-General of Works and Public Buildings (who had superseded a Board of Works — one of the economies of the Civil Establishment Act, 1782) were transferred to the Commission (2 Wm. IV, c.1) which was renamed Woods, Forests, Land Revenues, Works, and Buildings. The odd effect of this amalgamation, particularly since the Board was in effect an outpost of the Treasury, was to enable expenditure on the repair and maintenance of public buildings and parks to be charged against the income received by the Board from the Crown lands, thus avoiding Parliamentary control.

In 1851 (14 and 15 Vict., c.42) the functions of the Board in respect of Works and Buildings were made the responsibility of a Board of Works, and Public Buildings composed ex-officio of the Principal Secretaries of State, the President and Vice-President of the Board of Trade, and a First Commissioner as Chairman, who was entitled to sit in the House of Commons and to receive a salary not exceeding £2,000 a year. The land revenue side remained in the hands of three Commissioners, none of whom, however, was now entitled to sit in the House of Commons, so bringing this body in line with the Commissioners who managed the other revenues.

In 1863 there was a public outcry against the policy which the latter was pursuing in respect of certain royal forests. In order to increase the revenue from the Crown lands the Commissioners had encouraged enclosures and limited access to the public. When it was learnt that they were proposing to sell the rights of the Crown over the remaining unenclosed lands in Epping Forest the issue was raised in the House of Commons. In the absence of any representative of the Commission the House adopted the device of an address to the Queen 'that no sales to facilitate enclosures be made of crown lands or crown forestal rights within fifteen miles of the metropolis.' This was carried against the advice of Ministers. The negotiations for the sale were suspended. The House then appointed a Select Committee to deal with the specific proposed sale followed in 1865 by one which dealt generally with Open Spaces around the metropolis. This recommended that a new board should be appointed to act as trustees for the preservation of the forests etc. around London. Instead the government by legislation (29 and 30 Vict., c.62) transferred the forestal rights of the crown in Epping Forest to the Office of Works. This body, not being a revenue department but charged with the management of public property, could take a different view of the matter and even ask Parliament for the necessary appropriation to preserve the Forest for public use.[14] It has been suggested that this was an example of the problems that can arise when a public office is not represented in Parliament. It would appear fairly certain, however, that even if one of the Commissioners had been in the Commons he could not have won support for his policy. It was the Chancellor of the Exchequer, in effect hiding behind the Board, who could have pursued another policy. No doubt, however, the Treasury regarded the primary purpose of the revenue department as being to maximize the flow of revenue into the Exchequer. The lesson was that non-representative boards might be sufficient for taxes, supplemented by suitable appeal procedures, but the administration of the Crown lands was somewhat different.

The Post Office

From 1663 the net revenue of the Post Office formed part of the hereditary revenues of the Crown. George III surrendered them on coming to the throne in 1760, the money being paid into the Aggregate Fund and after 1787 into the Consolidated Fund. As with the Customs, the Post Office was occasionally charged with providing pensions and meeting other expenditure not arising out of the service. An Act of 1711 (9 Anne, c.10) estalished a General Post Office and empowered the Queen to appoint a Master by Letters Patent under the Great Seal to have the name and style of her Majesty's Postmaster-General. Having been established after the Act of 1707 it was a new office and therefore the holder was not eligible to sit in the Commons. Until 1823 the office was held by two persons, the usual designation being 'Postmaster-General', meaning the two combined.

The Post Office was regarded as a source of revenue and in matters concerning 'the management, ordering and government of the revenue' the Postmaster-General was required 'to observe such orders and directions' as the Treasury 'shall from time to time think fit to give him' subject, however, to the Acts concerning the postal services.[15]

It was apparent, however, that the Post Office was, in the words of the Select Committee on Finance of 1797, an Establishment 'executing other Services besides that of merely collecting the Public Money.'[16] Earlier Commissioners had recommended that the Postmaster-General should hold a board of senior officers once a week for the purpose of effectively superintending the management of 'this great Branch of the Revenue.'[17] In various forms this idea of a board was suggested for the next thirty or so years. If the Post Office were to be regarded purely as a revenue department then it was an anomaly, for the others were managed by boards. Even if it were to be treated as an ordinary department of State it was very unusal : no other public office of anything like its size was vested in a political head.

In the 1830s the Post Office came under strong criticism. Mr Robert Wallace, from inside the House, and Rowland Hill, from outside, led a vigorous compaign involving most of the Parlimentary devices — requests for Returns, Royal Commission and Select Committee, and Petitions. In 1836 the Chancellor of the Exchequer (T. Spring-Rice) promoted a Bill[18] to put the Post Office in commission. The person first named in the Commission was to be able to sit in the Commons and would be the Minister. The Chancellor of the Exchequer 'admitted that the present constitution of the Post-Office . . . was indefensible . . . a great office of administration like this, or a great revenue department, was not properly constituted in being placed in the hands of one officer, who retired from the office whenever a political change in the Government took place.' He asked the House to approve the general principle that 'a mere political officer, acting at the head of this department was as improper as such an officer would be at the head of the Customs, the Excise or the Stamp Department'. Despite a very able exposition by Lord Melbourne the Bill was rejected by the Lords. The Duke of Richmond, a former Postmaster-General (1830–4), said that the present situation could be remedied if the Treasury were to give the Postmaster-General greater latitude in disposing of the postal revenue. Lord Ellenborough used the classic argument against boards: 'There was', he said, 'no responsibility whatever where three or more persons were equally responsible' and experience had shown him that 'it was impossible to conduct any government well, unless you placed your whole confidence in, and intrusted the whole power to the individual.'[19]

The criticisms caused the Treasury to take other action. In

1837 an Act (1 Vict., c.32) repealed and amended 128 Acts concerning the Post Office and three years later a Penny Postage Act (3 and 4 Vict., c.96) was passed. At the same time Rowland Hill was given a two-year appointment in the Treasury, to become Secretary to the Postmaster-General in 1846 (in effect joint Permanent Secretary) and permanent head of the Office in 1854, serving in that position for ten years. The business of the Post Office in the Commons was initially handled by the Financial Secretary to the Treasury there being no Parliamentary Secretary to the Office. In 1866 (29 and 30 Vict., c.55) however, Parliament agreed that the office of Postmaster-General was not in future to be deemed to be a new office or place of profit within the meaning of the 1707 Act. The holder was, therefore, now free to sit in the Commons, but would still be subject to the requirement of having to seek re-election on taking up the office. After 1836 a higher calibre of politician was appointed Postmaster-General and it became more usual for him to be a member of the Cabinet. But it was not until 1910 that the Department had an Assistant Postmaster-General.

Other Subordinate Bodies

In general the growing activity of the Treasury after 1780 was met by increasing the number of clerks. In 1786, however, concern about the cost of stationery in the public offices led the Treasury to establish a Stationery Office under a Superintendent. As the existing contracts with private contractors ran out, this Office came to supply paper and stationery to an increasing number of departments and, sometime later, printing and binding. In the early years departments paid for supplies at cost price plus a small percentage to cover expenses but in 1823 a separate Vote of Supply was accorded the Office and charged with the cost of supplying the various departments. The Superintendent and his staff were appointed and employed by the Treasury. Three new subordinate or satellite bodies were also established for the Treasury. These were the Commission for the Reduction of the National Debt set up in 1786; the Exchequer Loans Commission set up in 1793 (later renamed the Public Works Loan Board); and the Civil Service Commission, set up in 1855.

The National Debt Commissioners were created as part of Pitt's scheme to reduce the debt by using a Sinking Fund of £1 million a year for the purchase of government stock. The Fund was to be removed from the immediate control of Ministers and Parliament.[20] The Commissioners named in the Act of 1786 (26 Geo. III, c.31) were all ex-officio: Chancellor of the Exchequer, Speaker of the House of Commons, Master of the Rolls, Accountant-General of the Court of Chancery, and the Governor and Deputy Governor of the Bank of England. They were required to lay an account of their proceedings before Parliament each year and also before the Audit Board. The Bank of England also had to lay a full annual statement before Parliament. The handling and reduction of the national debt was clearly a matter for the Treasury and the Chancellor of the Exchequer and there was never any doubt that he and not the other Commissioners was accountable to the House of Commons. They ceased to meet after 1860 the business being handled by a Secretary and a Comptroller under the eye of the Chancellor of the Exchequer.

The Exchequer Loans Commission was originally created to lend money to any body or to merchants, bankers, or traders mainly to foster trade and industry. The original Act of 1793 (33 Geo. III, c.29) placed £5 million at the disposal of a body of twenty persons named in the Act. Vacancies could be filled by the remaining Commissioners with Treasury approval. The Commissioners were required to give an account of their proceedings to the Treasury but otherwise the department was not involved.

A similar Act was passed in 1817 (57 Geo. III, c.34) but this also covered Ireland and specifically stated that the loans were to be made for the purposes of the carrying on of public works and fisheries and the employment of the poor. The Commission came to be known as the Public Works Loans Board. Parliament passed an Act regularly, usually every five years, naming the Commissioners and stating the sum placed at their disposal. About the middle of the century the Board started to lend money to local authorities. The approval of the Treasury was not necessary for the Board's decisions.

The Civil Service Commission was created in 1855 by an Order in Council which named three Commissioners. Their duties were to ascertain a candidate's qualifications for appointment and to certify him (a) as being within the limits of age prescribed for the post; (b) free from physical defect or disease likely to interfere with the proper discharge of his duties; (c) of character such as to qualify him for public appointment; and (d) possessed of the requisite knowledge and ability.

The Lord High Treasurer, one of the most ancient offices, was placed in commission in 1714. Until 1807 five Commissioners were named in the Letters Patent.[21] In that year the Chancellor of the Irish Exchequer became an additional Commissioner without salary (47 Geo. III, sess. 2, c.20) but when his office was merged with that of the English Chancellor two additional Irish Commissioners were appointed (56 Geo. III, c.98). After 1823, however, only one Irish Commissioner was appointed and in 1848 the number of Commissioners reverted to five, until 1868 when it was raised to six.

THE TREASURY BOARD

The office of First Lord of the Treasury had come to be regarded as most suitable to be held by the Prime Minister. When it was not held by the First Lord the office of Chancellor of the Exchequer was named second. But between 1714 and 1812 except for brief periods the two offices were in the same hands. When Lord Liverpool was Prime Minister, 1812–27, the office of Chancellor of the Exchequer was held in the House of Commons in recognition of the sovereign role of that House in finance. Canning held both offices in 1827 and so did Peel for a few months in 1834–5. From April 1835,* however, they were always held separately, a clear indication that either office was enough of a work load for any one man.

It was usual at first for all the Commissioners to attend each meeting of the Board. Issues were discussed and decisions reached. The joint secretaries took minutes of the proceedings which were read and formally agreed at the next meeting. The big increase in business particularly during the American and

* Gladstone held both offices in August 1873–February 1874 and again in April 1880–December 1882.

Napoleonic Wars made it impossible to continue to conduct the country's financial affairs in this manner. In 1827 the First Lord and the Chancellor ceased to attend. The Board, however, continued to meet until 1856, the junior lords in attendance acting as a kind of political check on the decisions of the joint Secretaries and certain senior permanent officials. Well before then, however, the Treasury was run as a department with a single political head — the Chancellor of the Exchequer — and this was well understood by Parliament.

The administrative role of the junior Lords declined, a fact testified by their salary being reduced to £1,200 in 1831 and to £1,000 in 1851. The Chancellor of the Exchequer (Lowe) claimed in 1869 that the junior Lords occupied a position which no one could regard as satisfactory. One of them generally assisted the Patronage Secretary to discharge his duties in the House, i.e. as a Whip, and the other two did little except settle the superannuation allowances of clerks. Yet the Treasury was greatly overworked, the pressure being too great, particularly on the (Financial) Secretary.[22] The junior Lords never, however, undertook the role performed in other departments by the Parliamentary Secretary, at least not until the Third Lord was created in 1868.

That role was performed by the joint Secretaries who by the 1830s had come to be known as the Financial and the Patronage Secretaries. These two political officers were in origin secretaries to the board: they were never members of it. Both had greater significance and status than that accorded to other Parliamentary Secretaries. The Financial Secretary, usually referred to as 'the Secretary', handled not only the Estimates of offices not represented in the House, but presented all the Civil Estimates. The Parliamentary or Patronage Secretary had an invidious and onerous role in the distribution of patronage at the disposal of the Treasury and had become the Chief Government Whip. The Chancellor of the Exchequer (Wood) told the Select Committee on Official Salaries[23] in 1850 that he did 'not know so difficult or so disagreeable an office' as that of Patronage Secretary and that 'all the heaviest work of the Treasury relating to business in the House of Commons' went to the Financial Secretary. Nevertheless the recommendation of the Committee that their salaries should be reduced from £2,500 to £2,000 was implemented.

The need to continue the Treasury Board was questioned by the Select Committee of 1848, who wondered whether public money could not be saved by getting rid of the junior Lords. Trevelyan, however, said

if the business of the Treasury was really transacted, as it professes to be, at a Board of six officers of equal authority, all of them discussing everything that comes before them, and enforcing their own opinion . . . it would have a most injurious effect . . . The real constitution of the Treasury is, that the Chancellor of the Exchequer is the effective head and all the business is really done by delegation from him, by each according to his degree;

Nevertheless he thought the junior Lords performed a very useful function. He admitted he could not defend the Board in theory but he could in practice. 'I consider that there is something in the fact, that the mind of the whole country has become habituated to the present constitution of the office, and that there is a degree of prestige, of authority connected with the name of the Lords Commissioners of Her Majesty's Treasury.'[24]

When Gladstone was considering a reorganization of the Treasury Board in May 1866 he wrote to Russell[25] recommending that the Patronage and Financial Secretaries should become members of the Board and three of the four junior Lords should be relegated to the status of Assistant Lords. He went on 'It would naturally follow upon a plan of this kind, that some at least titular changes should take place in the permanent staff. The Assistant Secretary (already recognized as a kind of head to the Permanent Civil Service — I suppose from the reflected light of the First Lordship) should be Secretary.' It is not clear what would have been gained by making the two Secretaries members of the Board now that it no longer met. As we have just seen, the only change was the creation of a Third Lord. The change of title of the Permanent Secretary was made in May 1867 by the Conservative

Administration which shows the continuity of British politics in administrative matters.

And so, though the Treasury in practice meant the Chancellor of the Exchequer, in legal terms it remained the Lords Commissioners of Her Majesty's Treasury. When in 1861 concern was expressed that the Patent commissioning the Lords of the Admiralty was at variance with the practice it was decided nevertheless not to amend it. To do so would have implied that the Treasury Patent would need to be correspondingly treated. It was better to let well alone.

OVERSEAS AFFAIRS

In 1780 very little of the authority of the Treasury was attributable to the royal prerogative. Taxation and borrowing depended on Acts of Parliament and, apart from the remaining hereditary revenues of the king, so did the spending of public money. In marked contrast the conduct of foreign and colonial affairs was almost wholly manifestations of the authority attributed to the king's prerogative, a fact which accounts in large part for the use made of the office of Secretary of State.

From the seventeenth century it had been customary for the king to have two Principal Secretaries of State. They entered office on receiving the Seals from the Sovereign and, as soon as convenient, took the required oath at a meeting of the Privy Council. In due course their appointments were embodied in Letters Patent under the Great Seal which granted the offices during pleasure. The Patents conferred the offices in similar terms on all their holders: the assignment of particular areas of responsibility and any subsequent transfer from one holder to the other being matters for informal communication from the king. It followed that if one of the holders was absent the other could act in his place. Nevertheless, certain conventions governing the distribution of functions came to be generally understood and accepted. Both Secretaries had a responsibility for English domestic affairs but the rest was divided between a Northern and a Southern department, each of which was the responsibility of one Secretary. During 1709–26 and again during 1742–6 a third Secretary was appointed with responsibility for Scottish affairs, otherwise handled by the Secretary for the Northern department. A third Secretary was again appointed between 1768 and 1782 to handle mainly American business, previously handled by the Southern department.[26]

The distribution of functions existing in 1780 was not very logical. Joint responsibility for home affairs in general would have been difficult to maintain once the House of Commons became increasingly interested in such matters. In March, 1782, a more understandable division was adopted — between home and foreign affairs. The new arrangement was muddled later that year when both the third Secretaryship of State and the Board of Trade were abolished, leaving the Home Department to handle matters concerning war and colonies as well as the internal affairs of the British Isles.

In July 1794, however, in order to facilitate the entry of the Whigs into Pitt's government, a third Secretaryship was again created. Originally Pitt intended this to deal with war and colonies but the Whig leader, the Duke of Portland, when agreeing to being Home Secretary, had assumed it would continue to handle the colonies and their patronage. Henry Dundas therefore became Secretary of State for War. 'The idea of a War Minister as a separate Department,' he told Pitt, ' . . . cannot exist in this country. The operations of war are canvassed and adjusted in the Cabinet, and become the joint act of His Majesty's servants; and the Secty of State who holds the pen does no more than transmit their sentiments . . . All modern wars are a contention of purse, and unless some very peculiar circumstance occurs . . . the Minister of Finance must be the Minister of War.'[27] Dundas favoured transferring his war functions to the Home Department and placing the colonies under a Secretary of State who would also be President of the Board of Trade. The Cape of Good Hope and Ceylon would have been included with India under the Board of Control. Pitt was replaced by Addington in 1801 and when Portland moved to being Lord President of the Council the king transferred 'all the correspondence with the governors of His Colonies' to the Secretary of State for War.[28]

This arrangement continued until 1854 when separate Secretaryships for War and for Colonies were created. In 1858 a fifth Secretaryship, for India, was created. Of these five Secretaryships, that for the War Office will be dealt with under Defence and that for the Home Office under Home Affairs. That for Foreign Affairs proved to be the most straightforward during our period, neither spawning new bodies nor raising problems of accountability.

Colonial Affairs

Though by 1810 the office was divided into war and colonial departments with an under-secretary concerned with each, the 'war' side dominated until the end of the Napoleonic wars. By 1814 the war department had seven and the colonial department eleven clerks. In addition there was a general department servicing both sides of the Office. In 1816, with the return to peace, the employment of the under-secretary for the war department and of four of the clerks ceased. The amount of specifically military business that remained in the hands of the Secretary of State was very small and mainly consisted of the formal transmission of the king's or government's decisions to the Commander-in-Chief and others with executive responsibility for the armed forces.[29] The titles of Colonial Office and Colonial Secretary came into general use quite early in the century.

The business of the Colonial Office presented problems both to the political and the permanent elements. Not only had the work load greatly increased by the 1820s but the nature of the business, dealings with numerous Colonies and overseas possessions, could be troublesome. Nevertheless most of it was handled by increasing the number of clerks, not by the creation of new departments. There were, however, four interesting exceptions;

(i) In 1814 a new office was established for auditing the accounts of certain colonies, an Act (54 Geo. III, c.184) authorizing the appointment of three commissioners for this purpose. The Colonial Audit Board was merged into the Audit Office for the United Kingdom in 1832 (2 Wm. IV, c.26);

(ii) In 1819 (59 Geo. III, c.120) the king was empowered to appoint a Registrar of Colonial Slaves whose principal duty was to receive the returns of slaves made regularly by the colonies and overseas possessions. He was not eligible to sit in the House of Commons. The office was financed out of the fees charged for registration. It came to an end with the emancipation of slaves;

(iii) In 1824 a Chaplain General for the Colonies was appointed to act under the immediate control of a Board consisting of the Archbishops of Canterbury and of York and the Bishop of London. His primary function was to improve the supply of duly qualified clergy in the Colonies. The Office came to an end in 1831;[30]

(iv) The Colonial Land and Emigration Commission.[31]

In the earlier years of the century there was considerable interest in increasing the flow of emigrants to the colonies. For a time the initiative was taken by the municipal authorities for some of the main ports and by some of the colonies. Lord Durham's Report of 1839 advocated a new policy for the disposal of land in the colonies and for encouraging a regular flow of immigration into Canada. He suggested commissioners should be created 'charged with the execution of the whole measure and rendered thoroughly responsible to Pasrliament'. The Colonial Secretary 'should still have the supreme control' [of the issue of rules for the disposal of public lands] and all regulations passed by the Commissioners should require his approval.

In January 1840 the Colonial Land and Emigration Commission came into existence. Three Commissioners were appointed and they took over the staff of the Agent General for Emigration created in 1836. They were responsible for the administration of the Passenger Acts and in 1846 took over from the Colonial Office responsibility for reporting on laws proposed in the Colonies. Sir George Grey told the Select Committee on Official Salaries in 1850 that the Commission was entirely under the control of his Office. Like the Board of Customs or Excise, he said, the Commissioners 'dispose of all ordinary business on their own responsibility'. It was only upon 'more difficult and important matters that they ask for instruction from the Secretary of State'. 'General directions' were given by the Colonial Secretary but 'it would be totally impossible to give directions as to the details.'[32] As the Australian Colonies took more responsibilities and immigration declined the work of the Board declined. The Merchant Shipping Act 1872 transferred to the Board of Trade the Emigration Board's duties under the Passenger Acts. It ceased to exist in March 1878.[33]

India

British interest in India had been developed very largely by the use of the chartered East India Company. Originally established for commercial activities it became more and more involved in the government of a vast and densely populated area. As a result Parliament came to take an increasing interest in Indian affairs which led to important legislation in 1773 and 1784. Though Dundas suggested the appointment of a Secretary of State for India the form adopted for stricter government control was that of a Board of Commissioners for the Affairs of India — popularly known as the Board of Control. The Act of 1784 (24 Geo. III, sess. 2 c.25) empowered the King to appoint, under the Great Seal, not more than six Privy Councillors, to include one of the Principal Secretaries of State and the Chancellor of the Exchequer. One of these two was to preside and have a casting vote but if neither was present the Commissioner with the seniority of appointment was to preside. In 1793 Parliament (33 Geo. III, c.52) bestowed the title of President on this senior Commissioner. He was paid a salary of £2,000 a year. By an Act of 1811 (51 Geo. III, c.75) the six members had to include two Secretaries of State and the Chancellor of the Exchequer. The President soon came to exercise all the powers of the Board and became a regular member of the Cabinet. He was, however, bound by the terms of the Act which, for example, required the signature of two Commissioners for formal orders and governed his relations with the Directors of the East India Company.

Compared with the wide prerogative powers available in respect of the colonies the king's powers as regards India were quite limited. For a number of years the king's approval of the Company's choice of Governor-General was not even needed but he had the power of removal. It was the Company which in addition to its commercial activities governed the country, even to the extent of having its own troops though the Board of Control could dictate policy and settle matters of peace or war.

The question of renewing the Company's Charter came up in 1793, 1813, 1833, and 1853 and resulted in exhaustive Parliamentary inquiries into Indian affairs. The renewal Act of 1813 declared the 'undoubted sovereignty of the Crown of the United Kingdom' over British India and the Act of 1833 assigned to the Company the position of trustees for the Crown. The Mutiny showed to many obsevers that the dual system of government — Board and Company — had failed and the Government of India Act 1858 introduced a new system of political responsibility.[34]

From its early days the Secretaries of State and the Chancellor of the Exchequer had played little or no part and the Board increasingly left its work to the President. He was usually a member of the Cabinet and frequently a member of the House of Commons, as were the joint Secretaries to the Board. Nevertheless the House of Commons found that it could not pin responsibility on the President because of the existence and powers of the East India Company. In Palmerston's words the affairs of India should be administered by 'Ministers responsible to Parliament for the manner in which that country is governed.[35] This pointed to the use of a Secretary of State, if the pattern of the Colonies were followed. The parallel was not, however, perfect for the Company had ruled and administered large parts of India and possessed knowledge and experience not readily available in London. Moreover India was a vast area with a population much greater than all the Colonies put together — it was an empire in itself.

There was therefore general agreement that a Minister for India would still need some body to advise him and even to exercise some form of check on him. The main argument turned on the composition of the body and its powers. The Act of 1858 (21 and 22 Vict., c.106) vested in the Queen 'the government of the Territories now in the Possession or under the Government of the East India Company' and all the powers in relation thereto which the Company had held in trust for the Crown. It declared that 'India shall be governed by and in the name of Her Majesty'. A Secretary of State for

India acquired all the functions hitherto exercised by the Board of Control and the Directors of Company subject to limitations imposed by the powers granted to the new Council of India.

This Council was originally composed of eight members appointed by the Queen and seven elected by the Directors but vacancies in the second group were to be filled by the Council as a whole. The major part of the fifteen must have served or resided in India for ten years and left that country within the last ten years. They were appointed to hold office during 'good behaviour' which, in practice, meant for life. Decisions of the Council were taken by majority vote, the member presiding, usually the Secretary of State, having a casting vote. The Council under the direction of the Secretary of State and subject to the provisions of the Act was 'to conduct the business transacted in the United Kingdom in relation to the Government of India and the Correspondence with India.'

Every 'order or communication' to India, and every order made by the Secretary of State in the United Kingdom was to be laid before it with the exception of 'secret' or 'urgent' orders. But neither secret nor urgent orders could be issued without the sanction of the Council on matters in which the Act required the concurrence of the majority of the members. The chief of these were grants or appropriations of the revenues of India or of any property transferred to the Crown under the Act and money borrowed in Grat Britain on the security of Indian revenues. Their concurrence was also required for the making of regulations for the distribution of patronage among the authorities in India; the restoration of an officer removed or suspended by the Indian authorities; and the appointment to certain scheduled posts of persons not belonging to the Indian Civil Service.

On all other matters the Secretary of State could overrule the Council, and a dissenting member had to be content with recording it in the Minutes. Any proceedings of the Council taken in his absence required his approval in writing.[36] Even so the position of the Secretary of State for India was different from that of those for Foreign and Home affairs. Indeed objection was taken at first to the arrangements on the ground that they hampered the free and independent action of the Secretary of State. But after a longer experience they earned more favourable opinions, especially from those who had served in that office. The arrangements were, however, described as 'intolerably cumbrous and dilatory.'[37] They do not though seem to have undermined the responsibility of the Secretary of State to Parliament. Occasionally as with Sir Staford Northcote in 1867 the Minister might have to defend overruling the majority opinion in the Council but save for certain limited matters his responsibility was complete and undivided. It should be noticed that the salary of the Secretary of State and the expenses of his Office were met out of the Indian revenues. The Act required the Secretary of State to submit to Parliament an annual statement of the revenue and expenditure of British India. In order to provide an independent check the Act established an Auditor of Indian Accounts, appointed not by the Secretary of State but by royal Sign Manual, countersigned by the Chancellor of the Exchequer. He held office during good behaviour and had to present an annual report to Parliament on the findings of his audit.

In 1869 (32 and 33 Vict., c.97) the appointments of all the Members of the Council were entrusted to the Secretary of State, not to the Queen. Moreover their tenure was altered from office during good behaviour to a fixed term of ten years, the Secretary of State having the power to reappoint for a further five years. This strengthened the hand of the Minister vis-á-vis the Council and showed that the House were by then more ready to trust him with fuller powers.

One peculiar consequence of the legislative form taken by the transfer of statutory powers to a Secretary of State was that the Secretary in Council became for the purposes of suits, but not for the holding of property, a body corporate which could sue or be sued either in England or India. Every person had the same remedies against the Secretary of State in Council as he might have had against the East India Company if the 1858 Act had not been passed.[38]

DEFENCE

The defence of the country and the conduct of war and peace were clearly central to the royal prerogative. But the administration of the land forces had presented quite a different problem from that of the naval forces. The army was regarded as a temporary phenomenon, its existence depending on whether or not the country was at war, whereas the navy was accepted as a permanent activity. Neither the House of Commons nor the country at large liked the idea of a permanent army, particularly one based at home. Permanence was prevented by the fact that the Mutiny Act, first enacted in 1689, on which the discipline of the army depended had to be renewed annually. Also the money for both the land and naval forces had to be voted annually. The distinction between the treatment of the two armed forces became increasingly unreal as war followed war in the eighteenth century. Nevertheless it partly accounts for the difficulties which had to be overcome before a coherent management structure could be provided for the Army.

Both services had at one time been headed by the king or some royal personage. The two 'fighting' posts were the Lord High Admiral and the Commander-in-Chief. The former office was, however, put into commission in the late seventeenth century and remained so, save for two very short periods, throughout our period. The Commander-in-Chief, however, remained an individual office, though for the greater part of the eighteenth century the office was not filled, the duties being exercised by the king assisted by a Secretary-at-War. This officer communicated the king's pleasure in matters of military administration and prepared for the royal signature the warrants which authorized the Treasury to pay to the Paymaster-General of the Land Forces the money voted by Parliament for the maintenance of the Army. In 1782 and 1783 statutes were passed (22 Geo. III, c.81 and 23 Geo. III, c.50) which placed on him responsibility for preparing and submitting estimates for expenditure on the land forces.

Under pressure from the war with France and the shock of the loss of the American colonies the office of Commander-in-Chief was revived in 1793. A year later, for reasons already mentioned, a Principal Secretary of State for War was created. There already existed an Ordnance Board and a Paymaster-General's Office both headed by political figures, the Master-General of the Ordnance often being in the Cabinet.

The strength of the Secretary of State's position lay in the fact that 'all warlike preparations, every military operation, and every naval equipment must be directed by a Secretary of State. Neither the Admiralty, Treasury, Ordnance, nor Victualling Boards, can move a step without the King's commands so signified.' In other words, any act, order, or instruction that required the King's signature involved the use of the Signet for which the Secretaries of State were responsible. But though the officer who authorized the use of the Seal was legally accountable for the act it thereby legitimized, this did not politically make him the Minister who decided the policy implied by the act. When the country was at war the Prime Minister and the Cabinet took the major decisions.

The Secretary-at-War was not a Principal Secretary of State and was a member of the Cabinet for only eight of the forty-four years 1783–1827. He shared with the Commander-in-Chief the duty of providing the forces decided upon by the Cabinet. When becoming Commander-in-Chief in 1795 the Duke of York asserted a right to control all promotions and questions of discipline and even contested the right of the Secretary-at-War to control finance. The Duke resigned in 1809. In that same year Palmerston became Secretary-at-War, to remain in that Office until 1828. As a result of Palmerston's efforts his relations with the Commander-in-Chief were clarified in 1812. His right of financial control was upheld but he was instructed not to issue any new order until it had been shown to the Commander-in-Chief. If the latter objected the issue was to be settled by one or all of three Ministers — the First Lord of the Treasury, the Chancellor of the Exchequer, or the Secretary of State for War and Colonies. Even so difficulties and disputes were not obviated but continued into the 1830s.[40]

If the test of an administrative system is whether it works successfully then the British war administration at the beginning of the nineteenth century was effective. Napoleon had been defeated and British arms reigned supreme in Europe. Nevertheless the Army did not escape the attention of the reforming zeal of the 1830s. In 1833 a Royal Commission under the Duke of Richmond was appointed to consider the practicality of consolidation but did not report. It was followed in 1835 by a more powerful Royal Commission with Lord Howick as Chairman and Palmerston, Russell, and Spring-Rice among its members. It reported in 1837.

The Howick Commission was asked to consider the possibility of consolidating the various officers and boards with powers and duties in respect of the management of the armed forces. It started by describing these various elements and the relations between them. In addition to the Secretary of State, Secretary-at-War and Commander-in-Chief the report mentioned:

(a) the Board of Ordnance: the size of the board had been reduced to three in December 1830 by the abolition of the offices of Lieutenant General and the Clerk of Deliveries. The Master-General directed personally and without the assistance of the Board, all those matters with reference to the Corps of Artillery and Engineers which in the rest of the army came within the province of the Commander-in-Chief — for example military appointments, discipline, and orders about deployment. The civil duties under the superintendence of the Board were the provision of arms, ammunition, and military stores for the whole of the Army and the Navy; clothing for the artillery and Engineers and part of the Militia; and various supplies, e.g. fuel and light for the Army at home and abroad and provisions and forage for the Army in Great Britain.

(b) the Commissariat Department of the Treasury: responsible for providing provisions and forage to the troops abroad. Until 1834 the Commisariat also had responsibility for providing supplies for troops within Great Britain.

The Commission[41] found these arrangements defective. The obvious defect which had been 'the frequent subject of remark in Parliament' was that 'the whole charge of the Army is nowhere shown in one comprehensive review. The cost of the land forces is only to be found divided in different Estimates, prepared and submitted to the Legislature by different authorities . . . contrary to the sound principles of finance, and calculated to throw difficulties in the way of a thorough investigation by Parliament of the military expenditure of the country'. They recommended that these various costs should be brought together in a single Estimate. There was, however, a much stronger objection to the existing arrangements: they caused 'an inconvenient separation not merely of account, but of the management of different branches of the same service . . . there should exist the most complete unity of purpose if the practical results of the absence of more concentrated authority are not to be traced in conflicts of opinion, diversities of system and delays exceedingly injurious to the public service . . .'

They rejected the proposal of the Duke of Richmond (in his draft report for the earlier Royal Commission) that there should be an Army Board, rather like the Admiralty Board, to take over all the civil business connected with the management of the military then performed by the War Office, Board of Ordnance, and the Commissariat. The military duties of the Master-General of the Ordnance would be transferred to the Commander-in-Chief. The Howick Commission thought the scheme would in some respects be an improvement but would not provide 'one authority having an efficient control over the whole military expenditure . . . and responsibile both for its amount and for the manner in which the sums voted by Parliament are applied'.

The Commission were particularly critical of the anomalous position of the Secretary-at-War: 'being the person upon whom the difficulties occasioned by Parliamentary objections to the amount of the estimates have principally fallen, while he has neither had any authority to take measures for reducing that amount, nor any responsibility for the efficiency and adequacy of the force kept up'. and so had been 'very frequently placed in a position of great embarrassment and difficulty both with respect to the Government . . . and also to the Commander-in-Chief.' The Commission proposed therefore that the greater part of the authority for the Army then vested in the Secretaries of State should be vested in the Secretary-at-War, who should always be a member of the Cabinet. He would be the Minister through whom the advice of the Cabinet as to the size of the military establishment should be laid before the king; should be the one to communicate on all points with the Commander-in-Chief on behalf of the Administration; and be immediately responsible to Parliament for all the measures of the government with reference to the army. The Secretaries of State would, however, continue

1780-1870 249

to signify formally the king's commands as to the employment of the Forces. Such orders, however, except in the most pressing emergencies, should be conveyed through the Secretary-at-War.

The civil duties of the Board of Ordnance were to be brought under his control by making the three Board officers responsible to him instead of to the Master-General and Board of Ordnance — in other words they would be converted into branches of the War Office. The Commission also proposed that the business of the Commissariat, exclusive of the pecuniary transactions committed to the Treasury, should be transferred to the War Office. This would enable this branch of military expenditure to be included in the general Army estimates. It would also avoid the inconvenience of having supplies furnished at one time by the Ordnance and at another by the Treasury according to whether the regiment was stationed at home or abroad. Above all, the change would relieve the Treasury from business 'which we consider it wrong in principle that it should undertake'. This large branch of the military service should be placed under the department which ought to be responsible to Parliament on all subjects connected with the army. 'The Treasury being charged with the general superintendence of the finances of the country, and with the duty of controlling the expenditure of each separate dept.' when it 'also takes upon itself the direct management of a service involving large expenditure, it leaves its proper sphere'. The Commission devoted a good deal of space to showing the wisdom of this particular recommendation: clearly they anticipated strong opposition to it from the Treasury.

Despite the status of the members of the Commission their main recommendations were not carried out. The major stumbling block was the relations between the civil and military control of the Army. The Duke of Wellington argued that the Secretary-at-War would become too powerful and the Commander-in-Chief a helpless instrument in his hands. The effctive command of the Army would be transferred from the king to the House of Commons, which was not a suitable body to exercise such detailed control. And underlying it all was an objection to the encroachment on the royal prerogative. It took the shock of the Crimean War to bring about a major change.

In June 1854, three months after the outbreak of the Crimean War the Secretary of State for War and the Colonies was relieved of his duties in respect of the Army and a new Secretary of State for War was created, to whom, in December, the Commissariat Office was transferred. In February 1855 Lord Panmure was appointed Secretary-at-War as well as Secretary of State, thus amalgamating the two offices. (The office of Secretary-at-War was abolished by statute in 1863 (26 and 27 Vict., c.12)) In March the general control of the Militia was removed from the Home Office. Next followed the abolition of the Board of Ordnance; its military functions being transferred to the Commander-in-Chief and its civil duties to the Secretary of State. The Board of General Officers and the Medical Department were next absorbed by the Secretary of State.

Thus by 1858, the year which saw the end of the Indian Mutiny, there was one War Office, housed in Pall Mall, under a Secretary of State who discharged all the civil administrative functions. The military functions of command and discipline remained in the hands of the Commander-in-Chief, housed in the House Guards, and now included the Artillery and the Engineers, hitherto the concern of the Master-General of the Ordnance. The Letters Patent of the Secretary of State for War conferred upon him 'the administration and government of the army and ordnance, including all matters relating to the pecuniary affairs, establishment, and maintenance of the army'. But a supplementary Patent contained the phrase 'the military command and discipline of the army, and appointments to and promotions therein, so far as the same may be exercised by the Crown through the Commander-in-Chief for the time being.' Though this reservation was subject to the responsibility of the Secretary of State it rather cast doubt on his supremacy. Moreover many influential people favoured a measure of independence for the Commander-in-Chief and disliked the idea of military patronage being in the hands of a party politician. They were not happy with changes which infringed the prerogative. And in 1856 the office of Commander-in-Chief had passed into the hands of the Queen's cousin, the Duke of Cambridge — and was to remain there until 1895.

Writing in 1858 Earl Grey felt it necessary to deal with the argument that the administration of the Army ought to be an exception to the rule that some Minister should be responsible for every act of the Crown. It was claimed, he said, that the administration of the army belonged solely to the Crown and that any interference with it by the House of Commons ought to be carefully guarded against as unconstitutional. Earl Grey then stated, 'Any direct interference on the part of either House of Parliament with the management of the army, would undoubtedly be a violation of the principles of our Constitution; but the same observation applies to every branch of the executive authority'. He then went on to point out that nothing could be done by the royal authority

for which some servant of the Crown must not be responsible to Parliament. There is no distinction in this respect between the exercise of the Royal authority over the army and over all other branches of the public service, and it certainly would not be for the true interest of the Sovereign that any such distinction should be drawn . . . nothing could be more dangerous for the Sovereign than to be subjected to such personal responsibility, by which the odium of having caused some great military disaster might be thrown upon the Crown instead of on its Ministers. Nor would the inconvenience be much less, if it were maintained that the Commander-in-Chief were to be singly responsible for all acts of military administration. The holder of that office would stand in a most unsafe position, if he could not depend on the support of the Ministers of the Crown in case of his measures being questioned in Parliament; and they cannot be expected to give this support, unless the officer who trusts to it communicates with them in the performance of his duties, in such a manner as to enable them to guard against his taking, or omitting to take, any step for which they will not be prepared to defend him.[42]

In 1870 Edward Cardwell succeeded in his aim to remove all reservations expressed or implied in his authority as Secretary of State for War. An Order in Council of June declared that

subject to the approval of the Secretary of State for War, and to his responsibility for the administration of the Royal Authority and

Prerogative in respect of the Army the Field-Marshall Commanding the Forces shall in addition to the military command conferred by the Letter of Service of July 1856 be also charged with the discipline and distribution of the Army, military education and training, enlistment and discharge.[43]

At the same time two institutional changes were made by the War Office Act (33 and 34 Vict., c.17). The Secretary of State was empowered to make two appointments: (i) a Surveyor-General of the Ordnance who, subject to him, was made responsible for certain matters, e.g. for providing food, forage, fuel, light, clothing, arms, and ammunition for the Army; (ii) a Financial Secretary, who *inter alia*, was to prepare the annual estimates for the Army and advise the Secretary of State on all questions of pay and pensions. He was eligible to sit in the House of Commons as was the Surveyor-General.

Thus, in 1870, under the control of the Secretary of State for War the work of the army was divided among three important offices: (1) the Officer Commanding-in-Chief; (2) the Surveyor-General of Ordnance; and (3) the Financial Secretary. The central department or Secretariat was the concern of two Under-Secretaries, one Parliamentary and one Permanent.

Navy

The management of the Navy was simple compared with the diverse arrangements for the Army. After 1673 save for three short periods, the last being in 1827–8, the ancient office of Lord High Admiral was in commission. Between 1718 and 1822 there were invariably seven Commissioners* for carrying it out, known as the Board of Admiralty, their full title in Acts of Parliament being 'the Lords Commissioners for executing the office of Lord High Admiral.' The Letters Patent by which they were commissioned treated all seven alike but in practice the first named, i.e. the First Lord, soon came to be recognized as having an ascendancy over his fellow commissioners. He was a regular member of the Cabinet.

---

* From 1802 to 1822, the First Lord with three civil and three naval lords (J Sainty, *Admiralty Officials*, p.13)

The Board of Admiralty was assisted by two other boards — the Navy and the Victualling Boards.** The Admiralty Board dealt mainly with the appointment and promotion of officers, the movement of ships and most important, had general control of the policy of the Navy. The primary responsibility of the Navy Board was the construction and maintenance of the ships, the Victualling Board being responsible for provisions, clothing and stores. The Board of Ordnance provided the guns and ammunition. There was also the Treasurer of the Navy, an important political post, through whose hands passed the funds voted by Parliament.

There was little doubt by the early nineteenth century that the Board of Admiralty was the dominant naval authority and that the First Lord was the Minister. The forces which led to consolidation in 1832 only partly arose from a need to clarify Ministerial responsibility. For some years there had been criticism of the board form of administration. Sir Samuel Bentham (younger brother of Jeremy) who was Inspector General of Naval Works, 1796–1807, argued strongly that joint management was an insuperable bar to efficiency, for one member of a board could always shift responsibility for a decision to another. For him, as for his brother, the recipe for success was individual responsibility. The Whigs accepted this argument and declared their intention to undertake a wholesale reorganization of naval administration. However they lost office in 1807 and did not regain it until 1830.[44] In November of that year Sir James Graham became First Lord of the Admiralty. When appointing him Earl Grey, the Prime Minister, who had been First Lord of the Admiralty in 1806, expressed a strong opinion that when Graham had had experience of the three boards he would conclude that some concentration was necessary[45].

So, by an Act of 1832 (2 and 3 Wm. IV, C.40), the Letters Patent commissioning the Navy and Victualling Boards and the Board for Sick and Wounded Seamen were revoked and all the interests, titles, authorities, powers, and duties vested in them were transferred to the Admiralty Board. The number of Commissioners was raised to six, of whom five were entitled

** Between 1794 and 1816 there also existed a Transport Board.

to sit in the House of Commons. The duties of the Treasurer of the Navy, except for the receipt and payment of money, were also transferred. The Act laid down that any two of the Commissioners could exercise any of its powers (previously the number had been three when the number of Commissioners was six or more).

In his Memoirs Sir John Barrow, Secretary of the Admiralty Board, 1807–45, said 'The whole plan [of the reform] hinged on two words *Individual Responsibility.*'[46] Sir James Graham said in 1861 that when he became First Lord in 1830 he found that the affairs of the Admiralty and the Navy Board were carried on very much as between independent bodies. The Comptroller of the Navy Board was rightly designated as Comptroller of the Navy for 'he exercised with regard to a great portion of the expenditure, a great deal more control than the Board of Admiralty, or the First Lord.' A very voluminous correspondence had to be conducted between the three boards. As for the junior Lords of the Admiralty they had very little to do.[47]

The Admiralty Board which emerged from the unification was a functional board rather on the lines of the Board of Ordnance. The administration of the Navy was divided between five principal officers appointed under the authority of an Order in Council: Surveyor, Accountant-General, Storekeeper-General, Comptroller of the Victualling and Transport Services, and Physician-General. They worked generally under the Admiralty Board and specifically under the direction of a particular junior Lord. In 1843 the Physician-General became Director-General of the Medical Department; in 1859 a Director of Engineering and Architectural Works was appointed; and in 1868 the office of Comptroller was merged with that of the Third Lord.[48]

The Select Committee of 1861 produced a number of opinions about the merits of having a Board and whether, if it were to be continued, the Letters Patent commissioning it should be modified to conform to the well-established practice. It was generally accepted that according to the Letters

* The number had been reduced to five in 1822 and was again so reduced in 1868.

Patent the First Lord had no greater authority than any other member of the Board. The current Patent, which took up three closely printed foolscap pages in the evidence, was examined and compared with that which constituted the Treasury Board where the same principle prevailed. Sir Charles Wood (First Lord 1855–8) said he had never read the Patent but was guided entirely by prescriptive usage. Graham argued against altering the wording of the Patent. He doubted whether it would be possible to frame one which would embrace the whole usage. He pointed out that under the present arrangement there was entire delegation by the Crown of all its prerogatives and so large a delegation might not be obtained if they were disturbed. The current First Lord (Duke of Somerset) along with Graham and Wood believed that the First Lord was fully and directly responsible for the administration of the Navy. But a previous holder (Sir John Pakington, 1858–9) and one or two Naval officers who gave evidence, did not agree, arguing that if the office of First Lord were in feeble hands he could be ruled by the board. They wished to have a Minister without a board. The reference to the delegation of the prerogative powers reflected the current arguments about Army administration — a Naval Captain even suggested there should be a Commander-in-Chief of the Navy.[49]

In January 1869 an Order in Council laid down for the first time officially that sole responsbility for the administration of the Navy was in the hands of the First Lord, making the other members of the Board subordinate to him. This was confirmed by another Order in Council of March 1870. When a Select Committee of the House of Lords examined Naval administration in 1871 they heard views to the effect that the Order of 1869 had made no real difference in the responsibility of the First Lord, but the Permanent Secretary said it had placed a much greater responsibility on his Minister. To complete the story: in 1872 the Letters Patent were shortened and simplified but all members of the Board remained equal and all orders continued to have to emanate from two members. At the same time an Order in Council made the First Lord 'responsible to your Majesty and to Parliament for all the business of the Admiralty' and made the Naval Lords responsible to him.[50]

HOME AFFAIRS

The redistribution of functions between the two Principal Secretaries of State in March 1782 and the subsequent transfer of responsibility for colonial affairs to the recently created Secretary of State for War in 1801 left the Home Secretary, as he quickly came to be called, a clear field for purely domestic activities, other than finance

Home Office

For some fifty years after its establishment the traditional work of the Home Office did not markedly expand and the new functions it acquired in respect of aliens and police were in effect statutory expansions of prerogative powers. Even so they were not handled by the small central core of clerks. The Aliens department created in 1793 was housed outside the main body of clerks who continued to concentrate on servicing the traditional functions of the Home Secretary. These new out-departments were responsible directly to the Minister. Even when the Minister's activities markedly increased in the 1830s this remained the case. As a result the Home Office was the only one of the offices of Secretary of State in which the number of clerks did not increase between 1822 and 1848.[51]

All the evidence is that the clerks in the Home Office were a tightly knit body, dominated by the traditional distribution of work and of relative status. Until 1795 their remuneration was based on the fees earned by the office. Even when, in that year, they began to receive fixed salaries, these were met out of the fee fund, which no doubt discouraged the recruitment of additional clerks, and would certainly discourage the loading of the fund with new appointments whose work did not bring money into it. Altogether then it was unlikely that the regular establishment of the Home Office were eager to acquire new functions.

The same was probably true of their political masters. Most of the subjects which Parliament and the various interests wished to see tackled raised difficult issues not only of policy but of administration: for example, reform of the poor law, control of the conditions of employment, popular education, and such aspects of church affairs as buildings and tithes. Moreover even without the addition of new powers and functions the load on the Home Secretary by 1830 was already substantial. In troubled times he could be fully occupied dealing with magistrates throughout the country. As Members became increasingly concerned about social and economic problems, he, as the main, if not the sole, Minister for home affairs, was always likely to be brought into discussion and controversy.

It is perhaps, therefore, not surprising that, though successive Home Secretaries were personally involved in most of the controversies on the home front, the resulting new functions were generally organized in such a way as to keep them at arm's length from the Home Office. They were vested either in new officers or in new boards, a good early example being the administration of the Factory Acts.

The Factories Act, 1833 (3 and 4 Wm. IV, c.103) empowered the king, by warrant under his Sign Manual, to appoint at pleasure, four persons to be Inspectors of Factories who 'shall carry into effect the Powers, Authorities and Provisions of the present Act'. These Inspectors were to have the power and were required 'to make all such Rules, Regulations and Orders as may be necessary for the due Execution of this Act.' They were also given substantially the same powers as the Justices who, however, retained their powers. The Inspectors were thus officers in the eighteenth-century meaning of the term. They were not part of the Home Office hierarchy, but exercised functions and powers vested by Parliament in the office which they held. They held their offices directly from the king, even though he would have acted on the advice of the Home Secretary. In contrast sub-inspectors were appointed by that Minister. Inspectors were required to keep full minutes of all their visits and proceedings and report them to the Secretary of State twice every year, or oftener if required; to report on the state of the factories and mills and whether these were conducted according to the Act; and to confer together so that their proceedings, orders, and rules should be 'as uniform as is expedient and practicable'.

The Act conferred immense powers on each Inspector personally, not as an agent or employee of the Home Secretary. It was the brain-child of Chadwick and those who devised the Poor Law Commission established a year later. It is little wonder therefore that the early experience of the Inspectorate revealed the problems that could arise for the working of ministerial responsibility when officers were exercising powers bestowed on them by Parliament.

In such a politically charged question as the conditions of work in factories the Home Secretary, and indeed the government generally, found it difficult to hide behind the statutory powers of four officers. Whilst the Minister could deny responsibility for particular prosecutions as being of a judicial nature, the rules and regulations were matters of general policy. In March 1837 the Home Secretary told the Inspectors that they were not to issue instructions 'until they have been submitted to the Law Officers of the Crown'. An amending Act of 1844 (7 and 8 Vict., c.15) removed the powers of Inspectors to act as magistrates or to make rules and regulations. The majority of the regulations to which the Inspectors had been working since 1836 were incorporated in the Act.[52]

When, in 1842, the control of child labour was extended to coal mines the Act (5 and 6 Vict., c.99) empowered not the king but one of his Principal Secretaries of State to appoint inspectors for the purpose. Moreover their function was to report on collieries, the condition of the miners, and the operation of the Act, not to undertake prosecutions.

In addition to its use of Inspectors (those for Constabulary created in 1856 being another example), the Home Office used Registrars, for example, for Births, Deaths, and Marriages and of Friendly Societies. The latter type of officer was also used by the Board of Trade, for example, for Joint-Stock Companies. Both Inspectors and Registrars like their eighteenth-century predecessors had powers vested in them, but in their case by statute and not by royal instrument. Their special status was, however, emphasized. In 1878 the Home Secretary announced that in future the Factory Inspectorate would carry the title of Her Majesty's Inspectors, as was already the practice for education and the police. The various Registrars were even empowered to charge a fee for their services, but their remuneration was not linked with their fee income.

More study is needed of these various offices in order to present a clearer picture of their precise relations with the

Home Secretary, or other Minister. It would seem, however, that they were not regarded as part of the 'Office', a role confined to the Minister, Secretaries, Clerks, and their ancilliary staff. Inspectors and Registrars, for example, came to be treated separately for the purpose of the Estimates and were usually in separate premises. The Home Office also used boards to deal with charities, church affairs, inclosures, and tithes. In addition to these satellite or subsidiary officers and boards, with varying degrees of independence, the Home Secretary had a general responsibility for Scottish affairs, through the Lord Advocate; for Irish affairs through the Chief Secretary for Ireland, and he was the Minister to whom the Law Officers looked for political guidance. He and his small body of clerks were thus by 1870 the centre of a large administrative web.

The Poor Law

Though the Home Secretary was the Minister principally concerned with the reform of the Poor Law in the early 1830s there is no evidence that either he or his officials wanted to enlarge their departmental empire. This was perfectly acceptable to the main exponents of the Poor Law Amendment Act 1834 (4 and 5 Wm. IV, c.76), Edwin Chadwick and Nassau Senior, who wanted to keep the administration away from politics and the House of Commons. Hence the Poor Law Commission.

The 1834 Act empowered the king to appoint three fit Commissioners to carry the Act into execution, to be styled the Poor Law Commissioners for England and Wales: two could sit as a board. None of them could sit in the House of Commons. Before taking office each was required to swear before a Judge or one of the Barons of the Court of Exchequer an oath that he would 'faithfully, impartially and honestly' according to the best of his skill and judgement 'execute and fulfil all the Powers and Duties of a Commissioner' under the Act.

Section 15 made the administration of relief to the poor subject to the direction and control of the Commissioners who were authorized to make and issue all such rules, orders, and regulations for the management of the poor, for the government of workhouses, and for the guidance and control of all guardians, vestries, and parish officers as far as related to the management of the poor, and the keeping, examining, auditing, and allowing or disallowing of accounts. These powers were, however, subject to an important administrative proviso: the Commissioners were prohibited from interfering in any individual case for the purpose of ordering relief, the local administration being vested in locally elected Boards of Guardians or, until they were established, in the Overseers of the Poor. Other Sections gave the Commissioners wide powers and functions — for example, uniting parishes for the administration of poor relief, directing the appointment of paid officers by the Boards of Guardians, and removing the masters of workhouses.

The Act contained very few references to the Secretary of State or to other Ministers. The Commissioners were required to record their proceedings, including a reference to every letter received, a minute of every letter written on their order, and a minute of the opinion of each Commissioner where they differed in opinion on some order or other proceedings. The record was to be submitted to a Principal Secretary of State every year or as often as he should require it. They were also to make a general report each year to the Secretary of State and to provide him with such information as he required. Their General Rules were not to take effect until forty days after being submitted to the Secretary of State. If within that time the rules were disallowed by the king in Council they ceased to come into operation. If disallowed subsequently they were to cease to operate. All such rules were to be laid before Parliament but for information, not approval. Treasury approval was required for the amount of the salaries of the Secretary, Clerks, Messengers, and other staff. Not more than nine Assistant Commissioners could be appointed by the Board without Treasury approval.

Thus the formal powers of the government were very limited. They could be criticized about their choice of Commissioners, but the Whig government took care to include a Tory among the three and avoided appointing Chadwick. They could control the issue of General Rules, but the Commissioners avoided this by issuing only Particular or

Special Orders until 1841. There was no distinction between the General and the Particular as to validity or force of law but the latter was issued in respect of a particular union or parish whereas the former was addressed to more than one of them.[53] The Minister could require the Commissioners to provide him with information, e.g. as to the progress of their work. None of these terms provided much scope for Ministerial intervention and therefore for Ministerial accountability. And as none of the Commissioners was entitled to sit in the Commons there was in effect nobody in the House either with a personal knowledge of the work and policy of the Commission, or with any responsibility for its work.

During the drafting of the Bill, Lord Althorp (Chancellor of the Exchequer), who was in charge of it, wished the Commissioners or one of them to sit in Parliament. He thought this would increase their responsibility and give them a mouthpiece to explain and defend their actions in one or other House. He abandoned it when confronted by the arguments of Nassau Senior that if in the House they would be thinking of their constitutents and not of their duties, and having to change with changes in governments, would make steady management and continuity of policy impossible. When in 1847 the Commission was replaced by a very differently constituted body Lord John Russell, who had been Home Secretary during the drafting of the 1834 Act, frankly admitted that it was he who had persuaded Lord Althorp to consent to the exclusion of the Commissioners from Parliament. He was now convinced that he had been wrong to do so even though he was quite aware of the dangers of connecting the administration of the Poor Law with party government.[54]

By 1847, however, most people were convinced that the absence of one of the Commissioners from the House of Commons had been a mistake. Sir George Nicholls, one of the three 'Kings of Somerset House' looking back long after the event wrote:

This separation from political influence would, it was believed, be a means of rendering their action more steady, vigorous, and independent, and less liable to popular or local bias. The result, however, showed that although these qualities might abound in a commission so constituted, there were countervailing circumstances connected with such an arrangement which rendered its policy doubtful, the commission being thereby deprived of the means of defending itself in the only place where defence could be effective. Public feeling and public prejudice, local or general, were represented and found utterance and supporters in parliament, where there was no Poor-Law functionary to explain or refute them; and charges made there, however vague, exaggerated, or groundless, spread through the country, and were received as undoubted facts, raising distrust and jealousy of the commission, and weakening its influence and impeding its action. It was denounced as being anomalous, tyrannical, irresponsible, and as exercising a power not recognised by the English constitution. This feeling prevailed within the House of Commons perhaps even more strongly than it did elsewhere, for every other department had its representative there, who might at once be questioned and called to account for whatever occurred; whereas the Poor-Law commissioners . . . could only be called upon circuitously through the medium of the home secretary, or by the more tedious process of moving for papers.[55]

Why were Althorp, Russell, and the House of Commons willing to accept an administrative arranement designed to exclude Parliament from any effective say in the management of the Poor Law? Had the Act been passed twenty years earlier it would have been more in keeping with the ideas of the time. It could not have been passed in that form twenty years later for by then Members and Ministers were well versed in the arrangements for securing ministerial accountability. Perhaps in the timing lies some part of the answer.

The Report of the Royal Commission had frightened many people and there was no division of opinion between Whigs and Tories that drastic remedies were needed. This was fertile ground for Bentham's ideas and Chadwick's vigorous advocacy. Bentham believed in individual accountability and Chadwick would have preferred a single Commissioner to three. Bentham did not want his Ministers to sit in the Commons and Chadwick distrusted politicians. Moreover in the early 1830s it was still believed that Ministers should actively run their offices whereas by the 1850s the major role of the permanent official was both recognized and accepted.

It is most unlikely that the Home Secretary or indeed any Minister of the time would have wished to accept direct responsibility for all that needed to be done to implement the recommendations of the Report, and in particular the changeover from outdoor relief to the rigorous application of the workhouse test. A new section would have been needed within the Home Office and many new appointments made. The alternative of a board was in effect the creation of a new department. Had one of the Poor Law Commissioners been able to sit in the Commons as was the case with the Commissioners for Woods, Forests, Land Revenues, Works, and Buildings he would have had to have ministerial status as did the First Commissioner. The revenue boards were not a suitable model, for a Minister accepted responsibility for their actions. Had the subject been church building or the commutation of tithes the board form might have worked as it did in those cases. But poor relief was a subject of far more political and popular concern. It could not be insulated from that concern by handing it over to an independent board. It can be argued that the arrangement would have succeeded had it not been for the disastrous years of 1838–42, when unemployment and poverty were at their very worst. It can even be claimed that what the Commissioners achieved and the speed at which they achieved it would not have been possible had the whole process been the responsibility of a Minister answerable to Parliament. By the time the arrangement was changed, the amalgamation of parishes into Unions, the creation of a large local staff of Poor Law officials and the restriction of outdoor relief had been substantially carried through.

During the passage of the Bill the government inserted a clause limiting the life of the Commission to five years. This was some comfort for those who were worried by the wide powers granted to the Commission. When the time came for renewal there was so much criticism that its life was extended only from year to year until 1842 when it was extended for five years. At the end of that time there was general agreement that somebody should be answerable in the Commons for the exercise of the powers conferred by the Act of 1834.

Instead, however, of the powers being placed in the hands of a single Minister, possibly those of the Home Secretary, the Poor Law Act, 1847 (10 and 11 Vict., c.109) empowered the Queen to appoint such persons as she saw fit to be Commissioners for administering the laws for the relief of the poor. In addition, the Lord President of the Council, Lord Privy Seal, Secretary of State for the Home Department, and Chancellor of the Exchequer were to be Commissioners ex officio. Only the President was entitled to receive a salary or remuneration for acting as a Commissioner. This implied that the President would not be a Commissioner ex officio, a view confirmed by the specific provision that the President and one of the Secretaries to the Board were to be capable of being elected to the House of Commons.

The new constitution altered the relations of the Commissioners with the government. They were no longer required to keep a record of their differences of opinion or submit any such record or report to a Principal Secretary of State. The general annual report was now to be submitted to Her Majesty. The report was still to be laid before Parliament. General Rules had no longer to be submitted to a Secretary of State but the Queen could, on the advice of the Privy Council, disallow any General Rule or part of it. Instead of Assistant Commissioners the Board were empowered to appoint Inspectors, the number and their salaries requiring Treasury approval.

In the event only one Commissioner was appointed. He was already a Member of Parliament as was one of the two Secretaries. So from July 1847 the powers vested in a central board by the Act of 1834 were vested in what had now become the normal combination of Minister and Parliamentary Secretary. The President of the Poor Law Board was not, however, like the Secretaries of State for in law the powers he exercised were vested in a board which contained four Cabinet Ministers with much greater prestige and political weight. It was accepted from the beginning, however, that the Board would not meet and that, as with the Board of Control and the Board of Trade, the office would be conducted by the President and his Parliamentary Secretary. But the Board was not prohibited from meeting and any one of the powerful ex-officio members could have requested a meeting had he been worried by the policy or the management of the Board. Those who were still worried about Poor Law policy no doubt felt the arrangement to be an added safeguard.

Sanitation and Public Health

When in the following year a new central office was established to deal with the new and growing public health
legislation, though the board form was adopted it was not
modelled on the Poor Law Board. The Public Health Act 1848
(11 and 12 Vict., c.63) established a General Board of Health
to consist of the First Commissioner of Woods, Forests, Land
Revenues, Works and Buildings, together with two other
persons appointed by Her Majesty by Warrant under the
Royal Sign Manual. The First Commissioner was designated
President of the Board. The powers and duties vested in the
Board could be exercised by any two members. One of the
members, but not the President, could be paid a salary.

The Public Health Act, 1854 (17 and 18 Vict., c.95) ended
the life of this Board. In its place the Queen was empowered
to appoint a President who along with the Principal Secretaries of State and the President and Vice-President of the
Committee of Council for Trade and Foreign Plantations were
to constitute a new General Board of Health. Only the
President was to receive a salary (of not more than £2,000 a
year) and he was entitled to sit in the House of Commons. All
the powers vested in the Board could be exercised by the
President alone or by any two or more members.

The Act provided for a life of only one year from the date of
its passing (10 August 1854) and thenceforth until the end of
the next Session. The Board was continued until 1858 when it
was allowed to expire. The Public Health Act of that year (21
and 22 Vict., c.97) vested in the Privy Council certain powers
vested in the Board, including the appointment of a Medical
Officer. The annual report of this Officer to the Privy Council
was to be laid before Parliament. The powers so vested could
be exercised by three or more members of the Privy Council,
the Vice-President for Education being one of them. It was
sufficient for any order, direction, or act of the Privy Council
in these matters to be signed by one of the Clerks of the
Council.

The Local Government Act of the same year (21 and 22
Vict., c.98), which was to be construed with the Public Health
Act as one Act, handed over to the Home Secretary the few

remaining functions of the Board which were mainly concerned with the establishment of Local Boards of Health. This
work was handled by a newly constituted Local Government
Act Office inside the Home Office but separate from the main
staff. In the six or so years which followed, the Home
Secretary, in the form of one of the Principal Secretaries of
State, was granted new powers — for example, the Sanitary
Act, 1866 (29 and 30 Vict., c.90) enabled authorities with his
consent to make regulations, for example, as to houses let in
lodgings.

Reporting in 1871 the Royal Sanitary Commission said it
was expedient that the administration of the laws concerning
public health and the relief of the poor should be presided over
by one Minister as the Central Authority, whose title should
clearly signify that he had charge of both departments. The
arrangement would probably render necessary the appointment of Permanent Secretaries to represent the respective
departments. It was essential on the public health side to
transfer to the new Minister the relevant powers and duties of
the Privy Council, the Home Office (the Local Government
Act Office), and the Board of Trade.[56]

The Commission did not indicate the form the new central
authority should take. However, the Local Government Act,
1871 (34 and 35 Vict., c.70) established a Local Government
Board, consisting of a President appointed by the Queen,
and the following ex-officio members, viz. Lord President of
the Council, all the Principal Secretaries of State, Lord
Privy Seal, and Chancellor of the Exchequer. The President
and one of the Secretaries of the Board were made eligible to
sit in the House of Commons. Any act of the Board could be
executed by the President or by any member or by a secretary
or assistant secretary if so authorized. But any rule, order, or
regulation of the Board to be valid had to be made under its
seal and signed by the President or one of the ex-officio
members and countersigned by a secretary or assistant secretary.

The Poor Law Board ceased to exist, and the Board took
over all its powers and those of the Principal Secretary of State
under the Poor Law and under various public health and local
government Acts, (including the Registration of Births,

Deaths, and Marriages) and the powers and duties of the Privy Council under the legislation concerned with Prevention of Disease and Vaccination. The Board was deemed to be established from the date of the first appointment of its President. This was 19 August 1871.

Elementary Education

In August 1833 the House of Commons agreed to a vote of not exceeding £20,000 in aid of private subscriptions for the erection of schoolhouses in England and Wales. Since no machinery had been created to administer the vote its distribution was carried out by the Treasury which, for England and Wales, did this at first through the National and British and Foreign School Societies. A vote for this purpose became an annual event. In 1853 grants were extended at so much per pupil to contribute towards running costs.

Several attempts were soon made to establish a board of Commissioners to administer the money. In June 1838 Thomas Wyse argued that 'with so many pressing public duties to perform, it was impossible that the Treasury . . . could discharge the necessary duties of superintendence, direction, control and correction, relative to the schools to which the grant was applied, in a satisfactory and complete manner'. The Home Secretary declined to take any immediate action. The government, he said, could not establish a board until there was more likelihood of agreement among the leading persons in favour of general education. Notwithstanding lack of government support and opposition from the Church, Mr Wyse's Address asking for the appointment of a board was defeated by only four votes.

Lord John Russell, as Home Secretary, took soundings among leading Anglicans in the hope of reaching agreement on the establishment of an independent and responsible board which had worked so well in Ireland since 1831. But he had to abandon the idea. The only viable alternative was the creation of a department of state with a political head responsible to Parliament. Aware that any Bill to achieve this would be defeated in the Lords, in April 1839, he used an Order in Council to set up a Committee of the Privy Council composed of the then Lord President, Lord Privy Seal, Home Secretary, and Chancellor of the Exchequer 'to superintend the application of any sums voted by Parliament for the purpose of promoting Public Education.' The original intention had been also to give the Committee the function of considering 'all matters affecting the Education of the People', but the wording was thought to be too vague and involve the Committee in too wide a scope. The constitutional propriety of such an administrative arrangement was not challenged: the precedent of the Board of Trade was generally considered to be good. The government had also avoided the kind of board typified by the recently established Poor Law Commission which had no members in Parliament. The Committee's main decisions, for example, the Grant Regulations, were recorded as Minutes. They were laid on the Table of the House of Commons. Volumes of Minutes were published annually between 1839 and 1857 after which they were included in the Board's Annual Report.

The Lord President of the Council was usually in the Lords, which was an important forum for the debate of education policy, the Church of England being well represented there. Debates in the Commons were usually handled by the Home Secretary but Members were becoming increasingly critical of their limited means of contact with a public office costing more and more money. By 1855 the grant for Schools was approaching £300,000. In that year Members introduced two Bills, one which would have established a 'Board of Public Instruction' and the other a Minister responsible to the Commons for the proper distribution of the grants. Neither was successful but dealing with the second Russell admitted that circumstances had changed since the Committee of Council had been originally established. He now thought

it would be for the benefit of the public service if the President of the Committee of Council were to be acknowledged as the Minister of Education, and that the department of education should be represented in [this] House by a person who might, perhaps, hold the rank of Privy Councillor, and who might be able to defend any measure that might be adopted, and who would be prepared at all times to explain the views of the Government with regard to the general question of education.[58]

The Lord President (Earl Granville) had already asked the Secretary (R. R. W. Lingen) to draw up a memorandum on the representation of the Education Department in the House of Commons. Lingen pointed out that the Home Secretary was much too busy with his other duties to answer, except at second-hand, for more than the general outlines of the department's work. He suggested that the Secretary's office should be made a Parliamentary one, leaving the two assistant secretaries, as the highest of the permanent officers. He supposed that the proposed Secretary would have about the same status as the Parliamentary Under-Secretaries at the Foreign and Colonial Offices. The government, however decided a politically more acceptable arrangement, but administratively less workable.[59]

In February 1856 an Order in Council placed the Education Department under the Lord President of the Council assisted by a member of the Privy Council who was to be the Vice-President of the Committee of the Council and 'act under the direction of the Lord President, and . . . act for him in his absence'. The Education Department was to include both the Educational Establishment of the Privy Council Office and the Department of Science and Art of the Board of Trade. The Department was also to inspect Naval and Military Schools. As the new officer could not be appointed and paid without Parliamentary authority an Act (19 and 20 Vict., c.116) empowered the Queen to appoint any member of the Privy Council to be Vice-President at a salary not exceeding £2,000 a year. He was to be capable of sitting in the House of Commons.

During the debate in the Lords[60] on this Bill Lord Derby thought it worthy of consideration to supersede the Privy Council altogether and have a Minister as the head of a department with no other duties to perform, unlike the Lord President who had many other duties. He also thought 'a single responsible Minister was much more efficient than a Board however respectable and able the Members constituting that Board might be'. Others also expressed a preference for a single Minister instead of a Committee. There was, however, no determined opposition to the measure.

Popular education became increasingly a political issue and

was the subject of several enquiries. The cost continued to rise and the Education Department was overburdened with work. The Revised Code of Regulations of 1862 introduced the system of payments by result, i.e. the grant to each school was made dependent on examination results and attendance. In 1864 and again in 1865 a Select Committee examined *inter alia* the top management of the department.[61]

The 1865 Committee did not have time to agree a Report but the draft prepared by the Chairman (Sir John Pakington) was published.[62] He argued that the Committee of Council was anomalous and unnecessary and tended to diminish the sense of responsibility of the Education Minister 'which is the best security for efficient discharge of official duties'. In the rare cases in which the Minister required advice from his colleagues it would be better for the whole Cabinet to be consulted. No doubt, he wrote, the Lord President was theoretically the Minister, but it seemed doubtful whether, in practice, the Vice-President had not the better claim to be so regarded. He proposed, therefore, that the Committee of Council should be replaced by a Minister of Public Instruction.

It was, however, not only the form of the central authority that was at issue. There was an increasing belief that a system of statutory local education authorities should be set up throughout the country. This became the basic feature of the Elementary Education Act, 1870 (33 and 34 Vict., c.75). It placed the local administration of elementary education in the hands of locally elected School Boards. In addition to receiving Treasury grants the Boards were empowered to levy a local rate for education purposes.

Strangely enough, apart from giving the Education Department certain statutory powers, it left its management politically just as it was. It was significant, however, that for the first time the Vice-President (W. E. Forster) was appointed to the Cabinet. Yet in early 1868 the previous government had introduced a Bill to authorize the appointment of a Secretary of State for Education but it had lapsed at the end of the Session. No doubt in view of the strength of the Church of England in the House of Lords it was advantageous to have a Minister in both Houses. It was also expected that the new

Local Authorities would relieve the Board of much of its work. And so when in 1884 the Permanent Secretary, Sir Francis Sandford, was asked about the management of the Education Department he told a Select Committee 'I should fancy that the Lord President is the Minister, I may say *de jure*, and the Vice-President very much the Minister *de facto*.'[63]

Board of Trade

The only other public office existing at the end of the eighteenth century which was to grow in importance in respect of internal affairs was the so-called Board of Trade. An Order in Council of August 1786 had given it the function of considering all matters relating to trade and foreign plantations. For a long time its duties were almost entirely consultative: advice to the Foreign Office about commercial treaties and to the Colonial Office on dealings with the colonies. In 1832, in response to the increasing demands by Parliament for statistics, the Treasury authorized the Board to establish a branch to collect and publish statistics on all aspects of national activity. But it was not until 1840 that the Department began to acquire executive functions. In that year it was given the power to collect railway statistics and to inspect railways (3 and 4 Vict., c.97). Companies could not now open new lines until after one month's notice to the Board which could appoint persons to inspect the work. Both the existing and future bye-laws of the railway companies had to be submitted to the Board which could disallow them. To undertake these new duties the Board set up a Railway Department and an Inspector-General of Railways was appointed. In 1850 (13 and 14 Vict., c.93) the Board was required to 'undertake the general superintendence of matters relating to the British merchant marine'. Four years later a Merchant Shipping Act (17 and 18 Vict., c.104) defined a mercantile marine code. Other functions were to follow. These new statutory functions were hardly relevant to the purpose for which the Board was established but the original Order in Council was not changed. They preferred to use the President and a Vice-President of the Board of Trade who had few functions to perform but a small staff that could be expanded to meet the new demands. Moreover by the 1840s ministerial responsibility for the Board's limited functions was clear. The Order in Council of 1786 had established a board composed mainly of holders of high offices of State, ex officio, viz. the Archbishop of Canterbury, First Lord of the Treasury, First Lord of the Admiralty, Principal Secretaries of State, Chancellor of the Exchequer, Speaker of the House of Commons, Speaker of the House of Commons of Ireland. To these were added ten named persons and the holders of the following offices providing they were members of the Privy Council: Chancellor of the Duchy of Lancaster, Paymaster-General of the Forces, Treasurer of the Navy, Master of the Mint.

But right from the beginning two of the members of the large committee were publicly designated as carrying the main responsibilities. They were the President and the Vice-President. Neither post carried any salary, being held in conjunction with another office. In 1817, (57 Geo. III c.66) however, a salary of not more than £2,000 a year was attached to the office of Vice-President followed in 1826 (7 Geo. IV, c.32) by a similar salary for the President. Even so it remained the practice for most of the first half of the century for the two offices to be held concurrently with other offices, in which case the salary from the Board was suspended.

From the early nineteenth century it was unusual for meetings of the Committee to be attended by any members other than the President and the Vice-President. The minute book of the Committee gradually degenerated into a catalogue or embryo register of papers until in 1853 it was finally abandoned and the normal system of registration was introduced in its place.[64] With three exceptons, made in 1846–8, new appointments of named members ceased in 1823.[65] The President became from the beginning a regular member of the Cabinet. There remained, however, the relations between the President and the Vice-President. The Select Committee on Miscellaneous Expenditure of 1847–8[66] suggested that there was no need for both to receive a salary as one could be remunerated by contemporaneous tenure of some other necessary office, e.g. Master of the Mint or Paymaster-General. The implication was that there was not enough work to warrant two salaries at the £2,000 a year level.

As the executive functions of the office grew the status of the

Vice-President came more into question. A Treasury Committee of 1866 put the problem clearly:

Whatever may have been the original position of the Vice-President, he has now fallen into the unsatisfactory state of an irresponsible officer, of almost equal rank with the President in the Office. In the absence of the President he is paramount. When the President is present he has no duties whatever, except such as he may undertake by arrangement with the President. He may refuse to do anything, or the President may refuse to allow him to do anything; and for these reasons, perhaps, he has also to fill another office which bears no relation to the Board of Trade, namely, that of Paymaster General without salary.

The Committee, therefore, recommended that a Parliamentary Secretary should be substituted who would have 'definite duties to perform in connection with office work' and he would be subordinate to the President.[67]

In 1867, therefore, (30 and 31 Vict., c.72) provision was made for the office of Vice-President to be replaced on the next vacancy by that of Parliamentary Secretary. This took place in December 1868. Thus the growing Department of Trade was in practice in the hands of a President assisted by a Parliamentary Secrtary but remained at law under a Committee of the Privy Council whose members had long since ceased to meet.

Other Offices

The ancient offices of Lord President of the Council and Lord Privy Seal were usually held by a member of the House of Lords and were usually in the Cabinet. In the debates on the abortive Education Bill of 1868 it was suggested that if the Lord President were to lose his education functions to a Minister for Education he would not have enough to do and perhaps, therefore, his office and that of the Lord Privy Seal could be merged. The then Lord President (Marlborough) thereupon produced a list of duties he had to perform other than education. They included Charters to municipalities, companies, and corporations; University statutes; Channel Islands' affairs; diseases of cattle; Diseases Prevention and Nuisances Removals Acts and the Medical Act 1858.[68]

In contrast, with the decline in the use of the royal Seals the

Lord Privy Seal had less and less to do departmentally. Indeed the Select Committee on Official Salaries of 1850 recommended that the office should be abolished and any administrative work transferred to the Home Office.[69] But Prime Ministers found it useful to have two or three paid political offices (the Chancellor of the Duchy of Lancaster and the Paymaster-General were others) with little or no load of administration. Not only did they enable him to bring leading members of his party into the Cabinet without their undertaking the burden of running a major department, it was also useful to have one or two Ministers not too weighed down with day-to-day business.

Law and Justice

One sphere of government which had been little affected by changes designed to concentrate and clarify ministerial responsibility was that vaguely labelled law and justice. The Home Secretary had a general responsibility, but his Cabinet colleague (the Lord Chancellor) was the head of the judiciary. There were also the Law Officers: the Attorney-General and the Solicitor-General for England and until 1872 the King's Advocate-General; the Lord Advocate and the Solicitor-General for Scotland; and the Attorney-General and Solicitor-General for Ireland. All these were political offices. Their general duties were to conduct prosecutions on behalf of the Crown and to deal with day to-day problems on which departments needed legal advice. The Solicitor-General was regarded as the deputy of the Attorney-General. The King's Advocate-General was adviser on international, maritime and ecclesiastical law.

The Lord Advocate was the nearest thing to a Minister for Scottish Affairs. When between July 1866 and December 1867 the person appointed by Derby was unable to find a seat, a Scottish Member suggested the addition of another Parliamentary Under-Secretary at the Home Office to perform the political functions of the Lord Advocate leaving him his professional duties. After some consideration the Home Secretary told the House that he did not think 'there was a sufficiency of business to render necessary the appointment of a distinct under-secretary of state for this particular purpose'.[70] In handling Scottish business the Home Secretary was apparently helped by the Scottish junior Lord of the Treasury. When the Lord Advocate secured election, albeit for an English Borough, the question of responsibility for Scottish affairs was dropped. It was not until August 1885 that a Secretary of State for Scotland was created.

Lord Brougham (Lord Chancellor 1830–4) advocated from time to time the creation of a Minister of Justice. The proposal arose partly out of his concern for the drafting of legislation and partly to provide for a national system of public prosecutions. It does not seem to have attracted much support.

BOARDS AND MINISTERIAL RESPONSIBILITY

Ministerial Boards

In his Cabinet at the end of 1870 Mr Gladstone had fifteen other Ministers. Of these, eight were the single head whilst the other seven had, legally at least, to share their authority with a board. The former were four of the Principal Secretaries of State (Colonial, Foreign, Home, and War), the Lord Chancellor, Lord Privy Seal, Chief Secretary for Ireland, and Postmaster-General. The seven were: Chancellor of the Exchequer, First Lord of the Admiralty, President of the Board of Trade, Lord President of the Council, Vice-President of the Committee of the Council for Education, President of the Poor Law Board, and the Secretary of State for India. As the Prime Minister was First Lord of the Treasury it may be claimed that half the Cabinet were involved in the board form of administration. The First Commissioner of Works, who had been in the previous Cabinet, was also so involved.

These boards were different from those which aroused criticism in the previous century in that they added little or nothing to the patronage at the disposal of the Crown. They were composed mainly of persons who already held office. The Board of Trade was a very good example of the new approach. The board abolished in 1782 was composed of eight paid Commissioners who were usually Members of Parliament. The board constituted in 1786 was composed mainly of ex-officio members and partly of unpaid nominated members. Appointments to the second category continued to be made until 1823 after which there were none except in 1846–8 when three were appointed. It was usual to prohibit the payment of an extra salary to ex-officio members.

By the 1850s that feature did not meet the general belief that effective government could be achieved only by insistence on the responsibility of individual Ministers. Mill stated the prevailing theory: 'As a general rule, every executive function, . . . should be the appointed duty of some given individual. It should be apparent to all the world who did everything, and through whose default anything was left undone. . . . Boards . . . are not a fit instrument for executive business; and are only admissible in it when, for other reasons, to give full discretionary power to a single minister would be worse.'[71] He was expressing a view commonly held inside the departments and in Parliament: it was part of the accepted wisdom. How therefore can that view be reconciled with the continued existence of the board form of departmental management?

It is first desirable to clear out of the way the suggestion that individual ministerial responsibility resulted from a dislike of the board form of administration and that, therefore, it reflected Bentham's views.[72] Bentham certainly believed in individual responsibility as the basis of public management but he aimed to achieve accountability by means other than by Ministers being in Parliament. His ideas were in keeping with the American constitution. Chadwick, his disciple, disliked elected officers whether or not in Parliament.

In contrast the British constitution had for a long time been based on the presence of Ministers in either the Lords or Commons. It was natural that advantage should be taken of this accessibility to make them answer there for government policies and activities. Eighteenth-century experience had shown the very great difficulty of holding a committee or board collectively answerable for all except major issues. In that sense Parliament and Bentham both believed in individual responsibility. In the case of Parliament, however, this did not mean outright opposition to the board, only that one of the members of the board, and one alone, should be answerable for its work. The energies of the House of Commons were directed not against boards *per se* but against allowing the board to obscure the full responsibility of a single answerable Minister.

Should the board not be represented in either House then either some Minister had to accept responsibility for it, as did the Chancellor of the Exchequer for the Boards of Customs and Excise and of Inland Revenue; or friction and irritation would occur, as with the Poor Law Commission during 1834–47; or the fact was accepted because the board's activities were not of much political interest.

This approach fitted in well with an unwillingness to change anything which had been in existence a long time. Sir Charles Trevelyan could not defend the Treasury Board in theory but he believed that the mind of the whole country had become habituated to the present constitution of the Treasury: there was 'a degree of prestige, of authority connected with the name of the Lords Commissioners of Her Majesty's Treasury.' In practical terms, the Treasury needed more than two Parliamentary Secretaries and, had the Treasury Board been abolished, would have had to have created other posts for the junior Lords.

Respect for tradition and its attendant advantages cannot account for the boards established around the middle of the century. There might be political advantages, for example, the ease with which the Education Department could be established by Order in Council. Yet, when the circumstances had greatly changed and there had been much talk of a Minister of Education the Act of 1870 continued the arrangement of 1839. The Local Government Act, 1871 adopted the constitution of the Poor Law Board of 1847, except for the omission of the Home Secretary.

In 1870 the boards in charge of public offices fell into two groups depending on whether or not they included the Minister among their membership. The eight listed earlier as having Cabinet or near-Cabinet representation formed one group.* In turn this group can be divided according to whether the other members of the board were equal or inferior

---

* The National Debt Office, Charity Commission, and Patent Office should be included in this group but did not have the status of a major department.

in political status to the Minister. If the First Lord of the Treasury is disregarded the Treasury fell into that group as did the Admiralty and the India Office.

The case for associating a council of advisers with a Minister was stated by John Stuart Mill. Having pointed out that the political head of a department would be unlikely to have adequate and professional knowledge of his department, he went on 'more frequently, it is not sufficient that the minister should consult some one competent person, . . . and act implicitly on that person's advice'. It was often necessary 'to listen to a variety of opinions, and inform his judgment by the discussions among a body of advisers'. He thought this was 'emphatically necessary in military and naval affairs'. The councils should be consultative in the sense that 'the ultimate decision should rest undividedly with the minister' but the members should not be looked on, or look on themselves as ciphers.[73]

This was the argument used in favour of the India Council and the Board of Admiralty and some would have applied it, as Mill did, to Army administration. It was also a justification for a Treasury Board in the early years of the century. It was, however, an argument which ran counter to the growing domination of the Permanent Secretary. It was later to blossom into the device of the advisory or consultative committee.

Mill's argument could hardly have been the reason for formally associating with one Minister a number of his ministerial colleagues. These could, of course, give him political advice but presumably he could have obtained that from any one of them either at a meeting of the Cabinet or informally. It might have been more understandable if the ex-officio Ministers had always been heads of departments closely linked with the work of the board. That can hardly be said of the Secretaries of State for Colonies and India who were members of the General Board of Health of 1854, but then that board was modelled on the Board of Control for India. Ex-officio membership of a departmental board either was window-dressing to impress the public or constituted a kind of Cabinet committee.

That last explanation was possible when the board took the

form of a committee of the Privy Council. Indeed the Cabinet was in origin a committee of the Privy Council; the Cabinet did not exist at law but all were members of the Privy Council which had a clear constitutional position. The Committees of the Privy Council for Education and for Trade were in effect ministerial committees. So were the arrangements made when some of the powers of the General Board of Health were handed over to a committee of the Privy Council in 1858. Had a similar arrangement been adopted in 1847 for the Poor Law Board it would have made more sense than a statutory board of Cabinet Ministers, yet its conversion to the Local Government Board was not made an opportunity to use the Privy Council committee form of management.

The Committee of Council for Education was used as a ministerial sounding-board for major issues. The Chancellor of the Exchequer and the Home Secretary were the two Ministers most concerned. Though by the 1860s it met only rarely, it met half a dozen times to secure agreement on the Revised Code of 1862. Usually the Lord President would circulate a draft Minute to members of the Committee and so get the views of Cabinet colleagues in that way, but occasionally he would take it to the Cabinet. Earl Russell thought there was 'great use in having the assistance of [ex-officio] members for the legislation of the Department;'. Members 'who concurred to a Minute' were 'to a certain degree, responsible for the general contents of the Minute'. C. B. Adderley (Vice-President, 1858–9), however, thought ex-officio members were 'worse than useless' an encumbrance to both, 'troubling them with consultations which they must feel to be a farce'.[74] That may have been an argument against revealing the names of those consulted but if accepted generally it surely went against the basis of Cabinet government.

Non-Ministerial Boards

In 1870 there existed in England and Wales a large number of public boards which did not include a Minister, but those usually listed as departments or public offices were:
Civil Service Commission
Copyhold, Inclosure, and Tithe Commission

Customs
Ecclesiastical Commission
Emigration Commission
Inland Revenue
Lunacy Commission
Public Works Loan Board
Woods, Forests, and Land Revenues

In the case of the three revenue departments — Customs, Inland Revenue, and Woods, Forests, and Land Revenues — the Chancellor of the Exchequer accepted responsibility in Parliament for their activities, as well as for their general policy. The Colonial Secretary answered for the Emigration Board, until it was abolished in 1878.

In the other cases, though a Minister might have to answer for certain matters, e.g. appointment of board members and the annual Estimates, there appear to have been a clear aim to keep Parliament at arm's length from the day-to-day decisions of the board. There was the argument that if Parliament had vested a function in a board it could hardly expect the Minister to behave as though it were his direct responsibiity. The Home Secretary (Sir George Grey) so defended the independence of the Ecclesiastical Commission: 'The Government', he stated, 'had no control over the matter. The law places the power in the hands of the Ecclesiastical Commissioners . . .'[75]

This was not, however, a watertight argument, for the Chancellor of the Exchequer accepted responsibility for the work of the revenue boards. The point turned more on the character of the work and can be illustrated by the Civil Service Commission. In 1860 a Member concerned about the failure of a boy to succeed in an examination for factory boys at Plymouth demanded that the papers and the answers thereto should be published. Gladstone, Chancellor of the Exchequer, opposed saying: 'I draw a broad distinction between . . . executive acts of an ordinary kind . . . and those particular cases where an essentially judicial function has to be performed.' So long as the Commissioners discharged their functions with honesty and general intelligence their acts should be exempt from review.[76] The motion was rejected. In their first annual Report the Commissioners said, 'As regards particular cases of the individuals subjected to our examination there has been an entire absence of interference, and a tacit but complete recognition of the judicial nature of our functions on the part of Your Majesty's Govt.'[77] 'The Treasury consistently refused to interfere with the decisions of the Commissioners or to act as a court of appeal.'[78]

The argument that a board was exercising a judicial function was used in other cases. When the Act of 1853, (16 and 17 Vict., c.137) which established the Charity Commission, was under discussion, one Member stated the views of the majority. 'It would be most objectionable that persons exercising judicial functions should be liable to be questioned in Parliament on the subject of their decisions ...'[79] A somewhat similar argument was used when the House of Commons occasionally attempted to question the decision in a particular case of the Copyhold, Inclosure, and Tithe Commission, Ecclesiastical Commission, and Lunacy Commission.[80]

It would have been quite consistent with this attitude for the salaries and other expenses of bodies of this kind to be made a charge on the Consolidated Fund, so insulating them from the inquiries possible during the consideration in Committee of Supply of Estimates which had to be voted annually. However the determination of the House of Commons to reduce the number of charges on the Fund led in 1854–5, to all except the Lunacy Commission being transferred to annual votes. Even that became an annual vote in 1869–70.

VII

INTERNAL ORGANIZATION

In the 1780s the typical Cabinet Minister had the assistance of only a few clerks. The Home Office contained only four rooms and sometimes handled less than twenty letters a day. 'It was an office administering to persons, not one administering programs and policies'.[1] True there were the two great empires of the Treasury and Admiralty Boards with their satellite and subordinate departments. But the offices directly servicing the First Lord of the Treasury and Chancellor of the Exchequer and the First Lord of the Admiralty were relatively small. If the description 'clerk' is taken to cover the administrative core of the office the Treasury employed some twenty-four and the Admiralty some sixteen in 1784–5. The Foreign, and Home Offices, about the same date, each employed less than a dozen clerks. Even if messengers, porters, and 'inferior' staff are included, the number employed in the Home and Foreign Offices in 1797 was only twenty-six and twenty-four. The hours of work were normally from 10 to 4 with numerous public holidays. Even so an office was more likely to be over than understaffed. The Commission on Fees were of the opinion that the general business of the Home and Foreign Offices was scarcely sufficient to furnish full employment for the clerks.[2]

Most of the time of these clerks and their assistants was spent either on the preparation and copying of documents of a formal kind for which fees were paid, or making drafts and fair copies of correspondence. Pens were expended in great quantities, two thousand being ordered in the Colonial Office in nine months during 1795–6 when there were only nine persons in the Office.[3] Even Ministers themselves spent some time making copies of their letters. It was not merely that much of the business was highly formalized involving several drafts and the writing of formal documents: it was that there then existed no method of retaining a copy of a letter except by copying by hand.

The non-routine work was done by the Secretary of State or other Minister. He usually had two Secretaries to whom he could turn for advice when making his decisions. The Chief Clerk might also come within this policy group. But even these two or three were very much assistants. The Secretary of State or Minister was thus not the public representative of a department which fed him with policy and had a life and driving force of its own. Instead he was the policy and decision maker, assisted by a small office staff, most of whom were engaged on copying and routine duties.

THE NEW PRESSURES

The simple personal character of the main public offices had changed almost out of recognition by 1870, because of the growth in the volume and character of business and the increasing emphasis on the accountability of individual Ministers to the House of Commons. The yardstick generally used to measure the growth in the business of a public office was the number of registered papers. Letters and papers received went in the first instance to the Registry where they were numbered and recorded before being passed for action to the appropriate secretary or clerk. If the experience of the Treasury was typical, some of the increase in the number of papers in the nineteenth century was due to a change in practice. Trevelyan said in 1848 that it had been the habit in late years to register every paper received in the office whereas in former times many papers were disposed of by private communications, either written or verbal.[4] The figures were used to justify claims for increases in staff or for the upgrading of particular posts. They are, therefore, more likely to exaggerate than to minimize the growth. They also imply that each item registered had the same weight. Nevertheless, they are the best available measure of the increase of public business.

In the case of the Treasury the number of registered papers, averaging 2,500–3,000 a year in the period 1783–93 had reached 4,812 in 1800. By 1820 the number was 22,288 and by 1849 was 29,914. The number of registered letters and papers at the Colonial Office rose from 2,731 in 1806, to 4,487 in 1816, to 8,499 in 1825, and by 1848 had reached 12,018. In 1849 the Admiralty were handling 36,859 registered letters and papers and the Home Office 13,553 letters alone.[5]

These statistics fail, however, to indicate the increasing amount of time and energy which the political head of a department had to devote to the business of the House of Commons and to political affairs generally. This burden did not become particularly noticeable until the 1820s and not sufficient to require modifications in the structure of most offices until ten to fifteen years later.

The House made various kinds of claim on Ministers. In the earlier part of the century it was mainly a matter of being present for debates sometimes of a general character but sometimes with a specific departmental content, e.g. on a petition. The Minister also had to keep an eye on any Select Committee which directly affected his office. From the 1830s the need to be in the House was increased by the part played by Ministers in the preparation of Bills which had then to be steered through Parliament, by debates arising out of the Estimates and by the growing use of Questions. The earmarking of days on which government business had priority emphasized the need for the government to be well represented on these occasions. Palmerston, then Prime Minister, told the Queen in 1861 that he sat in the House four days in every week from 4.30 p.m. until any hour however late after midnight at which the House adjourned. Even the earlier part of the day which once might have been wholly available for handling formal official business was now taken up with political matters.[6] When at the Home Office in 1853–5 Palmerston found that his whole day up to the time when he had to go to the Commons was 'taken up by deputations of all kinds and interviews with Members of Parliament, militia colonels etc.'[7]

The Minister was the person to whom not only Members but also the various interests turned to hear their complaints and suggestions.

A pointer is to be found in the development of the practice of Members giving Ministers notice of Questions by letter or orally in the House. Such notices first appeared on the Notice Paper in 1835. Members continued until 1886 to be able to ask Questions without notice, but well before then notice had become the normal practice. It was obviously to the convenience of Ministers that they should have notice and not be required to answer on the spot. It was also convenient to Members because it ensured that the Minister to whom the Question was directed would be present in the House to answer it. But over and above convenience the new arrangement must have reflected the fact that Ministers could no longer be expected to know intimately all the business of their offices. Preparing information for the answers became a function of the permanent staff. In 1858, for example, the Colonial Office started to procure an additional copy of the Notices so that the Registrar could cut out and place on the table of the head of each division notices which might relate to the subjects comprised within such division. This was to enable the Senior Clerk of the Division to collect the papers needed for answering the question. In January 1871 it was decided that the reading and circulation of the Notices should be done initially in the general department, not in the Registry. Another set should be provided to go to the Parliamentary Under-Secretary (Common's Notices) or to the Secretary of State (Lord's Notices).[8]

These pressures did not affect all offices equally. Those of the Lord President of the Council, Lord Privy Seal, and Chancellor of the Duchy of Lancaster, all of Cabinet status, were not greatly affected. This was one reason why, when departments had to be established for education and public health, they were made the responsibility of the Lord President until their political importance required their separate representation in the Commons. In contrast, as the reformed House was much more interested in domestic than overseas affairs, having to deal with such subjects dear to the hearts of all reformers as poor relief, factory conditions, prisons, police, and local government, made the job of the Home Secretary extremely heavy. The Foreign Office had little or no legislation and though from time to time major political issues arose these were likely to be handled by the Prime Minister, the Foreign Secretary being in the Lords for about half the period 1830–70.

The more time that Ministers had to spend in the House of Commons and on political affairs generally the less time they were able to devote to running their offices. As a result two changes had to take place in the internal structure of the major offices. On the one hand, most Ministers had to receive help on the Parliamentary side. On the other, there was a shift in the balance between the political and the non-political elements in the office, in favour of the latter.

UNDER-SECRETARIES

Ministers had, for a long time employed secretaries and other assistants. The only new issue posed by the nineteenth century concerned the status and tenure of these assistants. The position in 1780 was broadly that the great bulk of those employed in the various offices could count on tenure for life or until ill-health forced them to retire. It was not unusual, however, for the two or three closest to the Minister to change with the fortunes of their master or patron. For he naturally wanted to have somebody whom he knew and could trust and who had a similar approach to problems. He might even wish this person to undertake a great deal of the day-to-day work of the office or to be somewhat similar in function to a deputy even though Ministerial offices could not be executed by deputy. Should the Minister be in the Lords as was very likely at that time it was useful though by no means essential if he had an assistant in the Commons. There was, however, no issue of constitutional principle involved even if the Under Secretary stayed on to serve the next Minister: it was to a large extent a matter of personal choice. During the eighteenth century, therefore, we find the Minister's chief assistant sometimes changing and sometimes remaining stationary and serving one or more successors. The practice did not hinge on whether the secretary was or was not in the House of Commons. Throughout the century, for example, it was the custom at the Admiralty for the Secretary to be a member of the Commons and enjoy a tenure unaffected by ministerial changes.[9]

The situation changed when a Minister ceased to be wholly or mainly the personal choice of the king and became the choice of the Prime Minister and limited to one party. For Ministers then became the symbols, the individual attributes of that party: The political character of each office was emphasized. However good the Minister may have been, however much he enjoyed the confidence of the king and the esteem of Parliament he had to go out with the rest of the Cabinet when his party lost power. And, as politicians desire power, so the new arrangement emphasized the struggle for power and intensified and highlighted the fruits and consequences of securing power.

The late eighteenth century showed an awareness of the new forces at work without a deep understanding of where they would lead. This can be illustrated by the recommendations of the Commissioners on Fees. In their report of 1786 they thought that one Under-Secretary was sufficient in the Home and in the Foreign Office and that, to prevent the confusion and serious consequences that might arise from frequent changes, such office ought to be 'stationary'. Nevertheless the private and confidential business of each Principal Secretary of State might require the assistance of another person and, therefore, it might be expedient for him to be allowed 'on his coming into office, have the nomination of an Assistant Under-Secretary for the management of business of this description.'[10] When they examined the Treasury the Commission recommended that one of the two Secretaries should concentrate on the current business, be 'permanent', and be precluded from holding a seat in Parliament, whilst the other should be a Member and rotate with changes of government.[1]

It will be noticed that the Commission linked the rotating Under-Secretary with the personal needs of the Secretaries of State and did not imply that he ought to be in Parliament. In the case of the Treasury, however, the link was with changes in government, one being prohibited from membership of the Commons, the other being a Member. No doubt part of the difference can be accounted for by the differing Parliamentary needs of the departments. The Treasury already had a great deal of Parliamentary business whereas though the business of the Home and Foreign Offices could raise major issues, it was not then continuously a matter for the House.

This interpretation is borne out by subsequent events. The Commission's recommendations were rejected in each case, though for rather different reasons, yet the general principle came to be accepted. The Treasury Board decided that they needed two 'political' secretaries but in 1805 appointed a third Secretary known as the Assistant Secretary.* He was not to be a Member of Parliament. At the same time the Board decided to distinguish formally between the functions of the joint secretaries, one taking the financial side and the other the non-financial side, including the distribution of patronage. Around 1830 they came to be referred to as the Financial and the Patronage Secretaries. They changed with changes of government whereas the Assistant Secretary remained in office and in 1867 had his title changed to that of Permanent Secretary of the Treasury.

The Treasury also had the benefit of the junior Lords whose many Parliamentary duties came to overshadow their administrative duties. Speaking in 1850 the Chancellor of the Exchequer (Sir Charles Wood) said

latterly the constant supervision which is exercised by the House of Commons over matters of more minute detail than they ever before interfered with, renders it necessary to have a Parliamentary control in the Office over matters which formerly might very properly be trusted to the permanent officers; but now we must take very great care that the matter is seen by some Parliamentary officer, in order to be quite sure not only that that which is right is done, but that it is done in such a way as is consistent with the views which are known by persons in Parliament to be entertained by the House of Commons upon such subjects.

He also mentioned the need to attend Committees of the House: 'No person himself at the head of a heavy department can possibly spare time to do that; and unless there are some persons who are not so constantly employed, and who can be made available for such purpose . . . great public inconvenience would arise'.[12] The Chancellor was speaking particularly in defence of the junior Lords of the Treasury but his comments had a wider implication.

The offices of the Secretaries of State were more representative and provided the future pattern. The Principal Secretaries of State objected to being bound to have one stationary and one rotating Under-Secretary, even though this was the usual practice in the Home and Foreign Offices. The Order in

---

* Until 1816 he was also Law Clerk assisting in the preparation of legislation.

Council of 1795, which settled the establishment of the Home and Foreign Offices made provision for two Under-Secretaries in each without however differentiating between them. Both continued to hold office at the pleasure of their Secretary of State. Nevertheless one came to be regarded as stationary or permanent, with the other one having a marked personal or political flavour.[13] It was not until 1831, however, that the designations 'Permanent' and 'Parliamentary' were officially applied to the Under-Secretaries in the offices of the Secretaries of State, but by then the official designations reflected the practice already adopted in the Home and Colonial Offices and merely applied it to the Foreign Office.[14]

Though between 1782 and 1794 one of the Under-Secretaries at the Home Office was a Member of Parliament it was not until after 1806 that it became rare for him not to be a Member. In January 1822 when Peel became Home Secretary, he appointed his brother-in-law (G. R. Dawson) as his Parliamentary Under-Secretary. Dawson was told by Peel that the 'mere official duties were light . . . the parliamentary duties would be by far the heaviest, and also of greatest importance to me . . . the Parliamentary Under Secretary would be like my right hand . . .' He went on to say what these duties would be. There was attendance on committees of the House. He could not attend all these 'and must devolve on his Under Secretary the charge of attending such as he could not, and watching the progress of the business there'. Then, if the Secretary of State were unavoidably absent from the House, the Under-Secretary 'would have to conduct such business there as belonged to the office, for it would be a mortification to him to see that business in the hands of another . . .' The duties, Peel said, would be difficult at first but there was a material difference between the situation of an Under-Secretary whose principal was in the Lords and that of one whose principal was in the Commons.[15]

The differentiation took longer to develop at the Colonial and the Foreign Offices. When the colonies were brought under the Secretary of State for War, there was provision for only one Under-Secretary. In 1806 a second was established with a particular responsibility for war but was discontinued in 1816. Both offices were non-permanent and were usually held by members of the House of Commons. In 1825 the office of a second Under-Secretary was revived on a permanent, non-parliamentary basis.[16] In the case of the Foreign Office, although between 1796 and 1808 one Under-Secretary usually sat in the Commons, when C. Bagot was appointed in August 1807 he was told by the Foreign Secretary[17] that his duties would be too onerous to combine with membership of Parliament. He, therefore, vacated his seat in the following January. On no further occasion before 1831 did an Under-Secretary sit in the Commons, but two were in the Lords. Even after 1831 its tenure was not invariably associated with membership of either House until 1852.[18]

It took some time for the system to adjust itself to the distinction between parliamentary and permanent. Thus the separate pension arrangements made in 1817 for persons having held certain high and efficient civil offices applied to all Under-Secretaries as well as to the Principal Secretaries of State. The Act of 1834 showed recognition of the 'political' scheme by excluding, *inter alia*, all Under-Secretaries from what had become a 'non-political' scheme. When the superannuation scheme was under examination in 1857 the Royal Commission pointed out the anomaly. The exclusion of all Under-Secretaries and both Secretaries at the Board of Admiralty and the India Board from the general scheme meant that the Permanent Under-Secretaries or Secretaries were treated as 'political functionaries, although these offices are never held by members of Parliament, and are not vacated on a change of administration.'[19] The new scheme introduced by the Superannuation Act, 1859 applied to persons who had served in an established capacity in the permanent Civil Service, so for the first time the pension arrangements recognized the clear distinction which had developed between political and permanent elements in a department.

The distinction between the Parliamentary and Permanent Secretaries came to be extended to all departments which had substantial business in the Commons. In Palmerston's Administration of 1855–8 the Home, Foreign, War, and Colonial Offices each had Parliamentary Under-Secretaries, the Poor Law Board had a Parliamentary Secretary, the Treasury had a Parliamentary and a Financial Secretary, the

Admiralty had a First Secretary and a Civil Lord, the Board of Control had a joint Secretary, and the Board of Trade had a Vice-President. All these were political offices. The position was very little different in Mr Gladstone's Administration in 1870.[20] These posts offered opportunities to ambitious politicians to gain experience and perhaps establish a claim to be head of a department.

The concept of two 'Under' Secretaries left open the question of the division of functions between them and their relations with their Minister. Were, for example, the two to be equal or was the Parliamentary Secretary in effect to be a deputy Minister? The answer, it would seem, varied from department to department and changed over the period 1820–70.

The practice in the Colonial Office in 1848 was for the Assistant or the Permanent Under-Secretary, depending on the nature of the subject, to pass the papers to the Parliamentary Under-Secretary with his observations upon them, from whom they reached the Secretary of State to record his decision.[21] Earlier the Parliamentary and Permanent Under-Secretaries had had co-ordinate authority and divided the Empire between them on geographical lines. But this distribution of work was largely because sheer weight of business prevented the Permanent Under-Secretary from seeing every paper on its way to the Secretary of State. When the office of Assistant Under-Secretary was re-established in 1847 a block of lesser subjects was assigned to him and he was empowered to minute them direct to the Parliamentary Under-Secretary. This gave the Permanent head his chance to deal with every important matter and all drafts passed through his hands.[22]

There was for a long time a similar territorial division of function between the two Under-Secretaries at the Foreign Office.* But from 1860 the Parliamentary Under-Secretary

---

* Palmerston insisted that one or other of the Under-Secretaries should always be on duty; on Sundays as well as weekdays. They divided the supervision of the foreign world between them. He entrusted the 'Governmental' or Parliamentary Under-Secretary with such confidential duties as the management of the Press (C. K. Webster, *Foreign Policy of Palmerston 1830–41*, Vol. I, pp. 65–7).

began to lose ground. In that year he lost the New World and by 1865 he was mainly allocated the petty German states. By then all matters of office discipline had passed to the Permanent head who also had a privileged position as regards finance. Though the Parliamentary Under-Secretary continued, however, to see the papers on the way to the Foreign Secretary, he spent an increasing proportion of his time on purely Parliamentary affairs.[23]

At the Board of Education the status of the Vice-President was, as we have seen, somewhat ambiguous. When the Lord President was the only Minister the Secretary did everything, conducting the correspondence and arranging for his Minister to sign the orders for the payment of grants. When a Vice-President was created in 1856 the Secretary dealt almost wholly with him. The greater part of the current business was transacted by the Vice-President and the Secretary left it to him to decide whether a matter should be referred to the President. Nevertheless Lowe, had the impression that his position as Vice-President was closely analogous to that of an Under-Secretary in other Departments. This view was not shared by H. A. Bruce, Vice-President in 1865, who had a short experience as Under-Secretary at the Home Office. 'It certainly never would have occurred', he said, 'to Mr. Waddington [Permanent Under-Secretary] to apply to me for my decision upon any matter submitted to him; we were equals, and everything that we did not think right to decide ourselves, we referred to the Secretary of State, and the decision of the Secretary of State was always given in his own name.' In contrast, in the Education Office, all questions of administrative detail, except the appointment and removal of inspectors, were referred to the Vice-President 'and his decision in almost every case was final.'[24]

The variations between departments show that a standard pattern had not emerged even by the 1860s. The differences were due to the personalities involved and the character and traditions of the department. Hammond, for example, was a powerful, ambitious man who believed that he was bound to advise and recommend to the Foreign Secretary what he thought should be done and deliberately ousted the Parliamentary Under-Secretary from the diplomatic business of the

Office.[25] In contrast Lingen, who became Permanent Secretary of the Treasury in 1870 was, at the Board of Education at least, an official who 'simply did not believe that policy-making, still less policy-pushing, were within his province. These belonged to the politician ...'[26]

The general trend, however, was clear: it favoured the permanent officer. It was he, not the Parliamentary Secretary who, subject to the Secretary of State, became the head of the department. This was probably inevitable because the Parliamentary Secretary had neither the public prestige and accountability of the Minister nor the experience and expertise of the permanent official.

The strength and domination of the Minister *vis-à-vis* his Permanent Secretary, however short his period of office, lay in his membership of the Cabinet and his standing in his Party and in the House.

The Parliamentary Secretary never had the first and had little of the second to strengthen his position. The House of Commons wanted to deal with the Minister not with his Parliamentary Secretary. The latter was useful for any help he might be able to give in the department because of his knowledge of the Parliamentary scene. But he was not a deputy or substitute Minister. He was more important when his master was in the Lords but almost by definition any department which, by the 1850s, did not need to have its Minister in the Commons was unlikely to have a great deal of day-to-day business in that House.

The ability of the Parliamentary Secretary to act in the same capacity as a permanent official declined as he had to devote more and more of his time to the business and proceedings of Parliament. The trend was however accelerated by the political instability of the middle years of the century. Lord John Russell's Whig Administration which lasted from June 1846 to February 1852 was succeeded by Derby's Conservative Administration, which lasted barely ten months, then Aberdeen's Coalition government of just over two years, then Palmerston's Whig government for three years which was succeeded by another shortlived Conservative government of some fifteen months. In the 1850s there were five Home Secretaries, five Foreign Secretaries, six First Lords of the Admiralty, four Chancellors of the Exchequer and six Presidents of the Board of Trade. In 1852 the office of Secretary-at-War changed hands four times. There had been a similar period of instability with frequent changes of Ministers in the 1830s. From the beginning of 1830 to the end of 1870, there were fifteen new Home Secretaries, eight new Foreign Secretaries, eleven new Chancellors of the Exchequer, and fourteen new First Lords of the Admiralty.

Parliamentary Secretaries changed more frequently than their Ministers. There were twenty-five new ones at the Home Office and nineteen at the Colonial Office during the forty years 1830–70. In the 1850s there were eight at the Home Office (three in 1855), and seven at the Colonial Office.

These frequent changes at the political level coincided with periods of unusually long service in Permanent Secretaries. At the Home Office, S. M. Phillipps was Permanent Under-Secretary from July 1827 to May 1848, to be followed by H. Waddington who remained until August 1867. The Foreign Office had only three Permanent Under-Secretaries between 1827 and 1873, one of whom, E. Hammond, held the post for some nineteen years. C. E. Trevelyan and G. A. Hamilton were the only permanent heads of the Treasury between 1840 and 1870.

Thus about the middle of the century a number of factors came together to shift the balance of power within the main departments. The volume of business had grown beyond a point when even those able to devote their full time to it could not master it all. The time available to the political elements in a department was however being reduced by the increasing demands of Parliament and the public. The change came to be recognized in the relative salaries of the Permanent and Parliamentary Secretaries. After 1831 the Permanent received £500 a year more than the Parliamentary Secretary (£2,000 as against £1,500 and £2,500 as against £2,000 in the Treasury). In part the difference was defended on the ground that the office of Parliamentary Secretary 'frequently led to advancement in the higher offices of the Government' whilst that of Permanent Secretary was 'generally speaking, the commencement of a laborious course of profession of great trust and of close application'.[27] The fact that some members of the

Cabinet received only £2,000 a year (e.g. the Lord President, Lord Privy Seal, and President of the Board of Trade) was, of course, an argument in favour of paying Parliamentary Secretaries at a lower level. Equally the fact that this argument was not applied to the salaries of Permanent Secretaries reflected the importance attached to them.

The shift in the balance between the political and non-political elements by no means stopped short at the Parliamentary Secretary. The position of the Minister was also changing. The rate of change depended to a large extent on the character of the work of the department and the extent to which Parliament took an active interest in it.

The Colonial Office, for example, was peculiarly difficult for Ministers. It had to deal with colonies and territories scattered over the face of the globe. It was unlikely that any Colonial Secretary would have first-hand knowledge of many, if any of them. Moreover the Office dealt with all aspects of each colony — trade, finance, laws, and government and so on. As legal adviser, paid on a fee basis in the period 1813–25, James Stephen had to examine and advise on some 150–250 laws a year proposed by the different colonies.[28] Awkward issues such as slavery, degree of independence, and trading arrangements could raise political rows. Stephen in 1832 wrote that the Colonial Secretary 'must ever continue, dependent upon others for information and assistance in the discharge of his duties, to an extent scarcely known in other Departments, which are conversant with topics with which Statesmen are, from the nature of their ordinary pursuits, habitually familiar.'[29]

In 1839 Lord Durham, in his Report on the Affairs of British North America, stated:

The repeated changes caused by political events at home, having no connexion with colonial affairs, have left, to most of the various representatives of the Colonial Department in Parliament, too little time to acquire even an elementary knowledge of the condition of those numerous and heterogeneous communities for which they have had both to administer and legislate. The persons with whom the real management of these affairs has or ought to have rested, have been the permanent but utterly irresponsible members of the office. Thus the real government of the Colony has been entirely dissevered from the slight nominal responsibility which exists . . .'[30]

It should be noticed that frequent changes of Minister could affect the public attitude towards the department. The fact that there were no less than seven Colonial Secretaries during 1827–35 'made the Minister too elusive for the critics and pointed to the clerks as the real perpetrators of colonial misrule.'[31]

In contrast the Foreign Secretary had mainly to deal with areas and people reasonably familiar to him and with a fairly straightforward goal in mind, the furthering of British interests. The House of Commons was not greatly interested in foreign affairs, except when things appeared to be going wrong. The major debates could be taken by the Prime Minister, who kept in close touch with the day-to-day affairs of the Office. Therefore, though by the 1860s the Parliamentary Under-Secretary had ceased to play a major role the Foreign Secretary continued to dominate the Office until the end of the century.[32]

The ability of Ministers to run their departments depended on their capacity for hard work and their attitude to their role. At one extreme, Palmerston and Graham were both very hard-working and unwilling to be dependent on their permanent staffs. At the other extreme, Russell and Cornwall Lewis took an easier view of their ministerial duties.

It is pertinent, therefore, to compare the work of the same Minister at the head of the same or very similar office at different periods. We can do this for Palmerston.[33] He was Secretary at War from 1809 to 1828. In that office he dealt personally with much of the routine business, his duties involving a mass of the most petty and tedious routine. When he went to the Foreign Office in 1830 he ran it in a similar way. He told the House of Commons that he read 'every report, every letter, and every dispatch received . . . down to the least important letter of the lowest vice-consul.' He also answered them. He described his work as 'more intense and uninterrupted labour than almost any man ever went through before.'[34] In 1838 he explained to the young Queen Victoria: 'The Ministers who are at the head of the several departments of State are liable any day and every day to defend themselves in Parliament; in order to do this, they must be minutely acquainted with all the details of the business of their offices, and the only way of being constantly armed with such information is to conduct and direct those details themselves.'[35] In 1846 he returned to the Foreign Office after an absence of five years. He tried to run things as before but business got into arrears during the Parliamentary session. In 1850 he wrote 'I have been more entirely swamped by business during the whole of this last session of parliament than I ever was at any time.' He found the Home Office in 1853, 'on the whole . . . a much easier office than the foreign'. Even so he found he had little time for detailed administration while Parliament was sitting. In July 1853, arising out of his proposal that there should be attached to the Board of Control 'in lieu of a second political Secretary, a permanent Secretary,' he told the House that it was

impossible to overrate the advantages to the public service of having in each department of Government a permanent secretary, not belonging to any political party, not swayed by passion or feeling, or by the political contests which were from time to time carried on; but a man who, being the depository of the lore and the knowledge belonging to that particular department, was able, being a person also of judgment and discretion, to give the newcomer into office that information as to the past events, as to the principles regulating the department, as to the knowledge of individuals, and as to the details of transactions, without which it was impossible . . . for any man, let him be never so able and never so expert, when he first entered office, to perform his duties with that satisfaction to himself or advantage to the public which he would naturally desire.[36]

It is true that Palmerston was only 25 when he became Secretary at War and remained there for 19 years whereas he was 62 when he became Foreign Secretary for the third time in 1846 and 68 when he became Home Secretary in 1852, spending only three years in the last office. He was also a man of exceptional energy and devotion to duty. But, as Mr Parris has shown, similar evidence is available from an examination of the work of other Ministers. It was possible in the early years of the century for a Minister to handle substantially all the work of his office, and he was expected to do so. By 1850 this was no longer physically possible.

It is significant that the importance of permanent officials came to be publicly extolled around 1850. The statement in the Northcote–Trevelyan Report written in November 1853 and published in February 1854 would hardly have been made so confidently twenty years earlier and would probably not have been popular in Ministerial circles even ten years earlier. 'It cannot', they said,

be necessary to enter into any lengthened argument for the purpose of showing the high importance of the Permanent Civil Service of the country in the present day. The great and increasing accumulation of public business, and the consequent pressure upon the government need only be alluded to; and the inconvenience which are inseparable from the frequent changes which take place in the responsible administration are matter of sufficient notoriety. It may safely be asserted that, as matters now stand, the Government of the country could not be carried on without the aid of an efficient body of permanent officers, occupying a position duly subordinate to that of the Ministers who are directly responsible to the Crown and to Parliament, yet possessing sufficient independence, character, ability, and experience to be able to advise, assist and to some extent, influence, those who are from time to time set over them.[37]

THE 'CIVIL' SERVICE

It is perhaps also noteworthy that the term 'civil service' started to come into use during the 1850s — just how significant is difficult to say. The distinction between the civil and military servants of the Crown had been made for a long time. The Succession to the Crown Act 1707 referred to 'any Office, Place of Employment Civil or Military . . .' Nevertheless unless one was emphasizing the distinction between civil and military the general term in use was the 'public service'.

There are three possible explanations for its use in the 1850s. First, Trevelyan of the Northcote–Trevelyan report had been an employee of the East India Company where the term was in general use. Some of the main occasions for its early use were obviously inspired by the Treasury: the title of the report, the Civil Service Commission, and the Superannuation Act, 1859. Second, it was a label preferred by the public servants themselves. The interest group which actively and successfully compaigned against a contributory pension scheme called itself the Committee of Civil Servants and presented a paper to the Select Committee of 1856 headed The Pensions of the Civil Service. It may be that they merely wanted to distinguish themselves from the armed forces which had a separate scheme. Or they may have preferred the adjective 'civil' to 'public' as being more distinctive and linking them to the Crown rather than with Ministers and the public. Third, it is possible that the term may be a transfer from the Civil Services to those who provided the services. It was ugly to speak of Civil Services Estimates and quite often the phrase 'Civil Service Estimates' was used.

Mr Parris[38] claims that the epithet 'civil' implied a distinction between two branches of the executive government — the civil service as distinct from the political or parliamentary service of the Crown. This is what the term 'civil service' came to mean but that was not its origin nor was it yet its meaning by 1870. 'Public service' continued to be the general usage. The index to the two authoritative volumes by Alpheus Todd published in 1867 and 1869 reads 'Civil service: see public service'. Even the Superannuation Act 1859, probably the first Act to use the term, refers more often to the public service.

When it started to be used it covered both the political and the permanent servants of the Crown. Northcote and Trevelyan reported on the Permanent Civil Service, a contrast with the political not the temporary elements. A Table presented to the Select Committee on Civil Service Appointments in 1860 included both the political and the permanent elements in each department. An 'official' key to the Civil Service of the Crown by J. C. Parkinson, first published in 1859, still stated in its 1869 edition that the leading memebers of the Civil Service consisted of two classes: 'the one strictly civil and the other political; the one permanent, the other changing with the change of ministry'.[39] The modern sharp distinction between political and permanent did not exist. A Return of all persons receiving salaries, pensions, or emoluments exceeding £150 a year in 1860 placed them in alphabetical order. In the Treasury list Gladstone as Chancellor of the Exchequer appeared below a Mr Freemantle, a clerk earning £580 a year.

THE HIERARCHY OF AUTHORITY

From the earliest days there had been an allocation of functions within each public office, quite often indicated by specific titles. But even mong the various grades of clerk there was usually quite a well-defined, indeed on occasion a quasi-legal, allocation of duties. In the Treasury the business was divided under different heads, a part of which was allotted to each clerk, whose duty it was 'to execute everything relating thereto' and receive the fees on every instrument he prepared. The funding of fees in 1782 and the payment of fixed salaries undermined this personalistic method but it was not until 1805 that the nature of the duties to be performed rather than the rights of officials to certain quantities or kinds of business was explicitly made the basis of the division of labour.[40] It could be strengthened, as it was in the Home Office, even in the 1840s, by the payment of an allowance to a particular clerk for taking on extra work in respect of particular Office activity. The fact that much of the work performed depended on a long acquaintance with the precedents and legal formalities also emphasized the claims of particular senior clerks.

The character of the office arrangements also reflected the small number of staff involved, most of whom were engaged on copying and other routine tasks. There was little need or scope for chains of command or the hierarchical structures which emerged later in the century. The Minister and his two Under-Secretaries were in easy personal contact with the clerks with expertise and experience to offer.

The emergence of a more formal system related to levels of authority can be seen in the Colonial Office. When Stephen became Permanent Under-Secretary of the Office in 1836 he proceeded to institute changes in the handling of correspondence and the incoming business of the Office. The system as described in 1848 was as follows. The business of the Office was divided into five departments or sections, four being charged with the correspondence with specific colonies, the fifth having general office functions. Each was under a senior Clerk, Every incoming letter was registered and sent to the senior Clerk whose section dealt with that colony or business. It was his responsibility to minute each item with the prominent points which his experience and knowledge suggested. In ordinary cases he would propose the form of answer or a practical course of action. If the letter referred to a subject about which there had been prolonged or complicated correspondence which required analysis or explanation he had to send it forward with a statement which might assist in the practical consideration of the problem. Having done this the senior Clerk passed the papers to the Assistant or the Permanent Under-Secretary each of whom then passed them on to the Parliamentary Under-Secretary with their observation and from him they passed to the Colonial Secretary, who recorded his decisions on them. The papers were then returned to the senior Clerks whose duty it now became to examine the minutes and drafts to see whether any points in the instructions might be at variance to facts, regulations, or precedents not known to the Colonial Secretary or to the Under-Secretaries. Each departmental head also had to execute all the final instructions he had received including the preparation of any final drafts. These had to receive the sanction of the Parliamentary Under-Secretary and of the Secretary of State. In their various tasks the senior Clerks could draw on the assistance of other clerks in their departments.[41]

All this was in marked contrast to the arrangements of handling correspondence at that time in the Home Office. There the Minister's private secretary attended as soon as the letters arrived, the Under-Secretaries at ten o'clock. When the Home Secretary arrived at about eleven o'clock everything was brought to him by one or other of these three and he settled the answers with them, who then distributed the correspondence inside the department for action. At these daily meetings instructions to the clerks were minuted on the back of the letters. Sometimes this was just a single word such as 'Acknowledge' or 'Nil', at others, quite detailed instructions were given. The appropriate clerk took the necessary action, prepared the letter of reply as instructed which was dispatched after being inspected by the head of his department and the Under-Secretary. Under this system the knowledge and expertise of a clerk only had a chance to contribute to the process after the Minister's decision had been taken, when he might call attention to the disregard of a precedent or an ineptness in the reply. But their function was conceived as narrowly clerical.[42]

At the Treasury[43] the arrangements hinged on a number of senior posts created to meet new needs and pressure of business. The appointment of an Assistant Secretary in 1805 was followed in 1815 by the appointment of a Principal Clerk Assistant to the Secretaries. Two new senior posts were added in 1816, a Principal Clerkship of the Commissariat and the Auditor of the Civil List. By 1834 the latter was held to rank second to the Assistant Secretary. In 1832 a post of Principal Clerk for Colonial Business was created. These were over and above the Chief Clerks who presided over the several divisions into which the executive work of the Treasury was organized. In 1854, however, when a Principal Clerk for Finance was appointed he took over the Finance Division.

In 1848 all letters and incoming papers, after first being recorded, were distributed by the Registry in accordance with fixed rules. Everything relating to patronage and to Woods and Forests went to the Patronage Secretary; matters relating to the revenue departments and all important questions relating to civil contingencies went to the other 'Parliamentary' Secretary; matters relating to the Civil List and to Private and other Bills before Parliament which included clauses calculated to affect the revenue, and all matters relating to municipal corporations went to the Auditor of the Civil List; colonial business went to the Clerk for Colonial Business and so on. The Assistant Secretary was sent everything which did not come under any of those heads and everything relating to the Commissariat.

If the matter referred came under some established rule the Secretary or Clerk concerned prepared a minute on it which he read at the next meeting of the Board for the decision to be recorded. If it were a matter of importance, which did not clearly come under some established rule he submitted it, if he were a Clerk or one of the subordinate functionaries, to one of the Secretaries. Or, if he were one of the Secretaries, he submitted it to the Chancellor of the Exchequer. The higher and more important cases were all submitted to the Chancellor and in certain circumstances, even to the First Lord. In all cases, when the business had been settled by the proper authority, whomsoever he might be, it was put in the form of a Treasury minute and read at the Board which met on Tuesdays and Fridays.

After the minute had been approved it was sent back to the

Registry which after noting the date and nature of the decision passed it to one of the five executive divisions to carry out the decision, e.g. to turn it into a letter or to draw up a warrant. If it were a letter it was then brought to the appropriate Secretary to sign it. If it were a warrant it was laid on the table of the Board to be signed by three Lords, two after 1849 (12 and 13 Vict., c.89).

The arrangements at the Treasury were thus a mixture of decisions taken by permanent officers without reference to their political heads and those matters of great importance which were passed up to the political heads. The Board, however, provided a political check even on the first class of business. It will be noticed that the separation of those concerned with making the decisions from those charged with their execution was somewhat similar to the arrangements in the Home Office.

The Treasury Board ceased to meet in 1856 and in the same year major changes ended the distinction which had existed since the early years of the century between officials with general advisory functions and those with specific executive duties. The posts of Principal Clerk Assistant and Principal Clerk for Colonial Business were abolished and the work of the department was redistributed among six divisions, presided over by the Assistant Secretary, the Auditor of the Civil List, and four Principal Clerks. In 1859 and 1867 the Assistant Secretary and the Auditor of the Civil List were successively relieved of responsibility for divisions, which were as a consequence reduced to four.[44]

The process of delegation went further as the load on Ministers increased. When Earl Granville, a very experienced Minister, became Colonial Secretary in 1868; following Foreign Office practice, he authorized the two Under-Secretaries to sign dispatches for him. He said his time was too valuable to be used signing dispatches 'which merely convey acknowledgement, or transmit documents, or request formal information, or signify the acquiescence of the Secretary of State in arrangements of detail, on which it is not usual to interfere with the discretion of the Governor'. His successor Lord Kimberley continued the practice. Very critical of the slowness of the Office in answering its mail Granville introduced short cuts in the circulation of papers, e.g. when there was little doubt regarding the correct answer to a letter, then the draft reply or even a fair copy was to be sent to him in the first instance. He discontinued the geographical division of work between the Permanent Under-Secretary and the Assistant Secretary, desiring that 'the responsibility for the whole business of the office should rest with one person to whom [he] should be entitled [to] look primarily for assistance without distinction of Colony'.[45]

INTERNAL COHESION

The introduction of a chain of command had a unifying effect on a department. The procedure developed in the Colonial Office, for example, enabled the Minister to be presented with a departmental official view. To the information about precedents and the accumulated wisdom of the those familiar with the affairs of a particular colony was now added the views of the permanent head of the Office, based on a conception of the policy which the department would like to see pursued. It was therefore less possible for different sections or divisions to be pursuing contrary policies or giving contradictory advice to the Minister. The Permanent Secretary was put in a position to tender consistent advice which over the years could amount to the policy of the Office. This greatly increased his role and power.

The system was easier to introduce in departments where the increase in the volume of work had not taken the form of entirely new functions. For the extra load could be handled by the employment of more clerks either throughout the office or in particular divisions. This was not however the way that expansion could be handled in the Board of Trade or even, in the Home Office. In these two offices the development of new functions, for example, as regards railways or the inspection of factories, led at first to the creation of new sub-departments outside the main core of the clerks and even with a measure of independence.

The Board of Trade was a particular case in point. The new subjects added to the department were usually assigned to some new officer or some subordinate board. In 1853, there were four distinct 'departments' each with its own system of registry, staffs of clerks, and even separate staffs of messengers, and all in the same building. There were also five other sections or functions for which the President had some responsibility, housed in other buildings. The Mercantile Marine department was managed by a board of three who decided what was to be done about the letters they received. The attention of the President was called to matters which the board considered to be of sufficient importance. But the Joint Secretaries of the Board of Trade were not kept informed of the work of this body. The varied and somewhat haphazard relations between the President and the work of these different departments caused a Committee of Inquiry to suggest certain principles of organization.

'In all Executive Departments', they said, 'the arrangement of the responsible Offices should be in regular subordination and there should always be the means of calling a particular individual to account for his own share of the business, and allowing him no opportunity of sheltering himself by pleading the authority of any one but the person to whom he is immediately responsible.' In other words there should be a clear chain of command. In the case of the Board of Trade

there should be one Chief Officer to whom the President can turn for information with respect to any part of the business, and who is to be held responsible for the proper discharge of the whole. He should be assisted by competent persons in each subordinate Department upon whom he can rely for faithfully transacting matters of routine, and for bringing before him in a convenient form all such as require his especial notice and decision. The extent to which such Assistant Secretaries* should be trusted to manage the business of their Departments will depend upon the judgment which the Chief Secretary may form of their abilities and trustworthiness.[46]

The Committee recommended that the five departments which they had examined should be reduced to three —

* The term Assistant Secretary was first introduced into the Board of Trade in 1810 to denote those officials who, in the absence of the Clerks of the Privy Council were effectively the senior permanent officials of the department. From 1829 to 1867 it was increasingly the practice to refer to the two Assistant Secretaries as the Joint Secretaries. In 1853 the term was again adopted as a distinct grade (J C. Sainty, *Officials of the Boards of Trade*, pp 42 and 44).

General, Railway, and Mercantile Marine. Each should be headed by an Assistant Secretary who would be brought into regular and frequent communication with the President on matters concerning their departments. They thought this should be possible without weakening the legitimate authority or diminishing the responsibility of the Chief Secretary 'generally charged to look to the proper working of the whole machinery of the Office'. There should be only one 'Chief' Secretary not two. As regards the Inspectors of Railways and the professional members of the board of Mercantile Marine the Committee recommended that they should act as professional assistants to the President and Chief Secretary for the purpose of inquiring into and reporting upon matters referred to them in their respective fields.

The implementation of the proposal for a single 'Chief' Secretary was delayed, because of the special position of T. H. Farrer, who carried the whole responsibility for the Marine Department and who became the sole Permanent Secretary in 1867. The secretaries of the distinct Railway and Marine departments were given the title of Assistant Secretary but no such officer was appointed in charge of the General Department. In 1867[47] a further inquiry still found the Railway department conducted as an independent department and the existence of fragmentary subdivisions and therefore there was a want of cohesion. As a result the four departments (Commercial, Marine, Harbour, and Railway) were each put in charge of an Assistant Secretary under a single Permanent Secretary.[48]

IMPLICATIONS FOR RECRUITMENT

The increasing reliance of the political heads on their senior officials focussed attention in the 1840s on securing the best people for those positions and for making the best use of their time.

The bulk of the clerks were recruited at an early age and spent most of their working life in the same section of the office copying letters and documents and similar routine duties which required care but gave very little scope for initiative and intelligence. As a result they became expert in the accepted wording of the numerous formal documents in common use and the precedents for dealing with normal events. When, by virtue of seniority, they reached some form of senior clerkship, they had become in Palmerston's words, 'the depository of the lore and the knowledge' belonging to the department and were able to give a new Minister 'information as to past events, as to the principles regulating the department, as to the knowledge of individuals and as to the details of transactions'.

Sir Charles Trevelyan, the permanent head of the Treasury became highly critical of this single-tier system of organization.[49] He argued that it was expensive to use highly paid clerks on routine tasks. In his opinion there was a serious imbalance in the Treasury between the handful of Principal Clerks on whom the higher duties fell and who were overworked and the much larger number of clerks engaged on copying and routine duties and who were underemployed. Even more important he believed that long attention to such tasks dulled the intelligence of the better kind of recruit.* In 1848 he recommended that the Establishment of the Treasury should be reorganized on the basis of a distinction drawn according to the intellectual content of the work. Clerks were to be entrusted only with work with an intellectual content, the mechanical and routine duties being undertaken by an inferior class of writers or copyists specifically recruited for the purpose. His proposal was criticized by a former Chancellor of the Exchequer and by one of his predecessors as Assistant Secretary. The Select Committee did not favour his scheme.

In 1849, however, Trevelyan persuaded the Chancellor of the Exchequer that clerks on the general Establishment of the Treasury should be less employed on copying and that a number of 'Extra Clerks' should be recruited to undertake this work. Shortly after this he persuaded the Colonial Office to introduce by degrees 'a clear distinction between those kinds of labour which call for the exercise of the higher intellectual faculties and those in which good penmanship and common

* 'A young man comes from a public school full of energy, intelligence and excited hopes, but after two or three years' incessant copying he becomes disappointed and disgusted.' (Select Committee on Miscellaneous Expenditure, PP 1847–8, Vol. XVIII, Part 1, Q 1670.)

attention to exactness and regularity are all that is required'. There was to be a Superintendent of Copyists who would employ as many as were required to do the whole of the copying and other merely manual work of the department. In neither case, however, was the new principle fully accepted, for the copyists did not become part of the permanent Establishment.

In 1853 Trevelyan, however, managed to go even further with a reorganization of the Board of Trade. The President agreed that all mechanical work should be transferred to a copying department whose specially recruited staff were to receive all the benefits of established service, including superannuation, but were to be kept entirely separate from the 'Superior' Establishment with no claims to promotion to it. This two-tiered structure of a Superior and a Supplementary Establishment became the model for other Offices, including the Poor Law Board, the Board of Control, and the Post Office.

In their Report Northcote and Trevelyan stressed the importance of separating intellectual from mechanical labour. They talked in terms of superior and inferior positions. The latter would be engaged on copying, registering, posting accounts, and other routine duties. The competitive examination for the superior class should be on a level with the highest education in the country. The aim should be to secure first-class men from the Universities and the age limits for the competition should as a general rule be 19 and 25. These recruits with superior powers might 'rationally hope to attain to the highest prizes in the Service' which presumably meant that if the new system worked there would be one day no need to recruit Permanent Secretaries from outside the service.

For the lower class of appointment the age limits should be 17 and 21 and the examinations should be held in different parts of the country. These supplementary clerks could be available for work in any department according to the demand for their services.

The main argument used against the proposed distinction was that a detailed knowledge of the forms and procedures employed in a department was indispensable to senior officers and could best be obtained by working one's way up through the department. Trevelyan and Northcote admitted that care would have to be taken to ensure that those clerks who would be called upon to perform higher duties 'obtained a sufficient acquaintance with the details of the machinery of the departments'. Their proposal, they said, did not exclude such training. Although the superior clerks were to be employed on intellectual work from the beginning, they were to do a certain amount of mechanical work as well.

Not all departments adapted their organization to take account of the distinction. The War Office, for example, would not introduce a Supplementary Establishment. But even those which did, found it difficult to keep the two classes separate. In the Board of Trade the main difficulty arose from the substantial and continuing growth in the volume of business. As the pressure of intellectual work became too great for the Superior Clerks, clerks in the Supplementary Establishment were used and temporary (unestablished) clerks were engaged to deal with the routine business. The attractiveness of the conditions to Supplementary Clerks had resulted in the recruitment of men whose intelligence and qualifications were superior to those required for merely mechanical work. The blurring of the distinction led to dissatisfaction among those clerks who were coming to be employed on work similar to that done by the Superior Clerks but were denied similar pay and prospects of promotion.

Departments continued to make their arrangements according to the views of their Ministers and a conception of their needs. Even departments which continued to have a Superior and a Supplementary establishment found it impossible in practice to keep them distinct. In 1863, for example, the Board of Trade went back to a single-tier system combined with a number of unestablished temporary clerks.

Nevertheless the idea that the time of clerks should be devoted to intellectual activities took root. The problem was to find the best arrangement for handling the routine and mechanical business. The view of the Treasury in a letter to the Home Office in 1872 was that 'the number of senior and principal clerks should be no greater than is sufficient to place each of them in separate charge of a convenient portion of the official business under the Secretary of State'. When the smallest number of these had been settled thte Treasury thought that

the number of second and third class clerks of the Superior Establishment should not altogether be more than double of the number of senior and principal clerks. These relative numbers become feasible if such second and third clerks are relieved of mechanical work ... and are confined to the duty of assisting the senior clerks in the minuting of answers on the simpler cases and preparing the material for minutes on the rest.

Fair copying, registration, statistics, and accounts were to be undertaken by writers working under a small number of established clerks of a Supplementary Class.[50]

When around 1850 the Board of Trade were short of clerks to copy letters and documents one section turned to the recently developed copying press and gradually its use spread throughout the department. In 1873 Farrer, the Permanent Secretary, thought that the department would need another 6–12 clerks if it were to revert to hand copying. By then the device was used in the Admiralty and to some extent in the Customs. The subject had, however, never been thoroughly considered in the Treasury.[51]

One of the arguments used by Trevelyan against the single-tier system was that it discouraged the entry of able young men and dulled the intelligence of the ablest that did enter. As a result of these and other factors, for example, promotion by seniority rather than by merit, departmental heads were not infrequently obliged to go outside the office and appoint someone of high standing in an open profession or someone distinguished in other walks of life. In several departments the clerks were regarded as having no claims whatever to what were called staff appointments. This was discouraging to those who entered the service at an early age and looked forward to a career in the department.

At the time of the Northcote–Trevelyan Report it was rare for the permanent head of a department to have started his career as a junior clerk. Of the first six Assistant Secrtaries of the Treasury (1805–70) only two had entered as junior clerks and they covered only six of the sixty-five years. In 1850 the permanent heads of the Foreign, Home, and Colonial Offices had all been specially recruited. These top posts were ministerial appointments: when a vacancy occurred the political chief was anxious to appoint someone who was both able and politically trustworthy. The choice of outsiders for 'staff appointments' was particularly noticeable in a department such as the Board of Trade which had been required to take on a number of entirely new functions. This was understandable for the office employed only a handful of clerks none of whom could claim any expert knowledge of the new functions.

By 1870 the situation had not materially altered. Trevelyan's successor at the Treasury in 1859 had been a Member of Parliament for sixteen years and was Financial Secretary at the time of his appointment. With the exception of T. F. Elliot, promoted from the ranks in 1847, the posts of Assistant and Permanent Under-Secretary at the Colonial Office were filled from outside the Office until 1892.[52].

The system of limited competition introduced after 1855 produced a better educated class of clerk, and towards the end of the century it became more usual for the heads of departments to be secured by promotions from within. Twenty-two men entered the Treasury between 1856 and 1870 under this new system. Fifteen of these had been to a university as against only six in the years 1834–56. They were not academically distinguished as were those recruited when open competition was introduced. But in time they came to fill the top posts. Three became Permanent Secretaries to the Treasury: R. Welby in 1885, F. Mowatt in 1894, and Edward Hamilton in 1902.[53] Whether they and the other Permanent Secretaries appointed in this way were superior to Harrison, Trevelyan, Hammond, and Stephen appointed by patronage is an interesting but unresolved question.

ANONYMITY — THE MONOLITHIC DEPARTMENT

The increasing stress on individual ministerial responsibility, the intensification of party politics, and the more prominent roles of the Press and public opinion raised the question of the correct public behaviour of the non-political element in the public offices.

They posed little or no problem for those recruited at an early age. Had these wanted the public limelight they would hardly have chosen to enter the public service with its years of backroom drudgery. In any case, in their early years their status would not have given much weight to any public utterances they might care to make. By the time they had reached the topmost levels of their department they were well grounded in reticence about public business. This was not the case with those appointed at a mature age, usually because their party beliefs were palatable to the Minister or because they had already made themselves known in a particular field. Quite often such appointees were accustomed to writing and speaking in public and dealing with the Press, Select Committees, and other organs of opinion. They came in at the top, as Permanent Secretary or head of a sub-department, usually without any previous experiences of the public service. Their position brought them in close touch with the Minister and therefore with the politics and controversies of his policies. If they entered a well-established major department they might in time take on the traditions of the clerks under them. But the expansion of governmental functions in the period 1830–50 led to the creation of many new, somewhat specialized posts most of which were filled by outsiders. Such posts, if only because of their newness, provided considerable scope for individual initiative. For some twenty to thirty years, therefore, there flourished a small number of civil servants in influential positions who were not content just to advise a Minister in private but were prepared to advocate and press for their ideas in public.

The Board of Trade in the period 1830–42 is a very good example. Le Marchant, appointed as a joint Secretary in 1836, was a Whig supporter and in 1846 became a Whig Member of Parliament. McGregor who succeeded Deacon Hume as joint Secretary in 1840 was also a Whig. All the top posts in the Board of Trade, e.g. the Comptroller of Corn Returns and the head of the Statistical Department were filled from outside. All were pronounced free-traders. Moreover in their zeal for free trade they were prepared to advocate it in public and were neither 'anonymous nor neutral in controversial issues of economic policy'. They entered into discussions with Members of Parliament, encouraged the setting up of Select Committees, which they then fed with evidence to support their cause, and were prepared to work with groups favourable to their ideas.[54].

The semi-political public servants of whom Edwin Chadwick and Rowland Hill were two of the most prominent examples, were men of strong beliefs who wished to see their ideas put into practice. They moved in intellectual circles who shared these ideas. Their activities have attracted some approval in recent years: they are seen as reformers who got things done notwithstanding the apathy or dilatoriness of Ministers and Parliament. Their behaviour was not, however, consistent with the new pattern of individual ministerial responsibility. They were neither Officers in the old sense with their own rights and duties nor were they politicians who could be removed by the House of Commoms or the electorate. Those who believed in the policies these zealots were pursuing were ready to overlook the ambiguity of their position. But those who disagreed could only try and strengthen the new conventions which reduced the public status of such officials. They would either not have existed or not had so much influence at the beginning of the century if only because it was not a period which encouraged anyone who wished to promote new policies and functions. They were able to operate in the 1830s–50s because it was a period of reform, many new posts were being created and no firm tradition had emerged as to the correct public behaviour of public servants.

At a minimum, action of this kind by senior public servants was politically embarrassing. At its worst it raised in an acute form the precise relationship between the permanent staff of a department and their Minister. The implication was that if the Minister did not act on their advice they felt free to attempt to bring pressure on him from outside. Ministers were most unlikely to look favourably on anything which embarrassed them publicly, or to trust advisers who felt so strongly about views not held by the government.

Trevelyan committed a serious error of judgement in 1843 when after a visit to Ireland he wrote to the *Morning Chronicle* under a pseudonym but openly admitting the letter to be his handiwork. Sir James Graham, the Home Secretary, told him, 'In a critical state of affairs you have erred in judgement . . .' He asked whether the Prime Minister had seen Trevelyan's letter in the Morning Chronicle: 'Surely,' he said, 'it is highly improper that a Secretary of the Treasury should thus communicate to an Opposition newspaper intelligence which he made known to the government as of official importance'. Peel agreed. 'How a man,' he replied, 'after his confidential interview with us could think it consistant with common decency to reveal to the Editor of the Morning Chronicle and to the world all he told us is passing strange. He must be a consumate fool'. Peel also wrote to Graham about the same time, having MacGregor of the Board of Trade also in mind: 'It is really difficult in these times to place confidence anywhere, the love of talking and the desire for notoriety make people forget their duty'.[55] Trevelyan's lapse is difficult to reconcile with his very great care 'to keep aloof in public from party politics being so strict about this that 'he never voted in a parliamentary election whilst holding an official position' thinking this to be the only, correct conduct for a senior public servant[56]

These incidents were not, however, typical of the behavour the main body of public servants. They are evidence that no clear code of conduct had yet emerged. Yet thought was being given to it. In 1833 Lord Howick, who had just ceased being Parliamentary Under Secretary, at the Colonial Office, suggested to Sir James Stephen, the Permanent Under-Secretary, that Stephens's name should be publicly associated with his own in connection with the Bill abolishing slavery in the colonies. Stephen made two objections to the use of his name. First, that Howick would encumber himself with Stephens's unpopularity with the West India Body. Second, that 'as I fill no substantive or independent station, I have no just claim to arrogate to myself any part of the credit of any measure in the preparation or maturing of which I may have been employed. Exempted as I am from all public responsibility, it would be unjust were I to assume any share of the honour due to those who have rendered themselves responsible for my compositions'

In 1844 Stephen was attacked in an article entitled 'Reform in the Colonial Office' in the *Colonial* Magazine, whereupon Lord Stanley, the Colonial Secretary, wrote to him, 'For the administration of Colonial Affairs I am responsible and not you; and my responsibility is not to any portion of the Press, daily or Periodical, but to the Queen and to Parliament and to those two high authorities only'. He was indignant at the succession of calumnious attacks on Stephen, whose situation imposed on him 'the obligation of silence'. He authorized Stephen to make use of the letter showing his trust and confidence.

When Gladstone became Colonial Secretary in December 1845 Stephen wrote

Be assured that the last thing which I am in danger of forgetting is . . . that my office is, and ought to be, that of a mere Subordinate . . . I have no one wish . . . but to be a zealous, effective and submissive Servant to its Head . . . It is my daily relief and solace to feel that he sustains the undivided responsibility for every decision taken here and that I am responsible only for supplying him . . . with all the necessary materials for forming such decisions.[57]

Sir James Stephen was stating not merely his subordinate role to the Colonial Secretary, and for that matter to the Parliamentary Secretary, but also two principles which should govern the status of the Permanent Secretary, and therefore of his subordinates. First, that public accountability resided in the Minister alone: to the public the permanent official did not exist, he was anonymous. Second, as it was the Minister who had to stand up to criticism in Parliament and the Press, equally it was the Minister and not his officials who should receive the praise and the credit.

There was, however, another implication in these several examples. This was that a department could speak with only one voice in public: the voice of the Minister. Not even the Parliamentary Secretary could pursue in public a different line of policy. For the permanent staff in the department unanimity was more likely to be achieved if all their views had to pass through the Permanet Secretary, a further factor favouring the creation of a pyramid of command. It made it easier for a department to speak with one voice to the Minister, and, subject to that, equally with one voice to other departments and to the world in general.

The pyramid was readily achievable if the department could be organized into a series of subordinate divisions or branches, staffed mainly by clerks. But some departments, principally the Home Office and the Board of Trade, were very inclined to administer new functions outside the central core of the Office, an arrangement which could raise problems not only of the degree of control the department could exercise over them but also the public status of such officials.

We have already touched upon the ambiguous status of the early Factory Inspectors in respect of ministerial accountability. This ambiguity was emphasized by the publicity given to their reports. The Act of 1833 required the Inspectors to report to the Minister at least twice a year about their visits and proceedings and about the state and condition of the factories and mills and whether these were conducted according to the directions of the Act. The Act did not make publication a statutory obligation on the Home Secretary but nevertheless, from the beginning, the reports he received were printed and submitted to both Houses of Parliament.

In their early reports the Inspectors went beyond the statutory requirements.[58] They discussed and criticized the existing laws, referred to debates in the House of Commons, and quoted correspondence and instructions they had received from the Home Office. Naturally the Home Secretary found the polemical and revealing character of some of the Reports politically embarrassing for they were used by the critics of the government in Parliament and the Press. In June 1846 Sir James Graham let it be known that the reports should not include correspondence with the Home Office: 'for it would be irregular and inconvenient, . . . the propriety of publishing such correspondence and documents being a matter for the consideration of the Secretary of State.'

Three years later his successor (Sir George Grey) reiterated the point and added that he had also observed with regret, that 'while much valuable and interesting information is contained in [the] Reports, there is in some parts of them a controversial tone, which appears . . . to be inconsistent with the character which such Reports ought to bear.' He thought it ' very inexpedient that the results [of a conference between the Inspectors] should be to make their several reports the medium of argumentative discussion between the Inspectors on points wherein they differ in opinion, instead of being restricted to . . . the state and condition of the Factories within their Districts . . .' The Home Secretary had 'no wish to check the free expression of opinion on the part of the Inspectors' and he was always desirous of having 'the benefit of their experience and suggestions . . . but as such suggestions may in some cases be properly considered as confidential, it is not expedient that when of this nature they should be transmitted to the Secretary of State in a printed form and embodied in a Report to be forthwith laid before Parliament'. The Inspectors were therefore requested to revise their Reports accordingly. They were told that any observations which they wished to address to the Home Secretary outside the scope of their normal duties should be submitted in such a way that they did not come before Parliament as printed papers.

By the 1850s the reports came to conform strictly with the requirements of the Act. In February 1859, Sir George Grey, who had ceased to be Home Secretary a year earlier, told the House of Commons that, when an Inspector branched into irrelevant matters the practice of the Home Office was to refer it back to him pointing this out. Grey had generally found that the Inspector at once expunged it. The report, as revised by the Inspector, was then printed and presented to Parliament.[59]

Her Majesty's Inspectors of Education, first appointed in December 1839, were instructed in August 1840 that their reports were intended to convey such further information about the state of elementary education in Great Britain as to enable Parliament to determine in what manner the sum voted could be most usefully applied. It was intended that the reports would be laid before both Houses.

Encouraged by Kay-Shuttleworth, the first Secretary of the Education Department, to express their opinions freely and to place a wide interpretation on their duties, some used their reports to air their views generally on educational matters, far removed from the problems confronting elementary schools.[60] One Inspector submitted a report of 211 pages, mainly taken up with disquisitions on the differences between the Celtic and Anglo-Saxon races. As the number of Inspectors grew, the cost of printing and bulkiness of their reports caused the Treasury to protest and the department to attempt to reduce the volume of paper circulated. In 1851, for example, the Lord

President complained of the extravagant length to which the reports ran and requested Inspectors to be more concise.

In the 1850s however, a new factor began to affect the relations between the department and the Inspectorate — elementary education became an active political issue leading to the Newcastle Commission of 1858 and the introduction of a system of Payment by Results, the Revised Code, in 1862. Some of the Inspectors were strongly opposed to the change and to the policies being pursued by the department and felt independent enough to express their criticisms in public. The Minister and his Permanent Secretary attempted to curb their independence.

Lowe, with the support of his Permanent Secretary (R. R. Lingen), had already decided to discontinue publication of the Inspectors' reports in full, and merely to quote selected extracts from them. This led to a 'Grand Remonstrance', signed by most of the Inspectors, and a debate in the House of Commons. Some Members claimed that the reports were very widely read and feared that the department would omit from its digest any points made by Inspectors which criticized or reflected adversely on its policy.

In his defence, the Vice-President said: 'It would be a mischievous principle, to lay down that the heads of each Department . . . should be compelled to print indiscrimately at the public cost everything sent in to them by their subordinate agents'. What he asked, would be thought if the Prison Inspectors included in their Reports lengthy dissertations on moral philosophy. If the House were dissatisfied, when they saw the first of the new style reports it would have to agree a resolution requiring 'on its own responsibility that the Reports furnished to the Excutive should be published by them *in extenso* as first sent in'.[61] The Motion was withdrawn.

Early in July 1861, during consideration of the Education Estimates a Member called attention to the fact that one of the Inspectors of Roman Catholic Schools in his published report had claimed to show how much more admirable was the influence of Romanism on the social and moral conduct of nations and individuals than Protestantism. He thought this a great breach of duty upon the part of the Inspector, who had no right to make use of public time and money for the purpose. Lowe agreed that the remarks of the Inspector were irrelevant. He had taken measures to prevent the repetition of such observations.[62] At the end of the month, however, the same Member moved that an Address be presented to Her Majesty that She be graciously pleased to give directions that a copy of further reports of Inspectors of Roman Catholic Schools be laid before the House. He claimed that the volume of Reports for 1860 and 1861 omitted the reports of two out of the three Roman Catholic Inspectors. Lowe said he had not altogether been satisfied with the report of Mr Morrell so he had thought it better not to print it. He went on: 'When expressions were used which he did not approve, or when irrelevant matter was introduced, it was his duty to send the reports back to the Inspectors. He could not omit passages, or make alterations, without being charged with garbling, so that when the reports were returned to him unaltered, or still containing objectionable matter, he made it a rule to suppress them altogether'.[63] The Committee of Council had recently passed a Minute. 'inspectors', it read, 'must confine themselves to the state of the schools under their inspection, and to practical suggestions for their improvement. If any report, in the judgement of their Lordships, does not conform to this standard, it is to be returned to the inspector for revision and if, on its being again received from him it appears to be open to the same objection, it is to be put aside as a document not proper to be printed at the public expense.'[64]

In June 1863 the issue was raised again on going into Committee of Supply, this time by W. E. Forster. He interpreted a reply made by Lowe earlier in the Session to mean that the Minister intended 'to suppress everything in the Reports which did not coincide with his own views, and to publish only what he himself approved'. Forster claimed that the results of the experience of the Inspectors should not be confined to the Education Office but should be communicated to Parliament. Lowe agreed that the issue raised was one of great importance. It amounted to this: 'whether in the Education Department there shall or shall not be that discipline which exists, and is found necessary, in every other Department of the State'. After explaining the practice of the last two years and giving examples of the kind of material he did not think should be printed, he went on 'I hold it to be almost impossible to work any Department. of State unless these gentlemen who fill subordinate offices in it, and on whose assistance the chiefs must rely, are loyal to the Department.' They were not to surrender their opinions but,

at any rate, they should maintain silence if they cannot agree with the heads of their Department. No person will say that subordinates ought to be allowed to write controversial letters in the newspaper disputing the policy of their superiors. So with respect to official Reports laid before this House; I hold that it is the clear duty of every Department to prevent the writers of Reports from entering into controversy as to matters decided upon by the chiefs of the Office in other words, as to the policy of the Department . . . If the House chooses to say that the Inspectors are to report directly to it of course we shall instruct them to obey the order; but if the Reports are to pass through our hands, I hold it to be the first principle of official duty to enforce that sort of reticence and reserve which all official men are bound to practise . . . no public Department . . . can be expected to carry on its operations with success, if it is obliged to print controversies maintained against itself by the very persons whom it employs to carry out the objects intrusted to its charge.[65]

In April 1864 Lord Robert Cecil* moved a motion to the effect that the exclusion from the Inspectors' reports as published of statements and opinions adverse to the department's views, while favourable matter was admitted, were violations of the understanding under which the appointments were originally sanctioned by Parliament and tended to destroy the value of the reports. Lowe denied having personally altered any of the reports submitted by the Inspectors. Unfortunately the critics had obtained copies of reports that had been altered which they circulated to Members. As a result Cecil's motion was carried and Lowe at once resigned.[66] A Select Committee appointed to investigate the charge accepted Lowe's explanation and in July the House rescinded its earlier resolution.[67]

The Select Committee[68] learnt a good deal about departmental practice. Lingen, the Permanent Secretary, explained

---

* In the earlier debate he had claimed that there was but one thing more important than loyalty to a department and that was loyalty to the House of Commons.

that if an Inspector in his report argued about the future and if such arguments contradicted the policy of his department, then the report was not presented. The Committee concluded that 'supervision exercised in objecting to the insertion of irrelevant matter, of mere dissertation, and of controversial argument' was consistent with the powers of the Committee of Council. It had on the whole been exercised fairly. No objection was made to statements of facts observed by the Inspectors within their official experience, whatsoever might be their bearing on the policy of the department.

So the Inspectors, whether of the Home Office, the Education Department, or any other department, were brought into line with the practice of official reticence which applied to the general administrative side of a department, whether Permanent Secretaries or clerks. They were subordinates notwithstanding the publication of their reports. They could express their views within the privacy of the department but if they did not agree with their Minister's policy they had to be silent in public. By the end of our period each department presented a single, monolithic voice.

VIII

THE ADMINISTRATION OF LOCAL AFFAIRS

The factors which dominated the development of the public offices which served the king in London were not those which greatly affected the machinery for handling local affairs. For the latter was mainly in the hands of unpaid officers, indeed often a form of forced labour. The Clerks of the Peace and the Town Clerks in some Boroughs were possibly the only exceptions. The movements leading to the suppression or reform of the many sinecures and offices did not therefore affect it. Nor was there anything equivalent in local administration to the increasing emphasis on individual ministerial responsibility with its consequences for the external and internal organization of the public departments. The reform of the municipal franchise in 1835 was less significant than the Reform Act, 1832, if only because it was confined to a small part of the country.

Most of the changes in the administration of national affairs were brought about by a concern for improving the administrative machinery, whereas those made in the administration of local affairs arose out of a need to adapt and expand the public services to meet rapidly changing social and economic conditions. The dominant factor was the increase in population and, in particular, the resulting creation of comparatively large and densely populated towns. Between 1801 and 1851 the population of Birmingham grew from 71,000 to 233,000, of Bolton from 18,000 to 61,000, of Liverpool from 82,000 to 376,000, and of Manchester from 75,000 to 303,000. During the same period the total population of England and Wales rose from nearly 9 million to nearly 18 million.

The resulting large urban areas presented problems not usually found in small villages with their associated scattered farms, problems which could only be dealt with by some form of public or combined action — for example, disposal of refuse and sewage and supply of pure water. The factories also presented new problems. Finally, congested areas encouraged crime, drunkenness, and prostitution. Unfortunately, the forces which produced or exacerbated these problems also made the existing machinery less able to deal with them.

The traditional system of Justices and parish officers worked cheaply and quite well in areas in which the population remained stable, where people knew each other and where the ascendancy of the local squires and parsons was accepted. These favourable conditions disappeared when a locality experienced a large influx of strangers. Though numerically there were now many more people available for the various parish duties few of the newcomers felt any obligation to the parish and were generally unwilling to take on the onerous and invidious duties of the various parish officers. It had in any case never been easy to find suitable people to act as local constable or as overseer of the poor. The problem was further aggravated by the loss of identity of the parish as new housing, factories, and other building cut across and rendered meaningless the ancient boundaries.

Urbanization also had a detrimental effect on the supply of suitably qualified Justices of the Peace. The Webbs[1] have shown the breakdown in efficiency and purity of administration of the Middlesex and, in less degree, of the Surrey magistracies after 1780. Though outside Middlesex and Surrey corruption and disorganization did not prevail, there was still the problem of the lack of suitable candidates for the office. In many of the new mining and manufacturing areas it often became impossible to find resident gentlemen who were legally and socially qualified to fill the office of a Justice of the Peace. Lords Lieutenant refused to fill the Commissions with men whose circumstances laid them open to small pecuniary corruption. The County Benches were unwilling to allow the newly enriched manufacturers and traders to be appointed. The result was an intolerable tax on the time and energy of the limited number of Justices who held office. Not all who were commissioned bothered to take out their dedimus and so qualify themselves to act. In Sussex in 1835 out of a total of 294 commissioned, 99 had not done so.[2] In 1796 there were 2,656 magistrates in the country, excluding Lancashire; by

1818 the number had risen to about 4,000 and in 1832 to 5,371.[3] But many of these were not active.

In most of the long-established towns incorporated bodies or municipal corporations had mainly become self-perpetuating oligarchies concerned with the management of the corporate property, charitable trusts, and other traditional functions. Most showed little interest in tackling the new urban problems. Many of the new industrial towns did not have even this ancient machinery available.

Until the 1830s the initiative in dealing with the new problems was taken only by the localities themselves not by Ministers and Parliament. The changes which took place may therefore be conveniently considered in terms of two periods — that of local legislation and that of national legislation.

LOCAL INITIATIVE AND LOCAL LEGISLATION

The absence of any detailed legislation prescribing the structure and working of the numerous and diverse local authorities enabled them to adapt themselves to changing circumstances. But the flexibility did not enable them to take on new powers and functions, for example, to create new offences. For these, they had to obtain the authority of Parliament and this involved securing a Local or Private Act. Usually such Acts conferred the new powers on administrative bodies created for that specific purpose: they were additions to the existing machinery of Justices, parishes, and Boroughs. These new bodies may be grouped under three headings: Incorporated Guardians of the Poor; Turnpike Trusts; and Improvement Commissioners.

Guardians of the Poor

The original Poor Law Act of 1601 envisaged that the poor would be put to work, the overseers being required to provide a convenient stock of flax, hemp, wool, iron, or other materials for this purpose. From this developed the idea of a work house. Since it was not economic for each parish to provide such a working place, an amalgamation of parishes was needed. In 1696, for example, nineteen parishes within the City of Bristol were amalgamated. The responsibility of the overseers for the poor in these parishes was transferred to a

Corporation of the Poor which was given powers to provide work houses and hospitals and employ paid officers. Other towns also obtained local Acts to achieve this result.

In 1782 the Member for Lichfield, Thomas Gilbert, secured the passage of an Act (22 Geo. III, c.83) usually quoted as Gilbert's Act. It empowered parishes to unite for the purpose of maintaining a common poor house, provided that none was further than ten miles from the intended site. Ratepayers assessed at £5 or more were to elect three persons for each parish and from these the Justices were to nominate 'guardians' for a year. The Justices could also appoint a permanent Governor and a Visitor of the work house. The functions performed by the overseers, except the making and collecting of rates, were to be carried out by the parish guardians. A two-thirds majority of the ratepayers, assessed at £5 or more, could adopt the Act. Some 65 Gilbert's Act Unions were formed, involving some 924 parishes. But the procedure of the Local Act continued to be popular and altogether by 1834 there were 125 incorporated boards of guardians or corporations of the poor.

Turnpike Trusts

It was an ancient responsibility of the parish to maintain a free passage or highway from village to village. The Act of 1555 (2 and 3 Ph. and Mary, c.8) made this a statutory obligation to be fulfilled by four days (increased to six in 1563) 'Statute Labour' rendered by all householders under the superintendence of one of them, compulsorily serving as Surveyor of Highways; the whole under the authority of the Justices of the Peace. An Act of 1773 (13 Geo. III, c.78) enabled the Parish to pay the Surveyor and, with the sanction of Quarter Sessions, levy a limited Highway Rate in those cases in which the Statute Labour had proved insufficient to keep up the free passage. The traditional passage was for foot traffic of man or beast. The eighteenth century saw an increasing use of wheeled vehicles of every kind and the soft tracks suitable for horses and men proved quite insufficient. That and the increasing traffic called for new roads or for the remaking of existing roads. Neither the Parish nor any of the existing authorities had power to make a new road. Hence the recourse to a Local Act.

These Acts, dating from the early eighteenth century, established a body of Trustees and empowered them to construct and maintain a specified piece of road and to levy tolls upon certain kinds of traffic that used that piece. The powers were invariably given for a limited term of years, but every Trust in due course applied for and was usually granted a new Act continuing it for a further period. In addition to the powers conferred on each Trust by its Local Act they were given additional powers and their procedures were regulated by a succession of general Turnpike Acts, e.g. in 1773 (13 Geo. III, c.84).

By 1830 there were some 1,100 Turnpike Trusts in existence. They had a fairly standard constitution. The governing body consisted of persons named in the Act, who had to be qualified by the possession of a stated amount of property. These were reinforced occasionally by an ex-officio element, such as the Mayor, Alderman, and Recorder of an important borough through which the road passed. After 1820 it became usual for Acts to add, as ex-officio members, all the Justices of the Peace for a particular County or Division. In all cases the trustees were permitted, but not required, to fill vacancies arising from death or retirement, by the adoption of duly qualified persons.

Improvement Commissioners

These were established primarily for paving, lighting, cleansing, watching, and improving the streets. The Webbs claim that the first such body was the Commissioners of Scotland Yard established in 1662 for the Cities of London and Westminster. By 1830 there were some 300 in existence and it was rare for a town not to have a separate body of Improvement Commissioners.

The powers conferred by the Acts varied. Thus the Manchester and Salford Police Act, 1792 (32 Geo. III, c.69) was for 'cleaning, lighting, watching, and regulating the streets, lanes, passages, and places within the towns of Manchester and Salford . . . for widening and rendering more commodious several of the said streets . . . and for other purposes . . .' The other purposes included the regulation or suppression of public nuisances, e.g. letting off fireworks or playing football in the streets. The Police Commissioners were empowered to construct sewers and drains, make orders and bye-laws for the regulation of hackney-carriages, and for the proper construction of buildings, appoint watchmen, and provide a fire service. The large body of Commissioners included every owner or occupier of any dwelling-house or building of the yearly rent or value of £30 or more. The property qualification was stiff enough to exclude all the industrial wage-earners and small shopkeepers but nevertheless there were many hundreds of Commissioners. For the purposes of the Act the Commissioners were empowered to levy a rate of up to 1s. 6d. in the pound.[4]

Most of the Commissions, particularly those established by Local Acts between 1760 and 1820, were composed of a list of persons named in the Act, serving for life, and authorized to fill vacancies by co-option. After 1820 a small element of election came to be introduced and more use was made of an ex-officio element, for example, from the municipal corporation.

NATIONAL LEGISLATION 1834–70

As was to be expected from its attitude in respect of national administration, the interest of the House of Commons in local administration was mainly stimulated by the rising cost of local services, particularly of the relief of the poor. The usual techniques of inquiry were employed. A Select Committee on County Rates reported in 1825[5] and another on County and Highway Rates reported in 1834.[6] In 1830–1 a Return was made of the various rates levied for selected years from 1748–50 until 1829[7] In 1834 the House of Lords had its own Select Committee on County Rates [8] and this was followed by a Royal Commission which reported during 1835–7[9] But the the much more significant use of the Royal Commission was to inquire into the Poor Law, reporting in 1834, and into Municipal Corporations reporting in 1835, for both led to immediate legislation. For convenience, because the Municipal Corporations Act, 1835 was different in purpose and character from the Poor Law Amendment Act, 1834 and subsequent legislation, it will be dealt with first.

Municipal Corporations

The expansion of the population and the rapid development of new industrial towns would have posed serious problems even had those towns been administered by effective bodies. But the corporate bodies concerned were, in general, not effective. Many years earlier they had been enterprising and the leaders of the community. By the early nineteenth century many of the Common Councils had become oligarchies, with substantial property and with powers exercised through the Corporate Magistracy, which gave them eminence and authority, but with few links with the people of the town. Meanwhile other leading citizens had obtained from Parliament the power to establish a body of Commissioners. These facts might, in themselves, have caused the Reform Parliament to take action but there was another aspect which made change even more attractive to the Whigs. This was the close association between the Corporations and the election of Members of Parliament.

In 1830 the Boroughs returned 415 of the 513 Members for England and Wales. Most of the 212 Parliamentary Boroughs possessed a Municipal Corporation which exercised considerable influence at Parliamentary elections. Members of the corporation often welcomed a rich patron who could help their town or themselves. In many cases the corporation could secure the election of the candidates they favoured either on the strength of their own votes or by the manipulation of the number of Freemen. In 1817, for example, the Whig Corporation of Nottingham set out to make sure of both the town's seats through the wholesale creation of honorary Freemen. The Tories of Leicester enrolled 800 of their supporters as honorary Freemen more than a year before the dissolution of 1826. Some corporations also used their funds to assist favoured candidates with their election expenses. These practices were not new, but in the 1820s they received greater publicity with the growing circulation of newspapers. Also the standard of public conduct was rising.[10] Thus a large part of the impetus to reform these corporations was the same as that which led to the passing of the Reform Act.

The Municipal Corporations Act, 1835 (5 and 6 Wm. IV c.76) covered 178 towns. London was omitted as requiring exceptional and individual treatment. Other towns could gain incorporation subsequently by their inhabitants petitioning the king who was empowered, by and with the advice of the Privy Council, to grant charters with the powers and provisions of the Act. Each corporation was to be governed by a council elected by the votes of all ratepayers who had resided in the town for three years. For electoral purposes towns with a population of more than 9,000 were divided into wards, each ward returning three councillors. In addition to this elective element one quarter of each Council was to be composed of Aldermen, elected by the rest of the Council. Councillors were to serve for three years, one third retiring annually, and Aldermen for six. A fit person was to be elected each year by the Council as Mayor.

The Act was concerned primarily with machinery not with functions. It swept away all charters, privileges, customs, usages, and rights previously prevailing except where they were consistent with the provisions of the Act. The Councils continued to be responsible for their corporate properties and for any endowed charities for which they were trustees. Beyond that the Act gave them two main powers. First, each Council was empowered to make bye-laws for 'the good rule and government' of the borough and the prevention and suppression of such nuisances as were not already punishable in a summary manner by any Act in force throughout the borough. Bye-laws had to be passed by not less than two-thirds of the Council and could impose fines not exceeding £5. Second, each Council had to appoint a Watch Committee. This Committee was required to appoint 'a sufficient number of fit men' to act as constables for preserving the peace and preventing robberies and other felonies. For the rest, trustees or commissioners appointed under Local Acts for paving, lighting, cleansing, watching, etc., were empowered to transfer their functions to the municipal council for the area.

As was generally the case at the time when new bodies were established the Councils were empowered to appoint officials 'necessary for enabling them to carry into execution the various powers and duties'. But they were compelled to appoint a town clerk to hold his office during pleasure and a treasurer. These two offices could not be held by the same person.

The Act sorted out and put on a new footing the appointment and status of the Justices in these towns. The desire of towns to have their own magistrates and if possible to be free of the jurisdiction of the county Justices had been a major reason for seeking a royal charter. Its granting also saved the time of those who had to appear at Quarter Sessions and any fees or fines accrued to the municipal finances. Usually the Mayor and Aldermen were Justices for the town. In the legislation which added to the functions of the Justices practically no distinction was made between Justices who held their commission from the king and those created in towns with royal charters.

Most of the boroughs covered by the Act were granted their own Commissions of the Peace, but in future these were to be appointed by the king. A number of other boroughs were listed which could petition the king to grant them a commission. Councils could petition the king for the grant of a separate court of Quarter Sessions. Boroughs without their own court of Quarter Sessions were subject to the jurisdiction of the Justices for the County. They could also ask the king to appoint a paid police magistrate. Though radical in its broad intentions nevertheless the Act contained echoes of earlier days. Thus any constable who neglected his duty could be fined not more than forty shillings or imprisoned for not more than ten days by any two Justices. Again, every burgess elected to the office of Councillor, Alderman, Auditor, or Assessor, must accept the office or pay a fine not exceeding £50. Finally, persons holding any office of profit at the time of the passing of the Act whose office was abolished and who were removed from office were entitled to receive adequate compensation. If the displaced officer was aggrieved by the compensation offered him by the Council he could appeal to the Treasury, who were empowered to fix a sum binding on both parties.

Of the 178 Boroughs covered by the Act, 93 were to have the

boundaries already fixed for parliamentary elections and 85 were to retain their existing boundaries. This decision was considered provisional until Parliament should decide otherwise in the light of a more detailed study. The recommendations of a Royal Commission which reported in 1837, aroused strong local feelings and were not implemented. The adoption of the parliamentary boundaries usually resulted in a marked extension of the Borough's area and population.

The Relief of the Poor

In the 1780s expenditure on poor relief amounted to some £2 million; by 1820 this had risen to over £7 million and was about that figure in the early 1830s. Though by general admission times were hard much of the increase was attributed to the greater use of out-relief. In 1795 the Berkshire Justices had agreed a scale of relief for the poor and their families depending on the price of bread. Thus, when the gallon loaf of bread of second flour weighing 8 lb. 11 oz. cost 1 shilling then every poor and industrious man should have 3 shillings weekly for himself and 1s.6d. for his wife and family. If the wages he and his family earned were less than that the difference was to be made good from the poor rate. This breadscale, which became known as the Speenhamland Act, was extensively adopted by other Counties with a resulting big increase in poor relief. In the following year an Act (36 Geo. III, c.23) repealed so much of an Act of 1722 as prohibited relief being given to poor persons in their own houses. In future Overseers could, with the approval of the Vestry or the sanction in writing of a Justice of Peace, give relief to any industrious poor person in his or her own residence in case of temporary illness or distress.

There was some concern at the pauperization of a substantial part of the labouring class. There was probably more concern at the very high level of local rates, of which the poor rate constituted the main element. For thirty or so years there was talk of reform but it did not come until 1834, following the recommendations of a Royal Commission. This saw the problem as primarily that of the able-bodied in rural areas. The allowance system, i.e. the granting of outdoor relief particularly in relation to the level of wages, was the great source of abuse. The remedy was to make the situation of a pauper labourer less eligible than that of the man in work: — he would therefore prefer to work rather than exist on the lower level offered by poor relief. The way to achieve less-eligibility was that all who received relief 'should work for the parish exclusively' which in turn implied a well-regulated work house. This was not just as a place where people might undertake useful work. As envisaged by Chadwick and operated by the Poor Law Commission it involved such rules as the wearing of workhouse dress and maintaining silence at meals: in the words of Professor S. E. Finer, 'prison discipline for the crime of being destitute'.[12]

The Section on Remedial Measures, of which Chadwick was the author, argued that the principle of less-eligibility called for an *ad hoc* central and coercive agency, for the parishes would not apply the principle voluntarily and, because of the variety of local circumstances, Parliament could not legislate in the detail required. The workhouse test demanded the union of parishes and such establishments could only be managed by professional administrators. Thus the Report advocated a central agency, unions of parishes, and paid staff.[13]

The Poor Law Amendment Act 1834 (4 and 5 Wm. IV, c.76) did not, therefore, confine itself to local machinery, it also established a new national body — the Poor Law Commissioners for England and Wales. For the purpose of local administration the Commissioners were empowered to unite parishes. For each such Union a Board of Guardians was to be elected, the Justices of Perace for the area being members ex officio. The scale of plural voting found in the Parish Vestry Act, 1818 (58 Geo. III, c.69) was adopted for owners. For ratepayers the scale was one vote for property assessed at less than £200, with a further vote for the next £200 and 3 votes for £400 and above. In 1844 (7 and 8 Vict., c.101) the scale was amended and applied to both owners and ratepayers: one vote for each £50 of assessment with a maximum of six votes at £250 or more.

Though the Act established locally elected bodies its basic feature was a distrust of their exercising any real discretion. The Report claimed that the existing interests, passions, and local habits of the parish officers will, unless some further control be established, continue to sway and to vary the administration of the funds for the relief of the indigent; and that whatever extent of discretion is left to the local officers, will be used in conformity to those existing interests and habits. Wherever the allowance system is now retained, we may be sure that statuory provisions for its abolition will be met by every possible evasion. To permit out-door relief as an exception would be to permit it as a rule.[14]

So the Commissioners were empowered to make rules and regulations 'for the management of the poor'. Actually the Report recommended that the Commission be given power to 'disallow . . . relief . . . in any other mode than in a workhouse' whereas the Act merely enabled it to 'regulate outdoor relief'.[15]

The Commissioners were, however, specifically empowered to exercise some control over the employees of the Board of Guardians. They could direct the appointment of paid officers with such qualifications as they thought necessary. They could prescribe the duties, regulate the salaries, determine the continuance in 'office and the security to be given to such officials. The masters of work houses and the unpaid Union staff were to hold their appointments subject to the orders of the Commissioners and be removable by them.

The other feature of the administrative arrangements was the principle on which the areas were determined. The Commissioners were completely free to determine the number of parishes to be combined into a Union, the ten-mile limit embodied in Gilbert's Act being abolished. By July 1837 the Commissioners could report that they had united 13,264 parishes into 568 Unions. Most of the remaining 1,300 or so parishes in England and Wales had already been combined under the Act of 1782 or by Local Act or were very large parishes, mainly in London.[16] In 1856 there were still some 2¼ million people living in areas not under the 1834 Act and it was not until 1868 that the remainder were brought into the general scheme. By 1870 England and Wales was, for purposes of the Poor Law, divided into 667 Unions.

Though the Unions varied markedly in population the basic aim was the same in each case. In their First Report the

Commissioners said: 'The most convenient limits of unions which we have found has been that of a circle, taking a market town as a centre, and comprehending those surrounding parishes whose inhabitants are accustomed to resort to the same market. This arrangement was found highly convenient for the weekly attendance of the parish officers . . .'[17] The size of the Unions was limited by the need not to have too much business for the new Boards of Guardians to comprehend.[18] They were not confined to the boundaries of one County and indeed some 200 overlapped such boundaries.[19]

Public Health

In 1838 the Poor Law Commissioners wrote to the Home Secretary (Lord John Russell) calling his attention to the important part played by preventable disease as a cause of pauperism. Labourers were suddenly thrown by infectious disease into a state of destitution. In the case of death the widows and children were thrown as paupers on the parish. During the last two years there had been severe epidemics. The Commissioners asked therefore that the Guardians, who now had the services of an efficient body of officers, including experienced medical officers, should be enabled to exercise the powers, even if only temporarily, irregularly exercised by the parishes, for example, for the removal of nuisances and the causes of disease. The letter was accompanied by two reports based on investigations in London by the Commission's medical inspectors. The letter and reports were published in the Commission's Fourth Report, 1838.[20]

Upon publication, the Bishop of London, a member of the Royal Commission on the Poor Law and a friend of Chadwick moved successfully in the House of Lords an Address praying that the Poor Law Commissioners might be instructed to collect information about the causes of disease prevalent among the labouring population. Instructions were immediately given. The results were published in 1842 and included a report and recommendations written by Chadwick, Secretary of the Poor Law Commission, and issued by the Commissioners as distinctly his. In the following year he supplemented this by a special report on the Practice of Interment in Towns. The government thereupon appointed a

Royal Commission with the Duke of Buccleuch as Chairman. It published two reports, in 1844 and 1845. The general findings were clear: there was a need for new legislative measures applicable to all towns and populous districts to secure the introduction and maintenance of an efficient and economical system of house-drainage and sewerage, paving, and cleansing, and ample supplies of water.

In proceeding to consider the principles on which the legislation should be based the Royal Commission proposed, as a first necessity, 'that the Crown should have the power to inspect and supervise the execution of all general measures for the sanitary [*sic*] regulations of large towns and populous districts'; that the local authorities concerned should be armed with additional powers; and that their areas should in many cases be enlarged and made coextensive with the natural areas for drainage.[21]

The government promised general legislation but this was not achieved until the Public Health Act, 1848 (11 and 12 Vict., c.63). The Act created a General Board of Health, empowering it to establish Local Boards of Health either on the petition of not less than one-tenth of those who paid the poor rate in an area, or by compulsion in areas in which the average annual mortality had over a seven-year period exceeded 23 per 1,000. If the area was a municipal borough then the Borough Council acted as the Local Board. If the petition came from a parish or non-incorporated area then a new board came into being, elected on the same scale of votes as were the Boards of Guardians after the 1844 amending Act.

At the same time the Nuisances Removal and Diseases Prevention Act was passed (11 and 12 Vict. c. 123). First, a system of summary jurisdiction was established to deal with the main health nuisances, to be exercised by the Justices on complaint by the local health authority. Second, for periods of exceptional danger from formidable epidemics the Privy Council could by Order bring into operation certain special provisions of the Act whereby the General Board could exercise powers of imperative direction and the Local Authorities subject to such direction, were to have special powers of action.

Compared with the scientific manner in which the Poor

Law areas had been delineated and the recommendation that the sanitary authority areas should coincide with the natural drainage area the areas of the new Boards of Health were left to chance. The ratepayers in any Parish, however small, could adopt the Act. The Act was in essence seen as a method of making more cheaply and easily available the powers obtained mainly by Improvement Commissioners by way of Local Acts. Indeed about this time Parliament passed a series of Clauses Acts, e.g. the Towns Improvement Clauses Act 1847 (10 and 11 Vict., c.34) which set forth in 216 sections the provisions usually contained in Local Acts for paving, draining, cleansing, lighting, and improving towns. In the same year Clauses Acts were passed covering Markets and Fairs, Water Works, Cemeteries, and Town Police.

By the end of 1853 the General Board of Health had been memorialized by 284 places and had applied the Act in 182 places, with a total population of more than two millions[22] (the Act did not apply to the metropolis except for Woolwich). It had not made use of its power to compel an area to adopt the Act: a power, in any case, not of great value for the General Board had no power to compel the area to make use of the functions thereby bestowed on it. In 1858 the General Board of Health was allowed to expire and the Local Government Act of that year transferred its relevant powers to the Local Government Act Office of the Home Office. The powers in the 1848 and 1858 Acts could henceforth be adopted without the necessity for any further legislation or provisional order or departmental approval, by a resolution of a Borough Council or of an Improvement Commission or of owners and ratepayers in all other places having defined boundaries.

The small Parishes were given a special incentive to become Local Boards by the Highways Act of 1862, for the boards could not be compulsorily combined into Highway Districts. As a result 22 Parishes with a population of less than 100 and 130 with a population of between 100 and 500 quickly acted under the 1858 Act. The practice was stopped by the Local Government Act Amendment Act, 1863 which fixed a minimum population of 3,000 to qualify for adoption.

All the areas, whatever their size, which took advantage of the 1848 and 1858 Acts were subsequently rewarded in the

Public Health Act of 1872 (35 and 36 Vict. c.79) by being treated as Urban Sanitary Districts. Those who had not were designated as Rural Sanitary Districts.

Elementary Education

The Elementary Education Act, 1870 (33 and 34 Vict., c.75) adopted the same principle as the Poor Law and Public Health Acts, i.e. of creating new local authorities for a particular service. In marked contrast the Police legislation made use of existing local authorities. The 1870 Act also made use of another element in the Public Health legislation: local education authorities were not to be established universally, but only where needed or where requested.

The central authority, the Board of Education, was required to obtain returns from Boroughs and Parishes of the provision of elementary schools in their areas and the number of children requiring such education. Where the accommodation was judged to be insufficient the department could issue an order directing that additional places should be made available. If after six months these had not been provided or were not likely to be provided by voluntary effort the department could cause a School Board to be established. When, however, the Bill was before the Commons a new Section was added permitting the department to form School Boards on application by a Borough Council or the electors of a district. The shortage of school places in the metropolis was so apparent that the Act provided for the immediate formation of a London School Board.

Education so far had been provided by local voluntary effort assisted by Treasury grants. The legislation therefore made new public powers available and many areas wished to take advantage of the Act whether or not they already possessed sufficient provision. Most of the bigger municipal Councils, including Birmingham, Liverpool, Leeds, and Manchester, immediately requested that the Act be applied to their area. By June 1871 the department had issued orders for the election of School Boards for 96 Boroughs with a population of over 4.3 million and 188 civil parishes, with a population of nearly 900,000.

The size of each board was left to be determined by the

Education Department, which laid down a scale governed by the size of population. It ranged from 5 members for areas with fewer than 5,000 inhabitants to 15 members where the population was over 100,000. They were elected for three years, all retiring together. Notwithstanding there being several electoral systems already in existence the Act introduced an entirely new one. In the Boroughs the qualification for voting was the same as for elections to the Borough Council, in other areas outside London all ratepayers were qualified. Each voter could cast one vote for each vacancy to be filled. He could distribute his votes how he pleased and could even give them all to one candidate.[23]

Police

The provision of watchmen and police was one of the oldest local functions. Like the relief of the poor it was a Parish responsibility, and like that service many Parishes had proved unable to cope with the problems created by the growth of towns. Extra powers, for example, to employ paid officers, were in many towns provided in the Local Acts and were exercised by Improvement or Police Commissioners.

The metropolis, excluding the City of London, presented a particularly difficult problem with some million people divided among numerous parishes. It was also on Parliament's doorstep and therefore Ministers were particularly concerned about the need not only to suppress crime in it but also to control riots and agitations of a political character. It was for London, therefore, that Parliament first passed general legislation. Starting with the Middlesex Justices Act, 1792, the primary purpose of which was to substitute paid magistrates for the unsatisfactory unpaid Justices of the Peace, it culminated in 1829 with the Metropolitan Police Act (10 Geo. IV, c.44). Formulated and introduced by Peel, then Home Secretary, it placed the police in the metropolis, excluding the City of London,* directly under that Minister's control. Two** fit persons were to be appointed by him as

* The City of London Police were reformed by 2 and 3 Vict., c.14 of 1839 under a Commissioner appointed by the City Corporation.
** The force was placed under a single Commissioner by the Act of 1856.

paid Justices to take charge of the Police Office and were authorized to create and administer a police force composed of 'a sufficient number of fit and able men'. The Justices or Commissioners as they were called later, were to exercise their powers to direct and control the force under the authority of the Home Secretary and his approval was required for the orders they made for the government of the force. The financial aspects were made the responsibility of a Receiver appointed by the king and given the power to levy a police rate not exceeding 8*d*. in the £ throughout the metropolitan police district.

The Municipal Corporations Act, 1835 provided the next opportunity. The Watch Committee of each Borough Council became the police authority for the area, the police powers of any Improvement or Police Commissioners in the Borough being extinguished. The Committee was required to send quarterly reports to the Home Secretary giving information about the number of constables appointed, rates of pay, and rules governing the force. But the Minister was not given any powers to control the Borough forces.

In 1836 the government announced the appointment of a Royal Commission to inquire into the best means of establishing an efficient police in the Counties of Engand and Wales. Edwin Chadwick was one of the Commissioners. He and Colonel Rowan (a Metropolitan Police Commissioner) recommended a completely centralized body of trained policemen. In the words of the Report 'a paid constabulary force should be trained, appointed and organized on the principles of management recognized by the Legislature in the appointment of the new Metropolitan Police Force.' This meant the appointment of Commissioners of Police for the whole of England and Wales whose relations with the Home Secretary would be similar to those within the metropolitan area. In this case, however, the Justices of the Peace for the area were to be given certain rights, e.g. to call attention to an insufficiency of paid constables in any locality and to make representations calling for the dismissal of any superintendent. One-quarter of the cost was to be met from the Consolidated Fund and three-quarters from the County rate.[24]

In his Report Chadwick repeated the tactics he adopted in

the Report on the Poor Law, presenting a very alarming picture in the hope the public would stampede in his direction. He also conducted a publicity compaign. But he was vulnerable to criticism, being so closely associated with the unpopular Poor Law Commissioners. The government in the form of Lord John Russell, the Home Secretary, rejected the Royal Commission's main recommendations.

The County Police Act, 1839 (2 and 3 Vict., c.93) was a permissive measure. The Justices in Quarter Sessions could be empowered by the Home Secretary to establish a police force either for the whole County or for any division of it. The number of constables was not to be in excess of one to every 1,000 of the population. All appointments were placed in the hands of the Justices but that of the Chief Constable required the approval of the Home Secretary. That Minister was also empowered to make rules for the government and pay of the constables. The whole cost fell on the County rate. Where a County Constabulary was formed the powers of any Improvement Commissioners in the area to employ watchmen and constables were to cease.

Eight Counties adopted the Act in 1839; twelve in 1840; and four more in 1841. By then they were alarmed at the cost and only four more Counties had adopted the Act by 1856. In the meantime an attempt to improve the situation was made in 1842 by the Parish Constables Act (5 and 6 Vict., c.109). The obligation of each parish to police itself was reaffirmed by a requirement that Justices were to hold special sessions for the purpose of compiling lists of fit men between the ages of 25 and 55, all to be ratepayers of good character, who, with a few privileged exceptions, e.g. Peers and Members of Parliament, were to be sworn in as parish constables. Thus the principle of universal obligation to serve was given a last brief lease of life. At the same time Vestries were given the power to appoint paid constables. There could also be a superintending constable paid for out of the County rate who would have control over the parish constables in his petty sessional division. The measure was popular for a time as offering a cheaper means of providing police than that of the 1839 Act. Evidence to a Select Committee on Police in 1853 showed, however, that the experiment was a failure.

The Select Committee provided evidence that the existing arrangements were inadequate. In particular they stressed that efficiency had been impaired by the want of co-operation between borough and rural forces. To remedy this the smaller Borough forces should be consolidated with the County forces and the larger Boroughs should share a system of management with the adjoining County and where practicable under the same Chief Constable. They also recommended that the government should make a contribution towards the cost 'without essentially interfering with the local management of that Force.' Finally, they recommended urgent legislation to require police forces to be set up in every County.[25]

Palmerston, who was Home Secretary at the time tried to implement the spirit of the Report. His original Bill proposed that some Boroughs with a population of under 20,000 (some 120 of them) should surrender their police powers to the County Justices; that the five smallest Counties should be amalgamated with their neighbours; and that Watch Committees should lose some of their powers to the Chief Constable whose appointment in all forces was to be subject to the Home Secretary's approval. There was no mention of an Exchequer grant. The Bill aroused such protests from the Boroughs that it was withdrawn.

It was left to his successor (Sir George Grey) to secure the passage of a more acceptable Bill. His County and Borough Police Act, 1856 (19 and 20 Vict., c.69) compelled every County to employ a police force, the Justices of the Peace in Quarter Sessions becoming the police authorities for all the areas outside the Borough forces. The County police were given the same jurisdiction in the Boroughs that the Borough men had always had in the Counties. The main innovation in the Act was the provision of an Exchequer grant of 25 per cent of the cost of pay and clothing and linking this with inspection and a minimum size of Borough. The Bill and in particular the introduction of inspection, was opposed by the Boroughs but this time was accepted by Parliament. By 1869–70, 58 Boroughs had consolidated their forces with the Counties.[26]

London

Until 1855, apart from the special provision for the police, the metropolis was treated like the rest of England and Wales. The Justices for Middlesex, Surrey, and Kent exercised the conventional country functions for their areas, and the 80 or so parish vestries acted similarly to vestries in other parts of the country. The special urban problems were met very largely by the creation of various bodies of Improvement Commissioners by local Acts. In 1855 there were some 250 local Acts in force and London was administered by some 300 different bodies. The City of London, though a corporation, was not covered by the Act of 1835 nor, for that matter, by the Metropolitan Police Act.

The first major attempt at reform was the Metropolis Local Management Act, 1855 (18 and 19 Vict., c.120). This applied most of the provisions of the adoptive Hobhouse Act, 1831 (1 and 2 Wm. IV, c.60) compulsorily to 78 parishes within the Registrar-General's metropolitan area. Twenty-three, e.g. Kensington and Islington, listed in Schedule A, were regarded as large enough for the powers to be exercised direct by their own vestries. The remainder, listed in Schedule B, though retaining their vestries, were grouped for administrative purposes into 15 District Boards of Works. All the vestries were elected by rated householders on the principle of one man, one vote. The 55 grouped vestries then elected a given number of their members to serve on their District Board. The Schedule A vestries and the District Boards were responsible for the paving, lighting, and drainage of their areas and almost the entire sanitary powers, including the compulsory appointment of a medical officer of health. The Act also established a Metropolitan Board of Works elected by the City of London, the Schedule A vestries, and the District Boards. Its original purpose was to provide London with a main drainage network but it rapidly acquired other functions.

The 1855 Act provided the first example of the two-tier system applied to the Counties by the Local Government Acts 1888 and 1894. The Metropolitan Board of Works was replaced by the London County Council in 1889 and the Vestries and District Boards by Metropolitan Boroughs in 1900

LEGISLATION AND EXECUTIVE ACTION

The distinction between the periods of local and of national legislation though convenient as a method of exposition is likely to give two quite misleading impressions. First, it appears to imply that recourse to local legislation ceased in the 1830s and was replaced by national legislation. That was not the case except for police. For one thing the municipal corporations soon turned to this device to provide themselves with powers not conferred on them by general legislation e.g. to supply water and gas. For another, the public health measures primarily made available legislative provisions embodied in earlier local legislation: they were seldom in advance of their time and municipalities and other local authorities still found it necessary to resort to private Bills to meet new needs. Growing appeals to the doctrine of ultra vires, strictly interpreted by the courts in the case of statutory authorities, may also have encouraged cautious Town Clerks to advise their Councils to make certain that they had legal authority for all their activities.

Second, it conceals the great gap between legislation and performance. An Act of Parliament may prohibit or may confer powers but it does not administer itself. Its course through Parliament may produce many speeches by famous politicians but they do not thereby involve themselves in its administration. The national legislation just described was not administered by Ministers and civil servants except to a minor extent. Its purpose was to enable local authorities to act. This is obviously less true of the Poor Law Amendment Act, 1834, but even there it was the Boards of Guardians who had to deal with the poor and administer the Act throughout the land.

It is important to stress this point for most histories of local government during the nineteenth century, e.g. by J. Redlich and F. W. Hirst, and by K. B. Smellie, are the history of legislation not of administration.[27] In part this is because Ministers and Parliament are more glamorous than the much less well-known local figures who actually ran the services. It is also much easier to analyse an Act and the debates than to gather information about what was happening in several hundred localities. There remains a serious gap in our knowledge of the development of Municipal and County government between 1830 when the general studies of the Webbs end and 1888 when the County and County Borough councils began.[28]

Nor was the national legislation noticeably innovative. The 1834 Act applied to the country as a whole, the aggregation of Parishes of which there were numerous examples going back to the previous century. Most of the public health powers made available by national legislation had been fought for and paid for by the local authorities which had promoted private Bills. Police forces were being provided by many local authorities well before the 1839 and 1856 Acts, and elementary schools by voluntary bodies well before the 1870 Act.

The simple fact is that in the nineteenth century the only national officials employed throughout the country were those engaged in the levy and collection of national taxes and by the Post Office. Even the income tax continued to be administered to a large extent by those who administered the local services. The first Censuses of Population — 1801, 1811, 1821, and 1831 in England and Wales — were made a responsibility of the Overseers of the Poor assisted by other local officers, e.g. Clerks of the Peace and Town Clerks. When the Registrar General of Births, Deaths, and Marriages was established in 1836 he made use of the staffs of the Boards of Guardians both for the decennial census and the registration. The real significance of the various inspectorates was that they travelled throughout the country and were therefore in touch with day-to-day administration whereas the clerks stayed at their desks in London.

It has to be admitted, therefore, that this book does not devote the amount of space to the administration of local affairs that the contribution of the various local authorities would justify. Nor will it be possible to do so until far more study has been made of the working of more local authorities during the period. Instead we propose to compare in a general way how local administration developed in contrast to the trends revealed by the much fuller treatment of London-based administration.

THE TRENDS — NATIONAL AND LOCAL

Only in one respect was the trend in the administration of

local affairs really similar to the trend int the administration of the public offices in London, and that was in the movement from officer to employee. The numerous bodies of Improvement Commissioners relied almost wholly on paid staff working under the direction of the Commission or a committee of them. By 1800, for example, the Manchester Police Commissioners were employing 40 watchmen and some 20 firemen. In the case of the Turnpike Trusts the surveyors they appointed gradually took over the powers of the Parish Surveyors of Highways in respect of their sections of main road. The establishment of a Trust did not relieve the parish from its obligations under the 1555 Act. In most cases, however, the parish commuted its Statutory Labour by payment of a lump sum to the Trust raised by levying a rate.

A similar situation rose when the new statutory corporations of the poor were established. The Local Acts did not relieve the parishioners from their statutory duty to serve as Overseers nor did they exempt the Overseers from their duties or obligations. In effect, however, responsibility became vested in the Directors and Acting Guardians established by the Act. The various Houses of Industry or work houses were managed by paid officials, including a Steward or Governor and sometimes even doctors and school teachers. In any event, an Act of 1819 (59 Geo. III, c.12), empowered Parishes to appoint a salaried overseer, a servant of the Vestry and completely under its direction. In 1834 it was estimated that there were over 5,000 salaried Overseers of the Poor.[29]

There was the same trend in the Counties, Boroughs, and urban Parishes. Acting not by virtue of any statute, but rather by virtue of assumed common law powers, the authorities gradually developed a staff of paid officials in order to cope with the increasing work which either Parliament or changing social conditions had placed upon them. In the case of the Counties the staff originated in the office of the Clerks of the Peace for the work of Quarter Sessions and in those of the private clerks of the Justices, for other Sessions. During the eighteenth century it became usual for the Justices to appoint a County Treasurer and rather later a County Surveyor (to look after the County bridges). Some of the urban and suburban Parishes had, by the end of the eighteenth century, come to appoint a paid vestry clerk.

There was also a separation of the representative or political function from the administrative function. Before the Act of 1835 it was common for the Town Clerk and even the Treasurer and other officers to be members of the Common Council. In those Boroughs where the other members were not elected there was in effect no obvious difference between elected and appointed. The 1835 Act, which required Councillors to be elected, laid it down that neither the Town Clerk nor the Treasurer could be members of the council. This meant that the paid officials were employees of the elected and this became the general rule in other local authorities.

In striking contrast, whereas in national administration there was a strong trend towards the concentration of authority, the trend in local administration was towards diffusion. The Act of 1834 had, of course, led to a drastic reduction in the number of authorities responsible for poor relief, from some 15,000 parishes and townships to 667 Unions by 1870. Some consolidation had also been achieved in highway administration particularly following the Highways Act, 1862 (25 and 26 Vict., c.61), which led to the merging of parishes into Highway Districts.

There was, however, little or no attempt to create an administrative authority which would take responsibility for all the local services in its area. The areas of the Poor Law Unions did not become the general administrative unit. They were associated in the public mind with pauperism. Theoretically, it should have been possible to separate the area from the Board of Guardians. But the Unions were so new and so foreign to the rest of local administration that in the popular mind they were inseparable from their original purpose — to provide a catchment area for a work house. Even in 1869 when W. E. Forster, as Vice-President of the Board of Education was considering the local administrative bodies to be set up outside the municipal Boroughs by the Education Act of 1870 he felt that the balance lay in favour of the parish as against the unions 'as more simple, more in accordance with educational tradition, and less tainted with the idea of pauperism'.[30] The Royal Sanitary Commission of 1871 favoured the use of the Boards of Guardians as sanitary authorities but only for areas not already covered by Borough Councils and Local Boards.

The municipal corporations reformed and given a fresh life by the Act of 1835 were to prove suitable units for most purposes and gradually acquired more powers, e.g. by taking over those of any Improvement Commissioners in their areas. But they covered only a small part of the country. There remained the County as a possible unit and Joseph Hume and others tried in the 1830s and 1840s to provide them with elective bodies to match the municipalities. But the County was too large and remote for the handling of public health and sanitary matters. Its choice for the police was linked with the belief that the Justices of the Peace as custodians of law and order, were suitable for that purpose.

The absence of agreement on a suitably sized unit led Parliament to proceed service by service in an opportunistic manner. The parish being the unit of administration covering the whole country was favoured as the area irrespective of size or population.

By 1870[31] local administration in England and Wales was conducted by:

 65 county units and 97 Quarter Sessions Boroughs, with their Justices of the Peace.
224 Municipal Borough Councils
667 Unions under Boards of Guardians
852 Turnpike Trusts
117 Improvement Commissioners
637 Local Boards of Health
404 Highway Authorities — in the rural areas
15,414 Parishes, townships, and similar units
335 Burial Boards
     School Boards were on the point of being established

The citizen found his local services provided by three or more independent public authorities. Even if he lived in a Borough, there would be the Town Council, Board of Guardians, and School Board and, in some places, a body of Improvement Commissioners. His police might be provided by the County Justices. In rural areas his local services would be provided by the Parish Vestry, Board of Guardians, Board of Health, School Board, County Police, and possibly a Highway Board.

Each of these numerous bodies met their expenditure out of a rate on the assessable property in their area. Either they sent out their own rate demands or else they precepted on some other authority, i.e. that authority collected the money along with its own demands. In 1844 the Poor Law Commissioners reported that even leving out those created by local and special customs or by local Acts there existed, in the Common Law and the general Statutes, authority to impose and levy, for about 200 various and imperfectly defined purposes, some 20 different local rates. Most of these would, if the intentions of the law were to be carried into effect, be levied separately and distinctly in every district, many of them for raising sums of money quite insignificant in amount. The definitions of the persons and of the property on which these taxes were imposed varied greatly. Altogether they estimated that not less than 180,000 officials, the greater part of whom were unpaid and changed annually, were entrusted with the collection of these local taxes amounting at that time to not less than £12 million a year. The situation remained substantially the same in 1870. About that time there were 27,000 rating authorities and 18 different types of rate.[32]

Thus during a period when the House of Commons was with the help of the Treasury, consolidating and simplifying the handling of national taxation and expenditure they were adding to the variety and complications of the system of local taxation by creating new authorities with power to levy rates. The conception of a single fund was, however, introduced into local government by the 1835 Act. Each municipal corporation was required to establish a Borough Fund into which had to be paid the proceeds of all property possessed by the municipality and other money due and out of which could be paid certain salaries, e.g. of the Treasurer, and other officials, and certain expenses including, for example, preparing and printing burgess lists and the payment of constables. Should the income of the Fund prove insufficient the Council were empowered to levy a Borough rate to make good the estimated deficit. The requirement arose more out of concern about the use of the various trust funds at the disposal of the corporations and not, it would appear, in emulation of the Consolidated Fund. In any case the purposes for which the Borough Fund could be applied were limited. When a Council adopted the powers of a Board of Health, expenditure on that purpose came out of a separate fund.

At the national level a major factor making for concentration of both the financial and administrative arrangements was the stress on individual ministerial responsibility. There was nothing equivalent to this in local administration. It emerged in Parliament because the king as Executive could only be controlled through his advisers: the system of Ministers exercising the executive power being reinforced by the growth of a strong two-party system. Any attempt of the House of Commons to govern, and not many Members wished that to happen, was effectively rejected by Ministers, by an appeal to the royal prerogative or tradition in cases where an appeal to common sense looked likely to fail.

The development of local administration was quite different. In the case of the parish the voters i.e. the Vestry, were brought together from time to time to appoint Overseers and other Parish Officers. In the larger parishes with a load of work that could not be conveniently handled by holding full Vestry meetings occasionally it was natural to appoint a committee of their members to act. The right to do so was regularized by the Sturges Bourne Act, 1819, which provided that any parish might, by resolution of the inhabitants in Vestry assembled, nominate, for merely formal appointment by a Justice of Peace, a Select Vestry consisting of the Incumbent, Churchwardens, and Overseers and not less than five nor more than twenty other parishioners. Elected annually this committee did not supersede the authority of the Vestry but was expressly authorized to manage all matters relating to the relief of the poor, laying the minutes of its proceedings, together with a report of its work, before regular meetings of the Open Vestry to be held at least twice a year. The Overseers were required to conform to the directions of the Committee. By 1822 some 2,000 Parishes had chosen Select Vestries.[33]

The Borough Councils had long used committees for the conduct of their business. By the end of the seventeenth century Norwich Corporation had developed two standing committees and a host of special committees and these were more and more entrusted with the executive business which had formerly been done for the Assembly by the Court of Mayorality. The Webbs with many examples show that much of the executive work of Borough Councils was exercised through their committees.[34]

These committees were quite unlike the Select Committees used in the House of Commons. They participated in the executive process and were not just investigatory. The members had ready access to the chief officials of the authority and not merely for the purpose of taking evidence. Indeed the officials were servants of the Council as a whole, not as in the national government, of the king, i.e. of the ministerial element in Parliament.

Power to establish such committees became a feature of legislation. Many parishes had used committees even before the 1819 Act: the effect of the Act being to endow the committees with legal authority both over the distribution of poor relief and the assessment and collection of the Poor Rate. The Municipal Corporations Act, 1835, declared that it was lawful for any Borough Council 'to appoint out of their own body . . . committees, either of a general or special nature, and consisting of such number of persons as they may think fit, for any purposes which . . . would be better regulated and managed by means of such committees: Provided always that the acts of every such committee shall be submitted to the council for their approval'. The Act compelled them to appoint a Watch Committee which was even empowered to appoint and frame regulations for a police force, could take the decisions without the need for Council approval and was in effect the police authority for the Borough.

It might be assumed that the use of committees was a natural an administrative practice as the purchase of pen, ink, and paper. Why then should a public body require legal authority to appoint them? The answer in part is that in order for a committee to have any legal authority *per se* its establishment must be derived from some law. It was one thing to appoint a committee to enquire into a subject and report to the body which set it up, it was quite a different matter for a committee to exercise powers which legally were vested in the parent body.

There is, however, perhaps a more general explanation which may apply more to other administrative practices and processes. The traditional local authorities which flourished until well into the eighteenth century exercised some statutory powers, often very vaguely worded, but mostly their activities and forms of administration were derived from ancient usage, in other words the Common Law, In any case, the Parish, the County, and the Borough did not owe their origins to Statute.

The situation changed after 1834. The Boards of Guardians and Local Boards of Health were statutory bodies and even the Municipal Corporations were made so by the 1835 Act. It had always been possible to challenge the action of a public authority in the Courts on the ground that it had exceeded its legal powers — the prerogative writs of certiorari and prohibition were available for this purpose. Jurists had for a long time discussed the legal character of what they termed 'corporations aggregate'. Blackstone said that a corporation had the power 'To sue or be sued, implead or be impleaded, grant or receive, by its corporate name, and do all other acts as natural persons may'.[35] The courts, however, began to draw a distinction between corporations created by charter by virtue of the royal prerogative and those created by statute. The former were said to have common law powers, i.e. the common law attached to the capacities of ordinary individuals in so far as their exercise did not infringe any principle coexistent with their aggregate charaacter. In the eighteenth century this was even interpreted to permit the exercise of powers which conflicted with the terms of the charter.

A different view was taken of the capacity of statutory corporations. In the 1840s and 50s there were a number of cases, usually involving railway and canal companies established by Local Acts. These led in 1875 to a clear statement of the legal capacity of such bodies. In *Railway Carriage Company v. Riche* (1875) (LR, 7 HL 670) Lord Cairns laid it down 'If that is the purpose for which the corporation is established, it is a mode of incorporation which contains in it both that which is affirmative and that which is negative. It states affirmatively the ambit and extent of vitality and power which by law are given to the corporation, and it states . . . negatively that nothing shall be done beyond that ambit, and that no attempt shall be made to use the corporate life for any other purpose than that which is so specified'.[36]

Even so it might have been conceded that public bodies should be able to do those basic acts without which the functions they were set up to perform could not be exercised, for example, appoint staff. But even the parishes had to be given statutory powers to employ paid Overseers and Highway surveyors. The peculiar effect of this interpretation of the law is that the more the powers of the body are spelt out the greater the inference that what is not thereby included must be deemed to have been purposely excluded.

Thus the doctrine of ultra vires became a characteristic of the work of local authorities. It was possibly encouraged by the fact that the chief officer of most of these authorities, the Clerk, was a solicitor by training. In theory the same doctrine applied to the various central departments. New departments or boards established by Act of Parliament were specifically empowered to appoint officers and clerks. The General Board of Health were not empowered by the Public Health Act, 1848 to make permanent appointments of inspectors and therefore had to make do with engaging engineers in private practice to undertake specific local inquiries.[37] The doctrine did not loom so large, however, for two reasons. First, the statutory powers conferred on Ministers were usually in general terms and their exercise seldom affected particular individuals, whereas those conferred on local authorities were not only more detailed but directly affected property owners and other interests who were ever ready to plead that a Council was acting beyond its statutory powers. The power to sanction the setting-up of a Local Board was legally far simpler than the powers exercised by the Board in respect of nuisances, buildings, and so on.

Second, Ministers could always fall back on the doctrine that the Executive power was vested in the king, that the prerogative powers existed to enable him to perform this duty and anyhow he had a special status in the courts. By the end of the nineteenth century, even if not by 1870, local authorities had lost most of their earlier claims to act under Common

Law powers whereas the prerogative was still available to the central authorities.

Another contrast between national and local administration is to be found in the treatment of the electoral franchise. After the great struggle of 1832 the basis of the Parliamentary franchise remained unchanged until the Act of 1867. The basis was that of one man, one vote, the only point at issue being the voting qualification. In contrast the only local elections conducted on this basis were for the Municipal Corporations following the Act of 1835. Professor Keith-Lucas has shown that this franchise was somewhat narrower than that of the 1832 Act, but only if Freemen were taken into account.[38]

For Vestries, Boards of Guardians, and Local Boards of Health, a scale of votes gave the largest ratepayers up to six times as many votes as the ratepayers with the smallest assessable value. The origin of this basis is the Act of 1818. Sturges Bourne, its promoter, was greatly concerned at the way a number of small ratepayers could outvote the large property owners. He preferred the practice of a joint-stock company in which the stock holders had votes proportional to their holdings. It was natural in 1834 to apply the principle to the Board of Guardians and in 1848 to the Local Boards of Health, which outside the Boroughs, were mainly parishes.

Nothing had been done by 1870 to provide a representative system for County government, where the Justices of the Peace in Quarter Sessions continued to reign supreme. They were officers appointed by the king, not elected representatives, yet they had the power to levy the important County rate. At first sight it appears strange that the reform movement which produced the Acts of 1832 and 1835 left the Justices in charge of the County. The main reason was that they were regarded as judicial rather than administrative authorities. Their primary responsibility was, of course, the preservation of the peace and most of their work was of a law enforcement and judicial character. True they were made the police authority by the Acts of 1839 and 1856 but in the eyes of the Home Office their judicial, non-elective character was a significant attraction. The Home Secretary and Ministers were not happy at control of the police being in 'popular' hands.

The only change that would have made them more attractive in the eyes of some of their critics would have been to convert them into paid employees, i.e. stipendary magistrates. But this would have been costly and would have placed in the hands of the government a large number of paid offices, far more attractive than the onerous unpaid offices. Even the radicals preferred the status quo to the creation of a network of important paid officials appointed by and under the control of the government.

The Justices lost some ground during the century. In the early years they were given many additional powers, for example, in respect of aliens, employment of children in factories, friendly societies, savings banks, and the decennial census. But the Factory Act, 1833 made the Factory Inspectors equivalent to Justices in their power to prosecute offences against the Act. Power to approve the rules of Friendly Societies was transferred from the Justices in 1829 (10 Geo. IV, c.56) to the barrister appointed by the National Debt Commissioners to certify the rules of Savings Banks. A Friendly Society could, however, appeal to the Justices against the barrister's refusal to approve their rules. The title of Registrar of Friendly Societies was given to the barrister in 1846 (9 and 10 Vict., c.27). The Registrar was in future to receive a salary in place of the fees which he received from applicants. The Poor Law Amendment Act, 1834 removed their powers in that sphere even though they were made ex-officio members of the Boards of Guardians. They were given some powers under the new sanitary legislation but the administrative responsibility went to smaller units. Nevertheless notwithstanding their non-representative character they remained with significant responsibilities for local administration. In 1870 the County rate amounted to over £1½ million.

Several attempts were made to create elected authorities for the Counties but they came to nothing until 1888. An elaborate inquiry in 1835 into the County rate by a Select Committee revealed no financial corruption or scandals and unlike the Royal Commissions on the Poor Law and the Municipal Corporations did not provide evidence or make out a case for major reform. Joseph Hume, and later Milner Gibson, tried to secure elected County Boards and from time to time after 1835 they and other Members introduced Bills with that object. The Queen's Speech of February 1869 announced that a measure would be introduced 'for applying the principle of representation to the control of the county rate by the establishment of financial boards for counties'. A Bill was drafted and then withdrawn. As Lord John Russell told a deputation, there was no real or general demand for such a change.[39]

CENTRAL-LOCAL RELATIONS

Finally, something needs to be said about the relations between the bodies responsible for the administration of central and local affairs, or, in the context of the second half of the century, the relations between Ministers responsible to Parliament and Municipal Corporations, Local Boards, and similar bodies each responsible to its own electorate.

Judging only by the letter of the law it could be supposed that in the eighteenth century the Executive had large powers of control over the numerous local officers and bodies. The Lords Lieutenant and the Justices of the Peace were appointed and removable by the king. Through the judges of Assize or otherwise the Privy Council could issue instructions to the Justices. Local authorities could be indicted and fined for a breach of their duties on the presentment of a Grand Jury. But the fall of the Star Chamber and other conciliar courts had left the post-Restoration Privy Council with very little coercive power and this had been still further diminished by the Revolution. Since the eighteenth century the judges of Assize had confined themselves almost entirely to judicial work. Lords Lieutenant were, however, usually great noblemen and as such members of the House of Lords, and generally Privy Councillors, so they were in close touch with the king and the Executive. The Justices of each County were, as a rule, appointed on their nomination. In any case the practice of appointing only country gentlemen as Justices made Parliament and the rulers of the County very homogeneous. As a result it was improbable that the general policy which the Executive wished to pursue would be very distasteful to the

Justices. The link was less pronounced with the Boroughs but the same elements existed.[40]

Though these arrangements were likely to produce a harmony of outlook they did not provide the king and his Ministers with any power to control the decisions of local authorities. Acts of Parliament were needed.

In the legislation which greatly affected the administration of local affairs the question of the degree to which locally elected, bodies should be under ministerial control came up most strongly in respect of the relief of the poor. From the point of those who believed strongly in local self-government it was unfortunate that this was the service involved in the first major piece of local reform. It was even more unfortunate that Edwin Chadwick was a driving force both behind the Report of the Royal Commission and the Poor Law Amendment Act.

He and Senior, believing that those who ran the parishes could not be relied on to administer thoroughly a policy of less-eligibility, saw two possible forms of administration — a completely national service and a system of locally elected administration subject to a high degree of control by a national authority. Chadwick would have preferred the first alternative but for one drawback — a fully centralized service would prove too expensive since it would have to set up its own field agencies. The proposal would, in any case, have received little political support for it would, in the circumstances of 1834, have greatly increased the patronage available to Ministers.

The Royal Commission chose the second alternative. In doing so, however, they went as far as they could in subordinating the local to a central body. The Boards of Guardians were to be subject to a central board not only in a general way but, for example, in respect of the staff they employed. The Cabinet accepted most of the Royal Commission's recommendations but left out of the Act two powers on which Chadwick placed great weight: the right to commit Guardians for contempt, i.e. for not obeying the instructions of the central board, and the power to compel local boards to raise rates for building work houses.[41]. Nevertheless never before, nor during the nineteenth century, was a service vested in a local authority made subject to the detailed control provided by the 1834 Act.

Chadwick attempted in 1839 to repeat his triumph of 1834 and place the police in the hands of another central board of Commissioners. It was, however, the House of Commons and people generally, not the Home Secretary and the Cabinet, who rejected a central police force. Prominent Ministers then and in 1856 when the question came up again, favoured the idea. They were, however, up against stronger opponents than the mass of small parishes. The recently reformed Municipal Corporations had been specifically required to act as police authorities by the 1835 Act and in the rest of the country the Justices of the Peace had obvious claims to provide the service. Fears were also expressed about the danger to liberty of a national force. Anyhow the model of the Poor Law Commissioners and its Secretary (Chadwick) were not popular.

Having decided against a national force Ministers and Parliament inevitably went some way towards the Poor Law alternative of some degree of central control. The permissive 1839 Act gave the Home Secretary three new powers over the County forces. First, the Act stated that it was expedient that 'the Rules for the Government, Pay, Clothing, and Accoutrements and Necessaries of . . . Constables . . . be uniform, as nearly as may be' such Rules should be made by one of Her Majesty's Principal Secretaries of State but 'not so as to increase the Number of Men proposed to be appointed'. Copies of the Rules were to be laid before both Houses within six weeks of their being made. Second, the choice of Chief Constable was to be subject to the approval of the Secretary of State. Third, the Justices in Quarter Sessions could report to the Secretary of State the need for more constables to be appointed, subject to an upper limit of one per thousand of the population. The number decided upon was to be reported to the Secretary of State, and his consent was needed to any subsequent change in it. The powers were extended in the following year (3 and 4 Vict., c.88), e.g. to cover the numbers employed in each police district of a County.

The 1856 Act was primarily concerned with dealing with those Counties which had not acted under the 1839 Act and with dealing with the consolidation of Borough and County forces. It did, however, add three further devices. First, the Justices of every County and the Watch Committee of every Borough were required to send an annual statement to the Secretary of State of the number of reported offences and persons apprehended, the results of proceedings etc. Second, on the certificate of the Secretary of State that the police of any County or Borough had been 'maintained in a State of Efficiency in point of Numbers and Discipline', the Treasury could make a grant of up to one-quarter of the charge for their pay and clothing. This provision depended on the third device — the appointment by Her Majesty under her Sign Manual of Inspectors for inquiring into the state and efficiency of each police force. The Secretary of State could not withold payment of the grant without sending the report of the Inspector to the Justices or Watch Committee and laying that and any statement by the Justices or Watch Committee before Parliament. This gave added weight to the Inspector's judgement of the efficiency of any force. The Home Secretary's powers in the 1839 Act remained confined to the Counties

The Public Health Act 1848 contained few central powers of control though of course, the General Board of Health was actively involved in the establishment of the Local Boards: bye-laws made by any Local Board were not to be of any force or effect until confirmed by a Principal Secretary of State, and it was made unlawful for a Local Board to borrow at interest on the credit of the rates without the previous consent of the General Board of Health.

At first sight the requirement that central approval should be needed before a local authority could borrow money on the credit of the rates may appear of limited application. Clearly it was intended to ensure that like so many governments had done they did not pile up debt in order to keep taxation at a lower level. The Royal Sanitary Commission of 1871, however, took a wider view. They said the power to borrow must be given with much caution. So long as it was sought by a few towns and undertakings in local Acts it did not reach 'imperial proportions'. But when 'every community in the country is enabled to exercise these powers, even under control, the burden may become national'. They considered therefore that no only the financial viability of the local authority should be considered but also the character of the expenditure: 'No loan should be raised by a Local Authority for any works until the Central Authority have sanctioned the plans of the works, . . .'[42]

The 1858 Act continued those two provisions and added three more. First, every Local Board was required to make an annual Report to the Secretary of State of all works executed, money received and spent, and had to publish it in a local newspaper with a copy to the Secretary of State. Second, the power of the auditor was extended to enable him to disallow any item 'contrary to law' and surcharge it on the person authorizing or making the illegal payment. The auditor was as stated in the 1848 Act, 'the Auditor of Accounts relating to the Relief of the Poor for the Union' in which the Local Board was situated. Third, the Secretary of State was given the same powers in the case of an appeal as were possessed by the Poor Law Board in cases of poor law audit.

Under the Poor Law Amendment Act 1834 the Poor Law Commissioners had originally allowed each Board of Guardians to elect its own auditor. In 1844 (7 and 8 Vict., c.101) the Commissioners were empowered to combine Parishes and Unions into Audit Districts but the power of appointment was left in the hands of the Chairmen and Vice-Chairmen of each Board of Guardians. The auditors had the power to disallow items of expenditure which they considered to be contrary to the law, and those who had authorized or made the illegal payment had to reimburse the Board. An Act of 1848 (11 and 12 Vict., c.91) made it possible for Boards to appeal to the Poor Law Board against any such decisions which was given the power to set aside the surcharge. This power greatly strengthened central control for the General and Special Orders had the force of law. These Orders could be enforced by the surcharge power of the 'District' auditor subject to the discretion of the central authority to take a more lenient view or a different interpretation in particular cases. One Commissioner claimed: 'The audit is indeed the bridle by which the various local administrators can, with the greatest readiness and certainty, be guided to what is right, and restrained from what is wrong; and its importance therefore can hardly be over-estimated.[43] In 1868 Parliament agreed that the power of appointment of auditors should be transferred from the Guardians to the Poor Law Board (31 and 32 Vict., c.24). After 1847 the Treasury had made a grant to meet the auditors' salaries.

It was this system which the Public Health Act 1858 extended to the expenditure of Local Boards of Health and the Act of 1870 applied to the expenditure of School Boards. The District Auditor's Act, 1879 (42 and 43 Vict., c.6) reorganized the system and applied it to the accounts of sanitary authorities, counties, and district councils established by the Public Health Act, 1872 (35 & 36 Vict., c.79). The accounts of the Borough Councils continued in general to be audited under the provisions of the 1835 Act, viz. by two auditors elected by the ratepayers and one by the Mayor.

The Sanitary Act, 1866 (29 and 30 Vict., c.90) gave the Home Secretary what on paper seemed to be a drastic power but in practice proved less so. If, after an inquiry, he was satisfied that a Local Board was in default in supplying or maintaining sewers or in enforcing the provisions of the Sanitary Acts he could order it to remedy the omission and, if the default continued, appoint a person to remedy it, charging the cost to the defaulting authority. The powers were rendered useless until 1868 because the Home Secretary had insufficient power to meet the cost. In that year he was empowered to levy a rate and to raise a loan for the purpose. The Royal Sanitary Commission suggested that the central authority should, as an alternative, have the power to take legal proceedings in the courts.

Chadwick was the great believer in things being run from London either in the form of a completely national service or a service locally administered but subject to a high degree of central control. 'It is quite idle', says Professor S. E. Finer 'to pretend that Chadwick was not a bureaucrat'. His letters and papers reveal 'a glorification of the public official'. His experience at the General Board of Health made him believe that 'public opinion should be heard less and official opinion heard much more'.[44] Had his viewpoint prevailed the balance would have shifted away from the localities to London and from the elected representatives to paid officials. At the other

extreme there were somewhat romantic writers such as Toulmin Smith who claimed the idea of local self-government as a
glorious heritage and inherently superior in moral, if not also
legal, authority to Parliament.

The concept of local government as an entity contrasting
with central government did not emerge until the second half
of the century and it was only then that general thought came
to be given to the relations between the two.

In the words of the Royal Sanitary Commission in 1871

The principle of local self-government has been generally recognized
as the essence of our national vigour. Local administration, under
central superintendence, is the distinguishing feature of our government. The theory is that all, that can, should be done by local
authority, and that public expenditure should be chiefly controlled
by those who contribute to it. Whatever concerns the whole nation
must be dealt with nationally, while whatever concerns only a
district must be dealt with by the district . . .[45]

Those words were to prove to be open to widely different
interpretations as the years passed. In the context of 1870,
however, the emphasis lay on the freedom and independence
of locally elected councils to make their own decisions and
spend their own money, poor relief being the major exception.

IX

1780–1870: UNFINISHED BUSINESS

The political and administrative system in 1780 was already in a state of change, combining incongruously elements from a former age with some soon to become familiar in the following century. The factors which had been undermining the old system for a century or more had not yet advanced far enough nor elicited sufficient recognition and support to create a new structure. Blackstone's analysis of the constitution continued to be accepted, for it was not greatly affected by many of the subsequent administrative changes. But by the 1850s not only had the detailed working of the system greatly changed but so had such basic features as the status and authority of the king, the relations between him and his advisers and between his advisers and the House of Commons.

By 1870 the political and administrative system was considered to have reached, if not perfection, at least a high and stable state of excellence. The system of 1780 with its untidy diffusion of power and its reliance on formal legal procedures had been replaced by a concentration of authority in the hands of a limited number of political heads answerable to Parliament. The process of change had been going on for most of the period but developments in the 1860s had to contemporary eyes, removed most of the remaining blemishes.

The Exchequer and Audit Departments Act, 1866 embodied the accumulated wisdom and experience of the Treasury and the House of Commons in the control of public revenue and expenditure. The system of Estimates and Appropriations, the control of issues, the auditing of expenditure, and the powers and procedures of the Commons had been refined and perfected.

The distribution of functions and offices had been sorted out so that it was reasonably clear, even for the Navy and Army, which Minister was responsible for every segment of government policy and action. The structure still contained an odd mixture of sham boards, effective boards, and individual Ministers. But they were assumed not to obscure the realities, at least to those in the know.

Two important features had emerged as regards the public service. First, a clear distinction had come to be drawn between those who changed with changes in the political leadership and Administration and those who remained irrespective of such changes. The permanency of the latter was not a new feature of the system: they continued to be appointed at pleasure and so were removable for old age, illness, or incompetence, but not because a different political group had taken power. Their permanence was emphasized by the impermanence of the political element particularly in such periods as the 1850s when political leaders quickly came and went. Second, early steps had been taken to remove the permanent element from appointment by the political element and make it dependent on a capacity to pass examinations. By 1870 this move was still some way off the tight system which prevailed fifty years later. But already it was generally accepted that the permanent element was such an important part of the administrative system that its members needed to be very carefully chosen both as regards initial entry and subsequent promotion.

The Parliamentary franchise had become more generous as a result of the Act of 1867. Only the administration of local affairs remained untidy and diffused. The reform of the Municiapl Corporations in 1835, for political more than for administrative reasons, was not followed by creating similar elected bodies either for the Counties or for general purposes outside the Boroughs. Instead Parliament responded to the pressure of the moment, whether it be pauperism or cholera and provided a series of new administrative bodies. Nevertheless the appetite of the House of Commons to concern itself with every aspect of the life of the country was beginning to affect even the administration of local affairs. There was, however, little or no support for placing it in the hands of Ministers answerable to Parliament. Instead several devices had been introduced to enable a degree of central supervision, particularly detailed for the Poor Law, somewhat patchy for the police, and not yet much developed for other services.

The sense of pride in achievement can be gauged from four

authors who wrote, towards the end of our period, from very different backgrounds and viewpoints. In 1858 the third Earl Grey published his *Parliamentary Government*. He had held several political offices the last being Colonial Secretary, 1846–52. His father was Grey of the Reform Bill and he had, therefore, learnt about politics and government from an early age, indeed he was elected to Parliament at the age of 24. In 1861 John Stuart Mill published his *Considerations on Representative Government*. Mill had been brought up by his father (James) and Jeremy Bentham in the Utilitarian tradition. After their death he was recognized as the exponent of the philosophical radicals. Appointed to a clerkship with the East India Company, at the age of 17, he became head of his department in 1856, retiring in 1858, having refused a position under the reconstituted authority. Walter Bagehot published the first edition of *The English Constitution* in 1867. He was a political journalist and Editor of *The Economist*. Finally came *On Parliamentary Government in England* by Alpheus Todd the first volume of which was published in 1867, the second in 1869. Todd was Librarian to the Legislative Assembly of Canada and presumably received and had the leisure to read the Hansards and Parliamentary Papers sent from London.

Grey wrote from his experiences as a stateman; Mill was concerned to discern the principles on which an effective system of representative government should be based; Bagehot knew his way about the London political world and had the gift of the memorable phrase; and Todd converted what had been said in Parliament and Select Committees into a coherent exposition of the British system.

These writers were generally proud of the British system, particularly when comparing it with other constitutions, but several aspects gave Grey, Mill, and Bagehot cause for concern. In part their concern arose from the features which had been produced by the growth of government business, the intensification of the struggle between organized parties, and the desire of the Commons to exercise the fullest control over Ministers. Those familiar with the trend of the fifty years preceding 1870 and who believed that that trend would continue could in the light of the problems apparent in the

1860s, make a good guess at what strains and stresses might occur later.

We propose to deal briefly with three examples:
(1) the relations between Ministers and civil servants;
(2) the relations between the House of Commons and the Executive; and
(3) the administration of local affairs.

MINISTERS AND CIVIL SERVANTS

The trend of the 1850s and 1860s was quite clear. There was a steadily increasing pressure on the time of Ministers caused partly by their acquiring more functions but mainly by the much greater attention they had to devote to Parliament, the public, and interest groups. The lessening of the time that Ministers had to master the work of their departments was made worse by the shorter period they were in office.

Bagehot claimed[1] that the system whereby all the political heads changed upon a change of Administration produced three great evils: it brought in new and untried persons; it not only made new Ministers ignorant but kept present Ministers indifferent; and it could easily cause a mischievous change of policy. In reply or mitigation he showed that a worse situation would arise if the heads of departments were not chosen by Parliament. 'Nothing is more helpless', he said, than a department in Parliament 'if it has no authorized official defender'.[2] He went on, 'The incessant tyranny of Parliament over the public offices is prevented, and can only be prevented, by the appointment of a parlimentary head, connected by close ties with the present ministry and the ruling party in Parliament.'[3] He used the example of the Poor Law Commissioners created in 1834 to emphasize his point. In simple terms he was saying two things. First, that men with experience of the House and of politics were likely to be better defenders of a department or board than a clerk or outsider. Second, that Ministers and members of the same party stood together and could provide a protection for one of their number under attack.

Bagehot did not disguise the likely ignorance of Ministers produced by this system. A little while ago, he said, Lord Cranborne (later Lord Salisbury) had no more idea that he would now be Indian Secretary than he would be a bill broker. 'He had never given any attention to Indian affairs; he can get them up . . . But they are not 'part and parcel' of his mind; . . . A perfectly inexperienced man, so far as Indian affairs go, rules all our Indian empire.'[4] Who then ruled the Indian empire, that great possession of the Crown? Bagehot did not say.

The reader might have expected some attempt to explain the role of these who did not change with each change of Administration, with perhaps a word about their abilities to administer Empires and policies under Ministers who changed frequently and who were new and untried, ignorant, and indifferent. Instead, Bagehot only spent time on the defects of bureaucrats. They cared more for routine than for results; they tended to under-government in point of quality and over-government in point of quantity; they hated the rude, untrained public; protection was their natural inborn creed.[5]

To Bagehot the value of the political head was as a fresh mind, as the person who could ask awkward questions of the permanent chief 'skilled in the forms and pompous with the memories of his office'. He quoted what Sir George Cornewall Lewis had been fond of explaining: 'It is not the business of a Cabinet Minister to work his department. His business is to see that it is properly worked. If he does much, he is probably doing harm. The permanent staff of the office can do what he chooses to do much better, or, if they cannot, they ought to be removed'[6]. Sir George Lewis's conception of a Minister's role was very different from that given to the young Queen in 1838 by Palmerston. Ministers, he said, 'must be minutely acquainted with all the details of the business of their offices and the only way . . . is to conduct and direct those details, themselves'[7] So, at a time when the answerability of Ministers to Parliament was being held up as the significant feature of the British constitution Ministers were losing the capacity to master their departments. By the time he came to publish a second edition in 1872 Bagehot must have realized the weakness of his earlier exposition for he added at the end of the chapter dealing with Changes of Ministry: 'Recent experience seems, however, to show that in all great administrative departments there ought to be some one permanent responsible head through whom the changing Parliamentary chief always acts, from whom he learns everything, and to whom he communicates everything'.[8]

It may be that Bagehot was putting on a brave face to cover up the concern felt in some quarters that frequent changes of Ministers were a disadvantage, by stressing the freshness of their minds. Clearly the system worked differently in the 1850s than it had done during the fifteen-year reign of Lord Liverpool when there had been only two Chancellors of the Exchequer, Foreign and Home Secretaries. The 'deciduous governments' as Henry Taylor described them, which followed the break up of Lord Liverpool's Administration, had thrown the political heads into more dependence on 'the subordinate assistance'.[9] It was possible that the next fifty years would see Ministers staying long enough in office to be more in command of their departments. What was highly probable was that the load on them and their departments would continue to increase, with the consequential need to delegate more and more decision making to the civil service,

THE HOUSE OF COMMONS AND THE EXECUTIVE

One aspect of the working of the House of Commons which worried some Ministers, was the fear of *gouvernement d'assemblée*. The third Earl Grey,[10] for example, claimed 'there is a constant tendency . . . in the House of Commons, unduly to retard its proper work, by undertaking business for which it is unfit, and by indulging in discussions of unnecessary length'. He gave as an example the removal of 'various permanent charges from the Consolidated Fund' and the requirement that revenue receipts should be paid in gross not net. Their effect 'will be to encumber the House of Commons with a considerable amount of additional business . . . which it is impossible that it can perform properly'. He went on 'When an estimate is presented . . . to provide for the charge of a certain number of officers of different ranks, and receiving different rates of pay, . . . the Members who discuss the estimate in Committee of Supply have no means whatever of forming a sound judgment on the details . . .' There appeared to be, he said, 'a strong disposition on the part of the public to encourage the House in a mistake which, if persisted in, may detract materially from its usefulness'. It was right, he had stated earlier, for Parliament not to interfere directly in carrying on the Executive government 'since experience has demonstrated the unfitness of large deliberative assemblies for this function'. But every measure of Ministers was open to censure in either House and therefore those to whom power was entrusted 'must use it in such a manner as to be prepared to meet the criticism of opponents continually on the watch for any errors'.

Alpheus Todd, replete with the wisdom derived from his readings, stated quite categorically

Any direct interference by resolution of Parliament in the details of government is inconsistent with, and subversive of kingly authority, and is a departure from the fundamental principle of the British constitution which vests all executive authority in the sovereign while it ensures complete responsibility for the exercise of every act of sovereignty.[11]

It was not only Ministers who were worried about the desire of Members to involve themselves in the details of administration. Arthur Helps, Clerk of the Privy Council, writing in 1871 said 'Needless returns are called for, occupying the time and attention of public offices which ought to be otherwise employed; needless questions are asked in Parliament which sadly waste the time of Ministers . . . and what is a far more serious evil, the public Offices are hampered, worried, and weakened by a sense of their double responsibility; to their chiefs and their country on the one hand, and to Parliament on the other'. He asked for more consideration for Ministers, adding that the number of Questions asked was unreasonable.[12]

The usual way to deal with unreasonable demands was to appeal to the common sense of the mass of Members and get them to accept that certain kinds of detail should not be raised in the House. In 1857, for example, a Member moved an address for copies of all correspondence between a Battalion Paymaster and the War Office. Palmerston, then Prime Minister, warned the House that 'if they commence revising the decisions of the War Office upon the claims of individual officers they will embark on a sea of trouble to an extent of which, I am sure they can have no conception'. One great department of the War Office was 'daily and constantly employed in considering these personal claims. It forms an immense mass of business, and if the House of Commons erects itself into a tribunal of appeal against decisions of the Secretary for War upon claims of paymasters and regimental officers . . . a large mass of matter will have to be printed which nobody will ever read'. The House negatived the motion.[13]

The asking of a Question in the House was, for the ordinary Member, the best method of raising an individual case for it gave the Member publicity at least in the local Press. The rules governing the admissibility of particular kinds of Questions developed mainly after 1870. In 1872 the Speaker gave a ruling that an answer to a Question cannot be insisted upon, if it is refused by a Minister on the grounds of public interest.[14] Based on the character of those refusals Questions about particular matters, e.g. about the exercise of the prerogative of mercy or making charges of a personal character, came to be barred.

Second, there was the device of making certain expenditure a charge on the Consolidated Fund which, once agreed did not require to be voted annually in Committee of Supply. By 1870 this use was limited mainly to the Civil List, pensions to former public servants, the salaries of judges, the salary of the Speaker of the House of Commons and his Serjeant at Arms and the salaries of the Comptroller and Auditor-General and his Assistant. An earlier and not well thought-out attempt to insulate the salaries and expenses of certain boards and commissions from possible annual discussion in Committee of Supply had been abandoned.

Finally, there was the attempt to hold the curiosity of Members at arm's length by vesting the function not in a Minister but in a statutory agency, usually a Board. If the Minister did not have the power to make the decisions in particular cases he could not be questioned about any one of them. In the words of Erskine May: Questions should relate 'to any matter of administration for which the Minister is responsible'.[15] The Civil Service Commission, Public Works Loans Board, and the Inclosure, Tithes, and Copyhold Commissions were examples of this device. The Minister still remained answerable for any aspect which lay within his powers, for example, the appointment of Commissioners and the board's annual estimates. Also he could usually be held answerable for the general policy being pursued by the board either because his approval was required to its regulations or, because, being a statutory body there was an implied interest of Parliament in it. There would appear to have been an attempt at one time on the part of the Speaker to allow Questions to Members who were on a particular board, even though not Ministers. e.g. a Trustee of the British Museum or a member of the Metropolitan Board of Works and later the rule was applied to the Ecclesiastical Commission and the Charity Commission. But these were rare exceptions. The view seems to have been that if the matter was not the responsibility of any Minister it was not a concern of the House, at least at Question Time.

Control of time inside the Chamber did not lead Members to find other ways of investigating and criticizing the Administration. The period 1870–1920 saw no major permanent development of Select Committees. The Public Accounts Committee flourished and became a well-accepted feature of the constitution. But one had to wait a century before the House established Committees to investigate regularly the work of particular departments and by then the activities of government were many times greater than in 1870.

The fact is that for a long time after 1870 the tradition embodied in the words of Grey and Todd was accepted doctrine. Indeed they were reinforced by another trend of the nineteenth century — the belief that the process of government was a conflict between two parties — one in power and one in opposition. It was the business of the former to be the executive and of the latter to oppose, criticize and offer an alternative government. This placed an emphasis on the two front benches and on proceedings in the Chamber. The political conflict and the fact that the question of who should hold power was at issue placed emphasis on government secrecy, not disclosing any information that might be of use to the opposition. These factors, combined with the fact that the majority of Members had only a limited amount of time to spare for the House, inhibited Members from becoming involved in the detailed work of the departments.

THE ADMINISTRATION OF LOCAL AFFAIRS

Though the administrative arrangements for the provision of local services had been the subject of much legislation they had not reached the stage of perfection that many claimed for the national system. Of our four authors neither Grey nor Todd had anything to say about what was by the 1860s generally called local government. Bagehot made only few somewhat disparaging remarks:[16]

We love independent 'local authorities', little centres of outlying authority. When the metropolitan executive most wishes to act, it cannot act effectively because these lesser bodies hesitate, deliberate, or even disobey. But local independence has no necessary connection with Parliamentary government. The degree of local freedom desirable in a country varies according to many circumstances, and a Parliamentary government may consist with any degree of it.

As might be expected, John Stuart Mill took a much wider view of 'Local Representative Bodies':

It is but a small portion of the public business of a country which can be well done, or safely attempted, by the central authorities; and even in our own government, the least centralised in Europe, the legislative portion at least of the governing body busies itself far too much with local affairs, employing the supreme power of the State in cutting small knots which there ought to be other and better ways of untying.[17]

He then went on to indicate the principles on which the administration of local affairs should be arranged and in doing so touched on two issues not resolved by 1870.

First, he declared that

in each local circumscription there should be but one elected body for all local business, not different bodies for different parts of it. . . . The Government of the Crown consists of many departments, and there are many ministers to conduct them, but those ministers have not a Parliament apiece to keep them to their duty. The local, like the national Parliament, has for its proper business to consider the interest of the locality as a whole . . .[18]

In 1870 this principle was further from fulfilment than it had been at the beginning of the century.

Second, he tried to answer the question whether local bodies should have full authority within the sphere of their duties or should they be 'liable to any, and what, interference on the part of the central government'. Like others who have considered this question he could not find a clear-cut or simple answer. He thought that paving, lighting, and cleansing of the streets were clearly local functions but the administration of justice, police, and gaols were matters of general concern. His 'practical conclusion' was that the authority which was most conversant with principles should be supreme over principles, while that which was most competent in details should have the details left to it. He envisaged that for 'every branch of local administration, which affects the general interest, there should be a corresponding central organ, either a minister, or some specially appointed functionary under him; even if that functionary does no more than collect information from all quarters. and bring the experience acquired in one locality to the knowledge of another where it is wanted'. The central authority ought to keep open 'a perpetual communication with the localities . . .'[19]

His ideas were clearly a long way from those advocated by Edwin Chadwick but were they also not by any means the same as Toulmin Smith's concept of local self-government. By 1870 there was no clearly accepted doctrine about what later came to be called the relations between central and local government. There was the highly centralized system of control exercized over the Board of Guardians at one extreme and the freedom from central control embodied in the Municipal Corporations Act, 1835. The likely pattern for the future, however, was that being worked out between the police authorities and the Home Office and between the Local Boards of Health and the Local Government Act Office of the same department.

The trends up to 1870, however, contained two clues as to the future. First, the appetite of the House of Commons for information and the interest of Members in every aspect of the nation's social and economic life were unlikely for ever to be held in abeyance because a large part of public affairs was in the hands of locally elected bodies. Mill's analysis, though sympathetic to local independence contained arguments which could be used to justify various measures of central control, for example, to ensure that local bodies obeyed the general law or to secure a measure of uniformity. Nobody could for long stand up against the demands of a vocal group in the House of Commons.

Second, if there were criticism of individual local authorities or of a local service, there would be nothing more helpless than an interest without an authorized defender — to reword Bagehot only slightly. Who would answer criticisms directed at local government? Would a Minister defend the actions of bodies for which he was not responsible and might there not be a temptation for him to imply that had he had responsibility things would have been better managed? In that connection local government could not, like a central department, present a monolithic front. If several hundred authorities were administering the same service one or two were bound to be noticeably inefficient or behave in a way that irritated, even scandalized public opinion in the country at large.

These institutional influences had already begun to be reinforced by a financial factor. The only tax available to local authorities was a levy on the rateable annual value of land and buildings. In contrast the Chancellor of the Exchequer had a variety of taxes at his disposal — and the well-established Customs and Excise duties had been reinforced in 1842 by a Property and Income Tax which was to prove a very flexible and productive source.

The rateable value of England and Wales roughly trebled between the early years of the century and 1870. Considering that the main item of local expenditure — poor relief — fell after 1834 for some twenty years such an increase in taxable capacity was enough to meet the increasing expenditure on police, town improvements, and sanitation. Indeed there was a link between much of this new expenditure and rateable capacity which reflected the big rise in population and the provision of amenities and services which improved the value of property. This could not, however, be said of the purely agricultural areas. Agriculture continued to be a depressed industry and farmers and landowners complained about the burden of rates.

There emerged, however, a wider issue concerned with the

relative burdens on real property and on other forms of wealth. It could readily be shown that local taxation fell very largely on real property whereas national taxation fell mainly on other sources. This comparison inevitably led to demands that some part of local expenditure should be financed out of national taxation. Thus the Select Committee on County Rates reported in 1834 that certain charges borne on local rates, for example, criminal prosecutions and prisons, were charges of national importance and general utility and might therefore properly be charged on 'those funds to which the general mass of property throughout the country contribute more equally than it does to the county rate'.[20] As a result in 1835 the Treasury began to meet half the cost of criminal prosecutions and the movement of convicts. Following the repeal of the Corn Laws the Treasury took over the other half of these costs. The general argument had not got very far by 1870 but Mr Goschen's report of that year was particularly directed at the proportion of local and imperial burdens borne by different classes of real property.[21]

PART I, CHS. I—VII

[1] Sir William Blackstone, *Commentaries on the Laws of England*, 6th Edition (1775), Vol. 1, pp. 154–5.

[2] Ibid. p. 269.

[3] Ibid. p. 190.

[4] Ibid. pp. 237–80.

[5] Ibid. p. 267

[6] Ibid. p. 249.

[7] Finance Reports, PP. 1797–803, Vol. X. Appendix p. 7:.

[8] J. E. D. Binney, *British Public Finance and Administration, 1774–92* (1958), pp. 173–5.

[9] Blackstone, op. cit. pp. 254–5.

[10] J. C. Sainty, 'Tenure of Offices in the Exchequer', *English Historical Review* (1965), pp. 449–72.

[11] Blackstone, op. cit., Vol. II, p. 36.

[12] *Howell's State Trials*, Vol. 16 (1816), cols. 1273–4.

[13] *Parliamentary History*, Vol. XXI (11 February 1780) col. 48.

[14] This elementary exposition of the law concerning Officers and Offices is based on the section with that title in the 4th Edition (1778) of *A new abridgement of the Law* by Matthew Bacon, supplemented, where necessary, by the 9th Edition (1772) of the *New Law Dictionary* by Giles Jacob.

[15] Binney, op cit. p. 190.

[16] Sir William Holdsworth, *A History of English Law*, Vol. X (1938), p. 156.

[17] Ibid. pp. 146–51; and S. and B. Webb, *The Parish and the County* (1906).

[18] Commissioners for Examining the Public Accounts, 14th Report, (1785), HCJ XLI, p. 68.

[19] E. E. Hoon, *The Organization of the English Customs System, 1696–1786 (1938), pp. 197–8.*

[20] *Parliamentary History*, Vol. XIII, p. 93.

[21] Blackstone, op. cit. Vol. I, p. 246.

[22] Ibid. p. 336.

[23] A. S. Foord, 'The Waning of The Influence of the Crown', *English Historical Review* (1947), Vol. 62 B. Kemp, *King and Commons 1660–1832* (1957). I. R. Christie, 'Economical Reform and "The Influence of the Crown 1780"', *Cambridge Historical Journal* (1956), Vol. XII, pp. 144–54.

[24] David Hume, *Essays, Moral, Political and Literary* (World's Classics), (1903), p. 45.

[25] Blackstone, op. cit. Vol. I, p. 338.

[26] *Parliamentary History*, Vol. XX, p. 89.

[27] Commissioners for Examining the Public Accounts 12th Report (1784), *HCJ*, XL, p. 113

[28] *HLJ*, XXIX, p. 176, J. R. Western, *The English Militia in the Eighteenth Century* (1965), p. 140.

[29] W. R. Ward, *The English Land Tax in the Eighteenth Century* (1953).

[30] Western, op. cit.

[31] Blackstone, op. cit. Vol. III, p. 161 and Vol. II, p. 437.

[32] Binney, op. cit. pp. 120–1.

[33] Commissioners, op. cit. 6th Report (1782) HCJ, XXXVIII, pp. 712–13.

[34] Blackstone, op. cit. Vol. I, p. 272.

[35] Commissioners, op cit., 8th Report (1783), *HCJ*, XXXIX, p. 57.

[36] J. Torrance, 'Social Classes and Bureaucratic Innovation: The Commissioners for Examining the Public Accounts, 1780–87,' *Past and Present*, No. 78 (1978).

PART II, CH. II

[1] Blackstone, op. cit. Vol. I, pp. 190, 250, and 154–5.

[2] Miss B. Kemp, *King and Commons 1660–1832* (1957).

[3] Sir Thomas Erskine May, *Constitutional History of England*, 5th Edition, 1875. Vol. I, pp. 175–214. Report of Select Com-

mittee on Public Moneys, PP 1857, Series 2, Vol. IX, p. 579.

[4] E. L. Woodward, *The Age of Reform 1815–1870* (1938), pp. 21–2.

[5] Earl Grey, *Parliamentary Government* (1858), p. 4.

[6] *English Constitution* (World's Classics), p. 51.

[7] Blackstone, op. cit. p. 150.

[8] D. L. Keir and F. H. Lawson, *Cases in Constitutional Law*, Fourth Edition (Revised), (1954), p. 190.

[9] *Mersey Docks and Harbour Board Trustees* v. *Cameron* (1865); *Mersey Docks and Harbour Board Trustees* v. *Gibbs* (1866).

[10] Sir William Holdsworth, *A History of English Law*, Vol. X, pp. 293–9, 317–8.

[11] PP 1854–5, Vol. XX, p. 9.

[12] PP 1854/5, Vol. XX p.127.

[13] Parliamentary Debates, 3rd Series, Vol. 181, cols. 438–45.

[14] R. Pares, *George III and the Politicians* (1953), p. 148.

[15] Parliamentary Debates, 3rd Series, Vol. 176, col. 1909.

[16] Erskine May, op. cit. Vol. II, p. 85.

[17] Lord John Russell, *History of the English Government and Constitution*, 2nd Edition (1823), p. 151 and new edition (1865), p. 89.

[18] Earl Grey, op. cit. p. 9.

[19] Parliamentary Debates, 3rd Series, Vol. 61, col. 1061.

[20] Sir William Anson, *The Law and Custom of the Constitution*, 3rd Edition (1907), Vol. II, Part I, pp. 168–9.

[21] Select Committee on Public Moneys, PP 1857, Sess. 2, Vol. IX, pp. 529–30.

[22] Ibid.

[23] Earl Grey, op. cit. p.5.

[24] PP 1845, Vol. XVIII, p. 19.

[25] Collected Papers, Vol. III, pp. 244–70.

[26] Sir William Holdsworth, *Essays on Law and History* (1946), pp. 213–14.

[27] F. W. Maitland, *The Constitutional History of England* (1909), p. 417.

[28] Quoted by H. J. Hanham in *The Nineteenth Century Constitution 1815–1914*, pp. 33–4.

[29] Bagehot, op. cit. (World's Classics), pp. 30 and 67.

PART II, CH. III

[1] HCJ, Vol. LXX, p. 947.

[2] H. Robinson, *Britain's Post Office* (1953), p. 135.

[3] Select Committee on Miscellaneous Expenditure, PP 1847–8, Vol. XVIII, Part I, Q1156.

[4] J. C. Sainty, *Treasury Officials 1660–1870* (1972), p.58.

[5] Select Committee on the Printing of Returns and Papers, PP 1841, Vol. IX, pp. 623–8.

[6] J. C. Sainty, *Officials of the Boards of Trade 1660–1870* (1974), pp. 66–7.

[7] Select Committee on the Income and Property Tax Second Report, PP 1852, Vol. IX, pp. 467–95.

[8] Select Committee on Public Moneys, PP 1857 (Sess. 2), Vol. IX.

[9] See H. M. Clokie and J. W. Robinson, *Royal Commissions of Inquiry* (New York, 1969).

[10] M. W. Thomas, *The Early Factory Legislation* (1948).

[11] M. Brock, *The Great Reform Act* (1973), p. 20.

[12] D. E. Butler and J. Cornford, *International Guide to Voting Statistics* (1968), p. 333.

[13] J. P. Mackintosh, *The British Cabinet* (1962), p. 67.

[14] Butler and Cornford, op. cit.

[15] A. Aspinall, *Politics and the Press 1780–1850* (1949), p. 199.

[16] Select Committee on Printed Papers, PP 1835 Vol. xviii. See also Select Committee on Parliamentary Papers, PP 1852–3, Vol. XXXIV.

[17] Thomas Erskine May, *Treatise upon the Law, Privileges, Proceedings and Usage of Parliament*, 1st Edition (1844), p. 167.

[18] See P. Fraser, 'The Growth of Ministerial Control in the Nineteenth Century House of Commons', *English Historical Review*, Vol. 75, 1960, pp. 444–63. Also see J. Redlich, *The Procedure of The House of Commons*, Vol. I (1903).

[19] L. Radzinowiez, *History of English Criminal Law*, Vol. III, (1956), pp. 126–30.

[20] O. MacDonagh, *A Pattern of Government Growth* (1961), pp. 54–64.

[21] PP 1796, Vol. XIV, pp. 34–5.

[22] J. C. Sainty, *Home Office Officials 1782–1870*, p. 41 and *Treasury Officials 1660–1870*, p. 99.

[23] Parliamentary Debates, 3rd Series, Vol. 108, col. 974.

[24] Select Committee on Business of the House, PP 1861, Vol. XI, Report, p. vi.

[25] Select Committee on Public Business, PP 1847–8, Vol. XVI, Qq 2 and 21.

[26] C. Leys, 'Petitioning in the Nineteenth and Twentieth Centuries', *Political Studies* (1955), Vol. III, pp. 45–64.

[27] P. W. S. Thomas, *The House of Commons in the Eighteenth century* (1971). Erskine May, op. cit. (1844) said it was called the Treasury or Privy Councellor's Bench (p. 146).

[28] P. Fraser, op. cit. p. 460.

[29] D. N. Chester and N. Bowring, *Questions in Parliament* (1962).

[30] Erskine May, op. cit. p. 195.

[31] 10th Edition, p. 237.

[32] See O. C. Williams, *History of Private Bill Procedure*, 2 Vols. (1948); and F. Clifford, *History of Private Bill Legislation*, 2 Vols. (1885–7), reprinted in 1949.

[33] *Mirror of Parliament* Vol. V (1840), p. 4657.

[34] 3rd Edition, p. 557

[35] Clifford, op. cit. Vol. II, p. 678.

PART II, CH. IV

Section A

[1] Select Committee on Sinecure Offices 1st Report, p. 7, PP 1810, Vol. II.

[2] Commissioners on Fees, Gratuities and Public Offices. 2nd Report 1786, pp. 52–4, in PP 1806, Vol. IX.

[3] Ibid., 1st Report, p.7.

[4] Commissioners for Examining the Public Accounts, 11th Report, HCJ XXXIX, p. 779.

[5] 14th Report, *HCJ XLI, p.* 23.

[6] *Parliamentary History*, XXXIII, col. 87.

[7] George Rose, *Observations respecting* the Public Expenditure and the influence of the Crown, 2nd Edition (1810), pp. 9–10.

[8] J. Norris, *Shelburne and Reform* (1963), pp. 190–6.

[9] Select Committee on Sinecure Offices, PP 1810, Vol. II, Appendix A.

[10] Select Committee on Sinecure Offices, PP 1831, Vol. VI, Appendix I. See also Treasury Minute of 18 November 1834, PP 1835, XXXVII, p. 449.

[11] 14th Report *HCJ* XLI, p.23.

[12] 1st Report 1786, PP 1806, Vol. IX, p.14.

[13] Select Committee on Public Expenditure, PP 1808, Vol. III, p. 123. The Treasury Minute of 1803 is reprinted at p. 271.

[14] J. Norris, op. cit. p. 161.

[15] Parliamentary Debates 1st Series, Vol. XIV, cols. 48–68.

[16] Op. cit. pp 126–7. For the legislation 1807–12 see D. Gray, *Spencer Perceval 1762–1812* (1963) pp. 151–8.

[17] Return of Numbers Employed etc., PP 1830–1, Vol. VII, p. 45.

[18] Henry Roseveare, *The Treasury* (1969), pp. 104–5.

[19] 1st Report, op. cit. p.11.

[20] Select Committee on the Reduction of Salaries, PP 1830–1, Vol. III, p. 10.

[21] Select Committee on Finance. Proceedings 1797–1803, A, p. 58.

[22] Commissioners on Fees etc. PP 1837, Vol. XXXIV, p. 208.

[23] Commissioners on Fees etc., 1788, PP 1806, Vol. IX, p. 761.

[24] Commissioners for Examining the Public Accounts, 6th Report, *HCJ* Vol. XXXVIII, p. 707

[25] Op. cit. 6th Report, p. 712.

[26] Ibid. p. 714.

[27] J. Norris, op. cit. pp. 203–4.

[28] Second Report, PP 1806, Vol. IX, p. 57.

[29] Select Committee on Finance, 15th Report 1797, pp. 11–14.

[30] 2nd Report op. cit. p. 56.

[31] PP 1821, Vol. XI, p. 127.

[32] PP 1846, Vol. XXVI, p. 655.

[33] PP 1847–8, Vol. XVIII, Part I. Report, pp. viii–ix.

PART II, CH IV
Section B

[1] J. E. D. Binney, *British Public Finance and Administration 1774–92*, pp. 73–4, and Report of the Auditors of the Public Accounts 1808, in PP 1830, Vol. IX, pp. 141–64.

[2] 1st Report, PP 1806, Vol. IX, p.12.

[3] Commissioners for Examining the Public Accounts, 6th Report, *HCJ* XXXVIII, p. 714. Select Committee on Finance, 16th Report 1797, p. 4.

[4] Royal Commission on Superannuation, PP 1857, Vol. XXIV, pp. 150–1.

[5] Select Committee on Finance, 15th Report, 1797, p. 18, and J. C. Sainty, *Treasury Officials 1660–1870* (1972).

[6] First Report, op. cit. pp. 5–6, 11, and 14.

[7] The Order in Council is in the 16th Report of the Select Committee on Finance, 1797, pp. 37–46.

[8] Select Committee on Finance, Proceedings 1798–1803, A, pp. 60–61.

[9] Ibid. 15th Report 1797, pp. 20–1.

[10] Ibid. 16th Report 1797, Appendix B2, pp. 57–8.

[11] Return of Increase and Diminution of Salaries since 1793, PP 1821, Vol. XIII, pp. 6–7, 44–5.

[12] Ibid.

[13] Return of numbers employed, PP 1828, Vol. XVI, pp. 531–4.

[14] J. C. Sainty, *Treasury Officials 1660–1870*, pp. 30 and 34; *Home Office Officials 1782–1870*, pp. 4–5.

[15] Sixth Report, *HCJ* XXXVIII, p. 714.

[16] Third Report, PP 1808, Vol. III, p. 124.

[17] Second Report, PP 1828, Vol. V, p. 18.

[18] PP 1830–1, Vol. III, pp. 3–4.

[19] Select Committe on Official Salaries, PP 1850, Vol. XV, p. 183.

[20] Select Committee on Finance, 15th Report 1797, p. 3 and Proceedings 1798–1803, C 19.

[21] PP 1830–1, Vol. III, p. 450.

[22] PP 1830–1, Vol. VII, p. 494.

[23] J. C. Sainty, *Treasury Officials 1660–1870*, pp. 30 and 32.

[24] PP 1847–8, Vol. XVIII, Part 1, p. viii.

[25] PP 1854, XXVII, p. 18.

[26] M. Wright, *Treasury Control of the Civil Service* (1969), pp. 231–5.

[27] J. C. Sainty, *Office Holders in Modern Britain: Treasury, Admiralty, Home Office, and Board of Trade.*

[28] A. P. Donajgrodzki, *The Clerks of the Home Office 1822–48* in G. Sutherland (ed.), *Studies in the Growth of Nineteenth Century Government* (1972), pp. 93–5.

[29] Report of Civil Service Inquiry Commission 1875, Vol. XXIII, p. 7.

[30] Report on the Organization of the Permanent Civil Service, PP 1854, Vol. XXVII, p. 6.

[31] E. Hughes, 'Civil Service Reform 1853–5' *in Public Administration*, Vol. XXXII (1954), p. 20. See also his 'Postscript to Civil Service Reforms', ibid. Vol. XXXIII (1955), pp. 299–306.

[32] PP 1828, Vol. V, p. 19.

[33] E. Cohen, *The growth of the British Civil Service 1780–1939* (1941), p. 67.

[34] E. Hughes, op. cit. p.20. M. Wright, op. cit. pp. 91–3.

[35] PP, 1854–5, Vol. XX, p. 116.

[36] Select Committee on Civil Service Appointments, PP 1860, Vol. IX, pp. xiii–xiv; M. Wright, op. cit. pp. 67–8.

[37] The Order in Council of 4 June 1870 and also that of 21 May 1855 is printed in the Nineteenth Report of the Civil Service Commission 1875 (Vol. XXII). That Report also lists the changes already made to Schedules A and B in the Order of 1870.

[38] J. C. Sainty, *Treasury Officials*, pp. 40–3.

[39] A. P. Donajgrodzki, op. cit. pp. 104–5.

[40] Select Committee on Civil Service Superannuation, PP 1865, Vol. IX p. 434.

[41] See M. Raphael, *Pensions and Public Servants* (Paris, 1964) for the development of Superannuation in the Civil Service.

[42] 3rd Report, PP 1828, Vol. V, p. 491.

[43] PP 1856, Vol. IX, PP 1857, Sess. 2 Vol. XXIV.

[44] Royal Commission on the Opera-

tion of the Superannuation Acts, PP 1857 (Sess 2), Vol. XXIV, pp. xv–xvi.

[45] M. Raphael, op. cit. pp. 159–160.

[46] Parliamentary Debates, 3rd Series, Vol. XLIII, cols. 353–83. Wright (op. cit), p. 70 says that a limit of 25 had been the rule of the Civil Service Commission since 1855.

[47] PP 1830–1, Vol. VII.

[48] PP 1833, Vol. XXIII.

[49] PP 1854/5, Vol. XX, p. 441–5.

[50] PP 1860, Vol. IX, p. 398.

PART II, CH. V

[1] Commissioners for Examining the Public Accounts, 1st Report 1780 *HCJ* XXXVIII, pp. 36 and 74–6.

[2] 8th Report, 1797, pp. 6–7.

[3] Finance Reports, 1798–1803, A, p. 45.

[4] For the relation between revenue collection and the growth of country banking, see *Country Banking in the Industrial Revolution* by L. S. Presnell (1956).

[5] PP 1831, Vol. X, p. 15.

[6] See Treasury Minute, 22 December 1848 in Select Committee on Public Moneys PP 1856, Vol. XV, p. 511–31.

[7] Ibid. Qq 555–61 and 1293–9 and Memorandum, PP 1857, Sess. 2, Vol. IX, pp. 561–630.

[8] Ibid. 1857, Sess. 2, Vol. IX, p. 497.

[9] PP 1856, Vol. XV, Qq 939–40.

[10] 13th Report 1785, *HCJ* XL, p. 673.

[11] J. Ehrman, *The Younger Pitt* (1969), p. 271.

[12] *HCJ* CIII, p. 580.

[13] Select Committee on Public Moneys, PP 1857, Sess. 2, Vol. IX, p. 578 (Treasury Minute of August 1854).

[14] Ibid. PP 1856, Vol. XV, Q 958.

[15] PP 1847–8, VOL. XVIII, PART I, REPORT, P. VIII.

[16] SELECT COMMITTE ON PUBLIC MONEYS REPORT, P. 26, PP 1857 (Sess. 2), Vol. IX.

[17] See Treasury Returns in Appendix A to Report of Select Committee on the Charge on the Civil List Revenues, reprinted in PP 1830, Vol. IX.

[18] Select Committee on the Civil List 1815, p. 6 reprinted in PP 1830, Vol. IX.

[19] PP 1830, Vol. IX.

[20] Select Committee on Finance 1797, 3rd Report, pp. 10–11 and Finance Reports 1798–1803, H, 1 p. 71.

[21] PP 1830–1, Vol. III, pp. 1–4.

[22] Select Committee on Civil Government Charges, PP 1831, Vol. IV, p. 4.

[23] Op. cit. Report, p. viii.

[24] *HCJ* CIV, p. 190.

[25] Committee on Public Accounts, PP 1862, Vol. XI, pp. vi–vii.

[26] Select Committee on Public Moneys, PP 1856, Vol. XV, pp. 810–14.

[27] Ibid. Qq 1393–1401.

[28] *HCJ* LXXVI p. 87.

[29] PP 1856, Vol. XV, Q 1416.

[30] T. Erskine May, *Law, Privileges, Proceedings and Usage of Parliament*, 1st Edition (1844), pp. 319–20.

[31] Parliamentary Debates, 3rd Series, Vol. 170, col. 209.

[32] Ibid. Vol. 171, col. 1780.

[33] Select Committee on Public Moneys PP 1856, Vol. XV, Q 1427.

[34] PP 1867, Vol. X. p. 677.

[35] H. Roseveare, *The Treasury 1660–1870* (1973), p. 63.

[36] H. Roseveare, *The Treasury* (1969), p. 121.

[37] PP 1810, Vol. II, pp. 381–407.

[38] Sir Henry Parnell, *On Financial Reform*, 2nd Edition (1831), p. 160.

[39] J. Norris, *Shelburne and Reform* (1963) p. 288–9.

[40] H. Roseveare, *The Treasury* (1969), p. 129.

[41] 1st Report, PP 1817, Vol. IV, p.30.

[42] 3rd Report, PP 1817, Vol. IV, p. 111.

[43] PP 1828, Vol. V, pp. 7–8.

[44] J. Torrance, 'Sir George Harrison and the Growth of Bureaucracy in the early Nineteenth Century,' *English Historical Review* (1968), Vol. 64, pp. 64–7.

[45] See evidence of Sir Alexander Spearman and C. L. Crafer to the Select Committee on Miscellaneous Expenditure, PP 1847–8 Vol. XVIII Qq 1–51 and of W. G. Anderson to the Select Committee on Public Moneys, PP 1856, Vol. XV, Qq 1179–81 and 2196–2208.

[46] PP 1862, Vol. XI, Q 1495.

[47] Select Committee on Finance, First

Report, PP 1817, Vol. IV p. 8.

[48] Ibid. 3rd Report, p. 72.

[49] M. Wright, op. cit. p. 144.

[50] D. M. Young, *The Colonial Office in the Early Nineteenth Century* 1961, p. 147.

[51] PP 1837, Vol. XLIV, p. 151 et seq.

[52] Treasury Establishment, First Memorandum by Sir Charles Trevelyan, dated October 1855, Treasury Library.

[53] Select Committee on Public Expenditure, PP 1810, Vol. II, pp. 381–407, 5th Report (Second Part).

[54] Select Committee on Finance, 5th Report, PP 1819, Vol. II, p. 205.

[55] Royal Commission on the Public Accounts, PP 1831, Vol. X, pp. 3–4 and 22.

[56] Select Committee on Public Moneys, PP 1857, Sess. 2, Vol. IX, Appendix, Memorandum by the Chancellor of the Exchequer.

[57] PP 1831, Vol. X, pp. 17 and 23.

[58] Op. cit. pp. 28, 36, and 46–50.

[59] Ibid. quoted by Monteagle, Appendix 3, pp. 96–7.

[60] Torrance, op. cit. p. 65.

[61] PP 1856, Vol. XV, p. 68.

[62] PP 1857, Sess. 2, Vol. IX, pp. 52–3.

[63] Ibid. Appendix 2, pp. 53–4, and 59.

[64] Ibid. Appendix 3, p. 129.

[65] *HCJ* CXVII, 4 April 1862.

PART II, CH. VI

[1] 2nd Report 1781, *HCJ* Vol. 38, pp. 142–3.

[2] Select Committee on the Royal Mint, PP 1837, Vol. XVI and Royal Commission on the Constitution, Management and Expense of the Royal Mint, PP 1849, Vol. XXVIII.

[3] Royal Commission on the Royal Mint, PP 1870, Vol. XLI.

[4] Binney op. cit. p.1.

[5] 2nd Report, loc. cit. pp. 142–3.

[6] Select Committee on the Constitution and Management of the Customs, PP 1852, Vol. VIII, Part 1, Report p. xiv. Select Committee on the Inland Revenue and Customs Departments, PP 1862, XII Qq 33, 38, and 679.

[7] 2nd Report, PP 1806, Vol. IX, p. 51.

[8] B. E. V. Sabine, *History of Income Tax* (1966), p. 106.

[9] Quoted H. J. Hanham, op. cit. p.70.

[10] Parliamentary Debates, 3rd Series, Vol. 194, cols. 842–9, AND PP 1868–9, Vol. XXXIV, pp. 621–2.

[11] Sir Henry Parnell, *On Financial Reform*, 3rd Edition (1831), pp. 111–12.

[12] Select Committee on Miscellaneous Expenditure, PP 1847–8, Vol. XVIII, Part I, Q. 1245.

[13] PP 1851, Vol. XI, Qq 4980–92.

[14] Alpheus Todd, *Parliamentary Government in England*, Vol. II, (1869), pp. 243–6. For the Address to the Queen, see *HCJ*, CXVIII (1863) p. 49. and Parliamentary Debates, 3rd Series, Vol. 169, cols. 309–20. See also Select Committee on Open Spaces (Metropolis), PP 1865, Vol. VIII.

[15] Commissioners on Fees, 10th Report 1788, p. 760 in PP 1806, Vol. IX.

[16] Op. cit. Vol. IV, p. 7

[17] Commissioners for Examining the Public Accounts, 10th Report, *HCJ* XXXIX, p. 784.

[18] PP 1836, Vol. IV. p. 669.

[19] Parliamentary Debates, 3rd Series, Vol. 35, cols. 418–29 and 1159–70.

[20] J. Ehrman, *The Younger Pitt* (1969), p. 265 and J. E. D. Binney, op. cit. p. 114.

[21] See J. C. Sainty, *Officials of the Treasury 1660–1870* (1972) for the membership of the Treasury Board.

[22] Parliamentary Debates, 3rd Series, Vol. 194, col. 848.

[23] PP 1850, Vol. XV. Q 64 and Report p.v.

[24] Select Committee on Miscellaneous Expenditure PP 1847–8, Vol. XVIII, Part I, Qq. 1260–5.

[25] PRO. Russell Papers 30/22/16. I am indebted to Dr F. M. G. Willson for this reference.

[26] J. C. Sainty, *Office Holders, Secretaries of State 1660–1782* (1973), pp. 1–2.

[27] W. C. Costin and J. Steven Watson, *The Law and Working of the Constitution* (1964), Vol. II, p. 346.

[28] See the opening chapter in D. M. Young's *The Colonial Office in the Early Nineteenth Century* (1961).

[29] Ibid. pp. 14–22.

[30] Ibid. pp. 76–7.

[31] F. H. Hitchens, *The Colonial Land and Emigration Commission* (1931).

[32] Op. cit. Qq 1463–4.

[33] B. L. Blakeley, *The Colonial Office 1868–1892* (1972), pp. 106–9.

[34] Sir Malcolm Seton, *The India Office* (1926), pp. 11–20.

[35] Parliamentary Debates, 3rd Series, Vol. 148, cols. 1283–4.

[36] Seton, op. cit. pp. 30–2.

[37] Ibid. p. 33.

[38] Ibid. p. 34–5.

[39] Quoted D. M. Young, op. cit. p. 10.

[40] Royal Commission in the Civil Administration of the Army, PP 1837, Vol. XXXIV, Part I, p. 9.

[41] Ibid. Report, pp. 7–13.

[42] Earl Grey, *Parliamentary Government* (1858), pp. 8–9.

[43] See Royal Commission on the Civil and Professional Administration of the Naval and Military Departments, PP 1890, Vol. XIX, pp. 92–3.

[44] B. Pool, *Navy Board Contracts* (1966) pp. 116–37.

[45] Select Committee on the Board of Admiralty, PP 1861, Vol. V, Q 797.

[46] An Auto-Biographical Memoir (1847). p. 424.

[47] Select Committee on the Board of Admiralty, PP 1861, Vol. V, Qq 967–72.

[48] J. C. Sainty, *Admiralty Officials, 1660–1870* (1975).

[49] Select Committee, op. cit. Qq 1314–54, 2959–60, 5618–25. For the Admiralty Patent see Appendix I, pp. 641–4.

[50] For the administrative developments see the Royal Commission of 1890, op. cit.

[51] A. P. Donajgrodzki, in *Studies*, edited by G. Sutherland, op. cit. p. 85.

[52] M. W. Thomas, *The Early Factory Legislation* (1948).

[53] S. and B. Webb, *English Poor Law Policy* (1910), pp. 21–2.

[54] T. Mackay, *History of the English Poor Law*, Vol. III (reissue, 1904), pp. 130–1 and 328.

[55] Sir George Nicholls, *History of the English Poor Law*, Vol. II (1854), pp. 410–11.

[56] PP 1871, Vol. XXXV, pp. 9–11.

[57] See A. S. Bishop, *The Rise of the Central Authority for English Education* (1971), and P. H. J. H. Gosden, *The Development of Educational Administration in England and Wales* (1966).

[58] Parliamentary Debates, 3rd Series, Vol. 139, cols. 386–7.

[59] Bishop, op. cit. pp. 43–4.

[60] Parliamentary Debates, 3rd Series, Vol. 140, cols. 814–29.

[61] Select Committee on Education (Inspectors Reports), PP 1864, Vol. V, Select Committee on Education, PP 1865, Vol. VI.

[62] PP 1866, Vol. VII, pp. 123–31.

[63] Select Committee on Education, Science, and Art, PP 1884, Vol. XIII, Qq 46–52.

[64] Sir H. Llewellyn Smith, *The Board of Trade* (1928), p. 51

[65] See J. C. Sainty, *Officials of the Boards of Trade 1660–1870* (1974), for the composition of the Board.

[66] PP 1847/8, Vol. XVIII, Part I, p. xvi.

[67] PP 1867, Vol. XXXIX p. 220.

[68] Parliamentary Debates, 3rd Series, Vol. 191, cols. 1327–8.

[69] PP 1850, Vol. XV, Report p.v.

[70] Parliamentary Debates, 3rd Series, Vol. 188, col. 167.

[71] J. S. Mill, *Representative Government* (Everyman's Edition), pp. 332–3.

[72] B. B. Schaffer, 'The Idea of the Ministerial Department', *Australian Journal of Politics and History* (1957), Vol. III, pp. 60–78.

[73] Op. cit. pp. 333–4.

[74] Select Committee on Education, PP 1865, Vol. VI, Qq 56–83, 2890–5, and 948–67.

[75] Parliamentary Debates, 3rd Series, Vol. 88, col. 711.

[76] Ibid. Vol. 158, cols. 892–907.

[77] PP 1856, Vol. XV, p. 383.

[78] M. Wright, *Treasury Control of the Civil Service 1854–74* (1969), p. 66.

[79] Op cit. Vol. 129, col. 1490.

[80] On the peculiar status of the Ecclesiastical and Charity Commissions

see the unpublished Oxford D. Phil. thesis by F. M. G. Willson (1953). See also his *Ministries and Boards: Some aspects of Administrative Development since 1832 Public Administration* (1955). pp. 43–58.

PART II, CH. VII

[1] R. R. Nelson, *Home Office 1782–1801* (Durham N. C., 1969), p. 71.

[2] 1st Report, p. 10 in PP 1806, Vol. IX.

[3] D. M. Young, *The Colonial Office in the Early Nineteenth Century* (1961), p. 135.

[4] Select Committee on Miscellaneous Expenditure, PP 1847–8, Vol. XVIII, Part I, Q 1240. A regular Register of papers was started by the Treasury in 1783 (Select Committee on Finance, Fifteenth Report, 1797, p. 27).

[5] Select Committee on Official Salaries, PP 1850, Vol. XV, Q 42

[6] *Letters of Queen Victoria 1837–1861*, Vol. III (1907), p. 446.

[7] E. Ashley, *Life of Viscount Palmerston, 1846–1865*, Vol. II, (1879) p. 263.

[8] Office Minutes, Vol. 1A.99 and Vol. 4.61 (I am indebted to R. B. Pugh for these references.)

[9] J. C. Sainty, *Admiralty Officials 1660–1870* (1975), p. 34.

[10] Commissioners on Fees, First Report 1786, p. 12, in PP 1806, Vol. IX.

[11] Ibid. 2nd Report, 1786.

[12] Select Committee on Official Salaries, PP 1850, Vol. XV, Qq 46 and 49.

[13] Finance Proceedings 1797–1803, App. A, 137–47.

[14] M. Collinge, *Foreign Office Officials 1782–1870 (1979), p. 11.*

[15] C. S. Parker, *Sir Robert Peel* (1899), Vol. I, pp. 304 and 388–9.

[16] J. C. Sainty, *Colonial Office Officials 1794–1870* (1976), p. 9.

[17] E. Jones-Parry, 'Under Secretaries of State for Foreign Affairs, 1782–1855', *English Historical Review*, xlix (1934), pp. 308–20.

[18] M. Collinge, op. cit. pp. 11–12.

[19] Royal Commission on the Operation of the Superannuation Act, PP 1857, Sess., 2 Vol. XXIV, Report, p. 239.

[20] D. J. Heasman, 'The Emergence and Evolution of the Office of Parliamentary Secretary', *Parliamentary Affairs* (1970), Vol. XXIII, pp. 345–65.

[21] PP 1854, Vol. XXVII, pp. 47–8.

[22] R. B. Pugh, The Colonial Office in *The Cambridge History of the British Empire* (1959), Vol. 3, p. 719.

[23] E. Jones-Parry, op. cit. and V. Cromwell and Z. S. Steiner, 'The Foreign Office before 1914' in G. Sutherland, *Studies in nineteenth century government* (1972).

[24] Select Committee on Education, PP 1865, Vol. VI, Qq 1–55 and 827.

[25] Cromwell and Steiner, op. cit.

[26] R. Johnson, 'Administrators in education before 1870', in G. Sutherland, op. cit. p. 136.

[27] For full quotation see supra, p. 151.

[28] P. Knaplund, *James Stephen and the British Colonial System 1813–1847* (Wisconsin, 1953), p. 14.

[29] Quoted by J. W. Cell, *British Colonial Administration in the Mid-Nineteenth Century* (Yale, 1970), p. 7.

[30] PP 1839, Vol. XVII, pp. 37–8.

[31] R. C. Snelling and T. J. Barron, 'The Colonial Office: its permanent officials 1801–1914', in G. Sutherland, op. cit. p. 145.

[32] Cromwell and Steiner, op. cit.

[33] Henry Parris, *Constitutional Bureaucracy* (1969) pp. 106–10, and H. C. F. Bell, *Lord Palmerston* (1936), 2 Vols.

[34] H. C. F. Bell, ibid. Vol. 1, pp. 191, 258.

[35] *Letters of Queen Victoria 1837–1861*, Vol. I (1907), pp. 107–7.

[36] Parliamentary Debates, 3rd Series, Vol. 127, col. 825

[37] PP 1854, Vol. XXVII, p. 3.

[38] Henry Parris, op. cit. pp. 23–4.

[39] J. C. Parkinson, *Under Government: An Official Key to the Civil Service,*, 1st Edition (1859), 5th Edition (1869).

[40] J. R. Torrance, 'Sir George Harrison and the growth of bureaucracy in the early nineteenth century', *English Historical Review* (1968), Vol. 83, p. 59.

[41] PP 1854, Vol. XXVII, pp. 47–8.

[42] A. P. Donajgrodzki, op. cit., pp. 87–9 and Select Committee on Official Salaries, pp 1850, Vol. XV, p. 236.

[43] H Roseveare, *The Treasury* (1969); J. C. Sainty, *Treasury Officials 1660–1870* (1972); and Select Committee on Miscellaneous Expenditure, PP 1847–8, Vol. XVIII, Part I, Q 1203–15.

[44] J. C. Sainty, op. cit. pp. 14–15.

[45] B. L. Blakeley, *The Colonial Office, 1868–1892* (Duke, 1972), pp. 23–4.

[46] PP 1854, Vol. XXVII, pp. 129 et seq.

[47] PP 1867, Vol. XXXIX.

[48] J. C. Sainty, *Officials of the Boards of Trade 1660–1870* (1974), pp. 42–4.

[49] See Report on the Organization of the Permanent Civil Service and Reports from Committees of Inquiry into Public Offices, PP 1854, Vol. XXVII. Also M. Wright, *Treasury Control of the Civil Service 1854–1874* (1969).

[50] M. Wright, op. cit. p. 139.

[51] Select Committee Civil Services PP 1873 vol. VIII Qq 84–97 3201–16 and 3755–70.

[52] B. L. Blakeley, op. cit. p. 8 fn.

[53] H. Roseveare, op. cit. pp. 172–4.

[54] Lucy Brown, *The Board of Trade and the Free Trade Movement 1830–42* (1958).

[55] On this see G. Kitson Clark, 'Statesmen in Disguise': Reflexions on the History of Neutrality of the Civil Service'. *Historical Journal*, II (1959), PP. 19–39.

[56] Jenifer Hart, 'Sir Charles Trevelyan at the Treasury', *English Historical Review* (1960), Vol. 75, p. 109.

[57] For this correspondence see *Public Administraton* (1958), Vol. XXXVI, pp. 29–36. [58] See M. W. Thomas, *The Early Factory Legislation* (1948).

[59] Parliamentary Debates, 3rd Series, Vol. 152, col. 710.

[60] J. Leese, *Personalities and Power in English Education* (1950), pp. 45–77.

[61] Parliamentary Debates, 3rd Series, Vol. 152, cols. 698–701.

[62] Ibid. Vol. 164, cols. 756–8.

[63] Ibid. cols. 1788–91 and 1832–5.

[64] Select Committee on Education (Inspectors) 1864 Vol. IX p. 143.

[65] Op. cit. Vol. 171, cols. 717–23.

[66] Op. cit. Vol. 174, cols. 897–914.

[67] Op. cit. Vol. 176, cols. 2067–81.

[68] PP 1864, Vol. IX p. 17.

PART II, CH. VIII

[1] S. and B. Webb, *The Parish and the County* (1906), pp. 558–80.

[2] B. Keith-Lucas, *The Unreformed Local Government System* (1980), pp. 49–50.

[3] S. and B. Webb, op. cit. p.383.

[4] A. Redford, *History of Local Government in Manchester* (1939), Vol. I. pp. 191–213.

[5] PP 1825, Vol. VI.

[6] PP 1834, Vol. XIV.

[7] PP 1830–1, Vol. XI, p. 207.

[8] PP 1835, Vol. XIV.

[9] PP 1835, Vol. XXXVI; 1836, Vol. XXVII; and 1837, Vol. XXXIII.

[10] M. Brock, *The Great Reform Act* (1973), pp 19 and 26–8.

[11] Royal Commission on Municipal Corporation Boundaries, PP 1837, Vol. XXVI.

[12] S. E. Finer, *The Life and Times of Sir Edwin Chadwick* (1952), p. 85.

[13] Royal Commission on the Poor Laws Report, PP 1834, Vol. XXVII.

[14] Ibid. p. 161.

[15] S. E. Finer, op. cit. p. 89.

[16] Poor Law Commissioners, 3rd Annual Report, PP 1837, Vol. XI, pp. 1–2 and 114–16.

[17] 1st Report, PP 1835, Vol. XXXV, p. 12.

[18] V. D. Lipman, *Local Government Areas 1834–1945* (1949), pp. 36–54.

[19] Second Report of the Royal Sanitary Commission, PP 1871 Vol. XXXV, p. 19.

[20] PP 1837–8, Vol. XXVII, Appendix A1, pp. 62–96.

[21] Royal Commission on the State of Large Towns and Populous Districts, PP 1844, Vol. XVII and 1845, Vol. XVIII.

[22] Annual Report of General Board of Health, PP 1858, Vol. XXXV.

[23] P. H. J. H. Gosden, *Development of Educational Administration in England and Wales* (1966), pp. 127–35.

[24] Royal Commission on the Establishment of a Constabulary Force, PP 1839, Vol. XIX. Report, pp. 184–90.

[25] Select Committee, PP 1852–3, Vol. XXXVI p. 164.

[26] For this history see T. A. Critchley,

History of the Police in England and Wales, 900–1966 (1967).

27 J. Redlich and F. W. Hirst, *History of Local Government in England* (1903) 2 Vols. The First Volume has been edited and republished by B. Keith-Lucas (1958): K. B. Smellie, *History of Local Government* (1946).

28 See, however, D. Fraser, *Urban Politics in Victorian England* (1976); E. P. Hennock, *Fit and Proper Persons* (1973); A. Redford, op. cit.; Shena Simon, *Century of City Government (Manchester)* (1939), and B. White, *History of the Corporation of Liverpool* (1951).

29 S. and B. Webb, op. cit. p. 166.

30 P. H. J. H. Gosden, op. cit. p. 129.

31 These figures are from V. D. Lipman, op. cit. pp. 72–4. There are, however, small differences between some of them and the figures given by Dr Farr, head of the Registrar-General's Statistical Department to the Select Committee on the Areas of Parishes, Unions and Counties, PP 1878, Vol. VIII.

32 Report of Poor Law Commissioners on Local Taxation, PP 1843, Vol. XX.

33 S. and B. Webb, op. cit. p. 157.

34 S. and B. Webb, *The Manor and the Borough* (1908) Vol. II.

35 Blackstone, *Commentaries on the Laws of England*, Vol. I. p. 475.

36 D. A. Beattie, *Ultra Vires in its Relation to Local Authorities* (1936), pp. 1–4.

37 Sir John Simon, *English Sanitary Institutions* (1890), p. 209.

38 B. Keith-Lucas, *The English Local Government Franchise* (1952), p. 63.

39 J. Redlich and F. W. Hirst, Vol. I, op. cit. p. 174.

40 Sir William Holdsworth, *History of English Law*, Vol. X, pp. 128–36.

41 S. E. Finer, op. cit. pp. 90–1.

42 Op. cit. p. 68. See also Royston Lambert, 'Local Government Act Office 1858–71', in *Victorian Studies* (1962), Vol. VI, pp. 131–2.

43 Sir George Nicholls, *History of the English Poor Law* (1860), Vol. II, p. 445. See also S. and B. Webb, *English Poor Law History*, Vol. I. pp. 210–15.

44 S. E. Finer, op. cit. p. 475.

45 Op. cit. p. 16.

PART II, CH. IX

1 W. Bagehot, *The English Constitution* (2nd Edition) (World's Classics), pp. 157–9.

2 Ibid. p. 162.

3 Ibid. p. 165.

4 Ibid. p. 157.

5 Ibid. p. 172.

6 Ibid. pp. 176–7.

7 *Letters of Queen Victoria 1837–1861* (1907), p. 446.

8 Op. cit. p. 193.

9 *Political Studies* (1961), Vol. IX, p. 179.

10 *Parliamentary Government* (1858), pp. 76–83 and p. 20.

11 Vol. I (1867), p. 257.

12 *Thoughts Upon Government* (1872), pp. 36 and 168.

13 Parliamentary Debates, 3rd Series, Vol. 145, col. 447.

14 Ibid. Vol. 209, col. 466.

15 10th Edition (1893).

16 Op cit. p. 184.

17 *Representative Government* (Everyman's Edition). p. 346.

18 Ibid. p. 351.

19 Ibid. p. 357.

19 PP 1834 Vol. XIV.

21 PP 1870, Vol. LV.

Bibliography

This is a very limited list of sources. There is a large and growing literature in the learned journals and many of the particularly relevant articles are quoted in the footnotes. The Parliamentary Papers contain a wealth of material, much of it little used so far: here again there are many references in the footnotes. The list is in three sections. Works which contain specially full general bibliographies are marked with an asterisk.

I. General: covering all or most of the period 1780–1870
Aspinall, A. *The Cabinet Council 1783–1835* (1952)

Anson, Sir William R. *The Law and Custom of the Constitution.* 3 Vols. (3rd Edition 1907–8)
- Vol. I.   *Parliament*
- Vol. II.   *The Crown* Part I
- Vol. III.   *The Crown* Part II

Collinge, J. M. *Office Holders in Modern Britain* (Series)
- Vol. VII. *Navy Board Officials 1660–1832* (1978)
- Vol. VIII. *Foreign Office Officials 1782–1870* (1979)

Cook, C. and B. Keih *British Historical Facts, 1830–1900* (1975)

Hanham, H. J. *The Nineteenth Century Constitution. Documents and Commentary* (1969)

Holdsworth, Sir William *History of English Law.* 16 Vols. with an index of the whole as Vol. XVII (1972). The most relevant are Vols. I, X, and XI (1938)

Kemp, Betty *King and Commons 1660–1832* (1957)

Mackintosh, J. P. *The British Cabinet* (1962)

Maitland, F. W. *Constitutional History of England* (1909)

Mitchell, B. R. and P. Deane *Abstract of British Historical Statistics* (1962)

Parris, Henry *Constitutional Bureaucracy* (1969)

Redlich, F. *The Procedure of the House of Commons.* 3 Vols. (1908)

*Roseveare, Henry *The Treasury. The Evolution of a British Institution* (1969) *The Treasury 1660–1870* (1973)

Sainty, J. C. Compiler of the first six volumes in the invaluable series *Office-Holders in Modern Britain*
- I.   *Treasury Officials 1660–1870* (1972)
- II.   *Officials of the Secretaries of State 1660–1782* (1973)
- III. *Officials of the Boards of Trade 1660–1870* (1974)
- IV. *Admiralty Officials 1660–1870* (1975)
- V.   *Home Office Officials 1782–1870* (1975)

VI. *Colonial Office Officials 1794–1870* (1976)

Smellie, K. B. *A Hundred Years of English Government 1832–1939* (2nd Edition. Revised, 1950)

Todd, Alpheus *On Parliamentary Government in England*. 2 vols. (1st Edition, 1867 and 1869)

II. 1780

There are three invaluable series of reports which, though dealing with the years immediately after 1780, may nevertheless be taken to portray the administrative system of that date. They are:

(i) The 15 reports of the Commissioners for Examining the Public Accounts published in the *Journals of the House of Commons* between November 1780 and December 1786.

(ii) The 10 reports of the Commissioners for Enquiring into Fees, Perquisites, and Emoluments in the Public Offices (England). They are dated 1786, 1787, and 1788 but were not circulated to Parliament until 1806 (Vol. VII) Vol. IX in Bodleian).

(iii) The 36 reports of the Select Committee on Finance published in 1797–8, in the Reports from Committees Vols. XII and XIII. These were followed by copies of correspondence arising from the recommendations of this and the two earlier Commissions in Finance Reports 1798–1803.

Aylmer, G. *The King's Servants. The Civil Service of Charles I.* (1961)

Bacon, Matthew *A new abridgement of the Law* (4th Edition) (1778)

Binney, J. E. D. *British Public Finance and Administration 1774–92* (1958)

Blackstone, Sir William *Commentaries on the Laws of England*. 4 Vols. Eight editions by 1780.

Ehrman, John *The Younger Pitt* (1960)

Gratton, R. H. *The King's Government* (1913)

Hoon, E. E. *The Organization of the English Customs System 1696–1786* New York, 1938)

Jacob, Giles *New Law Dictionary* (9th Edition, 1772)

Maxwell-Lyte, Sir H. C. *Historical Notes on the Use of the Great Seal of England* (1926)

Namier, L. and J. Brooke *The House of Commons 1754–1790*. 3 Vols. (1964)

Norris, J. *Shelburne and Reform* (1963)

Pares, R. *King George III and the Politicians* (1953)

Thomas, P. D. G. *The House of Commons in the Eighteenth Century* (1971)

Thomson, M. A. *The Secretaries of State 1681–1782* (1932)

Thomson M. A. *Constitutional History of England* Vol. IV 1642–1801
   (1938)
Ward, W. R. *The English Land Tax in the Eighteenth Century* (1953)
Western, J. R. *English Militia in the Eighteenth Century* (1965)

III. 1780–1870
As many of the works quoted are relevant to more than one chapter
they are all included under this single heading.
Bagehot, W. *The English Constitution* (1867), (2nd Edition, 1872)
Bishop, A. S. *The Rise of a Central Authority for English Education* (1971)
Blakeley, B. L. *The Colonial Office, 1868–1892* (Duke, 1972)
Brown, Lucy *The Board of Trade and the Free Trade Movement 1830–42*
   (1958)
Cell, J. W. *British Colonial Administration in the Mid-Nineteenth Century*
   (New Haven, 1970)
Chester, D. N. and N. Bowring *Questions in Parliament* (1962)
Chubb, B. *The Control of Public Expenditure* (1952)
Cleveland-Stevens F. *English Railways* (1915)
Clokie H.M. and J. W. Robinson *Royal Commissions of Inquiry* New
   York, 1969)
Cohen, E. *The Growth of the British Civil Service 1780–1939* (1941)
Critchley, T. *A History of the Police in England and Wales 900–1966*
   (1967)
Cromwell V. *Interpretations of Nineteenth-Century Administration* (Victo-
   rian Studies 1966 pp. 245–55).
Edwards, J. Ll. J. *The Law Officers of the Crown* (1964)
Finer, S. E. *The Life and Times of Sir Edwin Chadwick* (1952)
Glover, R. G. *Peninsular Preparation: the Reform of the British Army
   1795–1809* (1963)
Gordon, Hampden *The War Office* (1935)
Gosden, P. H. J. H. *The Development of Educational Administration in
   England and Wales* (1966)
Grey, Earl *Parliamentary Government* (1858)
Hall, H. L. *The Colonial Office* (1937)
Hitchens, F. H. *The Colonial Land and Emigration Commission* (1931)
* Knaplund, P. *James Stephen and the British Colonial System 1813–1847*
   (Wisconsin, 1953)
Lipman, V. D. *Local Government Areas 1834–1945* (1949)
MacDonagh, O. *A Pattern of Government Growth 1800–60* (1961)
Mackay, T. *History of English Poor Law*. Vol. III (reissued 1904)
Mill, J. S. *Considerations on Representative Government* (1861)
Nelson, R. R. *The Home Office 1782–1801* (Durham N. C., 1969)
Nicholls, Sir George *History of English Poor Law* Vol. II (1854)

Parnell, Sir Henry *On Financial Reform* (3rd Edition, 1831)

Parris, Henry *Government and the Railways in Nineteenth Century Britain* (1965)

Pool, B. *Navy Board Contracts* (1966)

Pressnell, L. S. *Country Banking in the Industrial Revolution* (1956)

Prouty, R. *The Transformation of the Board of Trade 1830–1855* (1957)

Pugh, R. B. 'The Colonial Office 1801–1825', in the *Cambridge History of the British Empire*, Vol. III (1959)

Raphael, M. *Pensions and Public Servants* (Paris, 1964)

Redlich, J. and F. W. Hirst *The History of Local Government in England* 2 Vols. (1903). The first volume has been edited and reissued by B. Keith-Lucas (1958)

Roberts D. *Victorian Origins of the Welfare State* (Yale, 1960)

Robinson, Howard *Britain's Post Office* (1953)

Sabine, B. E. V. *A History of Income Tax* (1966)

Seton, Sir Malcolm *The India Office* (1926)

Smith, Sir H. Llewellyn *The Board of Trade* (1928)

Sutherland, G. *Studies in the growth of nineteen-century government* (1972) This contains ten extremely useful Essays, all except two of which cover part of the period up to 1870. These are:
1. S. E. Finer. 'The Transmission of Benthamite Ideas 1820–50'
2. A. Ryan. 'Utilitarianism and bureaucracy: The views of J. S. Mill'
3. J. Hart. 'The genesis of the Northcote–Trevelyan Report'
4. A. P. Donajgrodzki. 'The Northcote–Trevelyan Report and the clerks in the Home Office 1822–48'
5. R. Johnson. 'Administrators in education before 1870: patronage, social position and role'
6. R. C. Snelling and T. J. Barron. 'The Colonial Office and its permanent officials 1801–1914'
7. V. Cromwell and Z. S. Steiner, 'The Foreign Office before 1914'
8. M. Wright. 'Treasury control 1854–1914'

* Thomas, M. W. *The Early Factory Legislation* (1948)

Webb, Sydney and Beatrice *English Local Government*:
I.   *The Parish and the County* (1906)
II and III. *The Manor and the Borough* (1908)
IV.   *Statutory Authorities for Special Purposes* (1922)
V.   *The Story of the King's Highway* (1913)
VI.   *English Prisons under Local Government* (1922)
VII. *English Poor Law History* Part I (1927)
VIII and IX. *English Poor Law History* Part II *The Last Hundred Years* (1929)

Williams, O. C. *The Historical Development of Private Bill Procedure.* 2 Vols. (1948)

The Clerical Organization of the House of Commons 1661–1850 (1954)

* Wright, M. *Treasury Control of the Civil Service 1854–1874* (1969)

* Young, D. M. *The Colonial Office in the Early Nineteenth Century* (1961)

INDEX

Hastings, Warren 122
Hawkers and Pedlars Office 28, 47, 224
Health:
General Board of 88, 119-20, 265, 335-6, 352
Local Boards of 335, 347, 358-60
Helps, Sir Arthur (KCB 1872) 368
Hereditary Revenues 4, 58, 60, 190, 230
Hierarchy of Authority 27-30, 299-304, 315-16
Highways 325-6, 336, 345-7
Hill, Sir Rowland (KCB 1860) 231-2, 313
Holdsworth, Sir William 95
Holland, Lord (Henry Fox, 1st Baron 1763) 171
Home Office: 119, 197, 250, 256-9, 282, 284, 301
Inspectors' reports 316-17
staff and organization 110, 125, 140, 153-4, 162, 167-8, 256, 266, 282, 287-8, 336
Home Secretary 101-2, 145, 155, 238, 256-9, 260-3, 265-6, 274-5, 285, 336, 338-40, 357-8, 358-60
House of Commons 32, 35-41, 98-122, 367-71
control of finance 58-61, 98-9, 181-2, 192, 194, 205, 219-20 (*see also* Public Accounts Committee)
information and returns 99-103
publication of proceedings 108-9
time of 109-17
and Treasury 199-200, 203
House of Lords 32, 121-2
Howick, Lord 247-8, 314, *and see* Grey, Earl (3rd)
Hume, David 34-5
Hume, J. Deacon 312
Hume, Joseph 103, 347, 355

Ilay, Lord (3rd Duke of Argyll 1743) 32
Impeachment 1, 12, 19, 33, 37-9, 122
Improvement Commissioners 326-7, 329, 340, 345, 347
Inclosure Commission 120 (*and see* Copyhold, Inclosure, and Tithe Commission)
Income Tax 72-3, 103, 224, 344
India:
Board for the Affairs of/Board of Control 241-2, 297

Council 91, 241-4
Secretary of State for 239, 242-4
Inland Revenue 102, 224
Inspectors—publication of reports 316-21
Ireland:
Chief Secretary for 259; Lord Lieutenant of 151

Joint Stock Companies, Registrar of 102, 258
Judiciary:
Judicial power 2, 5, 7, 19, 49-51, 83-5
salaries 60-1, 179, 183-5
Justices of the Peace 10, 13, 17, 23-4, 50, 53-6, 141, 323-5, 330, 335, 338-41, 353-8
numbers 323-4

Kay-Shuttleworth, Sir James (1st Bt. 1849) 155, 317
Keith-Lucas, B. 353
Kemp, Betty 76
Kimberley, Lord (1st Earl 1866) 303
King 2-5, 12-13, 76-97
as corporation sole 6, 94-5
decline in status and authority 77-82
demise 6-8, 92-3
and Parliament 32-7, 81, 83, 106-7
King's Bench, Court of 49-50, 132
King's Remembrancer 23, 124

Lancaster, Chancellor of the Duchy of 43, 273, 285
Land Revenues of the Crown 228-30
Land Tax 49, 54-6, 73
Receivers-General of 16, 55, 133, 168-70, 173-4
Language—official 11, 65
Law Officers 274
Legislation 109-11, 342-4
King's powers re 3, 5, 32-3
Legislature—legislative power 1-5
Le Marchant, Sir Denis 312
Letters Patent 9, 13, 17-18, 25, 28-9, 43-4, 46, 90-1, 132, 254-5
Lewis, Sir George Cornewall (2nd Bt. 1855) 87, 158-9, 214-16, 296, 366
Lingen, R. R. W. (KCB 1878; Baron 1885) 269, 293, 318, 320-1
Liverpool, Lord (Baron Hawkesbury 1803; 2nd Earl 1808) 157, 234, 367